Peasants, Merchants, and Markets

Peasants, Merchants, and Markets

Inland Trade in Medieval England, 1150-1350

James Masschaele

St. Martin's Press
New York

PEASANTS, MERCHANTS, AND MARKETS: INLAND TRADE IN MEDIEVAL ENGLAND, 1150-1350

ISBN 0-312-16035-6

Library of Congress Cataloging-in-Publication Data

Masschaele, James, 1961-
Peasants, merchants, and markets : inland trade in medieval England, 1150-1350 / James Masschaele.
p. cm.
Originally presented as the author's doctoral dissertation (University of Toronto).
Includes bibliographical references and index.
ISBN 0-312-16035-6
1. England—Commerce—History. 2. Markets—England—History. 3. Peasantry—England—History. 4. Commerce—History—Medieval, 500-1500. 5. Cities and towns, Medieval—England. 6. England—Economic conditions—1066-1485. 7. Huntingdonshire (England)—Commerce—History. I. Title.
HF3515.M37 1997
381'.1'0942—dc21 96-52279

CIP

First St. Martin's edition: October, 1997
10 9 8 7 6 5 4 3 2 1

Table of Contents

In memory of Cam

Acknowledgments

In writing this book, I have been aided by many friends and colleagues, and I am pleased to be able to render public thanks for their generous help. This book began its life as a doctoral dissertation submitted to the University of Toronto, where I was mentored by a talented and diverse group of scholars, two of whom deserve special mention. Ambrose Raftis first introduced me to the sources and literature of medieval social history, and he proceeded to serve as a tireless source of inspiration and friendly guidance in directing my doctoral research. I am deeply indebted to him, above all else for imbuing me with the belief that creativity and imagination lie at the heart of the historian's craft. I hope he finds in this book some reward for all he has invested in me. Along with Ambrose, my graduate career brought me into contact with John Munro, who became my second principal creditor in Toronto. John held me to the same unflinchingly high standards he demands of his own work, and by deed as well as word he showed me the importance of careful thinking and writing in formulating historical arguments. Both of these mentors continue to give me generous access to their knowledge, wisdom and friendship, and both have helped to make this a better book than it would otherwise be.

Outside Toronto, I have been warmed at several scholarly hearths. While the bitter winds of cutbacks have been chilling academic life, my colleagues in the History Department at Rutgers University have kept the cold at bay, and I am grateful to them for the fire they have tended. I have also found warmth at numerous archives and libraries, among whom I would like to thank particularly the staffs of the Public Record Office, the British Library, the Institute of Historical Research in London, the county record offices in Shrewsbury and Norwich, and the libraries of Rutgers and Princeton Universities. I am also indebted to the community of historians engaged in studying the social and economic history of medieval England, for they too have kept a fire burning brightly in circumstances that are far from ideal. Many members of this community have read and listened to pieces of this book as it was being written, and their comments and criticisms have been of great help. Included in their number are Kathleen Biddick, Richard Britnell, Bruce Campbell, Anne DeWindt, Edwin DeWindt, Derek Keene, John Langdon, and Zvi Razi. I am particularly indebted to Maryanne Kowaleski, who read a draft of the entire manuscript. Her acute comments and observations caused me to rethink much of what I thought I knew and helped me to see more clearly what I really wanted to say in this book. Of course, responsibility for the work presented here remains entirely my own, but it is a responsibility borne more lightly with the encouragement of colleagues.

Numerous granting agencies have furnished me with some kindling to add to these hearths, and I thank them for their generosity. They include the

Research Council and the Dean of Arts and Sciences at Rutgers University, the American Council of Learned Societies, and preeminently the Social Sciences and Humanities Research Council of Canada, which funded two pivotal years of postdoctoral study. Funding for the humanities and scholarly achievement are inseparably linked; only a fool or a Philistine would think otherwise.

Comfortable as my professional environment has been, the warmest and coziest hearth in my life has been and continues to be tended by the members of my family, all of whom have shared with me the joys and frustrations of an academic career. My brother-in-law Cam Paquette drew—and often redrew as I changed my mind—all of the maps in this book except Map 8-1, which is reproduced with the kind permission of the Royal Commission on the Historical Monuments of England. His mapping skills were exceeded only by his good humor. My wife, Tia Kolbaba, has lived with this book as long as I have, and her role in helping me to write it is incalculable. My greatest debt is to my parents. Due to their family circumstances, neither pursued a formal education beyond their early teens, but both did everything in their power to imbue their children with a belief in the dignity and value of learning. I keep with me at all times a sense of gratitude both for the sacrifices they made to give me opportunities they did not have and for the values they instilled to help me understand what to do with them.

List of Maps and Diagrams

List of Tables

Manuscript Sources

British Library (BL):
Add. Ch.: Additional Charters
Add. R.: Additional Rolls
Harl. Ch.: Harley Charters
Stowe: Stowe Manuscripts

Corporation of London Record Office:
Recognizance Rolls

Norfolk Record Office:
Y/C4: Great Yarmouth Borough Court Rolls

Public Record Office (PRO):
C47: Chancery Miscellanea
C133: Chancery Inquisitions *post mortem*
C143: Chancery Inquisitions *ad quod damnum*
C255/12: Chancery Miscellaneous Files and Writs: Quiet Enjoyment of Privileges
E101: Exchequer K. R. Various Accounts
E163: Exchequer K. R. Miscellanea
E179: Exchequer K. R. Lay Subsidy Rolls
E358: Exchequer L. T. R. Miscellaneous Accounts
SC2: Court Rolls
SC6: Ministers' and Receivers' Accounts
SC11: Rentals and Surveys

Shropshire Record Office:
SRO 3365: Shrewsbury Borough Records

Suffolk Record Office:
C4/1: Ipswich Domesday Book

A Note on Measurements, Money, Dates, and Translations

One of the difficulties modern historians face when dealing with the economic configurations of the past involves the understanding of uncommon or archaic units of measurement. For the sake of clarity, the unusual measurements included in this book have been converted into ones more readily visualized by the nonspecialist; even specialists sometimes need to be reminded how many pounds of wool went into a sack. All units of measurement are described in terms of the Imperial system, itself something of an archaism, but the system that is most familiar to the Anglo-American community of scholars. Conversions between medieval units and modern ones have been based principally on Ronald Zupko, *British Weights and Measures* (Madison, WI, 1977), supplemented by R. D. Connor, *The Weights and Measures of England* (London, 1987) and the *Oxford English Dictionary*. All distances are given in miles and, in the absence of a consistent alternative, have been measured as the crow flies. This point bears some stressing, because a major concern of the book is to measure the spatial boundaries of commercial activity. The actual distances over which people traveled and carried goods would often have been greater than those noted in the text, in some cases considerably greater. For the sake of comparison, consider that a standard modern road atlas of Great Britain by the A-Z Map Company (*Great Britain Road Atlas*, 3rd ed., Sevenoaks, Kent, 1990) states that the distance between London and York is 198 miles, whereas the distance as the crow flies is about 175 miles. Medieval routes may have been more direct than modern motorways, but we cannot assume that this was always the case, and even a slight deviation necessitated by difficult terrain or an unsuitable river crossing would have been an important consideration for someone traveling with a cart.

The value of money poses similar problems of contextualization for historians. Values in the text are given in the units current at the time, in which £1 was worth 20 shillings (s.) and 1s. was worth 12 pence (d.). The mark (13s. 4d., equal to two-thirds of £1) was also commonly used in the period; in the text it is converted into equivalent amounts of shillings and pence. To visualize what a penny or a pound was worth in this period, it is useful to think of them in comparative terms of income and expenditures. A common laborer did well to earn 2d. for a day's work and had a good year if his annual income surpassed £2. A peasant with an income above £5 was considered to belong to his or her village's elite. Knights commonly assumed their status with incomes starting at £20 per year and sometimes with incomes as low as £15 per year. An income above £50 per year made the beneficiary a wealthy person. Only the very wealthiest members of the baronage counted their incomes in the thousands of pounds. On the other side of the ledger, in a typical year one penny (half the daily wage of a laborer) would have bought one gallon of ale, or about five pounds of good quality bread (wastel bread), or about two pounds of cheese. The relationship between wages and prices fluctuated quite substantially from one generation to the next over the course of this period, and the reader interested in tracing these fluctuations should consult David Farmer's essay "Prices and Wages," in *The Agrarian History of England and Wales,* vol. 2 (Cambridge, 1988), pp. 716-817.

Much of the economic activity of medieval England involved the production, trade, and processing of grain. The standard units of measurement used in the period for both grain and malt were the bushel and the quarter. The latter was a relatively straightforward measure comprising eight bushels. Why a unit of eight was called a quarter is a matter of conjecture; perhaps it was originally conceived of as equaling one-quarter of a cartload, as the *Oxford English Dictionary* suggests. Much more perplexing than the name of the quarter, though, is the actual size of the bushel on which it was based. Contemporaries tended to define the bushel by reference to weights of wheat held rather than by reference to volume or capacity, and they were consistent neither from century to century nor from region to region. References in contemporary sources suggest a minimum weight of 48 pounds avoirdupois and a maximum of 64 pounds avoirdupois. The interested reader can find a fuller discussion of this problem in the appendix of my article "Transport Costs in Medieval England," *Economic History Review,* 2nd ser., 46 (1993):277-79.

All primary sources quoted in the text have been translated into English. Translations have been used and cited from published sources when available, otherwise they are original to this book. For the reader's convenience, dates which were rendered by saints' feasts and regnal years have been converted in the text into modern calendar dates and years.

Manuscript sources have been cited in the style adopted by their archival repositories, beginning with the name of the archive followed by the document reference. Thus, a citation in the form PRO E179/242/8 refers to a document in the Public Record Office in London—the principal archive used in writing this book—with its specific class (E179) and piece numbers (242/8). Specialists often know from experience what types of documents are likely to be found in particular classes (E179, for example, refers to the well known class of Exchequer lay subsidy records), but they can seldom infer anything from the piece number unless they have used it in their own research (and also happen to have an outstanding memory). Uninitiated readers who wish to learn more about British archives would do well to consult *Record Repositories in Great Britain* (revised 9th ed., London, 1994), a handbook and summary bibliography published by the Royal Commission on Historical Manuscripts.

Introduction

In the 1120s, King Henry I directed a writ to the Bishop of Ely and the barons of Cambridgeshire informing them of his intent to restrict commercial activity within their county to the town of Cambridge.[1] Henceforward, ships were not to land, carts were not to be loaded, and tolls were not to be collected elsewhere than in the county town. In announcing this constraint, Henry paid homage to a tradition of commercial restriction that stretched back several centuries. "Let every market be in a city", says a tenth-century law of Athelstan, formulating a policy that several other Anglo-Saxon kings sought to emulate.[2] Henry's writ looked much more to this past than to the future. By the time his great-grandson and namesake—Henry III—was on the throne, such a policy had become virtually inconceivable. In 1265, after the grueling ordeal of civil war, the victorious king sought to reward the town of Shrewsbury for its loyalty during his recent travails. A blanket commercial monopoly of the sort given to Cambridge in the previous century was out of the question; in fact, the best Henry III could do for his loyal burgesses was to restrict sales of wool in Shropshire to the town *and* to other formally established markets and towns in the county.[3] It was no longer possible to pour all of a county's trade through a single funnel; all the merchants of an important county town could hope for was a limit on the number of other markets they needed to visit in the conduct of their business. And once the genie was out of the bottle, it would never go back in. By the time Henry III's great-grandson, Edward III, was on the throne, these other markets and towns had become firmly enmeshed in the economic order, so much so that the king, desperate for every penny he could find to finance the opening phase of the Hundred Years War, arranged to include in a parliamentary grant of taxes a special assessment on places that could not in any juridical or administrative sense be treated as towns but which nonetheless were home to merchants and mercantile possessions.[4] Henry I would have been astonished at how things had changed.

The goal of this book is to explain how this commercial transformation occurred. At the beginning of the period studied here, England had a skeletal network of towns producing goods for exchange and a thin veneer of commercial activity in the countryside; by the end of the period, the country had towns that were well integrated into national and international trading networks and a dense and articulated system of rural markets with a commercial infrastructure closely allied to developments in the towns. The significance of this change can be seen in many contrasts between life in the twelfth century and life in the fourteenth century. In the twelfth century, coinage in circulation in England amounted to less than £125,000; by the fourteenth century it had risen nearly tenfold, to about £1,100,000.[5] At the beginning of the twelfth century, the number of functioning marketplaces in the country can be counted in scores; by the fourteenth century the number has to be counted in hundreds. In the twelfth century, a town with a few thousand residents ranked among the leading urban centers in the country; in the fourteenth century, towns of that size were commonplace, and a large provincial town such as Norwich had a population ten or twelve times as large.[6] In the twelfth century, most peasants paid their rents by providing their lords with manual labor; by the fourteenth century virtually all peasants paid at least some of their rent in money, and villeins in many parts of the country had reached agreement with their lords to commute obligatory work services into cash payments. No matter where we look for comparison, we find a substantially more sophisticated level of economic life in the fourteenth century, with local forms of production and distribution firmly ensconced in the orbit of regional networks of trade.

Many parts of this story have already been told. In fact, interest in the commercial life of medieval England has a long pedigree, stretching back into the nineteenth century to such historiographical giants as F. W. Maitland and James Thorold Rogers. The first half of the twentieth century produced several sophisticated syntheses on the subject, notably those by E. Lipson and L. F. Salzman, as well as dozens of local and regional studies that attempted to illustrate the interconnections between a developing commercial framework and the history of particular towns, villages and counties.[7] Some of this momentum dissipated in the aftermath of World War II, as social and economic historians shifted their attention to demography, estate studies, and the techniques and productivity of agriculture. As in much advanced scholarship in these generations, big pictures were presented on small tableaux: the individual estate, the individual village, the individual town. Commercial life came to be studied only in specialized contexts, chiefly in studies of international exchange and in histories of particular towns.

This phase of relatively benign neglect ended rather suddenly in the 1980s with a spate of new works dealing with issues in commercial history: Richard

Britnell established a framework for the systematic study of rural markets; Rodney Hilton and J. A. Raftis explored small towns and their bonds with the countryside; John Langdon investigated the history of transport; Christopher Dyer studied consumption patterns; Kathleen Biddick introduced the notion of choice and competition among rural markets; Bruce Campbell redefined the parameters of agricultural productivity; and numerous others adopted a commercial framework in studies of towns and regions.[8] The seeds planted by these scholars are now yielding a bumper crop, including an impressive number of research monographs and works of synthesis. In 1993, a team of scholars working under the auspices of the Center for Metropolitan History at the University of London (Bruce Campbell, Derek Keene, James Galloway, and Margaret Murphy) published an extended study of London's grain trade in the first half of the fourteenth century, documenting commercial contacts in the period that regularly extended up to a distance of 100 miles from the city.[9] In the same year, Richard Britnell produced a synthesis of research into commercial developments over the half-millennium between 1000 and 1500, emphasizing the institutional framework of commercial change and the social context from which it sprang.[10] Three other books devoted to commercialization found their way into circulation in 1995: Richard Britnell and Bruce Campbell edited an important collection of essays by a number of leading scholars in the field; Edward Miller and John Hatcher sought to coalesce current thinking about the role of towns and trade in the period; and Maryanne Kowaleski published a ground-breaking study of the regional commercial networks that developed in and around the town of Exeter, focusing on the interaction between an important regional town, its port and maritime connections, and its surrounding hinterland.[11]

These recent studies have shed much light on the role commerce played in transforming the social and economic life of medieval England, but they have not illuminated all areas of the subject equally well. A particularly deep shadow still falls over rural commerce and the relationship between country markets and other, better known, commercial institutions. Rural trade is inconsistently documented in surviving records, and much of the evidence is episodic and scattered indiscriminately across an array of different archives and sources. It is widely assumed that our knowledge of particular rural markets does not and cannot extend beyond the minimal details recorded in the royal charters that authorized their existence. Subjects such as the ultimate success or failure of a market, the relationships between different markets in the same area, and the interaction between markets and towns—the stock in trade of anthropologists and geographers who study peasant marketing in other periods and places—have not yet received their due from historians seeking to understand commercialization in a medieval context. The vast majority of knowledge about commercial activity in the period is based on developments in the towns, and while it is natural that historians should use urban economies as springboards to study commercial development across society as a whole, in practice the approach can be problematic. Most urban history in recent years has been local history, with the records generated by the town under investigation inevitably defining the boundaries of inquiry.[12] Depending on the quality of surviving records, commercial relations with the countryside have been either omitted from the field of inquiry or described only as subsidiary elements of the town's economy. Typically, the urban historian seeks to discover what is distinctive about the particular town he or she studies—distinctive not only in the sense of how the given town differs from other towns but also in the sense of how it differs from a vast and amorphous countryside. Consequently, towns are often seen as entities that managed to extricate themselves from what went on in the countryside rather than as constituent elements of regional market systems that embraced both town and country.

This book interprets medieval commercialization from a different perspective, one that sees the process as involving the countryside as deeply as the towns. Such an interpretation requires a rethinking of both sides of the rural-urban relationship, insinuating towns more assiduously into the rural matrix of the overall economy, while also insinuating the countryside more assiduously into the regional matrix of commercial activity. To facilitate such rethinking, this book taps an array of sources that other historians interested in the subject either have not used or have used in different ways. Most of these have been drawn from the central archives of royal government, a treasure trove for historians of all persuasions. By the end of the book, the reader will have a passing familiarity with the local assessors responsible for evaluating their neighbors' property in parliamentary grants of taxation, the sheriffs responsible for requisitioning and transporting foodstuffs for the king's army, and the plaintiffs and defendants who found their way into the king's courts to assert their rights to profit from trade in one way or another. Because of this intimate involvement of royal government in commercial life, we have at our disposal a far richer body of material to investigate rural trade and the interaction between towns and markets in the High Middle Ages than is commonly thought. Indeed, the sheer volume of material in central government sources related to commercial activity is eloquent testimony to the importance of the changes this book seeks to explain.

The kind of market-based trade explored in the following chapters occurs in a wide array of economic, social, and political settings. In spite of extreme differences from one place to the next, economic anthropologists and geographers have discovered that most systems of exchange have certain structural elements in common, elements that allow us to make meaningful comparisons among widely differing social and economic environments. A common model used to explain these similarities is central-place theory, which attempts to explain the interrelationship between different kinds of markets within a given area and to account for the way these markets form themselves into integrated, hierarchical systems of exchange.[13] According to central-place theory, if a region attains a reasonable level of security for the possession and exchange of private property and simultaneously develops marketing institutions without any strongly distorting political interference, it will eventually move toward an integrated system featuring a hierarchy of commercial venues. Certain markets, usually those based in larger towns, will serve as regional clearing houses, or central places, while other markets will provide contact points between the central places and the surrounding areas. The configuration of each central-place hierarchy is unique, depending on the entire range of cultural, geographical, and technological features that distinguish one region from the next, but the fundamental relationships between different elements of the marketing system are relatively consistent, whether they are observed in a region of peasant farmers or in a region of the consumption-crazed, post-industrial modern world.

Every market in every commercial system serves as both a "bulker" and a "breaker" of the common goods in circulation, and central-place theory helps to explain the kind of bulking and breaking occurring in any given site. The essential difference between a lower-order center and a higher-order center derives principally from the scale on which the site bulks and breaks. A simple rural market typically bulks only the agricultural commodities produced in its vicinity and breaks modest consignments of consumer goods acquired elsewhere into individual retail units. A city functions the same way for the producers and consumers living in its vicinity, but it also bulks and breaks on a larger scale, bulking for exchange with other cities the produce first assembled in the outlying markets of its hinterland and breaking for distribution to the same hinterland markets large wholesale consignments of goods imported from other regions. In a well-articulated central-place system, both the rural market and the city benefit from this relationship: Both sites expand the demand for goods generated or obtained locally beyond the level attainable within the site itself or within the vicinity of the site, and both sites give access to a wider array of imported goods than would be the case if they functioned in isolation. In other words, by articulating themselves with other commercial sites in the region, all markets are able to tap into broader and deeper pools of supply and demand than would otherwise be available—the whole is invariably greater than the sum of its parts.

Although first formulated in the nineteenth century, central-place theory was not systematically applied to the study of preindustrial peasant economies until the 1960s, when G. William Skinner used it in his study of markets in China.[14] Skinner divided traditional Chinese market centers into three basic types: standard, intermediate, and central.[15] Trade in the standard markets was the first stage in the circulation of goods upward from the local peasant economy and the terminus before peasant consumption for goods moving downward from higher-order centers. The intermediate market was defined geographically and commercially as the threshold between the small scale trade of the standard markets and the capital intensive trade of the central markets. Traders at these intermediate sites sometimes engaged in wholesale trading with merchants from the central markets, but they did so primarily as a consequence of their bulking and breaking for the standard markets. The central market, ordinarily a strategic transportation site, was distinguished by its dominance of wholesale trade. It was the link between the lower order centers of its region and the commercial universe outside the region. In this capacity, it did the final bulking of goods destined for trade with the central markets of other regions and it also served as the gateway for wholesale goods sent from these other regions, which would eventually percolate down to the intermediate and standard markets of its own region.

Among medieval historians, central-place theory has had an ambivalent reception.[16] Several studies of the markets in particular counties, such as Tim Unwin's study of the markets of Nottinghamshire, have attempted to apply tenets of the theory in a medieval context but have failed to generate conclusive results from the effort.[17] On the other hand, regional studies that have eschewed the theory have sometimes reached conclusions that suggest the viability of the model. A good example is Étienne Fournial's study of the Forez region of France, which proffered a description of the region's exchange network that has much in common with Skinner's description of China.[18] Fournial distinguished the area's markets into three basic types. At the base of the system were a large number of markets that existed solely for the purchase and sale of basic provisions, local commercial venues in which transactions involved small quantities of goods destined for domestic consumption. Above these local markets were a limited number of higher-level centers functioning as internal redistribution points, places where merchants from the highest-order centers went to sell internationally traded mercantile goods *(le grand commerce)* and to buy local specialties such as leather and cloth. These intermediate centers were also the focus of merchants residing in settlements without formal markets, who sought to buy merchandise to resell in their home communities. At the top of the trading hierarchy were a few major towns with active year-round trade. These were the centers controlling *le grand commerce* and involved in trade with similar centers in other regions. Fournial did not consciously adopt central-place theory in his study, but his conclusions fit readily within the theoretical framework of the model.

This book is not intended to be a commentary on the applicability of central-place theory, but it is written in the belief that many of the premises of the theory are demonstrably applicable in a medieval context: the premise that rural markets can be categorized according to their importance in a larger regional context; that different kinds of markets were integrated with each other into larger regional systems; that these systems revolved around the leading towns; that economic integration between town and country occurred by means of these hierarchical constellations of markets; and that regional constellations were in turn integrated with other constellations to form a rudimentary national economy. The regional constellations of markets that bound town and country together began to develop in the latter part of the twelfth century, gained momentum through the thirteenth, and reached a relatively mature state by the fourteenth century. This mature structure formed the basis of much of English economic life in the following centuries, right up to the Industrial Revolution and the allied urbanization of the nineteenth century—in other words, for as long as England retained a predominantly rural economy. Much of what has been written on commercialization in England in this period has concentrated on external indicators of economic change. This book examines the underlying infrastructures without which such change would not have occurred, or at least would not have occurred in the way it did.

The book is divided into four sections. The two chapters of part 1 explore some of the economic characteristics of towns and villages that shaped commercial relations between the two. Chapter 1 looks at patterns of employment and wealth in a number of towns, drawing attention to the prominence of agricultural commodities as the principal basis of both consumption and production in urban economies. Even in towns, most of the goods in circulation originated in the fields and pastures of the countryside, and, consequently, most objects first became commodities of trade in a rural context, or at least in a nonurban context. Yet at the same time, much of the processing and distribution of these goods took place in an urban setting. This symbiosis lay at the heart of the medieval exchange economy: Towns depended on rural producers for their supplies of industrial raw materials and basic sustenance, while the countryside depended on urban consumers and producers to generate a level of demand that made market production a rewarding enterprise. Chapter 2 builds on this premise by examining more directly the production of agricultural commodities, with particular emphasis given to the role of peasant producers. Many historians see the production and distribution of commercial goods in a peasant society as an incidental byproduct of an economy overwhelmingly oriented toward subsistence, arguing that only an industrialized, capitalist system of production has the capacity to generate a consistent and sustainable supply of commodities for exchange.[19] Transferred to a medieval context, this presumption has frequently led historians to turn to the great estates of the privileged classes when seeking to explain the market in agricultural staples. But though lords undoubtedly took advantage of the towns' demand for agricultural commodities, the central premise of chapter 2 is that they took a back seat to their tenants. Collectively, the peasantry was the most important group of commodity producers in the medieval economy; when urban workers spun yarn and brewed ale, the wool and barley they worked was more likely to have come from peasant producers than from any other source. Consequently, the commercial networks that arose to transfer goods from the countryside to the towns necessarily bore the imprint of a rural economy that was dominated by small-scale producers.

The second part of the book moves from production and consumption to distribution, describing the principal commercial nodes in the economy and their relationship to each other. The number of rural markets in the country increased dramatically over the course of the period investigated here. At first glance, the very multiplicity of sites suggests a highly fragmented commercial system characterized by isolation and the absence of integrating regional structures. But as discussed in chapter 3, this view is based on a misunderstanding of how and why the founders of new markets sought to establish new venues. Attempts to establish new markets were deliberate, premeditated acts by individuals and corporations, involving a number of rights and procedures prescribed and protected by the crown. By investigating the institutional apparatus that the founders of markets used to establish their rights and the legal framework in which they preserved them, we can analyze the expectations and assumptions that founders brought to the enterprise. Founders knew very well that their creations had to fit into preexisting regional structures of trade if they were to be successful, and they also knew that their creations had to attract trade on a level beyond that conducted by local households if they were to justify the effort of creation. Over the course of the thirteenth and early fourteenth centuries, these markets met a variety of fates: Some failed entirely; others barely established a toehold in the regional hierarchy; yet others became thriving centers generating substantial volumes of trade. At first glance, the number of sites and the diversity of their fates seems to put almost insurmountable obstacles in the way of anyone who tries to define the boundaries of the regional systems in which they operated, but the problems are not quite as intractable as they seem. Towns were the anchors of all regional trade, and we have numerous sources to gauge the size, wealth, and commercial significance of different towns. Thanks to a unique experiment in taxation undertaken at the end of our period, described in chapter 4, we can also isolate the most important rural markets in many parts of the country. By cross-referencing these different sources, we can develop an overview of the spatial horizons and internal structures of the prevailing regional commercial networks of the period, identifying some of the variety in regional networks, and distinguishing common traits over larger areas.

These networks involved several different levels of exchange, and the third part of this book seeks to identify and distinguish the different levels. Each of the chapters in this section addresses a different kind of commercial activity: Chapter 5 deals with trade between towns, almost invariably conducted by merchants; Chapter 6 deals with the penetration of the countryside by merchants based in towns but facing competition from other commercial agents based in the countryside; and Chapter 7 deals with trade into towns by residents of the surrounding countryside. Most of the actual transactions we can observe in this period were recorded in the context of establishing rights of access to different kinds of commercial venues. Disputes over access to markets arose in many contexts, but they fall into recognizable patterns: situations involving the corporate rights of two towns; situations involving the access to an urban market by residents of the surrounding countryside; and situations involving the corporate rights of a town and the private rights of an individual or corporation based in the countryside, such as the holder of a market franchise. Thus, although the division of trade into these different types is largely a modern analytical construct designed to impose order on a disparate body of evidence, it is not entirely divorced from the contexts in which individuals with commercial interests were likely to find themselves.

To illustrate the structure and dynamics of regional trading networks in as concrete a fashion as possible, the fourth part of this book explores the infrastructure and operation of a single regional marketing system. The main focus of the section is the network of markets functioning in the county of Huntingdonshire, but consideration is also given to the interplay between these markets and those of neighboring counties. Chapter 8 develops a method for distinguishing between different levels of rural markets and offers a model defining the spatial and temporal boundaries of the region's interlocking marketing networks. In the case of Huntingdonshire, the county came reasonably close to forming a single marketing network, although this overlap was more a product of the size of the county than of its administrative boundaries. One of the essential criteria determining the extent to which a particular group of markets will coalesce into an integrated network of trade is the efficiency of transportation and communications within the network. This topic is taken up in chapter 9, which reconstructs the transportation infrastructure developed in Huntingdonshire and its environs in the period. By setting the physical and technological parameters within which trade occurred, roads, rivers, and bridges exerted a profound influence over the development of individual commercial sites and the shape of larger regional networks. Both the design of Huntingdonshire's transportation infrastructure and the concern for its maintenance are consistent with the view that the county's markets operated as elements of a regional system. Further corroboration of the regional context of trade is furnished in chapter 10, which documents the flow of people and goods within the region. Merchants from neighboring counties can be found attending rural markets in Huntingdonshire, and traders from the county can be found operating in a variety of commercial settings well removed from the towns and villages in which they normally resided. Huntingdonshire had particularly strong ties with King's Lynn, the coastal port that serviced the county's two principal rivers. These ties overlapped internal marketing arrangements and drew the area into the currents of national and international trade.

This book seeks to be as thorough as possible within the adopted chronological and thematic limits, but it makes no claim to exhaustiveness. Some important veins of material have scarcely been scouted out, let alone mined. The role of fairs in developing regional structures of trade, for example, is only dealt with in passing, partly because Ellen Wedemeyer Moore has recently traversed the subject's upper reaches, and partly for thematic reasons.[20] The goal of this study is to convey a sense of regional trade as a regular and routine part of social and economic life for a broad spectrum of society, and fairs by definition were exceptional events. Smaller regional fairs, which were nearly as abundant as local markets, come closer to meeting the set criteria than the great international fairs, but they generally operated as an expansion of the weekly market rather than as an entirely distinctive form of commercial activity. In the course of a market dispute in Great Yarmouth in 1228, for example, an investigating jury noted in its verdict that a nearby weekly market was "augmented" at fair time by sales of horses and oxen but otherwise functioned in the same way.[21] As S. R. Epstein has recently demonstrated, fairs were more durable institutions than most historians have thought, but they were less important in the development of regional networks of trade in the period investigated here than were towns and markets.[22] Consequently, this book concentrates on the latter. The field of mercantile practices, involving such issues as credit arrangements, contracts, partnerships, and recordkeeping, is likewise not covered systematically in the following pages. For commercial historians interested in England, many of these subjects continue to be areas of *terra incognita,* though a few trails have been blazed in recent years.[23] Occasional forays onto this terrain are made in the text in order to provide a context for a particular case history or archival source, but at the moment the undergrowth is too thick to permit a deeper penetration of the subject, desirable though it might be.

England went through many enduring transformations in the period covered in this book. The thirteenth and early fourteenth centuries saw the issue and reissues of Magna Carta, the origins of Parliament, the maturing of the common law, and revolutionary changes in the use of written records and the conduct of government. Intertwined with these fundamental changes, influenced by certain of them and influencing others, we need to place the formation of regional marketing systems, which gave at least some people a reason and a means to participate in the world beyond the confines of their individual village or town.

Part I

Commodity Production in Town and Country

1

The Urban Commodity Economy

In most descriptions of medieval English towns, economic diversification is presented as a quintessentially urban trait and rightly so, since towns typically accommodated large reservoirs of skilled artisans whose variety of skills greatly enhanced the diversity of material life enjoyed by the rest of society. The economic complement to a diversified labor force was, of course, a diversified realm of commodity production. Outsiders to the field of urban history still tend to see the medieval economy in faded monochromes, emphasizing the limited size of the market and the correspondingly limited variety of consumer goods, but insiders prefer to use richer splashes of color in their depictions, employing hues and tones that are sometimes as vibrant as the stained glass and luxury textiles of the period itself. Both perspectives contain important elements of truth, for the essence of urban life lay in the transformation of a limited range of raw materials into a much broader spectrum of specialized consumer commodities. While both sides of this equation are important to our understanding of the economies of medieval towns, the range and origin of raw materials is both the more striking feature of urban commodity production and the more powerful explanatory tool to describe the relationship between towns and their hinterlands. Such is the premise of the present chapter, which explores the symbiosis between rural and urban production by looking at the deployment of labor and the nature of wealth in towns of the thirteenth and early fourteenth centuries and thus draws attention to the community of interest that bound town and country together.

I

In any pre-industrial economy there is a close correlation between the scale and variety of employment opportunities and the availability of raw materials and the levels of output. Western economies of the late twentieth century are, in this respect, the anomalies of history: In most of the world for most of history, labor inputs have predominated over capital inputs in all areas of manufacturing and processing; the very word "manufacture," of course, literally means "to make by hand." To compensate for the scarcity of capital, nonindustrial economies typically saturate the products of the earth with labor. Because of this intrinsic correlation between raw materials and inputs of labor, levels of employment in particular sectors of an economy can serve as a rough guide to the relative importance of both the raw materials available for processing and the finished products put into circulation.

The labor market of medieval England was characterized first and foremost by considerable occupational diversity.[1] As P. D. A. Harvey has recently shown, even in relatively nondescript peasant villages of the twelfth century we can find local villagers pursuing specialized lines of work.[2] One measure of the panoply of specialized skills in existence is the extraordinary diversity of surnames of occupation: There are at least 165 Middle English surnames derived from the cloth industry alone, and more than 100 each from the metal and victualing trades.[3] Another measure is the ingenuity with which laborers used things that we would consider useless. The butchering of a cow, for example, could give employment to at least 25 different artisans, not including the farmer who raised and the butcher who slaughtered the animal.[4] Several specialized skills were called upon in the sequence of procedures by which the hide was turned into leather, and others were needed to make use of the fat (for tallow), the guts (for cord), and the horn (for glue and opaque glass for lanterns) of the slaughtered animal. The scraped-off hair of the butchered animal served the plasterer as a binding agent, and even the cores of the horns were employed by those in the building trades.

Paradoxically, the same artisans who achieved such levels of specialization also frequently occupied themselves with more than one trade. Like those above and below them in the social scale, artisans and their families grasped at whatever opportunity presented itself.[5] As part of the household economy, wives might brew ale, spin, and produce petty goods such as eggs and fowl for the market in addition to assisting in their husbands' trade. Even seemingly specialized male occupations were often combined with other economic activities: A merchant might be involved in agriculture, for example, or a tanner in the cloth trade. This versatility partly explains both the support for and the invective against guilds and their efforts to eliminate interlopers. Guild members inevitably felt threatened by the seemingly endless supply of cheap labor willing to acquire specialized skills at its own expense, while those outside the guild saw no reason why the most remunerative fields of employment should be the ones most difficult to enter.[6] The result was an ongoing tension that could and often did break out into riot. On the surface, there seems to be a contradiction between a worker's ability to create a tiny niche in the market by developing a microspecialty and the same worker's willingness and ability to be a jack-of-all-trades. This is, however, apparent only to modern, western eyes, used to a world in which material goods are so plentiful that simply disposing of them has become an ecological nightmare. In a pre-industrial economy, the specialization and versatility of labor are branches of the same tree, grounded in the discrepancies between nature's bounty and human reproduction first described by Thomas Malthus.

Specialization and versatility inevitably impose limitations on any attempt to classify the occupational structure of medieval towns. They need not, however, be taken as a counsel of despair, at least not insofar as they relate to the economy of commodities. The scarcity of raw materials and the abundance of labor meant that occupations involving manufacturing and processing were generally ones that contemporaries valued highly, and as such they are the ones that most commonly yielded some form of distinctive occupational labelling. They were also the pursuits commonly monopolized by male heads of households, the individuals most likely to leave traces in Clio's storehouse. There is little doubt that the legions of people involved in "service" in the towns—the nebulous group of apprentices, servants, and others who emerge so strikingly in the poll taxes of the later fourteenth century—were routinely omitted from most sources describing occupations.[7] But members of this group had only an indirect relationship with the economy of commodities: They frequently played a role in transforming raw materials into goods for exchange, but their role was determined by the household in which they lived rather than by the raw materials they transformed. Classifying occupations with sources surviving from before the Plague inevitably skews analysis toward male heads of household of at least moderate wealth involved in the processing or handling of commodities. But though this privileges some sectors of the economy at the expense of others, in the present context we can assume that occupations related to commodity production are well represented.

Data on the occupational structure of four towns are presented in table 1-1.[8] The data for Norwich in the period between 1285 and 1311 and Winchester and Coventry prior to 1300 have been extracted from the reconstructions of Serena Kelly, Derek Keene, and Joan Lancaster, respectively, based on the occupational designations recorded in deeds of property transactions in the three towns.[9] The fourth town is Wallingford, progenitor of a remarkable series of tallage rolls that begin in 1227 and arrange the town's taxpayers into occupational categories, possibly meant to reflect the town's guild structure.[10] The sectoral categories of table 1-1 are adapted from those used by Keene for Winchester.[11] Each category combines a range of specialized occupations: the leather trades, for example, included skinners, tanners, tawyers, glovers and several other specializations. For all of the towns, clerics are excluded from the table and analysis, as are government and service occupations and rarer pursuits that do not fit any of the main sectors presented in the table. The aim of the exercise is not to give a complete and definitive account of urban employment but rather to convey a sense of the relative proportions of workers associated with the principal commodities being produced and exchanged. In all cases, the core groups involved primarily with commodity production constitute substantial majorities of identified occupations, accounting for 72 percent of all occupations recorded in Norwich, 79 percent in Winchester, 88 percent in Coventry, and 100 percent in Wallingford. Clerics make up almost all of the individuals excluded from the Norwich data and about half of those excluded from the Winchester data. A miscellany of occupations was excluded in the Coventry data, with carters and coopers being the most prominent. Although no occupations were excluded from Wallingford, the data presented by that town's tallage rolls are the most artificial of the set, having been molded by the town's administrators as part of a bureaucratic exercise.

TABLE 1-1:
Sectoral Profile of Primary Occupations in Four English Towns (%)

	Norwich 1285-1311 (N=691)	**Winchester ante 1300 (N=150)**	**Wallingford 1227 (N=193)**	**Coventry ante 1300 (N=267)**
Victualing	19	27	22	22
Leather	25	19	18	16
Textiles	21	20	5	20
Clothing	7	11	32	6
Mercantile	14	5	9	12
Metal	8	8	10	16
Building	6	10	5	8

NOTES: Clerical, administrative and miscellaneous occupations are omitted from this table, as explained in the text. In Wallingford some textile workers may have been grouped with clothing trades. In Coventry some clothing workers may have been grouped in mercantile trades. Wallingford percentages do not total 100 because of rounding.
SOURCES: S. Kelly, "The Economic Topography and Structure of Norwich, c. 1300" in *Men of Property,* ed. Ursula Priestly (Norwich, 1983), p. 16; D. Keene, *Survey of Medieval Winchester,* vol. 1, part 1 (Oxford, 1985), pp. 252, 352-65; J. Lancaster, "Crafts and Industries," in *A History of the County of Warwick,* vol. 8, ed. W. B. Stephens, Victoria History of the Counties of England (London, 1969), p. 153; *Sixth Report of the Royal Commission on Historical Manuscripts,* part 1 (London, 1877), pp. 576-79.

Given the nature of our sources, it would be unwise to put too much interpretive weight on either the precise numbers or the variations between towns observable in table 1-1. Far more significant is the broad consensus we can discern among the four towns. Taken as a whole, the data suggest that the leather, textile, and victualing trades dominated the labor market in urban economies, constituting considerably larger shares of employment than any other category. The prominence of each of these sectors was probably even greater than the data in the table convey, particularly in victualing and textile production. Designations of primary occupations tend to obscure the work performed by women and part-timers, work that was more heavily oriented toward victualing and textiles than toward other activities involving commodity production, as Maryanne Kowaleski has shown in her analysis of the occupational profile of Exeter in the later fourteenth century.[12] By cross-referencing local households against the town's voluminous court records, Kowaleski reconstructed in considerable detail the range of secondary employment commonly practiced in Exeter. Her work corroborates the prominence of all three of the main employment sectors documented in table 1-1, both as primary occupations and as secondary or part-time occupations.[13] It also suggests that victualing represented a significantly higher share of total urban employment than is revealed by explicit designations of primary occupations, particularly when the nearly ubiquitous brewing of ale is included.

In spite of the source limitations, there is no reason to suspect that any major economic sectors involving commodity production are entirely hidden from view. Individuals whose status and nominative descriptions did not derive immediately from their work typically occupied economic niches in one of the sectors defined by the groups that are better documented; if anything, they weight urban economies even more heavily toward the most prevalent areas of production. What is clear and consistent in all analyses of urban occupations is the extent to which the economies of towns were dominated by the processing of raw materials produced in the countryside. Victualing, the leather trades, and textile production accounted for at least half of the economic activity in virtually every town, possibly as much as two-thirds. Understanding this orientation is an important step toward understanding the symbiosis between town and village in medieval England, for each of the "big three" sectors of urban employment and production ultimately depended on the fields and pastures of the countryside. Consequently, the growth and prosperity of most towns went hand in hand with the development of commercial links with the countryside, a countryside that supplied not only the foodstuffs necessary to support the burgeoning urban populations of the period but also the goods that underpinned a significant proportion of industrial activity. This in turn suggests some of the commodities likely to have accounted for a substantial share of trade in the period: cereals, fish, and livestock as the principal staples of victualing; hides and wool as the basic raw materials of manufacturing; and victuals, textiles, and leather goods as the principal consumer products. When, in 1275, King Edward I laid the foundations for a national customs system by imposing tariffs on wool, wool fells, and hides, he clearly knew how best to butter the bread of his treasury.[14]

II

An alternate approach to assessing the relative importance of the different commodities in circulation is to cull the evidence about material possessions available in the local rolls of the lay subsidies, particularly the local rolls that survive for towns. These rolls list the goods held by individuals at the time of assessment and furnish an estimate of the value of the different goods making up each individual's personal portfolio of commodities. By aggregating this information, we can measure the relative value of different commodities existing in specific places at specific points in time.

The subsidy was the principal means of taxation in medieval England, intimately associated with the needs of war financing and thus frequently employed during the reigns of the three Edwards.[15] It was a tax assessed on chattels, with a prescribed fraction (varying from one-sixth to one-fortieth) of the appraised value of the chattels owed as tax. Prior to the standardized levies introduced in 1334, every parliamentary grant of a subsidy to the king involved a massive administrative effort to evaluate the property of virtually every household in the country. Grants of subsidies were irregular, and thus each subsidy required a fresh appraisal of the country's resources. The appraisals of chattels were made by local jurors empaneled for the purpose, who had the dubious honor of going from house to house in the town or village to appraise the chattels of their fellow householders.[16] These local boards of assessment were required to make a precise record of what they found—how many bushels of wheat an individual held on the day of assessment and how much they were worth, how much livestock was owned, and so on—and send it to the chief taxers appointed by the king to supervise the collection in each county.

As is well known, the records of these taxes exist in various stages of redaction. At the local and county level, the documents survive principally in two forms. The most common form is a simple listing of the names of the taxpayers in each town or village and the amount of tax owed by each individual. These county lists were drawn up from more detailed local assessment lists—the second common form—which give not only the name of the taxpayer and the amount of tax owed but also the portfolio of chattels evaluated by the assessors, often including appraisals of the value of each item. The county lists recorded all the information that was needed by the officials responsible for collecting and auditing the tax. Consequently, they were routinely preserved at the Exchequer, while the local assessment rolls, with their mass of details about individual commodities and their values, proved to be too unwieldy for the Exchequer to work with and thus rarely found their way into the safety of storerooms in Westminster. Nevertheless, a small number of local assessment rolls did manage to escape the parchment recyclers, sometimes as evidence in contested appraisals, sometimes as appendages to county rolls that a weary auditor chose to overlook when consigning the rolls to storage, and sometimes by cautious local officials who wanted to keep a record of the taxpayers in the community chest for future reference.

Because they itemize individual goods and estimate their value, local subsidy rolls are an exceptionally useful source with which to study the commodity market of the period—although not always a completely accurate one. In theory, the assessors who appraised the goods of their peers evaluated all chattels, but in practice they allowed certain types of goods to escape notice. Some of their generosity in this regard resulted from explicit exemptions mandated in the parliamentary grants authorizing collection of the tax.[17] Among these official exemptions, three are worth mentioning as influencing every subsidy assessment. The property of the Church derived from "spiritualities," such as tithes and glebes, was exempt, although "temporalities," such as the produce of a manor, were liable for assessment. In order to protect the poor, those with chattels worth less than a specified minimum amount were also officially relieved of most of the levies. The third major exemption entailed specific kinds of clothing and household furnishings. These are specified in the writs sent to the chief assessors, known as the "forms" of taxation. The items specified varied slightly from year to year, but generally included a suit of clothing for the husband and wife, the couple's bed, and a few other items of adornment.

Those who have worked closely with the assessments made prior to their standardization in 1334 have also suggested that the assessors regularly incorporated certain unofficial exemptions into their appraisals. These tacit allowances bedevil any attempt to correlate a settlement's total wealth with its recorded taxation value, and the analysis of the subsidies in this chapter makes no claim to resolve this conundrum. James Willard observed long ago that the basic working stock of farmers and artisans seldom appears as a tax liability and that the holdings of grain attributed to most households would not suffice to keep the family alive from year to year. He concluded from these observations that a family's working capital and basic subsistence needs were normally considered to be beyond the limits of taxation. Working from this observation, Willard suggested—and others who have worked with the subsidy records have accepted—that what was ordinarily assessed in a lay subsidy were the chattels that were surplus to the minimum consumption needs of the household.[18] This position was, in fact, explicitly noted in the assessments made in the reign of Henry III. In 1225, the form of taxation specifically exempted a merchant's riding horse, household tools, and basic foodstuffs, and a villein's tools, foodstuffs that were not for sale, and hay and forage that were not for sale.[19] Later forms of assessment are not as explicit on this point, but the local assessment rolls reveal that the 1225 rules continued to influence the practice that Willard described as "customary exemption." What we typically see, then, when we look at a local lay subsidy roll is a partial rather than a complete listing of the principal forms of property in a community. Hidden from view are the belongings of the poor, the goods held for simple consumption and reproduction in all households, and possibly other indeterminate goods that the assessors tacitly exempted when they made their rounds.

Limited though they are as a measure of total wealth, local subsidy rolls are our most comprehensive registers of movable property, and they cast considerable light on the basic configuration of urban economies in the late thirteenth and early fourteenth centuries. Local assessment rolls from a number of towns have survived,[20] and although the level of precision and rigor inherent in these rolls fluctuates considerably from one assessment to the next, particularly thorough examples survive from Ipswich in 1283, Shrewsbury in 1306, and Colchester in 1301.[21] These three places furnish a good cross-section of medieval English towns: Ipswich was a thriving port and prosperous town in the period; Shrewsbury was of comparable size and wealth, but its distributive function is more accurately described as that of an inland regional capital; and Colchester was a smaller and less wealthy town than the others in this period, although like the other two it served as the central urban focus of its county.[22]

Data on the absolute and relative values of the various commodities assessed in the three towns are presented in tables 1-2 through 1-4. These represent the sum total of all of the individual assessments given in the subsidy rolls. In each table, the first column indicates the kind of asset assessed and the second the number of taxpayers holding that asset as part of their portfolio of taxable property, also expressed as a percentage of all taxpayers included in the assessment (or, in the case of Ipswich, the percentage of all taxpayers with itemized inventories in the assessment). The third column indicates the sum of all holdings of the relevant commodity in the assessment, accompanied by a statement of the percentage of all assessed property that commodity represents. Thus, in the case of Shrewsbury in 1306 (see table 1-3), the relevant entry indicates that 120 people paid tax on malt and barley in the town and that their total stock was appraised at £51. These 120 holders of brewing grain comprised 48 percent of all taxpayers recorded in the assessment, and their stock comprised 11 percent of the total property assessed in the town. As in the case of malt and barley, most of the entries in the tables consist of categories of related goods rather than the specific items listed in the documents—the entry for grain, for example, includes individual assessments of wheat, rye, oats, and peas. The aim of this amalgamation is to distinguish more clearly the principal sectors of economic activity, as was done with the employment sectors discussed earlier in this chapter. The idiosyncrasies of each assessment and the methods used to deal with them are described more fully in the following pages, and technical details about the categories and the treatment of unusual entries in the sources are provided in Appendix 1.

Partly because of the widespread acceptance of customary exemptions, some historians have questioned the reliability of the itemized listings.[23] Clearly, the property found in the subsidy rolls cannot be equated with the total wealth possessed either by an individual town or by an individual taxpayer, nor is it certain how well the values calculated from subsidy records reflect total wealth in the different towns.[24] But although the omission and possible undernumeration of some types of wealth requires us to be circumspect in interpreting the subsidy rolls, their limitations should not be allowed to overwhelm their virtues.[25] For present purposes, their limitations as registers of total wealth are less problematic than they might initially appear to be. The comparison of three different subsidies from three different towns in three different years compensates somewhat for possible defects in any single assessment; similarities in the subsidies are more likely to have resulted from real situations than from coincidence. Furthermore, focusing on the relative proportions of wealth exhibited within each subsidy rather than on the absolute totals eliminates the hopeless task of translating between taxable wealth and total wealth and instead allows concentration on what the subsidies reveal about the different forms of wealth and their relationship to each other. The assessments do not furnish an exact facsimile of any community's entire store of wealth, but they do furnish a realistic representation of its principal constituents.

The earliest of the three subsidy rolls, and probably the most thorough, survives from a tax of one-thirtieth collected in Ipswich in 1283 to finance the war in Wales.[26] The assessors' instructions required them to tax all the movable goods of towndwellers held as of January 20 (the octave of the Feast of St. Hilary) but to exempt people whose goods were worth less than 6s. 8d. Their instructions did not mention any official exemptions on goods, but they did mandate that the customary practices of earlier assessments be followed. The roll documenting their appraisals lists assessments for 276 individuals with a remarkably high assessed wealth of almost £1,800. Data about the total worth of the commodities assessed in Ipswich in 1283 are presented in table 1-2. The data in the table represent taxable commodities worth £1,426, or about four-fifths of all assessed wealth in the town. The remaining fifth included assessments of cash and debts (totalling just under £120, or about 7 percent of all assessed wealth) and assessments that did not distinguish the values of individual commodities. These latter entries occur either as lump sum valuations for all possessions or as single valuations for multiple goods. Apart from the fact that household goods are often involved, the latter form of combination assessment appears to be haphazard and thus unlikely to skew the data in the table to any significant extent.

Table 1-2 lists the commodities in descending order of total assessed value in the subsidy roll. As can be seen in the table, household and personal goods, consisting principally of clothing and undifferentiated utensils, formed the largest reserve of taxable wealth in Ipswich, as they did in each of the other two towns considered here. While this prominence in the assessment suggests in a general way the importance of domestic consumer goods in local economies, the category is too nebulous to be of much help in assessing the principal foundations of urban economic life. More significant in this regard are the other, more precisely identified commodities taxed in Ipswich. Ranking just behind household goods as a store of taxable wealth is the town's aggregate stock of malt and barley, which totaled approximately 16 percent of the value of all the goods included in the table. In most instances

TABLE 1-2:
Commodities Taxed in Ipswich, 1283

Commodity	No. of Holders	Aggregate Value
Household/personal goods	168 (80%)	£238 11s. (17%)
Malt and barley	93 (44%)	£233 18s. (16%)
Ships and boats	36 (17%)	£157 3s. (11%)
Cloth	17 (8%)	£135 19s. (10%)
Wool	21 (9%)	£87 2s. (6%)
Stone	5 (2%)	£73 18s. (5%)
Livestock	63 (30%)	£68 4s. (5%)
Grain	49 (23%)	£64 13s. (5%)
Hides and leather	28 (13%)	£64 11s. (5%)
Horses and carts	44 (21%)	£62 19s. (4%)
Wood	26 (12%)	£47 11s. (3%)
Mercery	11 (5%)	£46 13s. (3%)
Iron and coal	11 (5%)	£39 3s. (3%)
Wine	5 (2%)	£31 17s. (2%)
Textile supplies	8 (4%)	£20 3s. (1%)
Meat	9 (4%)	£17 7s. (1%)
Salt	9 (4%)	£16 1s. (1%)
Miscellaneous	13 (6%)	£20 9s. (1%)

NOTES: "Miscellaneous" includes lime, gold, turves, candles, wax, bows, hempseed, lard, tallow, grease, spices, fish, cheese, and butter. Percentages in aggregate value column do not total 100 because of rounding.
SOURCE: E. Powell, "The Taxation of Ipswich for the Welsh War in 1282," *Proceedings of the Suffolk Institute of Archaeology* 12 (1906): 137-57.

the record simply gives a cash value for individual stores, but in a few instances the assessors appraised the stores at a value of 4s. per quarter of eight bushels, suggesting an assessed stock of well over 1,000 quarters (or 8,000 bushels). Barley was the predominant cereal crop in most parts of Suffolk, although its predominance over other grains is greater than one would expect from the agrarian practices of the town's hinterland.[27] Following malt in total assessed value is the category of ships and boats, which constituted a bit more than one-tenth of discernible assessed wealth. Cloth held a position of roughly equal significance to the maritime sector as a source of taxable wealth. Each of the remaining commodities—wool, stone, livestock, grain, hides and leather, horses and carts, wood, mercery, iron and coal, wine, textile supplies, meat, and salt—constituted a relatively small share of assessed wealth. Of these commodities, the occurrence of a significant stock of stoneware—comprising millstones and gravestones—is particularly interesting. Ipswich's role as an importer of stone is attested in another contemporary source; the item's unusually high profile in the subsidy reinforces the impression that the town's assessors were exceptionally meticulous in carrying out their assignments.[28]

The concentration of wealth in particular commodities in the town varied markedly from one commodity to the next, as can be seen in the second column of table 1-2, which records the number of people holding each of the commodities. Not surprisingly, household goods were the most widely distributed taxable item in the town, the only one held by a substantial majority of taxpayers. Apart from household goods, simple agricultural produce—malt and barley, livestock, and grain—constituted the most widely distributed forms of taxable property. The market in malt and barley had a few heavyweights, such as Hugh Golding, who held £40 worth, and Hugh Lyn, who held £24 worth, but it was characterized more by a disparate group of people holding stocks assessed at amounts ranging from about 10s. to about 30s., the probable equivalent of somewhere between two and eight quarters. By contrast, the ownership of goods that had a more strictly mercantile or industrial orientation, such as cloth, stone, and watercraft, tended to be concentrated in fewer hands. This is a pattern we might expect: goods that could be processed within the household as an extension of basic subsistence production were held widely, whereas goods demanding specialized manufacture and heavy initial investments were not. The principal exception to this rule is wool, which can be worked at the household level in small amounts yet proves to be a market dominated by a relatively small group of people. In fact, well over half of the stock of wool assessed in Ipswich was held by a single merchant.[29] The stock of wool assessed in Ipswich is smaller than one might expect, though it is prominent enough to suggest that it was not omitted from the assessment as a customary exemption. It is possible that possessors of wool were more successful at evading the eye of the assessor than were the holders of other goods, although it is difficult to see why wool could be concealed when cloth was so commonly assessed. It is more likely, though, that there is a structural explanation for the apparent shortage of wool in the urban assessments, a point that will be developed more fully after the subsidy data from the other towns have been set on the table.

Like the thirtieth collected in Ipswich in 1283, the twentieth collected in Shrewsbury in 1306 involved a relatively low fractional rate and thus may have netted a greater share of total property than other, more onerous subsidy assessments.[30] Shrewsbury's assessors were instructed to exempt individuals with property worth less than 10s. but to record all other property held by residents of the town on Michaelmas (September 29).[31] The assessors appraised the property of 251 residents of the town, with chattels worth approximately £500. Other sources from the period suggest that Shrewsbury was somewhat larger and wealthier than Ipswich, suggesting in turn that its assessors were not as thorough in 1306 as their East Anglian counterparts had been in 1283.[32] On the other hand, a comparison of the roll with records surviving from a number of other subsidy assessments conducted in the town suggests that the assessors were exceptionally precise in listing and evaluating local property in 1306, a precision that was probably due to the presence in the town of the king's court—including the Keeper of the Wardrobe, who had been put in charge of the collection in Shropshire—while the assessment was in progress.[33]

Data on the relative values of the different commodities taxed in Shrewsbury are presented in table 1-3. Because the assessors scrupulously assigned a value to every item listed in the personal inventories, the table includes well over nine-tenths of the commodities occurring in the subsidy roll, with only holdings of cash, totalling about £30, left out. As can be seen in the table, the range of commodities in Shrewsbury is similar to that in Ipswich, although somewhat more restricted. The most noticeable difference between the goods assessed in the two towns is the virtual omission of maritime equipment and stoneware in the Shrewsbury roll. Shrewsbury's assessors also included negligible amounts of a few other goods that were more visible in the Ipswich assessment such as salt and textile supplies, but on the whole the similarities of the assessed inventory are more noteworthy than the differences.

While Shrewsbury's range of goods is similar to that of Ipswich, the taxable amounts of the different commodities are fairly different. Given the imperfect nature of our sources, however, it would be unwise to attach too much significance to minor variations in assessment from one subsidy to the next. Undoubtedly, some of the categories in Shrewsbury are seriously underrepresented, wool being the most obvious example. Shropshire was one of the leading wool producing regions in the country, and by the fourteenth century Shrewsbury's merchants had acquired national standing as major players in the marketing of the region's clip.[34] The poor showing of wool in 1306 can only be attributed to a deliberate policy of excluding it from taxation. Other major differences in the profiles of assessed wealth in Shrewsbury and Ipswich, though, are much more likely to reflect real economic differences than procedural inconsistencies. The most noticeable of these differences is Shrewsbury's much greater concentration of wealth in cereals, comprising 20 percent of assessed wealth there as opposed to only 5 percent in Ipswich. Malt and barley were important stores of wealth in both towns, although they were less prominent in terms of relative aggregate value in Shrewsbury than in Ipswich and considerably less prominent in relation to other cereal crops. Pastoralism also appears to have found greater favor in the Salopian town, a feature suggested by the greater proportional shares of horses, other livestock, and hides and leather goods. Considering Shrewsbury's reputation as a center of the leather industry at this time, one might have expected an even greater concentration in hides than occurs in the subsidy, but even in its muted form, the figure suggests a different economic emphasis. Despite these differences, a number of closer parallels in the two subsidies exist, particularly in the categories involving industrial and mercantile goods such as mercery, iron and coal, and, to a lesser extent, cloth.

TABLE 1-3:
Commodities Taxed in Shrewsbury, 1306

Commodity	**No. of Holders**	**Aggregate Value**
Household/personal goods	251 (100%)	£116 18s. (26%)
Grain	152 (61%)	£88 8s. (20%)
Malt and barley	120 (48%)	£51 6s. (11%)
Horses and carts	81 (32%)	£50 6s. (11%)
Livestock	83 (33%)	£36 19s. (8%)
Hides and leather	36 (14%)	£33 0s. (7%)
Cloth	22 (9%)	£22 16s. (5%)
Mercery	19 (8%)	£9 16s. (2%)
Wood	53 (21%)	£7 13s. (2%)
Iron and coal	17 (7%)	£6 11s. (1%)
Meat	16 (6%)	£6 3s. (1%)
Fish	8 (3%)	£6 2s. (1%)
Wool	9 (4%)	£3 18s. (1%)
Miscellaneous	25 (10%)	£12 10s. (3%)

NOTES: "Miscellaneous" includes candles, spices, swords, armor, lard, tallow, grease, woollen thread, caps, woad, salt, painter's pigment, gold, cheese, one breviary, and one boat. Percentages in aggregate value column do not total 100 because of rounding.
SOURCE: D. Cromarty and R. Cromarty, *The Wealth of Shrewsbury in the Early Fourteenth Century* (Shrewsbury, 1993), pp. 89-99.

Unlike the rolls of Ipswich and Shrewsbury which document the wealth assessed in two of the country's wealthier provincial towns, the local roll from Colchester serves as a window on the world of a relatively modest regional town. Two local rolls survive from Colchester, one from 1296 and one from

1301, both fortuitously copied into the Rolls of Parliament.[35] Of the pair, the roll from the fifteenth of 1301, a tax earmarked for the war in Scotland, is the more inclusive and forms the basis of the following analysis. The town's assessors appraised property held on Michaelmas, but, in a departure from traditional practice, they were not instructed to exempt the chattels of the poor.[36] As a result of this unusual circumstance, the assessors evaluated the property of 399 people, a remarkably high number considering Colchester's size, one that may represent upwards of three-quarters of all households in the town at the time.[37] Their evaluations covered property worth a bit more than £500, a similarly impressive amount for a middling town. Like their counterparts in Shrewsbury a few years later, Colchester's assessors in 1301 were particularly fastidious in recording the precise nature of their neighbors' goods, which suggests a careful and patient process of evaluation.

Information concerning the goods that were taxed in Colchester is presented in table 1-4. As in Shrewsbury, virtually all of the goods valued in

TABLE 1-4:
Commodities Taxed in Colchester, 1301

Commodity	No. of Holders	Aggregate Value
Household/personal goods	343 (86%)	£167 7s. (33%)
Livestock	154 (39%)	£160 10s. (32%)
Grain	186 (47%)	£52 1s. (10%)
Horses and carts	63 (16%)	£24 3s. (5%)
Malt and barley	92 (23%)	£23 15s. (5%)
Hides and leather	30 (8%)	£22 18s. (4%)
Cloth	19 (5%)	£9 7s. (2%)
Wool	26 (7%)	£7 15s. (2%)
Mercery	14 (4%)	£7 6s. (1%)
Boats and nets	16 (4%)	£6 9s. (1%)
Wood	35 (9%)	£5 7s. (1%)
Meat	7 (2%)	£4 4s. (1%)
Miscellaneous	31 (8%)	£9 11s. (2%)

NOTES: "Miscellaneous" includes iron, spices, fish, bread, onions, garlic, wine, grindstones, rope, oil, bows, mustard seed, vinegar, flax, glass, salt, and wax. Percentages in aggregate value column do not total 100 because of rounding.

SOURCE: G. Rickwood, "Taxations of Colchester, A.D. 1296 and 1301," *Transactions of the Essex Archaeological Society,* n.s., 9 (1906): 126-55; *Rotuli Parliamentorum,* vol. 1, pp. 243-65.

Colchester can be distinguished as separate items in the tax roll. Cash worth about £16 (or about 3 percent of the total) is the only item included in the assessment but not in the table. Apart from the strikingly precise description of household and personal goods in Colchester, the range of goods taxed there corresponds well with the other two towns. Like Ipswich, Colchester's assessors directed their attention toward maritime resources in the form of boats and nets. The only puzzling discrepancy of any note is the absence of any appreciable assessments on smithies in the Essex town, an omission that is particularly incongruous in a document that supplies so much detail about pots, andirons, and other household metalware.

With the data from all three towns now on the table, we can turn our attention more fully to comparing their similarities and differences as a prelude to formulating some broader conclusions about the nature of wealth and capital investments in medieval English towns. To illustrate more completely the points of comparison between the three subsidies, table 1-5 presents in summary form the data about the relative shares of aggregate wealth represented by each commodity listed in the preceding tables. To make the data more useful as a measure of possible market orientation rather than as a measure of total taxable wealth, table 1-5 excludes the assessments made on household and personal goods to give a clearer picture of marketable commodities. Undoubtedly, many household and personal items should be seen as commodities that formed part of the exchange economy; one can assume, for example, that iron implements and precious objects of gold and silver were not ordinarily fabricated within the household. But though they unquestionably accounted for a significant portion of material wealth in all settlements, domestic possessions probably did not form an important part of medieval trade. Even in the nineteenth century, linens and clothing were commonly the handiwork of women working in the household, and it is unlikely that this practice was any different in the thirteenth century. Adding these household and personal goods to the list of other excluded stores of wealth—cash, debts, and joint valuations—removes a substantial portion of total assessed wealth in all three towns, but it still leaves us with commodities that constituted approximately two-thirds of all wealth taxed in Colchester and Ipswich and about three-quarters in Shrewsbury.

The most striking feature of table 1-5 is the prominence of simple agricultural commodities in the subsidies of all three towns. The three main agrarian categories in the table—malt and barley, grain, and livestock—account for about a third of assessed wealth in Ipswich, about half in Shrewsbury, and more than two-thirds in Colchester. Studies of the local subsidy records of 1297 surviving for Grimsby and four taxation boroughs in Bedfordshire (Bedford, Dunstable, Leighton Buzzard, and Luton) have found similarly strong orientations toward agrarian staples in the assessed wealth of those towns.[38] If we are correct in assuming that lay subsidy assessments ordinarily did not extend to household subsistence stores, we would have to conclude that the share of urban resources dedicated to agricultural staples was considerably higher than even the subsidy data suggest. This orientation toward agrarian goods illustrates the extraordinary extent to which medieval towns dedicated their resources simply to reproducing themselves from one generation to the next, a task that required them to put the procuring and processing of foodstuffs at the very heart of urban life. It also explains why the development of commercial ties with the surrounding countryside was a matter of utmost importance for all towns; without secure and cost-effective access to the produce of surrounding fields and pastures, urban life of any real magnitude was simply not possible.

To a lesser extent, the subsidy data also illustrate the importance of rural commodities in facets of urban life other than basic subsistence. If we combine

TABLE 1-5:
Relative Aggregate Values of Commodities
Assessed in Three Towns, Excluding Household and Personal Goods

Commodity		**Town (%)**	
	Ipswich	**Shrewsbury**	**Colchester**
Malt and barley	20	15	7
Ships and boats	13	0	2
Cloth	11	7	3
Wool	7	1	2
Livestock	6	11	48
Stone	6	0	0
Grain	5	26	16
Horses and carts	5	15	7
Hides and leather	5	10	7
Mercery	4	3	2
Wood	4	2	2
Iron and coal	3	2	<1
Textile supplies	2	0	0
Wine	3	0	0
Salt	1	0	0
Miscellaneous	2	7	4

NOTES: "Miscellaneous" goods are identical to those noted in Tables 1-2 through 1-4, with the addition of meat, fish, and foodstuffs in Shrewsbury and Colchester. Percentages do not necessarily total 100 because of rounding.
SOURCES: See Tables 1-2 through 1-4.

wealth derived from horses, wool, and hides—a troika of nonsubsistence pastoral products—we find that these three elements constituted about one-sixth of all assessed wealth in Ipswich and Colchester and one-quarter in Shrewsbury (had the latter's wool been assessed more completely, the figure there would be even higher). We need to moderate these figures somewhat to allow for the inclusion of carts with horses in the table's data (a relatively insignificant part of the total) and the inclusion of finished and semi-finished leather products with the hides (a much more consequential distortion), but the general point about the prominence of pastoral wealth is still sound. As with foodstuffs, the development of supply lines facilitating the transfer of resources from country to town was critically important to the economic well-being of English towns. For merchants and tradespeople living in the towns, gaining access to the raw materials on which their wealth was ultimately based was as important as knowing how to transform them into finished consumer goods.

III

Both the occupational data described in the first section of this chapter and the subsidy data discussed in the second give us a sense of the relative importance of the principal orientations of urban economies in medieval England. There is a good deal of overlap in what they reveal. Both indicate that a relatively small range of commodities accounted for a very large share of economic activity. Both methods suggest that medieval English towns had three primary economic sectors that absorbed large portions of total available capital and provided large numbers of available employment opportunities: victualing, textile production, and the processing of hides and leather. Towns did achieve some degree of specialization in one of these commodities or sometimes in a more specialized commodity as in the case of stone and stonework in Ipswich. But a basic constellation of goods and jobs derived from the three principal sectors can be found in almost every town, a constellation that accounted, by a conservative estimate, for at least half (and more likely two-thirds) of all urban economic activity.

The pursuit of each of these leading areas of economic activity was heavily dependent on goods originally produced in the countryside and draws attention to the critical symbiosis between urbanization and rural commodity production that accompanied the growth of towns in the centuries before the Black Death. As F. W. Maitland observed long ago when describing thirteenth-century Cambridge, medieval towns commonly had fields attached to them, and in many of them, agriculture was as much a part of life as was manufacturing and trade.[39] But towns as large as Ipswich and Shrewsbury could not possibly meet demand from local resources; as R. H. Britnell has shown, even a more modest town like Colchester, with a generous endowment of land and other agricultural resources, needed to draw on its hinterland to meet its basic consumption needs.[40] Both their size and their numbers (a subject that will be taken up in more detail in chapter 4) meant that the collective urban appetite for bread, ale, and meat could only have been met by the development of well-articulated links with rural producers. The same can be said for the leading industrial pursuits of the period. The textile trades were ultimately dependent on the acquisition of rural wool, and the hide and leather trades were equally dependent on the acquisition of rural livestock, or at least on the acquisition of processed hides and skins from the countryside. The remarkably consistent interest in these commodities, both within England itself and to a great extent in other parts of Europe, created a dynamic and highly competitive market for rural producers who could generate the appropriate raw materials. To a considerable extent, the analysis in this book of rural marketing in the thirteenth and fourteenth centuries is simply a commentary on this binding of urban brewers and spinners to their suppliers in the countryside.

At first glance, the employment data and the subsidy data considered in the second part paint different pictures. The leather trades, for example, accounted for as much as a quarter of employment in some towns, yet in none of the towns with subsidy rolls, including one known for its leather industry (Shrewsbury), did leather and leather products account for more than 10 percent of assessed wealth. Likewise, metal appears more prominently as a source of employment than as a repository of taxable wealth. Significant though they are, these discrepancies may not be as great as they initially appear to be. The subsidies essentially provide us with a picture of urban economies engaged in what modern business consultants refer to as the "just-in-time" approach to carrying inventory, a strategy that has been trumpeted in recent years as a way to improve corporate balance sheets. The "commodities" of the medieval economy were principally raw materials, largely because the production of most goods involved relatively few intermediate steps between the raw material and the finished consumable product. There was little need, as there is in an industrial economy, to transform a raw material from its natural into its semi-finished or finished state until it could be sold. Whenever possible, "commodities" were left in their natural state. Once they were reduced from this state, they were turned into finished products as quickly as possible and subsequently removed from the commodity market altogether. At all stages of production, producers and entrepreneurs sought to minimize the amount of capital they needed to tie up in inventory. To put the concept in concrete terms: shoemakers earned their living because they had specialized tools and skills, not because they held a ready stock of prefabricated shoes available for sale.

Nature, however, did not fully cooperate in this strategy; it insisted on injecting raw materials into the economy in a timeless annual cycle that bore little connection to human inclinations. Sheep were sheared in late spring and early summer, wheat was reaped at the end of summer. However people may have wanted to arrange their economic calendars, by necessity they had a whole year's mass of raw materials thrust upon them at a few relatively short periods of the year. Accommodations were therefore necessary. One accommodation was to move the commodity to the next or, if possible, the finished stage of production as soon as possible. Wool, for example, was marketed with alacrity to the large textile towns or to the hungry looms across the Channel: In Lincoln in 1292-93, more than two-thirds of the town's annual toll receipts from wool were collected in the seven weeks between June 15 and August 9.[41] The relatively poor showing of wool in the subsidy assessments in Shrewsbury and Colchester may indeed be partially due to the swiftness with which merchants snatched up available supplies and dispatched them to the leading textile centers. By Michaelmas, much of Shropshire's spring clip may already have found its way into the hands of drapers in Ghent.

A second accomodation called for the preservation of nature's bounty in its original form right up to the moment of consumption or at least as near to the moment as possible. Wheat, for example, was stored as grain rather than as flour; frequency of social contact rather than scale of enterprise explains why millers loom so large in the literature of the period. Such behavior made perfect sense in a world without refrigeration, chemical preservatives, or anaerobic containers. Thus, the subsidies reveal plenty of grain and livestock, but relatively little bread and meat—the transition from raw material to consumable product happened so quickly that the assessors of the subsidies could not regularly record it. This rapid transformation was effected by the armies of laborers that we see involved in the victualing trades. They were the natural complement to the need to keep foodstuffs in their natural state as long as possible.

But even though the discrepancies between the employment data and the subsidy data are not as great as they initially appear to be, they are nonetheless real. Ultimately, the disparity between labor resources and capital resources can only be accounted for by enlarging our focus from the town to the region. Towns were overwhelmingly oriented toward transforming agricultural commodities into consumer goods, but such transformations could take place only after they had established reciprocal relations with producers in the countryside. Most towns were agricultural producers in their own right, but towns the size of Ipswich and Shrewsbury, and several dozen others of similar ilk, could not possibly produce enough from their own soil to keep their workers occupied. Only by drawing on the resources of the surrounding countryside could the towns develop their "industrial" sectors. Without a supply of wool there was (as the towns of Flanders learned to their dismay in the early phases of the Hundred Years War) no textile industry. Without a supply of cereals and animals, there was only a rump victualing sector. Without a supply of livestock, or at least of hides and skins, there was no leather industry to speak of. This interdependency between town and country was not simply an incidental part of the economy; it was the very bone and marrow of economic life. The contrast between the employment data and the subsidies furnishes more than an explanation of the internal workings of the towns; it also provides a part of the explanation for the integration between town and country. The "just-in-time" approach was a feature of an integrated structure in which raw materials were generated *and stored* in the country, while their transformation, and to a large extent their consumption, occurred in the towns. Until industrialization rewrote the rules, rural villages were, in effect, the reservoirs of capital in the economy, while towns were the reservoirs of labor. Such an arrangement, a hallmark of the High Middle Ages, could only have materialized once the economy had developed a mechanism for binding the two together. The development of towns and the commercialization of the countryside went hand in hand; without the one, the other would never have amounted to very much.

2

Peasants and the Production of Agricultural Commodities

Peasant agriculture played a crucial role in creating and perpetuating the inland marketing networks dealt with elsewhere in this book. As discussed in chapter 1, the driving force behind the exchange economy of the period was a symbiosis between rural production of staple agrarian commodities and urban demand for these same commodities as foodstuffs and as industrial raw materials. Few historians of the period discount the contribution peasants made to the production of agricultural staples, but most see this contribution as being overwhelmingly oriented toward subsistence needs rather than toward market exchange. While we have no reason to doubt the priority peasants gave to subsistence needs when allocating their resources, we should not conclude from this that peasants had only limited involvement with the burgeoning market economy of the period. Quite the opposite is true: Peasant producers were more significant in the production and circulation of marketable agricultural commodities than either the great lords or the gentry. Substantiating this claim, which runs contrary to several generations of received wisdom about the relative economic performances of peasants and manorial lords, is the main goal of this chapter.

Much of the argument for a subsistence-dominated model of medieval peasant agriculture can be related to a conceptual model first adumbrated by the influential Soviet economic theorist A. V. Chayanov.[1] Chayanov argued that peasants practice a distinctive form of economy, one that structurally precludes the incentives that a market economy uses to entice producers into the market. In any economy in which the household is the fundamental unit of both production and consumption, Chayanov posited that changes in a household's level of production or consumption would depend entirely on changes within the household rather than on changes induced by external economic factors. As its numbers grow, a peasant household applies greater inputs of labor to its productive activities and seeks to add land to its capital base; when its numbers begin to decline, the reverse process occurs. Chayanov saw peasants essentially as economic satisfiers rather than economic maximizers: As long as every one in the household has a full belly and dry feet, the individual members of the consuming unit see no point in working harder. Chayanov's peasants are woefully ignorant of the opportunity cost of labor, and they exhibit no desire to augment individual levels of capital. Consequently, they neither expect nor desire to produce commodities surplus to the needs of the household and thus do not engage in regular market transactions.

While Chayanov's model has a certain inner consistency, it has not held up well under empirical scrutiny. Studies of modern peasantries have found that production of some surplus is characteristic of all peasant economies, and many economic anthropologists now prefer to speak of peasants as engaging in simple commodity production rather than the kind of subsistence farming visualized by Chayanov.[2] Advocates of this model define a simple commodity producer as one who produces goods for the market on a regular basis but who does so as an extension of, rather than as a substitute for, a household economy oriented toward subsistence. Commodities are held to be "simple" in the sense that they require neither extensive labor specialization nor significant inputs of capital beyond those invested in subsistence pursuits. A peasant household raising chickens—an enterprise common to most peasantries—simultaneously engages in both subsistence and market production when it sells the eggs of hens ultimately destined for the family's table. Households might also add a few hens beyond consumption needs without having to alter significantly the share of land or labor devoted to subsistence. Similarly, some fruits of household production are necessarily subsistence-market hybrids because they are not amenable to complete consumption within the domestic unit. When a cow is butchered, for example, the supply of highly-perishable comestible innards often exceeds the consumption capacity of the producing family, and the transformation of the byproducts—hooves, horns and hide—into consumable goods ordinarily requires skills and specialized capital beyond those available in most domestic units.

Shorn of an anachronistic association with later forms of capitalism, simple commodity production is a useful concept for historians of medieval peasants. The model allows us to speak of the production of goods for the market as an intrinsic part of peasant production without requiring us to hunt for proto-capitalists in thirteenth-century villages. We do not need to see subsistence and surplus as antithetical concepts, nor do we have to deny one to advocate the other: Peasants can simultaneously produce for their own household and for the market. The production of commodities for exchange was—and still is in most modern peasantries—structurally integrated into the household, reflecting a conscious strategy to augment household income without sacrificing the security of direct production and consumption of essential staples. Essentially, we can return to the commonsense position staked out by Daniel Thorner more than 30 years ago:

> We are sure to go astray if we try to conceive of peasant economies as exclusively "subsistence" oriented and to suspect capitalism wherever peasants show evidence of being "market" oriented. It is much sounder to take it for granted, as a starting point, that for ages peasant economies have had a double orientation toward both.[3]

To substantiate the role played by the peasantry of medieval England in generating commodities for the exchange economy, this chapter will concern itself primarily with peasant production of a limited number of staple agricultural commodities, principally grain and wool. The range of commodities produced in a peasant village was much greater than this, greater indeed than we will ever know for certain. Intramural exchange of livestock was ubiquitous, although our sources give us only occasional indications of its vitality.[4] Most villages had a smith, who supplied his neighbors with plow shares, locks, and handtools and whose products regularly turn up in excavations of deserted village sites. Poultry, eggs, firewood, and peat turves likewise changed hands in a commercial context within the village, as did butchered meat, bread, fish, cheese, carts and cartwheels, cloth, candles, hay, and dozens of other commodities.[5] Much of this trade bypassed formal marketing structures, and much of it was probably conducted by women as part of their routine household management.[6] But if we do a disservice to the complexity of village economies by limiting our attention to a few primary agricultural goods, we can at least take solace in the fact that these goods accounted for an important share of every village's productive activity. Our evidence about peasant land use and capital deployment is mostly indirect, but it consistently depicts the production of cereals and wool as mainstays of the English peasant economy. We know, for example, that the "great" tithes collected on wool, lambs and grain accounted for the vast majority of parish income and that the "small" tithes, paid—in theory at any rate—on almost all other forms of production seldom amounted to more than about one-quarter of the amount collected from the great tithes.[7] On a rough estimate, in most parts of the country the production of grain and wool probably accounted for somewhere between one-half and two-thirds of all available land and capital resources in the two centuries prior to the arrival of the Black Death. When we consider the production of these basic staples, we can safely assume that we are dealing with the preeminent commodities generated in the peasant economy of the period.

The chapter will be divided into three sections. The first section will focus primarily on peasant grain stocks recorded in royal purveyance accounts in the first half of the fourteenth century. These records show peasants in possession of significant household surpluses of foodstuffs, principally cereals but in a few instances butchered cattle and swine as well. By cross-referencing the purveyance accounts with other records of village life, we can develop a sense of who these individual suppliers were and why they were capable of parting with some of their store of grain and other produce. The second section will look at a range of evidence documenting peasant livestock holdings, with an emphasis on peasant sheep flocks and wool production. Peasants have long been overlooked as producers of livestock and livestock products but both estate records and local tax records suggest that they were deeply immersed in the pastoral economy. In the third and final section, a telescope will be substituted for the microscope employed in the two previous sections in an attempt to gauge the significance of peasant surplus production within the economy as a whole. Individually, each peasant's surpluses were relatively modest when compared to the holders of estates and manors, but what we really need to know to establish the relationship between production and exchange is the aggregate share of different kinds of producers. In other words, precisely how petty was the commodity production of the medieval English peasantry?

I

Unlike the wealth of their lords, peasant assets are often better documented among state records than among local records. We will probably never be able to match the magnificent wealth of detail about economic resources and productivity among the peasantry that manorial account rolls allow us to establish for the lords, but the dearth of sources documenting the peasant economy is not nearly as complete as is commonly thought. Peasants feature prominently in all of the attempts made by the English crown to harness the nation's resources for war, and, fortunately, the Exchequer proved to be nearly as safe a repository for a document generated in the period as a monastic archive. With a little prodding, sources such as tax lists and purveyance accounts are capable of divulging considerable detail about the peasants' economic resources. Indeed, the very fact that most of the crown's wartime financing came directly from peasant producers rather than from other social groups is itself testimony to the central role the peasants played in the English economy.

Royal purveyance records furnish a particularly good example of the light central administrative records can shed on the subject of peasant surplus. As part of their planning for major military campaigns, English kings targeted selected counties to supply specified quotas of needed foodstuffs for shipment to the troops stationed in Scotland and France.[8] Logistical arrangements for these collections were ordinarily entrusted to a local sheriff, who sent a handful of bailiffs to scour the countryside in search of the requisitioned goods. These purveyors typically acquired the foodstuffs on credit, with the crown agreeing to settle its debts after the military crisis giving rise to the purveyance had passed. Payments by the crown were, from the suppliers' point of view, frustratingly slow—a contemporary moralist, referring to the wooden tally sticks used to record the crown's debts, complained that the king should have eaten off wood and paid silver for his victuals rather than vice versa—but they were seldom disregarded.[9] But the system that frustrated contemporaries is a boon to historians. Because purveyance established a multitude of credit relationships, sheriffs and their agents were required to keep meticulous financial accounts for each purveyance campaign, recording the names of individual creditors and the amounts of money they were owed. Among the voluminous surviving purveyance records are scores of these accounts, many of which itemize not only the creditors' names and anticipated remuneration but also the kind and quantity of goods they supplied. As J. R. Maddicott has observed, peasants bore the brunt of most purveyance campaigns, and consequently they account for the vast majority of the individuals recorded on these lists of royal creditors.[10] But lords also found themselves caught up in the purveyors' nets, and we should be careful not to view purveyance as a completely arbitrary and unfair imposition on defenseless peasants.[11] Peasants loom large in purveyance records because they loomed large as the holders of purveyable commodities. Their role as the principal suppliers of foodstuffs to the army was due more to their predominance as agrarian producers than to their subservience in the political system.

Purveyors could, and often did, raise significant stocks of provisions in relatively short periods of time. Large counties sometimes contributed up to several thousand quarters of grain: Lincolnshire's purveyors collected more than 2,700 quarters in 1297, while Kent's came up with more than 4,800 at roughly the same time.[12] The royal victualers who collected these supplies in places near the front—Bordeaux, Calais, Carlisle, Berwick—managed correspondingly large stocks. In 1300, for example, receivers in Carlisle and Berwick accounted for reserves on hand of more than 20,000 quarters of grain.[13] Impressive though they might appear at first glance, such stocks probably accounted for a relatively small share of the country's total production of foodstuffs. Maddicott has calculated that the particularly heavy imposition on Kent in 1297 represented the produce of about 5,000 acres; not a negligible sum to be sure, but one that represents less than one percent of the county's total acreage.[14] Of course even in a land-hungry age some of Kent's acres were deemed unsuitable for cropping, and if we allow for fallow and inhospitable weald, we might extrapolate that purveyance involved as much as five percent of the county's productive land. But this is an upper limit for a particularly intense campaign; in most counties in most purveyances, the demands of the crown could not have involved more than one or two percent of the total pool of arable land.

Purveyance records are thus of marginal value as guides to absolute productive capacities. They are, however, considerably more useful as measures of surplus at the level of the individual producer. For understandable reasons, purveyors preferred not to have to deal in occasional bushels in every village they entered. From their point of view, it made sense to engage in fewer but larger transactions with a more restricted number of producers; they may not have known it but essentially what they sought was to keep their transactions costs as low as possible. Their main problem in doing so was not a shortage of supply so much as a shortage of cash, or at least a shortage of goodwill. For producers asked to turn over a portion of their year's harvest for a purveyor's tally stick, the speed of repayment for purveyed goods was a legitimate concern. We still have much to learn about the local circumstances surrounding contacts between peasants and purveyors, but the available evidence suggests they more often involved negotiation based on customary behavior than capricious and unilateral seizure of property. Ultimately, negotiation led to a compromise: Individuals turned over stocks that were large enough to make the system viable, but not so large as to put their own welfare in jeopardy if repayment was slow or otherwise problematic. Thus, when we use purveyance records as a guide to the holders of surplus, we are essentially observing the amounts that individuals could turn over without exposing themselves to too much risk. In other words, we can document only minimal holdings of individual surplus; we cannot assume that purveyors took the entire surplus of any of the households they visited.

Because the mass of purveyance data is rather unwieldy and strewn across several different archival classes in the Public Record Office, we are well advised to limit our focus to a single county, the administrative basis for the original campaigns and consequently for most of the surviving records. A good candidate for study is the county of Huntingdonshire, visited with great frequency because of its high productivity and convenient access to eastern ports, and one that will be featured in later sections of this book. We have four lists of individual contributors to purveyance campaigns in Huntingdonshire, two from the reign of Edward I and two from that of his grandson Edward III.[15]

The two earliest lists of individual suppliers in Huntingdonshire are derived from purveyances undertaken to provision Berwick with wheat and malt in 1301 and with wheat, malt, and beans in 1303.[16] Both are arranged to reflect the contributions made by the hundreds, the principal administrative districts of the county. The 1301 list records the names of 79 individuals residing in 23 villages in one of the county's four hundreds, while the 1303 list deals with 69 individuals in the same hundred without giving a consistent indication of village of residence. As was common in purveyances, individuals typically contributed standard amounts, often divided evenly between the sought-after goods. In 1301, 25 of the 79 contributors turned over one quarter (eight bushels) of grain, 9 a combined total of one-and-a-half quarters, and 26 a combined total of two quarters. Only 10 people supplied less than one quarter, while 9 supplied more than two quarters, 7 of whom supplied three or more quarters. The 1303 contributions parallel those made two years earlier, with 29 individuals supplying a single quarter, 3 supplying between one and two quarters, 13 supplying two quarters and 18 supplying three quarters, the last figure reflecting a common habit of providing one quarter of each kind of commodity. Only 6 of the contributors in 1303 handed over less than one quarter. The largest contribution in the pair of lists came from two residents of Yaxley, one who supplied two quarters of wheat and two of malt in 1301 and one who supplied three quarters of wheat and one of malt in the same year.

While these contributions of grain represent only a portion of each supplier's available surplus, they are still significant quantities. One quarter of wheat weighed nearly 400 pounds, enough to supply someone with a little more than a pound of bread every day for a year.[17] Estimates of subsistence needs in the past vary enormously, depending on the values one assigns to such variables as daily caloric needs (a function of sex, age, climate, size, and work patterns), conversion rates of cereals to foodstuffs (involving assessments of loss in milling and baking), and nutritional values of the various cereals. As a rough rule of thumb, we can say that one quarter of wheat would have kept one person alive at a bare-bones subsistence level for nearly a year.[18] Accordingly, we can view the amounts contributed by most Huntingdonshire peasants in the early fourteenth century—representing only the stock taken by a purveyor, not necessarily the household's total available surplus—as representing minimum annual subsistence requirements for one or two people.

A surprising number of the contributors to these purveyance campaigns can be traced in other series of records, particularly in the county's extensive Hundred Rolls.[19] Of the people recorded as contributors in 1301, for example, 20 (25 percent) can be found as landholders in the tenurial surveys of the Hundred Rolls, and a further 13 (16 percent) can be linked on the basis of distinctive surnames to families holding land in the same village. In most instances, contributors stand out as people of substance in their native villages. About half (16 of 33) of the identifiable contributors held a virgate (approximately 30 acres in most Huntingdonshire villages), and about a third held a half-virgate. Two others held multiple virgates, while the remainder held less than a half-virgate. John Oreby of Sawtry is a good example of the kind of individual likely to find himself caught up with the demands of the crown. Oreby contributed to purveyance in both 1301 and 1303, supplying four bushels of wheat and four of malt in the former year and one quarter each of wheat, malt and beans in the latter. In the Hundred Roll survey of Sawtry, we find Oreby as the tenant of one virgate of freehold land in the village, held for relatively light rent.[20] Another good example is Robert de Overton of Yaxley. Overton provided purveyors with two quarters of wheat and two of malt in 1301. Like John Oreby, Overton held a virgate in his native village, but unlike Oreby, his property was held in villein tenure, owing substantial work services to Thorney Abbey, the principal lord of the village.[21] As these two examples illustrate, identifiable suppliers in 1301 include both freeholder and villeins, with no obvious correlation between personal status and the size of their contribution.

In the case of Elton, one of the villages involved in these two purveyance drives, we possess a number of manorial court rolls in addition to the Hundred Roll extent. Elton belonged to Ramsey Abbey and typified the manors of that estate, with a large demesne and a substantial number of customary tenants charged with relatively heavy labor services.[22] Four of Elton's peasants supplied foodstuffs in 1301 and an equal number in 1303. Six of these eight supplied one quarter of wheat and one of malt, the seventh half as much as his peers, and the eighth handed over two quarters of beans. We can find six of these contributors in the village's Hundred Roll entry: All six held virgates, one as a freeholder and five as customary tenants.[23] All eight of the contributors can be traced in Elton's surviving manorial court rolls, where they appear among the village's elite.[24] All but one member of the group had held at some point in their lives the influential post of juror, in most instances on multiple occasions. All members also served regularly in other official capacities within the village, as pledges, ale tasters, and in one instance as reeve. Their activity in the court similarly reveals their wealth and prominence in the village: Several engaged in multiple land transactions, one acted as a creditor to other villagers, one employed a servant, one took charge of the goods of a hanged felon, and so on. These are precisely the kinds of people we should expect to find as the producers of surplus in the English countryside: the thriving upper ranks of peasant villages.

A second opportunity to observe the role of individual peasants as creditors of the kingdom's war effort comes in the middle of the fourteenth century, with a pair of documents recording provisions taken to supply Calais in 1348 and 1351.[25] While these later campaigns differed in some respects from earlier ones, they tapped a similar pool of resources and confirm the primary role played by wealthier peasants in supplying provisions to the army.[26] Indeed, the most noticeable changes in purveyance in the intervening half-century—the inclusion of meat and animals, an increase in the size of individual contributions, and a greater zeal in recording prices for all goods—emphasize even more emphatically the capacity of peasants to generate surplus.

In 1348, 18 suppliers can be found on the sheriff's account as suppliers, hailing from all parts of the county. All but two of these suppliers turned over stocks of at least three of the five commodities sought by the sheriff: wheat, malt, peas, beef, and pork. The contribution of William Wade of Hemingford Abbots is typical of the others. Wade gave the sheriff two quarters of peas, three quarters of malt, half a side of beef, and five bacon flitches, worth a total of £1 13s. 7d. These victuals probably would have sufficed to give a family of five a protein-heavy diet for about a year. Like Wade, nearly two-thirds of the contributors (11 of 18) furnished goods worth more than £1. Many of the suppliers provided beef and pork, suggesting that at least better-off peasants ate meat on a regular basis. At the head of the group of suppliers in 1348 stood John Godwyne of Godmanchester, who showed remarkable faith in Edward III's credit by turning over four quarters of wheat, four of peas, five of malt, an entire ox carcass, and two bacon pigs, worth in total more than £4. Godwyne's contributions would have sufficed to feed perhaps a dozen people for an entire year.

Similar portfolios of goods passed through the sheriff's hands three years later, when 108 individuals are recorded as suppliers to the king. As in 1348, both grain and meat were taken. Although none of the 1351 contributors matched John Godwyne, most gave amounts that were comparable to those supplied three years earlier: 23 individuals gave more than £1 in goods to the purveyors; eight of these gave more than £2.[27] Surprisingly, with one possible exception, none of the contributors in 1348 recurs in 1351.[28] We do not know if such spreading of the burden reflects a conscious policy adopted by purveyors, or perhaps by local communities themselves; whatever the cause, the spread drives home the point that we are looking at substantial numbers of peasants capable of generating meaningful amounts of surplus. The size of the contributions in 1351 takes on added significance if we consider the timing of the campaign, which occurred in the months of April and May, in response to a writ for purveyance first sent in January.[29] These two months are near the nadir of the annual food cycle, the so-called "hungry gap" affecting virtually all peasant societies.[30] Villagers had lived off their fall harvests for an entire winter when the purveyors made the rounds, and they could not expect to replenish their larders with new crops for at least another month or two. Stocks held in early spring were inevitably smaller than those available in the fall, and yet we still find peasant villagers able to turn over substantial stores when called upon to do so.

As was true of their predecessors, the mid-century contributors were drawn from the ranks of peasant elites. Thomas le Coupere of Broughton, for example, who contributed £1 11s. 6d. in goods to the purveyance in 1351, was a juror in his village's manor court in 1359 and on many occasions thereafter.[31] William le Coupere, probably Thomas's father, had one of the highest assessments in the subsidy of 1332, and John le Coupere was listed as a former holder of a virgate in a rental of the village in 1380-1381, a virgate that was probably worked by Thomas when he lent provisions for the garrison in Calais.[32] Elton's mid-century contributors were likewise cut from the same cloth as their forerunners. We can find four of the six contributors in 1351 serving as jurors in the manorial court in 1350, and a fifth as a bailiff involved with the reeve in the annual account of the manor in the year of the purveyance.[33]

The picture that emerges from all of these purveyance lists in Huntingdonshire is relatively consistent across the half century, and it probably represents reasonably accurately the situation in the country as a whole. When purveyors made their rounds of the countryside looking for foodstuffs to support the war effort, they consistently directed their attention to the upper echelons of peasant society. In most of the villages they entered they found at least some peasants with healthy stores of surplus produce, stores that were large enough to make expeditious collection feasible without imposing excessive suffering on the contributors. Purveyance records illuminate peasant surplus with the partial light of a flickering candle rather than the direct rays of a noonday sun, but in an area with such great depths of darkness, a flickering candle is a welcome sight.

II

In addition to cultivating cereals, peasants also devoted their capital and labor to animal husbandry. Indeed, peasants' desire to combine animal husbandry with crop production goes a long way toward explaining the predominance and longevity, and possibly even the genesis, of the common field systems adopted throughout much of the country: In return for abiding by communal dictates about crop rotations in the fields, peasants enhanced their individual pasture resources by creating temporary grazing space on the stubble of a harvested part of the arable.[34] Nevertheless, rural historians have traditionally focused their attention on cereal production as the central concern of the agrarian regimes of the medieval world. This attention has not been wholly misplaced, but it has tended to move study of the pastoral economy to the margins, in both a geographical and a metaphorical sense. Recent work by Kathleen Biddick and Bruce Campbell has helped to redraw the boundaries between corn and horn in the manorial economy, and Maryanne Kowaleski's work on the circulation of hides and leather goods has helped to do the same for the commercial and industrial exploitation of livestock products, but we still are woefully ignorant of the part played by peasants as producers of livestock, particularly in the centuries before the Black Death.[35]

This ignorance can be attributed at least partly to historiographical factors. In one of his many celebrated essays, Michael Postan investigated village livestock in a seemingly thorough and convincing fashion.[36] By looking principally at a sample of thirteenth-century local lay subsidy rolls, Postan claimed that peasants had "exceedingly low" or "exiguous" numbers of livestock in their possession, a conclusion that fit neatly with his interpretation of the period as one of growing impoverishment caused by overpopulation.[37] In Postan's view, peasants responded to the rapid demographic expansion of the period by curtailing their production of livestock, converting land that had once been used as pasture into arable. Inevitably, the erosion of livestock production reduced the supply of manure and this in turn limited the fertility and productivity of the land dedicated to cereal crops.[38]

Postan's model possesses the virtue of interpretive consistency, but his analysis of peasant livestock resources is riddled with evidentiary and even logical inconsistencies.[39] He described thirteenth-century village livestock totals as "exiguous" because they compared poorly with the totals found in surveys of the same regions undertaken by the Ministry of Agriculture in 1867 and 1908.[40] While comparing stocking totals in different eras is certainly a worthwhile enterprise, using a tax assessment as one benchmark and a benign census as the other is not a particularly good way to do it. Many unanswered questions remain about how subsidy assessors went about their business, but among the score or so of scholars who have either edited or analyzed these valuable sources, Postan has been the only one to argue that they document completely all peasant wealth above the taxable minimum.[41]

On the basis of this highly questionable interpretation of what the subsidies do and do not record, Postan proceeded to transform the data of the subsidies, in a remarkable piece of statistical legerdemain, into a kind of balance sheet designed to show that livestock totals were low not only relative to later centuries but also relative to the concurrent holdings of arable wealth revealed in the same documents. In making this comparison, Postan put oxen and horses, as plow animals, entirely on the arable side of the ledger.[42] These two animals certainly had a central role to play in cereal production, but to argue that they had more in common with a bushel of barley than with a cow is unusual to say the least. And as if this did not sufficiently tilt the balance against pastoralism, Postan went on to claim that the data available from the 1225 Wiltshire subsidy records—one of only three sources of subsidy data used in the article—should not be included in the calculation of pastoral wealth because the assessment took place around Easter, when peasant grain stocks were at a low ebb.[43] While it is certainly reasonable to make allowances for seasonal fluctuations in grain stocks, it is hard not to suspect that Postan excluded the Wiltshire evidence because it flatly contradicted his interpretation.[44] Wiltshire's peasants did indeed have modest stocks of grain in the assessment, but Postan's model suggests that they should also have had meager holdings of livestock, and this was simply not the case. The 85 taxpayers in the village of Martin, for example, paid tax on 2,691 sheep, 190 horses and oxen, 243 cows and calves, and 59 pigs.[45]

In the three decades since Postan's analysis was first published, numerous scholars, working from divergent points of view, have presented more constructive insights into the role livestock played in the peasant economy. John Langdon has documented the widespread ownership of horses among the peasantry and has argued that peasants played a leading role in substituting the use of horses for the use of oxen during the thirteenth century.[46] Mavis Mate has pointed to peasant demand for pasture as the best explanation for the scale and buoyancy of pasture rentals in southeast England in the period, an argument that could readily be applied to other parts of the country.[47] Several scholars have drawn attention to the trespasses by peasant livestock documented in manorial court records; Jack Ravensdale, for example, found individuals fined for trespassing with flocks of up to 300 sheep in the village of Landbeach in Cambridgeshire.[48] Mark Bailey's analysis of folding rights (delimiting when and where sheep flocks were grazed) likewise points indirectly to the prominence of peasant sheepholding in the Suffolk Breckland—landlords' preoccupation with folding only makes sense if peasant flocks were large enough to warrant sustained concern.[49] Once we remove Postan's heavy neo-Malthusian filter, we find extensive evidence to document the viability of peasant livestock production; indeed, the very sources Postan used to dismiss the issue can be turned on their head to reveal a substantial peasant commitment to pastoralism.

One of our most revealing sources about the viability of peasant livestock production comes from descriptions of customary stinting arrangements. In most parts of the country, pasture resources in the thirteenth and fourteenth centuries were scarce enough that parties interested in raising livestock found it wise to define the density of stocking permissible on village commons and other grazing lands. Such defining involved the rights of villagers vis-à-vis each other as well as the rights of villagers vis-à-vis their lords. Stinting allowances were designed to limit the number of animals individuals could graze on common land by assigning quotas commensurate with holdings of arable land in the village. Although stints were probably ubiquitous by the middle of the thirteenth century, if not earlier, they seldom come to our attention because they were subsumed in the large body of consensual custom observed by peasants as members of a village community, and thus rarely needed to be written down. But as manorial lords advanced their possessory claims over village wastelands during the thirteenth century, stinting rights came to be defined as appurtenances of tenure negotiated between lord and tenant rather than as simple matters of custom within the village. It is in this guise that precise statements of stinting allowances found their way into our sources, less frequently than one might like but nonetheless often enough to convey a sense of common practice.

While their aim was to limit the number of animals grazed by any single individual, the limits set in most stinting allowances were surprisingly high.[50] A Hundred Roll entry for the village of Swyncombe in Oxfordshire in 1279, for example, notes that each of the ten villein tenants of the Norman Abbey of Bec Herlouin could pasture 1 horse, 6 oxen, 6 pigs, and 50 sheep on the common pasture over the winter months. Remarkably, these tenants each held only eight acres of arable in the village. On the Ramsey Abbey manor of Therfield in Hertfordshire, an incoming tenant in 1347 was given common for 120 sheep as part of his bundle of tenurial rights. Holders of a bovate of land in Mowthorpe in Yorkshire could, as the allotment of their tenures, stock 1 horse, 2 cows, 3 pigs, 4 geese, 15 ewes and as many lambs as these ewes produced. Virgaters and half-virgaters in Heytesbury, Wiltshire, could each maintain 35 sheep on the common pasture, and tenants in several other Wiltshire villages had similar rights. According to a local jury in 1245, a virgater's stocking allowance in Croxton Kerrial, Leicestershire, traditionally included 40 sheep with offspring, 2 oxen, 1 cow with offspring, 1 boar, and 1 sow. Several other Leicestershire villages at this time limited the stint to 30 sheep but offered more generous provision for other livestock. In Sussex at about the same time, the Bishop of Chichester granted stints of 25 sheep, 2 cows, and 1 horse to his virgate tenants in Ferring and similar amounts to his tenants elsewhere. As these examples illustrate, the precise terms of stinting varied from place to place, but the variation tends to fall within recognizable boundaries. Throughout the country, substantial peasant tenants could typically expect their share of village resources to include pasture for 30 or 40 sheep, a handful of oxen and cattle, a few pigs, and a horse. They would also, of course, have kept chickens and geese in their yards, probably in some numbers.

More detailed evidence of peasant livestock holdings can be found in an unusual listing of "recognitions" *(recogniciones)* paid by tenants of the Abbey of Bury St. Edmunds in a few Suffolk villages in 1302.[51] The format of these lists is similar to that found on extant local lay subsidy rolls, except that livestock is the only form of property explicitly enumerated. The lists give no indications about their purpose, but they appear to be related to the internal affairs of the Abbey rather than to the exigencies of a national tax assessment. They may record some kind of payment for grazing rights or access to the abbey's pastures, but it is more likely that they stem from a tallage or an aid collected by the abbey and hence that the totals document the bare minimum number of animals in the respective villages. Postan referred to them to establish the veracity of the subsidy records he used in his article on village livestock but he failed to elaborate on what they have to say in their own right.

The most thorough inventory recorded in this unique source comes from the village of Coney Weston, a modest Breckland-edge settlement about ten miles northeast of the abbey town. Five freemen and 77 villeins in Coney Weston—probably the entire body of householders in the village—paid recognitions to the abbey, but only the villeins occur in the list as holders of livestock. The list describes 3 of the villeins as too poor to contribute anything and lists 20 others as owing varying sums of money without mentioning any associated livestock. The remaining 54 villeins held differing combinations of horses, oxen, cattle, sheep, and pigs. All but four members of the group held at least two different animals, and a quarter of the group held at least four different kinds. The aptly named N. Richeman had the most impressive portfolio in the village: 4 horses, 6 cows, 10 pigs, and 40 sheep, for which his recognition amounted to half a mark (6s. 8d.). Considering the group as a whole, we find that these 44 villeins held 60 horses, 51 pigs, 117 head of cattle, and 342 sheep. As a statement of minimal livestock resources held by a group of disadvantaged tenants living in a notably infertile part of the country in an era of exceptional demographic pressure, these numbers do not warrant a particularly pessimistic view of peasant pastoralism. They do, however, suggest an important distinction within the ranks of the peasantry, in that ownership of livestock was not spread evenly through the village. A core group of 16 men dominated Coney Weston's livestock resources, accounting for more than half of the horses and cattle, about two-thirds of the pigs, and more than four-fifths of the sheep.[52] In this concentration of capital in the hands of a select group of residents, Coney Weston's livestock figures conform to what we know about many other facets of peasant life: Peasant society was not a society of equals. This pooling of resources in the hands of select groups of peasant producers helped to create the circumstances that allowed peasants to assume a leading role in the production and exchange of agricultural commodities in the economy as a whole.

Another valuable inventory of livestock resources can be found among the recently excavated records of the royal manor-cum-independent borough of Godmanchester, in the form of an unusual pair of documents that records the number of fleeces and lambs held by individuals in the town, along with land under crop.[53] Although the compilers of these registers omitted holdings of all other kinds of property—including other kinds of livestock—from consideration, they did enumerate sheep with some degree of precision. Their interest solely in crops, fleeces, and lambs suggests a connection between the two documents and the Nonae assessment of 1341, and hence a slightly later date for one of the documents than was advanced by its excavator.[54] Whatever their precise dates, it is clear that both lists arose as part of contemporary tax evaluations and as such share the limitations of all tax records in this period. Indeed, the considerable discrepancies between the two lists, both of which ostensibly record the same information within a short span of time, attest to the likelihood that these sources convey what the town was willing to admit to owning for the purposes of taxation rather than what the town owned *in toto*. As with the recognitions of Bury's tenants and our entire collection of subsidy documents, we can use these sowing lists only to establish minimum levels of property ownership.

The more extensive of the two lists will form the basis of analysis here. This fuller list documents the sown crops, fleeces, and lambs held by 199 individuals in the town, but manuscript damage affecting some of the fleece and lamb entries eliminates 35 of these taxpayers from consideration. Of the remaining 164 individuals, about a third (59 total) produced neither fleeces nor lambs. Virtually all of the remaining members of the group held fleeces, and most held both fleeces and lambs. The list records a total of 1,330 fleeces and 362 lambs in the town, yielding a total of 8.1 fleeces and 2.2 lambs per recoverable taxpayer, or 12.7 fleeces and 3.4 lambs per taxpayer involved in sheep production. As in Coney Weston, averages are somewhat misleading because individual flocks were not of uniform size. Holdings ranged all the way from the single lamb owned by the unnamed widow of Robert Rede to the flock of 160 sheep and 10 lambs recorded for John Peysel. The 20 most substantial producers in Godmanchester accounted for nearly 60 percent of the town's assessed flock and exactly half of its lambs—in other words, many people in the town engaged in the enterprise, but only a select few committed significant resources to it. Bartholomew Hildemar was one of these select few. In addition to cultivating 5 different crops on 21 acres of arable, Hildemar tended a flock that produced a recorded total of 32 fleeces and 9 lambs in the year in which the sowing list was compiled. This close connection between arable and pastoral production was typical of the holders of large flocks in Godmanchester and indeed of much of the rest of the country as well. Wealth in one pursuit typically found its parallel in the other.

How much of the livestock in places like Coney Weston and Godmanchester circulated outside of the household economy? Livestock and livestock products feature prominently in contemporary lists of the tolls collected in fairs and markets, and as noted in chapter 1, towns had an insatiable appetite for the hides and wools that fueled the leather and textile trades. We also know from surviving customs accounts that hides and especially wool left the country in vast quantities, destined for the burgeoning cities of Flanders and Italy. At the very least, we can say that peasants did not lack for incentives to profit from their pastoral endeavors. Occasionally, we are vouchsafed glimpses of their production of marketable surpluses, as in Edward III's ill-fated manipulations of the wool trade in the 1330s and 1340s. Two villeins in the village of Needingworth in Huntingdonshire, for example, lost nearly two sacks in a seizure made by royal purveyors in 1339, and producers of similar ilk accounted for the vast majority of the clip collected in the more orderly direct tax in wool of 1341.[55] Despite the value of such anecdotal evidence in illustrating the prominence of peasants in the market for pastoral products, we are more likely to appreciate their role by comparing it with the other major producers of the period, the lords and the gentry. How did these individual peasant flocks and herds of a few dozen animals measure up against their palpably wealthier social superiors?

III

To answer this question, we need to turn our gaze away from the microcosm of the single village or individual producer to look instead at the larger economic macrocosm of the national economy. Regardless of whether we frame our social comparison using relative shares of total wealth and surplus or using production of a single commodity, such as wool, we invariably find the peasantry as the paramount creators of wealth and marketable surpluses in the economy.

That the peasantry collectively owned the lion's share of the country's total wealth is beyond question. E. A. Kosminsky's meticulous analysis of the Hundred Rolls reveals that peasant landholders held about two-thirds of the productive land in the regions covered by the source, and most historians accept this figure as the norm for the country as a whole.[56] If anything, we would expect to find even less demesne land in the parts of the country not included in the Hundred Rolls. A similar figure can be offered for relative shares of annual national income, or gross domestic product. Nicholas

Mayhew has recently attempted to quantify the aggregate wealth held by different social groups at the beginning of the fourteenth century, and his work deserves serious consideration.[57] Using Christopher Dyer's calculations about the annual incomes enjoyed by different social levels and moderate demographic estimates, Mayhew has calculated that at the dawn of the fourteenth century peasants accounted for 66 percent of total gross domestic product, towndwellers 18 percent, and gentle and clerical society the remaining 16 percent. These figures, of course, are highly conjectural, and other historians have offered significantly different versions of both total output and social demographics in this period.[58] But Mayhew's estimates do find support in the distribution of wealth revealed in national tax records, and as orders of magnitude they are probably not too far off the mark.[59] As one would expect, peasants' total wealth did not match their aggregate share of the population, but even with substantially lower levels of per capita income than more privileged echelons of society, collectively they still held far more of the country's wealth than any other group. As Mayhew has observed, his calculation "shows clearly how far GDP was dominated by the work of agricultural laborers and peasant farmers at the bottom of the social pyramid."[60]

Of course aggregate wealth and aggregate commercial share do not go hand in hand: If lords directed most of their production to the market and peasants directed theirs to subsistence, we could still imagine a commercial sector dominated by the demesnes. Undoubtedly, a substantial part of the peasants' share of gross domestic product should be attributed to subsistence activities. But we must be careful not to err in the other direction by attributing the lords' total share of GDP to production for the market. On many estates, cash rents formed a considerable part of total income, and absentee rentier income had even less to do with producing commodities in the thirteenth and fourteenth centuries than coupon-clipping does today. For most large estates, cash rent was the single largest item of annual revenue. The precise mix of rents and demesne production varied from estate to estate, but even in the heyday of direct manorial production, rents often constituted half or more of a lord's annual income.[61] In addition to rents, most lords had other forms of direct cash income, derived from such things as court amercements, entry fines, milling perquisites, and market tolls. None of these items generated anywhere near the amounts derived from tenant rents, but cumulatively they helped tilt the balance even further towards cash revenues, at least on the larger manors.

Indeed, the very notion of the manor as primarily a market-oriented producer is problematic. As Kathleen Biddick has demonstrated in the case of Peterborough Abbey, manorial lords were wont to accord a higher priority to the needs of internal consumption and reproduction than to the potential gains of commercial involvement.[62] Bruce Campbell's study of more than 200 manors in the counties surrounding London—where we might expect to witness the country's highest level of commercial activity—has revealed that only one-quarter of total manorial produce actually found its way to market.[63] Such findings are corroborated by evidence about lords' capital investments in the period. Rodney Hilton has found that prior to the Black Death major landholders seldom dedicated more than about 5 percent of their annual income to investment in capital.[64] Hilton concluded from this that lords must have ranked conspicuous consumption well ahead of capital investment in their scale of economic values. This is not the behavior one would expect of a social group interested in producing commodities for the market. In a similar vein, J. A. Raftis has recently shown that lords of the period relied heavily on peasant capital to turn their manors into productive assets.[65] Raftis's work indicates that lords sought well-endowed peasant tenants for their estates just as avidly as modern corporations seek educated and experienced employees for their management positions. Unlike modern chief executives, though, medieval lords were often content to leave fundamental production decisions in the hands of their underlings, even decisions about what to produce and how to produce it.[66]

All of these studies are weighted heavily toward the traditional manors of the wealthiest lords. Many historians have suggested that smaller estate holders—those at the knightly and gentry level—were not as insulated from the market as the great magnates, and both the logic and the evidence for this position are sound. The holders of smaller estates seldom had villein tenants providing work services on their demesnes, and they typically dedicated most of their landed endowments to direct production.[67] Kosminsky, whose work brought these differences between manors to the fore, argued that the holders of such estates had to earn their living by hiring labor and producing for the market.[68] His position has held up well under scrutiny. Such gentry estates were far more numerous in the countryside than were the classical estates of the peerage, although their smaller average size meant that they accounted for only about the same aggregate share of the country's land.[69] Still, because of their numerical preponderance and distinctive estate structure, we can recognize in the knights and gentry a significant group of producers sending agrarian commodities to market. On four small estates in Essex in the first half of the fourteenth century, for example, sales of agricultural produce accounted for about 90 percent of all manorial income.[70]

According the gentry a significant role as commercial producers, though, does not require that peasants be pushed to the margins of the market economy. Even with a predominantly commercial inclination, gentry producers could have supplied only a limited part of total market demand. They had neither the numbers nor the resources to do otherwise. In the thirteenth century, England had somewhere between 1,000 and 1,500 knights, a figure that can be derived independently from at least two different sources.[71] One of these sources, distraints for knighthood, explicitly linked knightly status to income levels. In 1256, a knight's minimum income was set as low as £15 per annum; by the beginning of the fourteenth century, the figure had risen to £40. Even at their fourteenth-century level, and even if they derived every farthing of their income from sales of agricultural produce, the knights' aggregate share of the entire national market must have been negligible. We have to descend to the lesser gentry, those with incomes between £5 and £20, before we encounter a group sufficiently large and prosperous to have significantly influenced the commercial world. Estimates of the size of this lower tier of gentry range between 10,000 and 20,000, still a small number in a population that may have approached seven million people, but one large enough to have had a meaningful impact on the market for agricultural produce.[72]

Once we descend to this level, though, we find ourselves cheek-by-jowl with the upper echelons of the peasantry. Our sense of peasant incomes comes largely from hypothetical models based on knowledge of their landholding and assumptions about their yields. These estimates generally place the income of an upper-rank peasant family in the vicinity of £4 per annum, although a somewhat higher figure is certainly not beyond the range of possibility, judging by the amounts that peasants paid as tax and supplied to purveyors.[73] Peasants with this level of income typically possessed a virgate (or yardland) of land, usually comprising about 30 acres of arable, along with a messuage of an acre or two and rights of access to common pasture and local woodland. Now, if we picture one of the lower gentry as working somewhere around 100 acres and enjoying an annual income somewhere around £10, we should picture the wealthiest peasants as operating on a scale somewhere around one-third that of the lower gentry. While such a difference undoubtedly constituted an important social and economic divide in the village and beyond, it also signals the peasantry's predominance as marketers of agricultural commodities. For the lower gentry numbered in the thousands; the peasants in the millions.

Virgaters and their ilk were, of course, a distinct minority in the village, but they were a substantial minority. Kosminsky found that about one-quarter of all landholding peasants in the Hundred Rolls, including both free and unfree, held a virgate, and a further 4 percent held larger holdings; Postan arrived at a similar figure using estate records; and Miller and Hatcher have tentatively suggested a figure of one in five.[74] The number certainly varied from one region to the next: East Anglia had few peasants working more than about 20 acres of arable, while in the West Midlands estate surveys commonly show a third or more of tenants at the virgate level. The number could also vary from one village to the next in the same region: Villages that were part of the great estates, for example, tended to preserve the integrity of virgate holdings, while freehold villages with diffuse lordship tended to favor splintering of holdings. Even in villages where the virgate persisted as a standard formal holding, subletting and occasional alienations could reduce the amount of land actually held by a particular family. In spite of all this variation, though, in most villages in most parts of the country we can document the presence of a core group of wealthy peasant families continuously endowed with holdings at or near the 30-acre range of a typical virgate.

The peasant population of late-thirteenth-century England was probably close to five million, if we assume that peasants made up 80 percent of a total population of somewhere between six and seven million.[75] In the country as a whole, then, we can estimate a population of upper-rank peasants somewhere around one million, if we accept Miller and Hatcher's estimate of the proportion of virgaters, or 1.5 million if we accept Kosminsky's. Using the lower estimate and the venerable multiplier of 4.5 members per household in England before the Plague, we arrive at a total of 222,222 households at this rank in the country as a whole. As Zvi Razi has documented in the case of Halesowen, virgater households were probably larger than those of other peasants, but even a calculation that assumes an average size of six members per household yields a total of 166,666 virgater households.[76] Such an estimate would require us to believe that every one of the 14,000 or so settlements recorded in Domesday and the 1334 lay subsidy rolls had about a dozen resident families enjoying virgater or equivalent rank.[77] Numerous studies of English villages suggest that such a figure falls well within credible grounds.[78]

Given these estimates of wealth and numbers, it is easy to see why upper-rank peasants dominated the production of agricultural commodities. While their lands and incomes per capita were perhaps a third or so as large as the averages for the gentry, virgate-level peasants were about ten times as numerous. If both groups marketed the same proportion of their produce, peasants would have supplied the market with more than three times the amount of produce supplied by gentry producers. Subsistence needs probably took a greater share of a wealthy peasant's total production than was the case for gentry farmers, although one might argue that the latter kept larger households, with disproportionately more servants and fine horses. We cannot pretend to precision with so much hypothetical underpinning, but it would probably not be too far off the mark to accept that peasants marketed somewhat less of their produce and postulate that upper-rank peasants generated somewhere around twice as much agricultural produce as their social superiors.

The peasant share of market activity was by no means limited to the wealthy virgaters, significant though they were in the village hierarchy and in the economy as a whole. Even if only a small proportion of the less wealthy peasantry was involved in producing agricultural commodities, and even if they produced meager individual surpluses, their collective importance should not be forgotten, given their numbers. But though they undoubtedly pushed the production of agricultural commodities even further toward the peasant side of the ledger, their impact was probably not as great as their numbers might suggest. As we move into the less exalted ranks of peasant society, we come closer to true subsistence producers, peasants who had neither the land nor the capital resources to generate agricultural goods beyond what could be consumed within the domestic unit. Such households still participated in the commercial expansion of the period but only in a limited way as producers of the staples that formed the heart of the exchange economy. Their role in commercial activity lay principally in other spheres: in producing exchange goods derived from specialized labor rather than from ownership of land and capital; in providing the labor that allowed the gentry and wealthier peasants to augment their production of surplus; and in the provision of a mass of consumers for the petty retailers of village society. Peasants endowed with a handful of acres undoubtedly participated in various kinds of commercial exchange, but at least as regular producers of agricultural surplus they took a back seat to the upper echelons of the village. Thus, even though they formed upwards of three-quarters of peasant society, it is unlikely that they generated nearly as much agricultural surplus as the wealthiest quarter. With their occasional bushels of wheat and pounds of wool, multiplied several hundreds of thousands of times over, they swelled the peasantry's total stock of marketable surplus, but the bulk of that stock came from the households of their wealthier neighbors.

A good illustration of how the social division of economic resources and productive capacity might have manifested itself in a real market setting comes from one of the best-documented branches of medieval commerce: the wool trade. Customs accounts reveal that England exported about 30,000 sacks of wool—nearly 11 million pounds—in an average year in the early fourteenth century.[79] Traditionally, historians have turned to the great estate-holders to explain this remarkable commercial feat.[80] But as Eileen Power and more recently A. R. Bridbury have pointed out, the great estates could in no way have generated the sums of wool that left the country.[81] Few Benedictine houses produced more than 50 sacks of wool annually: Peterborough and Ramsey Abbeys produced between 30 and 40 per year, and Westminster Abbey perhaps less than 20.[82] On the basis of such figures, it is difficult to imagine the 100 or so Benedictine foundations in the country coming up with more than about 2,000 sacks of wool in any given year. The Cistercians devoted more of their resources to sheep than did the Benedictines, but they had fewer houses and their total production was probably lower than that of the black monks. Pegolotti's late-thirteenth-century listing of major wool producers, which renders a nearly complete account of Cistercian houses and their wool production, shows the white monks producing a bit more than 1,200 sacks yearly.[83] His list also shows the smaller religious houses—Premonstratensians, Gilbertines, and Augustinian Canons—collectively producing roughly the same amount as the Cistercians. We are less well informed about episcopal estates, but we do know that around 1290 the Bishop of Worcester had a flock of 5,650 sheep, which would have produced less than 20 sacks of wool annually.[84] If this is anywhere near the average for a bishopric, it would be difficult to imagine aggregate episcopal production in excess of 500 sacks per annum. Taking all ecclesiastical estates together, total production figures would not likely be more than about 5,000 sacks per annum, less than one-sixth of the total exported.

The rest of the country's wool, of course, had to come either from lay estates or the peasantry. Unfortunately, we know much less about the wool produced on secular estates than we do about their ecclesiastical counterparts, although we can make some rough estimates. In his sample of manors near London, Bruce Campbell calculated that wool accounted for just under 10 percent of all manorial income from sales of agricultural produce.[85] If we assume similar production levels for the rest of the country and use Mayhew's calculation of the share of annual national income held by the lay groups above the rank of peasant (£425,000), we end up with an estimate of annual wool revenues for all social levels of secular society above the peasantry of £42,500.[86] Since Mayhew's calculation included rents and many other forms of income not derived from agricultural production, this figure probably overstates actual wool income by a considerable amount. Even such a generous allowance, though, still leaves the lords and gentry producing less wool than the peasantry. At a price of £5 per sack—a common price for wool of middling quality in the various parliamentary price schedules of the period—the £42,500 of hypothetical annual wool production by peers and gentry represents 8,550 sacks. This figure is considerably larger than the estimate for the production of ecclesiastical estates, but it still leaves the peasantry as the most significant body of producers in the country, responsible for more than half of the wool exported in an average year in the early fourteenth century. If the domestic market was only one-quarter the size of the export market, we would need to conclude that peasants undertook roughly two-thirds of the country's wool production.

Similar conclusions can be drawn regarding the ownership of taxable wealth revealed in the lay subsidies. As was discussed more fully in chapter 1, assessors of the lay subsidies ordinarily taxed only those goods that were surplus to the needs of domestic consumption; they did not tax basic working stock, nor did they tax foodstuffs likely to be consumed within the household. No one has yet undertaken the monumental task of categorizing on a national scale the social rank of all taxpayers documented in these sources, but several scholars have done so for single counties or regions. Our earliest lists of subsidy payers derive from the fifteenth collected by Henry III for his Poitevin expedition in 1225 and include local assessment rolls for one wapentake in Lincolnshire and a deanery in Wiltshire, as well as the county roll for a single village in Cambridgeshire. The editor of these valuable sources calculates that somewhere between two-thirds and three-quarters of all the wealth taxed in that subsidy belonged to peasants.[87] A similar preponderance of peasant wealth can be found in the more plentiful records of later subsidies. In the hundred of Blackbourne in Suffolk, the 1283 subsidy returns reveal that peasants owned a remarkable 85 percent of all the chattels assessed for taxation.[88] In three Bedfordshire hundreds in 1297, lords made a better showing than their counterparts elsewhere, but they still accounted for only one-third of the area's assessed wealth.[89] Every close investigation of the lay subsidies yet conducted, either at the village or the county level, has reached the same conclusion: Peasants held at least two-thirds of the country's assessable surplus, possibly significantly more. They could have achieved such preponderance as taxpayers only if they similarly dominated the production of marketable commodities.

IV

Recognizing the leading role peasants played in generating agricultural commodities is an important step toward understanding the structure and dynamics of commercial activity in medieval England. As described in chapter 1, agricultural commodities formed the matrix of urban economic life, providing the critical core of materials for industrial and commercial enterprise as well as the essential means of subsistence and reproduction. As towns grew in size and complexity over the course of the thirteenth century, the intensity of their interest in capturing the surplus of the countryside grew apace, since wealth and well-being could be attained only through winning a share of the wheat and wool produced in surrounding villages. The growth of urban demand and the intensification of peasant production were thus complementary developments of the period. Towns offered powerful incentives to all rural producers to produce beyond subsistence level, and those peasants able to do so responded to the incentive with great vigor. The commercial economy of the period was firmly rooted in this elementary symbiosis between urban demand and peasant commodity production.

In addition to explaining the extent of commercial activity in the economy as a whole, peasant surplus production also helps to explain the prevailing types of commercial institutions. Peasants, after all, are the quintessential type of small producers; the surplus each household produces is not sufficient on its own to warrant anything more than local interest. As the organization of the monastic wool trade teaches, large producers typically had opportunities to sell their surplus without ever making use of local markets; had the production of surplus been a preserve of the great estates, or even of the gentry, the network of rural markets that formed in England in the twelfth and thirteenth centuries might never have come into existence.[90] Transactions involving sacks of wool or granaries full of grain were readily conducted by means of direct—and private—negotiations; it was preeminently the peasantry, with their stones of wool and odd bushels and quarters of grain, whose commercial prospects were intimately linked to the public world of the market.[91] The key to commercialization in all peasant societies lies in the development of commercial venues and networks of exchange that can pool modest individual surpluses in a manner that is sufficiently cost-efficient, time-efficient and space-efficient to make the circulation of commodities beyond the limits of the village a viable proposition. Explaining how and why English peasants and merchants managed to create such networks of exchange will form the principal concern of the remaining chapters of this book.

Part 2

Nodes of Exchange

3

A Flurry of New Markets

By the year 1300, a healthy proportion of the English economy was involved in producing goods for market exchange. Many of these goods found their way into the burgeoning towns of the period, but, as the preceding chapters revealed, a large proportion of the goods in circulation originated in the countryside. There were numerous means by which the products of the country flowed into and out of towns. Lords and peasants residing near the towns could bring goods directly to market, and towndwellers could likewise venture beyond the confines of their community to acquire directly from rural producers the food and raw materials they desired. Both of these alternatives were, in fact, commonly employed in this period, and will be discussed in greater detail in chapters 6 and 7. But as the populations in towns grew, so did the need for improved lines of supply. Alongside the need for better supply lines grew the chance to tap a new consumer market beyond the confines of town and court, one that would be able to absorb some of the increasing industrial output that resulted from the growing urban labor market. In other words, the situation was ripe for the development of intermediary trade arrangements, ones that could increase the materials brought from and the products sent to an extended hinterland while decreasing the search and transport costs involved in doing so. The principal means by which this was accomplished was the foundation of a plethora of new rural marketplaces all across the country and the formation of these markets into multiple, integrated systems, each revolving around an urban hub. To understand how this great transformation occurred, we need to look first of all at how the country came to have so many markets.

Doing so takes us along a path that winds through the great halls of Chancery and Exchequer and leads to the meetings of the county courts and, occasionally, to the sessions of the king's court. Even in the thirteenth century, England was a much governed country, and the seemingly simple act of establishing a new market was hedged around with a welter of rules and regulations governing when and where one could be held. By the thirteenth century, the right to hold a market was considered to be a form of royal franchise, sometimes kept in hand by the king, but more commonly given over to be exercised by an individual or corporation. This conception of a market—one among a number of similarly conceived notions of rights and jurisdiction at the time—generated a copious body of grants, claims, and counterclaims, which has been something of a mixed blessing for historians. On the one hand, we have rich sources of information that allow us to investigate the precise location and foundation chronology of new markets. Considerable progress has been made in this investigation to date, largely on a county by county basis, and the prospects for drawing up a complete inventory of medieval marketplaces at some point in the near future are very good. But, on the other hand, the abundance of information has created some daunting problems of interpretation. Markets created in the period from about 1200 to 1350 number more than a thousand, and it is often thought that this multiplicity resulted from trade being a strictly local phenomenon. Why else, after all, would the country need so many markets unless each was capable of servicing only a narrowly circumscribed area? This seemingly commonsensical view is, however, based on a misconception of the legal rights and privileges inherent in a market franchise. A close analysis of these legal rights reveals that there was not necessarily a direct correlation between the number of markets recorded in royal records and the type of trade occurring in the economy. In fact, an appreciation of the legal basis of the market franchise points to precisely the opposite conclusion. Markets, even rural markets, were created in this period not to facilitate purely local trade but rather to facilitate trade between localities and regions. In other words, rural marketplaces were not self-contained enclaves catering strictly to a local population; they were parts of larger integrated economic systems, caught up in the gravity of places like Ipswich, Shrewsbury and even London.

To clarify this point, we need to explore more fully three of the steps by which new markets were licensed and nurtured in the thirteenth century. First, we need to analyze the precise terms of the legal franchise defined by the courts. Aspiring founders of markets were legally bound to respect the rights of the holders of preestablished sites. Among other things this meant that founders had to be able, when necessary, to convince a court that a proposed market would augment the number of outside traders active in the area and thus would not simply shift local trade from one site to another. A second illustration of the external orientation of rural markets can be gleaned from the procedural methods used by prospective founders to set up their new sites. To be successful a market had to be publicized, and the means by which this was done sheds light on the expectations of the franchise holder with respect to his or her new venture. Finally, a third clue to the type of trade conducted in rural markets is offered by the theory and practice of toll collection, which also reveals the importance of outside traders in the designs of those holding market rights. Not all buyers and sellers had to pay toll when trading in a market. From the holder's perspective, the most lucrative group of market users were traders hailing from places other than the market site. Without such traders, possession of a market franchise was not worth very much. From several different perspectives, then, we can detect a hustling and bustling world of regional traders behind the seemingly endless squabbles about the precise nature of the market franchise.

I

Markets existed in England many centuries before the arrival of the Normans. We know little about the nature of these early markets beyond the fact that a number of them developed into important urban centers in later centuries. According to Richard Hodges, prior to the general economic and political collapse of the ninth century, markets were located almost exclusively in major towns and ports, and trade occurred between and around these centers but did not extend far beyond them.[1] There was, in effect, an international commerce made possible by the English Channel and the North Sea, but little inland or regional trade to speak of. Many towns and ports persisted as sites of settlement through the disintegration of the ninth century, but their trade was reduced to the merest shadow of what it had once been. With the onslaught of Dane and Norse in England and the disintegration of the Carolingian order on the Continent, bare survival was the best that could be hoped for. According to Hodges, when a modicum of political stability reemerged late in the ninth century, the exchange economy assumed a new configuration, one that had narrower horizons but better-developed articulations between the surviving urban centers and the interstices between them.[2]

Whatever the early history of markets in England, there is no question that they were relatively few in number before the thirteenth century. Hodges's evidence, most of it archaeological, suggests that thirteenth-century growth started from a higher plane than has been generally recognized, but the written evidence leaves no doubt that integration between different levels of markets was still fairly rudimentary before the second half of the twelfth century. Domesday Book, for example, recorded only 60 markets in the country.[3] While it is true that the Domesday commissioners were not particularly interested in recording markets and fairs, the paucity of evidence found in other sources supports the view that there were relatively few markets operating in the eleventh century. Indeed, the extremely well-documented surge of market foundations in the thirteenth century would never have taken place if rural markets were already plentiful two centuries earlier.

The arrival of the Normans did, however, set in motion a change in the conception of what a market was and how it should be governed. In ancient Rome, regulating public markets was an imperial prerogative, exercised through special officials, the ediles.[4] This tradition persisted in some small degree among the Anglo-Saxon kings, as among their counterparts on the Continent, but their resources were inadequate for doing much more than passing the occasional decree insisting that sales take place in public places, sometimes specified as recognized towns and ports.[5] Norman and Angevin kings, on the other hand, gradually succeeded in reclaiming markets as an area of public jurisdiction vested in the crown. The culmination of this trend toward resumption of jurisdiction was reached in the aggressive Quo Warranto campaign initiated by Edward I shortly after his accession to the throne in 1272, when market holders, along with holders of other types of franchises, were called before royal justices in eyre to legitimate their rights to hold their markets.[6] Those unwilling or unable to do so were liable to lose their market rights.

As anyone with experience in government can attest, one person's right to do is often another person's obligation not to do. In the case of thirteenth-century markets, having accepted the king's monopoly to create new sites, and having acquired a royal franchise to do so, would-be founders of markets expected the king to help them guard against interlopers seeking to establish rival venues that would siphon off some of their trade. If its authority was to be anything more than a pretense, the crown necessarily had to devise methods not only to grant rights in the first place but also to see to it that the rights were respected after the grant was made.[7] And so, almost from the moment kings began to assert their monopoly over the creation of markets, the royal courts were called upon to adjudicate between rival claimants seeking to extend their rights as far as possible, even if doing so meant, as it often did, infringing upon the rights of other holders. Though these disputes were probably a headache at the time, we are fortunate that they arose a time when greater attention was being paid to preserving the records of the king's courts. The litigation between rival holders of market rights allows us to watch the unfolding of the marketing network in one of its most formative stages, a stage in which it acquired the shape it was to bear into and beyond the Industrial Revolution.

Inherent in the grant of a market franchise were several fundamental rights.[8] One was the right to jurisdiction over any disputes that arose in the course of the market day, and, more importantly from the market holder's perspective, any resulting fees and fines. One of the ruses used by royal prosecutors seeking to seize unchartered markets from their holders during the Quo Warranto proceedings was to ask a jury if the holder observed the letter of the law by providing a pillory at the market site to punish offenders, knowing full well that many did not bother to do so, preferring instead to collect fines. A related right of jurisdiction—and of profit—was the authority to enforce in the marketplace the royal assizes of bread and ale and to pocket the fines imposed on transgressors. A third right inherent in the grant of a market was the privilege of receiving toll from those using the market. There were, however, a number of important qualifications to this right of toll collection, ones that will be dealt with in more detail below. These three sources of revenue—fines on trading disputes, fines on illegal measures used in sales of bread and ale, and tolls on sales in the marketplace—help to explain why a market franchise was worth having, and why it was worth protecting from rival claimants. But there was a fourth right inherent in the grant of a market, one that did not, strictly speaking, generate any revenue for the holder, but one nonetheless that gave the other three rights their principal attraction. This was the right to a monopoly of sales transactions in the area surrounding the market. This last right is fundamental to an understanding of what a market was, and as such is worth considering in some detail.

Beginning early in the reign of King John, when the king granted someone a market, he invariably did so conditionally, because the grant of a market franchise established the recipient's rights not only vis-à-vis the king, but also vis-à-vis other franchise holders. The king and the king alone could grant a market, but even the king could not grant a market that was prejudicial to one that was already operating. This end was achieved by inserting a special proviso in the charters granting markets: New markets were permitted "unless they be damaging to other markets," *(nisi sit ad nocumentum aliorum mercatorum).*[9] The *nisi sit ad nocumentum* clause was first used in 1200 and became a standard phrase in market grants from then on. The "damage" prohibited by the *nisi sit ad nocumentum* clause was defined in practice as the redirection of established patterns of trade. A new market damaged a preexisting one if it attracted trade that traditionally took place in the other market. By diverting trade, the holder of a new market gained toll revenue and rent payments at the expense of the holder of the preexisting market, whose franchise was "damaged" as a result. In effect, once a market was legally established, only the holder of the rights was entitled to the profits that could be garnered from sales transactions. Furthermore, any and all sales that occurred within the purview of the market franchise had to be made in the market. Sales in any other place were illegal.

The possession of this sales monopoly is implicit in one of the earliest cases involving markets to appear in the Curia Regis rolls after the introduction of the *nisi sit ad nocumentum* clause. In 1202 the Abbot of Bury St. Edmunds claimed that the market founded the previous year by the Abbot of Ely in Lakenheath, Suffolk, was harmful to his market in Bury.[10] Although Lakenheath was 17 miles by road from Bury, the jurors decided that the new market was prejudicial to that of Bury "because live and dead flesh, fish, grain, and sundry merchandise, which used to be carried to St. Edmunds and sold there, and upon which the Abbot took toll, now is carried to Lakenheath and sold there, so that the Abbot loses his toll."[11] On the basis of this finding, the king banned the Lakenheath market. Bury then decided to take matters into its own hands. According to Jocelin of Brakelond, Bury gathered together 600 men to tear down the market and to arrest those buying and selling in it.[12] Forewarned of this, Ely ensured that all the buyers and sellers had deserted the market by the time Bury's group arrived in Lakenheath. Undaunted, the mob proceeded to dismantle the market stalls and to carry off a number of animals, forcing Ely to submit while a more peaceful settlement was reached. Ely had attempted to disrupt Bury's monopoly of sales transactions and was foiled because such an attempt was, as the roll states, contrary to "the custom of England."

Over the course of the next century, the courts struggled to give precision to the general tenet that a market franchise contained within it the right to monopolize sales.[13] Disagreements inevitably arose because of uncertainty over how extensive the monopoly should be. Sales made in the same town or village holding the market and on the same day as the market were clearly meant to be included within the terms of the monopoly. But what about sales made in neighboring settlements? What about sales made the day before or the day after the market day? Where should the limits of the monopoly be set?

One of the most commonly questioned limitations on the sales monopoly was based on distance from the market site. A passage from the legal treatise ascribed to Henry Bracton, written sometime around 1250, has become a *locus classicus* in research on medieval trade because of its precise description of permissible distances between markets. Bracton's rule of thumb was that two markets should not be located closer than 6 2/3 miles together, which the author considered to be a feasible distance for one to travel to a market, sell one's goods, and return home before nightfall.[14] A new market founded more than 6 2/3 miles distant from a preexisting one could be detrimental, Bracton stated, but it could not be considered neighboring and therefore could not be forbidden. Bracton did not enunciate a formal legal principle, and there are many instances where the rule was not applied, but in practice the courts generally adhered to a similar definition.

A second principle limiting the extent of a market's monopoly of sales transactions was based on the timing of potentially conflicting markets. Medieval markets were periodic, held on a specific day or days of the week. On that day there was little question that the monopoly was effective within the locational limits set by the courts. But other markets held on other days of the week could seriously affect the volume of trade of a preexisting market and thus necessitated some guidelines concerning what was and what was not acceptable as a limitation of a market monopoly. Bracton himself mentioned the importance of timing, although this part of his discussion has received considerably less attention than his discussion of location. Bracton said that a neighboring market, by which he meant a market within the 6 2/3 mile radius, was not necessarily harmful if it was held on the second or third day after a preexisting market. Indeed, though situated nearby such a market could even be beneficial; harm accrued only if the new market competed temporally with the preexisting market.[15] The legal treatise *Britton*, written about 1291, spells this out with even greater clarity. If a plaintiff wished to implead a competing market, *Britton* holds that he must specify that the new market had been set up "on the same day in the same town, or in another town within 6 miles and a half and the third part of a mile from his market."[16] If the market had been set up on another day, the plaintiff would lose his case.

Application of the restrictions based on timing can be seen in many instances. In 1220, a plea was brought by the Prior of Sidmouth, Devon, against the infamous Fawkes de Breauté, "an able, unscrupulous, and godless man," as the *Dictionary of National Biography* describes him.[17] In this instance, however, de Breauté does not appear in a particularly sinister light: He simply tried to change the day of his market in Sidmouth, which customarily had been held on Sunday, to Saturday. There was no question of any change in location involved, yet the attempt to change the day on which the market met led the Prior of Sidmouth to claim that de Breauté's market would now be detrimental to neighboring markets. The case was postponed, and the final verdict has not survived, but the fact that a case would be brought at all is indicative of the importance of timing. A similar example occurs in a dispute over a proposed market in Prittlewell, Essex. In 1289, the king instructed his sheriff in Essex to inquire about potential damages if a market were granted to be held either on a Monday or a Friday.[18] The sheriff assembled a jury for the purpose, which found that the market would not be prejudicial to other markets so long as it was held on a Monday, the implication being that a Friday market on the site would be. Another illustration of the importance of timing occurs in a dispute over the market in Great Dunmow, Essex.[19] The new market of Richard, son of Simon de Dunmawe, in the village of Great Dunmow was challenged by Gilbert of Clare, the Earl of Gloucester, as being harmful to Gloucester's market in Bardfield, about five miles away. In his defense, Richard claimed that there was no damage done because his market was on a Tuesday, whereas the market in Bardfield was on a Saturday. Richard went so far as to make the claim that the case should not even be put to an inquisition to establish damages for the sole reason that the two markets were on different days. We do not have a verdict in the case, but we do know that Great Dunmow had an active market a few generations later, so presumably the court agreed with Richard's position.[20]

More detail about the reasoning behind the timing restrictions occurs in a case in 1240 involving the markets of Swaton and Folkingham in Lincolnshire.[21] The newly created Friday market in Swaton was said to damage the established Saturday market in Folkingham because "merchants who ought to go to market at Folkingham are prevented from doing so by the market in Swaton." William Longespée and Idonea, his wife, creators of the market in Swaton, defended their interests not by challenging the principle that the timing was detrimental but rather by pointing out that they had constructed a trench allowing ships to reach Swaton with goods that could be taken on to Folkingham after the close of the market in Swaton. In other words, there were extenuating circumstances that alleviated the harm normally associated with establishing a new market the day before a preexisting one. Unfortunately, no judgment in the case is given.

As these examples indicate, interested parties were well aware of the basic rules governing the location and timing of new markets. Indeed, knowledge of the rules became so common that the issue of damages almost proved to be a Pandora's box. Could concourses of buyers and sellers over which nobody claimed jurisdiction or levied tolls, in places such as churchyards, be in conflict with chartered markets?[22] Did the acquisition of a charter alter the relationship between two markets established before King John's change in franchise law?[23] Did a market that had fallen moribund enjoy its original privileges if revived?[24] To fight their way through these thickets of interpretation, the courts inevitably tried to keep sight of a few basic principles by which to judge the specific circumstances of each case. Legal texts such as Bracton and Britton describe the most transparent of these principles, the ones involving distance and timing. But if we probe a bit deeper, we find two other underlying assumptions about how the market franchise was supposed to operate. One of these was that new markets were unacceptable if they did nothing more than simply shift trade from one place to another. In other words, only markets with the potential to establish new trade were allowed to get off the ground. The other was that a market encouraged new trade by bringing outsiders to the site. Many of the conflicts over markets in the period were grounded in the fear that itinerant merchants would be "intercepted" by rival venues. That courts treated the interception of trade as a real problem implies that the merchants originated in places suitably removed from the trading sites.

II

While it became a necessary step for prospective market holders to take, acquisition of a royal charter did not by itself guarantee a monopoly of sales transactions in the area surrounding the proposed site. The charter guaranteed the security of those rights if the market were established in a proper manner, which meant, essentially, if it did not conflict with other markets. But the king did not take potential conflict into account when granting a charter; rather, it was the responsibility of the one seeking the charter to ensure that the market met the necessary requirements allowing it to be held. As R. H. Britnell has noted, charters were granted on the principle of *caveat emptor*.[25]

At the same time, however, the crown did more than simply write up the charter and collect the requisite fee. After the charter was granted, the king saw to it that knowledge of the grant became publicly available. In this way, he could minimize the prospects for future litigation based on harm to a preexisting market, and he could also help the new market establish its first roots in its new environs.

In the days before the billboard and the television commercial, the diffusion of information about new goods and services was a large hurdle to be overcome if a new venture was to succeed. Acquisition of a market charter did not guarantee that people would begin to buy and sell at a given place. Before people would come to a new market, its existence had to be made publicly known, preferably as far afield as possible. This was accomplished by means of the sheriff and the county court.[26] As part of the grant of a new market, a recipient normally received the services of the sheriff to announce in the county court and elsewhere that a new market would henceforward be held at the time and place specified in the charter. In 1205, for example, the Bishop of Rochester was granted a weekly market in Bromley, Kent, and the sheriff of Kent received a writ to that effect, ordering him to have the grant proclaimed throughout his bailiwick.[27] Other early examples of similar writs instructing the sheriff to proclaim a new market include ones issued to the sheriff of Devon in 1207 and to the sheriff of Shropshire in 1214.[28] In 1227, the sheriff of Gloucestershire was ordered not only to make public proclamation of a new market but also to have both the charter granting the market and a letter patent of protection for the market read in a full session of the county court.[29] The pace of founding new markets had slowed considerably by the fourteenth century, but as late as 1343 a writ was issued to the sheriff of Yorkshire with identical directions about publicizing the new market in Skipsea.[30]

The sheriff's proclamation must have been a source of some anxiety for the person who had acquired the charter. Part of the purpose of making the proclamation was to allow other franchise holders the opportunity to contest the grant before it was translated into a potentially rival venue. In fact, the writs ordering proclamations also regularly instructed the sheriff that the grant was conditional on the new market's not damaging any neighboring markets. If another market holder was able to establish that the proposed site had the potential to injure a preexisting one, the sheriff was expected to take measures to protect his or her rights. Consequently, just as the sheriff played a fundamental role in creating and overseeing the markets in his county, he was also responsible for prohibiting markets that were improperly founded or found to be damaging to other markets.[31] Prohibiting a market entailed making a public proclamation that henceforward the market would not be held and could even involve the physical dismantling of the buildings erected in a marketplace.[32]

We have a particularly illuminating example of how this system of public announcements and challenges worked in the case of the disputed market rights in Swaton and Folkingham, mentioned earlier. In 1240, William Longespée and his wife Idonea sought and received a royal charter granting them a Friday market in Swaton, Lincolnshire.[33] Gilbert de Gaunt challenged the grant, alleging that it would damage his market in Folkingham, about five miles southeast of Swaton.[34] Folkingham's market was held on Saturdays, and Swaton's was proposed for Fridays. On the surface it would appear as though de Gaunt had a legitimate gripe. The Longespées argued that they had followed all the requisite steps for creating a market and that everything had been in order at each step. They had, first of all, secured a royal charter. Then William had taken the charter and a writ ordering proclamation of the market at the county court to the sheriff. When the charter was read at the court, Walfrid de Stowe—not Gilbert de Gaunt, as the Longespées' attorney pointed out—opposed the market, saying that it would damage the market in Sleaford.[35] Sleaford is situated about six miles northwest of Swaton; in later centuries its market was held on Mondays, and this was probably the case in the thirteenth century as well. The sheriff conducted an investigation of Stowe's claim, but found no basis for the allegation. As a result, the sheriff ordered his bailiffs to proclaim the new market in Swaton.

Determining how to assess the validity of a formal plaint raised upon the proclamation of a new market was a matter usually left in the sheriff's hands. On one occasion the king wrote to the sheriff of Gloucestershire to tell him that he had learned "with certainty" that a market was damaging and consequently had to be prohibited.[36] But the instructions sent to the sheriff of Bedfordshire were more typical: "you should diligently inquire into the truth of this matter and if it seems legitimate to you, then you should have [the offending market] prohibited and proclaim publicly that it will no longer be held."[37] "Diligent inquiry" effectively meant creating an ad hoc jury to investigate the problem. In 1205, when the sheriff of Norfolk was told to inquire into potential damages, he did so by empaneling a jury of lawful and oath-swearing knights.[38] Over the course of the thirteenth century, such investigating juries were to become standard elements of procedure whenever someone challenged the validity of a newly chartered market.[39]

As even this cursory discussion demonstrates, the creation of a new market in the thirteenth century could be a fairly complicated affair. Several of the procedural steps reinforce the view that these rural markets were intended to develop trade that encompassed something more than local producer-to-consumer exchange. The choice of the county court as the proper forum to announce or denounce a proposed market is itself significant. Issues that were of interest only to a single village or even to a group of neighboring villages were traditionally handled at the level of the hundred or wapentake, administrative districts immediately below the level of the county. An average hundred contained several dozen villages and covered an area in excess of 100 square miles. If newly founded rural markets were expected to cater only to local trade, pronouncement at the hundred court would have sufficed to establish whether or not a new market would harm a preexisting one. Instead, the issue was deemed appropriate for treatment at the county level because it was assumed that merchants and others from beyond the hundred might be interested in making use of a new market. The procedure used to evaluate potential damages caused by the proposed market in Swaton demonstrates this in unambiguous terms. When the plaint against the market was raised in the county court, the sheriff of Lincolnshire had inquiries made in ten neighboring wapentakes, comprising about one-third of the entire county, an area greater than 500 square miles.

III

Not including the profits arising from jurisdiction, the revenues that a market generated can be divided into two basic types: revenue deriving from possession of the soil on which the market was held and revenue deriving from the right to collect toll on transactions occurring in the marketplace. Among the former types of revenue were those known as stallage, a rent for a table or stall from which to sell and by far the most common property-related revenue, and pickage, a payment for the right to break ground with stakes to set up a booth. Market tolls were primarily a form of sales tax, sometimes collected from the seller of a good, sometimes from the buyer and sometimes from both buyer and seller.[40] Market tolls also included payments for the use of the market holder's official weights or measures. The most common type of these weighing tolls was tronage, a toll collected for the use, often mandatory, of a market holder's weigh beam.

To realize a profit from the tolls collected in a market, holders of the venue had to succeed in attracting trade beyond that required for the basic sustenance of the people in and around the market site. All market holders assumed that petty retailing would occur in their markets without any special incentives. In most towns and villages where new markets were established, such trade had gone on informally for generations before the market was founded. But petty local retailing was not the main interest of founders of markets in the period, chiefly because it was incapable of yielding sufficient toll revenue to justify the costs of running the market. In all markets, the aspirations of toll collectors were hampered by two important limitations. The first limit derived from restrictions on the rates of toll that could be levied, and the second derived from the prevailing custom of exempting trade oriented toward simple household provisioning. Both of these limits shed important light on the aims of market holders in founding and managing their venues, and both merit closer investigation.

Contrary to popular belief, the rates of toll collected in most markets and towns of the period were extremely low, seldom above one percent of the value of the goods being exchanged.[41] The rates were, in fact, so low that a significant volume of trade had to be taxed to yield any appreciable revenue. This was partly the result of royal regulation, and partly the result of competition. The right to collect any type of toll was a royal franchise kept within conventional bounds, and the crown sometimes acted on behalf of the users of market facilities to maintain rates at an appropriate level.[42] The First Statute of Westminster prescribed that anyone taking excessive toll was liable to have his or her right to the market where the offense occurred confiscated.[43] Market holders appear to have been free to set their own rates, but they clearly were not allowed to collect tolls that were out of line with those commonly collected in other markets. In one instance in 1275, the Abbot of York was said to charge excessively high rates in Hornsea, including the exalted sum of one farthing (1/4d.) for a horseload of goods carried into the market.[44]

Government intervention was, however, probably less important than straightforward competition in keeping down the rates of toll collected in markets. Holders of markets knew that the users of their facilities were likely to be savvy comparative shoppers. In a few instances, overly energetic toll collection even led to organized boycotts against the offending market. London merchants, for example, carried out a two-year boycott of the market in Bury St. Edmunds in the late twelfth century to back their claim for toll exemption there.[45] The burgesses of Lincoln were particularly adept at voting with their feet. In 1235, the Bishop of Lincoln complained that the bailiffs of the town had caused the townsmen who customarily bought and sold in his market in Horncastle to withdraw from the market because of a dispute over toll collection.[46] Forty years later, the Lincoln burgesses effected a boycott of the fair in Boston while their grievances about toll collection were presented to the king.[47] Irregular toll exaction was a shortsighted policy from which market holders quite likely stood to lose more than they could gain. Whenever market participants withdrew because of grievances over toll, a holder lost not only further toll revenue but also revenue from the rents of stalls and shops.

In very few of the rural market sites founded in the thirteenth century could the holder expect local inhabitants on their own to generate enough trade to make toll collection a worthwhile enterprise. Market holders were well aware that the most effective way to increase revenue was to encourage greater volumes of trade rather than to increase charges levied on a fixed quantity of trade, and this ordinarily meant enticing people from elsewhere into the market site. By encouraging greater use of their facilities, holders sought to augment both the rents received through stallage and pickage and the tolls collected on transactions in the market.[48] To achieve this end, some holders were even willing to make short-term sacrifices in toll revenue for the sake of the longer-term health of a fledgling site. In 1246, for example, the tolls of the market in Hadleigh, Essex, were relaxed for three years in order to encourage the use of the new market there.[49] Similarly, a toll-free period of five years was offered as an inducement to traders in 1285 to use the market of Brading on the Isle of Wight.[50] The most detailed example of the motives and consequences of toll remission is supplied in the record of a five-year grace period offered by the Abbot of St. Osyth in his market at Brentwood.[51] In 1241, the Abbot of Battle took St. Osyth to court for exacting tolls from Battle's men who frequented the market in Brentwood, contrary to Battle's right to freedom from toll throughout England and contrary to the initial practice of the market in Brentwood. The Abbot of St. Osyth explained in his defense that after he had acquired the market charter he had instituted a five-year period during which no tolls were collected "in order to attract men from the area to his market." When the five years were up, St. Osyth began to collect toll "in such wise that the men [of Battle] willingly and without solicitation gave toll and the Abbot of Battle himself gave toll on his granary." Whatever one makes of St. Osyth's claim that subsequent payments were voluntary, it is clear that a very conscious policy of encouraging trade was in place and that toll incentives played a large part in this policy.

As well as having to accept low rates, holders of markets had to accept a second major limit to their toll receipts in the form of customary exemptions claimed by those who used the market for household provisioning rather than as a source of profit. According to both custom and law, those making use of a market solely to acquire their basic household needs were exempt from toll. Ordinarily, only sales beyond the level of private consumption were eligible for taxation. We know about the exemption from toll for household trade primarily from instances when it was overlooked. The Hundred Rolls of 1275 furnish a particularly good sample of complaints raised against overly aggressive toll collectors. Those farming the market town of Lutterworth, Leicestershire, for example, were accused of taking toll on grain bought for sowing and consumption and on other small articles that were normally exempt from toll.[52] Similarly, the burgesses of Wallingford were cited for taking toll on grain and other foodstuffs purchased by "the men of the area" *(hominibus patrie),* contrary to their custom of exacting toll only from merchants.[53] Villagers in Lugwardine and Marden in Herefordshire told the justices that the Bishop of Hereford had begun to charge toll in all of his markets in the diocese, even though people "were accustomed from time out of mind to be free to buy and sell for their own use as long as they were not general merchants."[54] In a dispute over tolls in King's Lynn, the goods involved were emphasized rather than the status of the seller: toll could not be taken on small goods such as cabbages, apples, or butter in earthen pots, but it could be taken on larger wares such as wool.[55] A few of the claims opposing the right to exact toll on small transactions of goods destined for household consumption explicitly state that a general point of law and custom was at issue. A challenge to toll collection in Stamford claims that "knights and free tenants of all districts may freely purchase their food, such as bread, meat, fish and things of this sort, in all towns of England without toll."[56] When the Bishop of Lincoln was cited for taking toll improperly in Sleaford, the jurors reported that the bishop "takes toll, contrary to royal law and custom, from small articles such as linen for the carcasses of oxen and sheep, small baskets, seeds, and similar things which are not merchandise."[57]

In these examples, it is clear that contemporaries sought to distinguish between simple household trade and trade engaged in for the sake of profit. Only those involved in the latter were expected to pay tolls on their forays into the market. Even trade that might appear to involve economic considerations beyond simple household subsistence needs sometimes qualified for toll exemptions. A particularly revealing dispute in 1330, pitting the rural inhabitants of Northamptonshire against the burgesses of the county town, suggests that even cattle could be viewed as items of household trade rather than as commodities traded for profit. In this case, the residents of the county testified that Northampton's bailiff had recently begun to demand toll on all sales of cattle in the town, although traditionally toll had been paid only at fair time, and even then "only from dealers and not from those who bought cattle for stock."[58] A similar complaint was made a few generations earlier by residents of Nottinghamshire against Richard Foliot's bailiffs in Wellow, who "[took] toll on beasts and other goods bought for private use from tenants of the royal demesne and from others who are not merchants."[59]

The limiting of tolls to transactions motivated by profit suggests once again that the goal of founding a market in the thirteenth century was to attract a level of trade beyond the petty local exchange of basic foodstuffs. Medieval markets, even markets in peasant villages, were held not only to satisfy local consumption needs but also to facilitate the exchange of commercial wares, commodities in the Marxist sense of goods possessing exchange value rather than simple use value. Not every market functioning in the country was able to attain this higher level of trade, but most aspired to it. Only by facilitating trade for profit could a market holder expect to profit from his venture. If a local farmer sold a bushel of grain to a cottager, the market holder could not collect anything from the cottager and at best might collect a fraction of a pence from the farmer, although even that was questionable. If, on the other hand, a virgater or gentry farmer from an outlying village sold several quarters of grain to a baker or cornmonger, the transaction might yield a penny or two from both buyer and seller because neither party's engagement in the sale was necessitated by subsistence considerations. Even taxing virgaters and bakers probably did not lead to windfall profits for the holders of most rural markets. But if enough of these more substantial profit-oriented traders could be enticed to use the market on a regular basis, then the resulting toll revenues might make the effort of collection worthwhile.

IV

The preoccupation with the founding and regulation of markets in the thirteenth century inevitably left its clearest traces in disputes involving particular markets and individuals. In these disputes, discussion ordinarily centered on the immediate impact of a new market on a neighboring market, but the issues involved much more than simply regulating the trade of local people living in the area of the contending markets. Rival holders were instead constantly jockeying for position within a larger marketing structure. When we piece the particular disputes together we find that those affected by the rules, as well as those making them, conceived of individual markets as part of larger networks of trade rather than as isolated entities. The emphasis on the timing of neighboring markets as an essential criterion in assessments of potential damage to preexisting markets is particularly revealing in this regard. To locals interested in acquiring food for their tables, there is some significance to having a regular time to trade, but there can be an indifference to when the time is. To the market holder hoping to attract outside traders to his market, however, timing is a crucial consideration, because the market must be held at a time when it is feasible for outside traders to participate.

In any periodic trading network, there is a strictly limited supply of days and places that can be accommodated within a broader preexisting cycle. As the marketing structure of medieval England filled in, it became increasingly difficult for a new market to carve a niche for itself. The temptation was great to try to jump the line by shunting a preexisting market to the side in order to take over its position within the established hierarchy. A particularly explicit example of this behavior, and the motivations behind it, occurred in a dispute between the Abbot of Bury St. Edmunds and the founder of a new market in the village of Barrow, situated about four miles away.[60] The abbey complained that the Saturday market in Barrow was prejudicial to its Monday market in Bury, offering two reasons for the claim. First, local people had begun to take their corn, wool, and hides to Barrow rather than to Bury. Secondly,

> the men and merchants of various districts farther off, as Huntingdonshire, Cambridgeshire, Bedfordshire, and Hertfordshire, used to come with their great wares, such as horses, oxen, cows, sheep, hides, and so forth, to Bury St. Edmunds, but for the last five years they have been stopping and staying on Saturday at Barrow and there sell their wares and return to their own country so that they do not come to sell or buy at the market of St. Edmunds, to the great nuisance and injury of the vill of St. Edmunds.[61]

The abbot claimed that he had suffered losses of £100 because of the loss of trade. His claim for damages may have been excessive, but it is clear from the abbot's complaint that Bury's market was attracting traders from within a radius extending up to 50 miles away. It is not at all surprising that we find so many examples of such behavior in surviving records; what is more surprising is how effectively the organs of law and government were able to deal with them.

The end result of the hundreds upon hundreds of attempts to establish new markets in the thirteenth century was the creation of a closely articulated marketing system allowing frequent and substantive contact between town and country. As will be described more fully in chapter 8, many of the attempts made by hopeful founders failed to result in functioning markets that were able to find a niche within the system.[62] Some fell afoul of the rules guarding preexisting sites and were quashed before they saw the light of day; many more that abided by the rules found it impossible to enter the charmed circle when forced to swim upstream against the prevailing current. Coincident with the surge in enthusiasm for founding new markets was an equally strong winnowing of speculative ventures unable to entice traders to attend, a process that will be investigated in more detail in later chapters. But even with some of the seeds landing among the rocks, there was enough fertile soil to yield a rich harvest of active and prosperous rural markets. These succeeded in cross-breeding with the vigorous urban stock, creating a hybrid that would last for half a millennium.

4

The Distribution of Towns and Markets

By the fourteenth century, sites of commercial activity in England were both numerous and diverse. Even if we restrict ourselves to formal nodes of exchange—towns, ports, markets, and fairs—we are dealing with a group the members of which can be counted in thousands rather than hundreds. Beyond these formal nodes an even greater number of informal places of exchange are discernable: monasteries, festival sites, pilgrimage sites, aristocratic households, and peasant households by the hundreds of thousands involved in the retailing of basic foodstuffs.[1] At first glance, the diversity of these sites is almost bewildering. Among the towns, for example, ancient centers such as Winchester can be found, dating back into the mists of the early Anglo-Saxon centuries, but there are also recent creations such as Kingston upon Hull, founded deliberately by King Edward I in 1299. Places such as London, operating virtually as an independent state within a state, are found alongside places such as Abingdon, fighting an endless, and ultimately fruitless, struggle to emerge from the shadow of a jealous feudal overlord. Some places functioned as major international entrepôts, buzzing with merchants from divers parts of Europe, and hundreds of others functioned as humble markets for the produce of the surrounding countrysides, struggling to attract merchants from nearby towns, let alone those with international horizons.

The presence of so many sites of exchange suggests a potentially prominent role for commerce in the economy of the period, but it also suggests an environment in which trade was extremely fragmented and localized. Towns, for example, served as the heart of regional distribution networks, but it is hard to imagine all—or even most—of England's approximately 600 medieval "boroughs" functioning in this capacity.[2] A high density of commercial sites does not necessarily preclude the presence of larger and more complex hierarchies of trade, but the tendency among historians has been to stress the fragmentation at the expense of the larger networks, largely because of the difficulty in devising appropriate criteria to distinguish the roles of different elements in the commercial hierarchy. If we want to speak of broader commercial networks, though, we need to categorize different settlements according to their role in regional trading networks. This involves two related tasks. The first is to distinguish between towns that functioned as central nodes of regional exchange and places that had some urban traits but only modest commercial horizons. The second task involves making a similar distinction within the ranks of rural market sites, isolating venues with commercial functions beyond those inherent in every gathering of buyers and sellers at a fixed time and place. By segregating towns and markets in this manner we can see in a preliminary way how individual sites might have fit into larger commercial hierarchies, and we can also make broad comparisons of commercial patterns in different regions. This chapter aims to do just that by delving into sources that reveal how people of the time differentiated between different levels of the commercial hierarchy. The thicket of medieval urban and commercial locations is in bad need of pruning—it turns out to have a lot of dead wood obscuring its living parts. Fortunately, our sources sometimes direct us where to use our hooks and shears, so that much of the trimming simply needs to follow the pattern traced by contemporaries themselves.

I

A good place to begin the pruning is within the ranks of urban communities. Among the 600 or so places that showed minimal traits of urban life by the middle of the fourteenth century, only a relatively small minority had both the capital and the human resources needed to exercise a significant economic or commercial influence over an entire region. In fact, the vast majority of places that have been classified as "towns" by medieval historians were commercial lightweights, exercising less influence over the flow of commodities within a particular region even than some of the village markets located in the same vicinity. Ultimately, such things as borough tenure—the distinctive form of urban real estate—and independent local courts had little real significance unless they were translated into concrete economic advantages: Few of the residents in and around Winchcombe could have known or cared as they plowed their fields and tended their sheep that the town had once been the capital of a shire. But rejecting such readily documented indications of a special economic organization as borough tenure opens up a Pandora's box: Which communities then deserve to be elevated to the status of regional town and which demoted to the status of glorified village? There is no simple answer to this question, but by pooling different pieces of evidence we can establish a few guidelines to distinguish the mountains from the foothills.

One of the most reliable guides to the economic orientation of different settlements in this period resides in the record of decisions made by contemporaries in the course of distinguishing between towns and villages. Such decisions were sometimes the result of actions taken internally by the residents of a particular community intent on acquiring special privileges for their place of residence and sometimes the result of appraisals made by outsiders in the course of administrative exercises created by the state. In the category of internal decisions we have two significant indicators: first, the effort to acquire a charter of incorporation granting special legal, fiscal, and tenurial privileges, and, second, the effort to establish a guild merchant and thereby to secure special commercial privileges. Virtually nothing is known about how communities reached either of these decisions; all that exists is evidence of the tail end of the process, the granting of the coveted corporate privileges. Charles Gross, Adolphus Ballard, and James Tait have established with some degree of certainty which places felt warranted in taking these steps and which did not, and we can use this knowledge as part of our effort to classify the commercial role of different settlements.[3]

External appraisals of a community's economic orientation occurred on numerous occasions in the latter part of the thirteenth and first part of the fourteenth centuries. Perhaps the best known of these is the selection of towns required to send representatives to Parliament. The reign of Edward I (1272-1307) was a period of considerable experimentation in the composition of Parliament, and, as May McKisack has described in her study of borough representation, the boroughs were the principal laboratory.[4] Because the rules and precedents about representation were still inchoate, we find substantial variation in the lists of summons that survive from the reign. On a few occasions prior to 1295, the king sent summons directly to the towns that were to attend, but more often he sent a writ to the sheriff ordering him to cause the towns in his bailiwick to elect representatives for the imminent gathering. Apart from the instruction that representatives were to be elected for every city and town (sometimes every city, town, and market town), the writs gave no further direction to the sheriffs about the places meant to be included. The decision about which communities fit the description of city, town, or market town was, in other words, left entirely in the sheriffs' hands. And as is clear when one works through the lists, the sheriffs did not refer to lists of towns with charters or adopt any formal rules about places with burgage tenure when they made their choices; they simply acted on their experience as administrators and, presumably, as consumers. In effect, if a sheriff thought that a particular settlement was urban, it was.[5]

Much the same thing can be said about the selection of places liable for taxation at the differential urban rate in the lay subsidies. Prior to 1294, the fractional rate set in the subsidy, while varying from one assessment to the next, was the same for towns as for villages. But in 1294, towns were assessed at a higher rate than villages, and this double rating system was adopted in most subsequent subsidies. We do not know precisely why the new system was adopted, but it seems likely that there was a sentiment that urban chattels could be concealed more easily than rural ones, and consequently that a higher fractional rate would bring the contributions of the towns more into line with those of the villages.[6] As in the case of parliamentary representation, there was neither a fiat from the king nor hard and fast rules defined by central administrators about which places were expected to contribute at the urban rate. Indeed, particularly in the early double-rated subsidies, it is unlikely that the king and his Exchequer officials even knew what to expect under the new rules. The instructions issued to the chief taxers in the various counties were as vague as those sent to the sheriffs about selecting representatives for Parliament. On the basis of his careful sifting of the mass of records that these subsidies produced, James Willard concluded that the most important criterion on which the decisions of the chief taxers hinged was "trading activities rather than size" of the communities involved.[7] The chief taxers were ordinarily prominent men living in the counties to which they were assigned, and their decisions were pragmatic ones based on their knowledge of the economic composition of the settlements with which they dealt on a regular basis.

On two other occasions in the first half of the fourteenth century, experiments in taxation created moments of definition. One of these came in the attempt in 1340 to emulate the great tithes of the church when assessors were asked to tax grain, wool, and lambs in rural communities but merchandise in urban ones, giving rise to the Nonae Rolls, a source that will be described in greater detail below. The other was part of a survey undertaken in 1316 to assign responsibility for military service, recorded in a source known as the *Nomina Villarum.* In this exercise, the sheriffs were required to enumerate the hundreds and wapentakes in their bailiwicks and to record the names and, if applicable, the lords of all cities, boroughs, and townships within their jurisdiction. Cities and boroughs were exempt from the burden placed on the villages to supply soldiers in this levy, an exemption that required the sheriffs to distinguish between urban and rural settlements. In both these cases, the instructions issued to the officials responsible for gathering the information were as ill defined as those issued for the selection of members of Parliament and taxation boroughs. Sheriffs made the decisions concerning the levy of troops and probably followed precedents set in the summons to Parliament, but the tax of one-ninth involved an alternate group of decision-makers, ordinarily consisting of jurors reporting on the parishes in a particular deanery.

All told, then, we have six contemporary indices of urbanization: possession of a charter; presence of a guild merchant; representation in Parliament; payment of an urban rate of taxation in the subsidies; description as a city or town in the *Nomina Villarum;* and assessment as a town in the Nonae Rolls. Of these six, four derive from people outside the site in question but familiar with it, and three are directly and unequivocally based on the economic life of the settlement. Noneconomic factors were more prominent in the securing of a charter, selection as a parliamentary borough, and designation in the *Nomina Villarum,* but even in these instances the economic life of the settlement exerted great influence over the determination of status. When we compare the results of these indices, it is clear that we are working with nets of differing mesh size. The subsidies have the finest mesh of any of our sources, recording 221 different places as boroughs in at least one assessment between 1294 and 1336.[8] A much wider mesh is evident in the case of guild merchant locations, which yield a total of 79 urban places.[9] The summons to Parliament and the charter evidence align themselves more closely with the subsidies than with the guild merchant evidence, each documenting about 180 places with some claim to urban status.[10] Neither the Nonae Rolls nor the *Nomina Villarum* provide coverage for the entire country, but it is clear from the parts of the country that are covered that they had an intermediate mesh size, netting more specimens than the guild charters but fewer than the parliamentary summons.

While there is much overlap between the sources, there are also many towns that make only cameo appearances, particularly in the subsidies and summons to Parliament. Indeed, it is largely by aggregating these sources, and then combining them with isolated references to burgage tenure, that Maurice Beresford and H. P. R. Finberg managed to document the existence of more than 600 medieval boroughs.[11] The correlation between the number of places that show flickers of urban life and the number of places with prominent commercial functions, is, however, a very loose one. Beresford and Finberg used extremely generous criteria as search parameters when compiling their list, and there is little question that their results exaggerate the number of settlements that can legitimately be considered to have had urban traits of any real significance.[12] Even our most inclusive contemporary source, the lay subsidies, identifies only about a third the number of sites identified by Beresford and Finberg as having urban characteristics. Many of the planted boroughs, in particular, need to be treated with caution, as these tended to be little more than handfuls of burgage plots embedded within communities that continued to be geared almost entirely towards agriculture, as Beresford himself has pointed out.[13] Some of the plantations were spectacularly successful over the long haul: Leeds and Liverpool were both founded in 1207, although Salisbury and Stratford-upon-Avon, founded at roughly the same time, were considerably more important economic centers in their first centuries of existence. Far more commonly, though, the hopes that a planted town would emulate the success of a Salisbury or a Stratford proved to be chimerical, particularly by the late thirteenth century. Typically, in these later attempts at borough foundation the burgage plots were let to the same kinds of artisans that could be found in any village. In these instances, the offer of burgage tenure did little to change the commercial complexion of an area; frequently a burgage plot was just a tenanted cottage by another name.

We have, then, a large number of unsuccessful urban seedlings, places that failed to develop the root system necessary to bear commercial fruit. But even places that are not immediately culled from the bin need further sorting and grading. There are few disagreements among historians about which towns should be put at the head of the list of major commercial centers in this period, but there is as yet no agreement about how to handle places lower down the scale. Any system of classification inevitably distorts what was in reality an extremely nuanced sliding hierarchy, but the hierarchy itself cannot be understood without divisions. The six indices described above offer probably the most meaningful guide to where the lines might be drawn. One of the obvious places to look is the consistency with which particular places struck policy-implementers as urban sites. About 45 of the places netted by the lay subsidies, for example, are not described in any of the other sources as boroughs, and about half of these are described as such in only one of the 13 dual-rate subsidies between 1294 and 1336.[14] Likewise, although some 180 places were asked to send representatives to at least one early Parliament, the number of places that were consistently asked to send members was about half that total.[15]

Recognizing the discrepancy between the total number of places making fleeting appearances as towns in the subsidies and the number of towns uncovered by the other five available indices mentioned above, Willard has drawn up a useful comparative table to measure the consistency of contemporary appraisals.[16] His data show a total of 41 places that occur as boroughs in all six of the sources, or in five out of five indices in the cases where records are incomplete.[17] It is also fairly certain that towns that are missing from just one of the sources should be considered to be in the same league. Some of these places were overlooked through administrative oversight in one or other of the royal exercises (Lincoln and York, for example, were not returned in the *Nomina Villarum*), but more often they were not home to a guild merchant, a curious anomaly that has yet to be fully addressed by urban historians. Included among this group are places such as Norwich and Northampton, which no one would question as belonging among the prominent towns of the country. There are 38 towns in this group, which, when combined with the 41 places recorded in all possible sources, yields a total of 79 major settlements consistently identified as towns in contemporary appraisals.[18]

A handful of other towns that were in anomalous constitutional positions merit consideration for membership in this group. The case for Chester and Durham is fairly straightforward. Because of their palatinate status, neither was included in any of the royal initiatives that brought the other towns to light. Both places had charters and guild merchants, and there can be little doubt that both were important commercial centers.[19] A third place—Coventry—can also be added rather easily. It fails to occur as an urban center in only two sources, the lay subsidies and the *Nomina Villarum,* and in both cases this can be attributed to a special agreement made with the crown allowing the town to be taxed as a village.[20] An argument can also be made for ranking

Boston among the major towns of the country, although its absence from several of the sources is less easy to explain. In the 1280s, Boston was the leading wool-exporting port in England, and its wealth is clearly reflected in fourteenth-century tax records.[21] While it did have a guild merchant, the town did not receive its charter until the middle of the sixteenth century.[22] More mysteriously, it never sent a member to Parliament and was treated as a village in the lay subsidies, the *Nomina Villarum,* and the Nonae Rolls.[23] It is possible that its constitutional position as part of the honor of Richmond accounts for some of the anomaly, and it is also possible that its sprawling inclusion of surrounding lands was a factor in its treatment by administrators.[24] Whatever the explanation, on balance it seems reasonable on account of its exceptional wealth and prominence as a port to include Boston among the principal towns of the country. Adding Chester, Durham, Coventry, and Boston to the list of leading towns netted by the other sources results in a total of 83 towns in this category. Not surprisingly, this is about the number that were regularly invited to Parliament after the initial stage of experimentation was over.

The 38 towns that failed to appear in two of the available sources would, in most cases, still be of some commercial significance, but at this rank we are probably moving away from what might be described as regional towns and into the rank of local marketing centers.[25] A good example of a town found in this category is Andover in Hampshire. A good series of records illustrates the activities of the town's guild merchant at this time and includes a number of disciplinary issues related to the trading activities of members of the guild.[26] Even a quick perusal of these records reveals that the affairs dealt with in Andover were typical of any number of small towns in the country. In the sessions held in 1279, for example, the guild dealt with the behavior of butchers, fishmongers, and regraters (petty retailers) of various description (including a regrater of timber) and passed a resolution concerning the weighing of wool and yarn. Yet at the same time, Andover struck neither the sheriff making the return for the Nomina Villarum nor the deanery jurors responsible for assigning tax status in the Nonae Rolls as belonging in the ranks of the county's towns. More surprisingly, in only one of the lay subsidies between 1294 and 1336 was Andover assessed at the urban rate; in the other nine for which records exist it paid the rural rate. These exclusions indicate that, in spite of its guild merchant, Andover's economy was more likely to be considered rural than urban, that the veneer of urbanism did not penetrate very deeply into the settlement's grain. In the trilogy of "city, town, and market town" commonly inserted in royal writs concerned with decisions about community status and description, Andover, and with it most towns in this group, straddled the border between town and market town. Differentiating these communities from places like Dunstable in Bedfordshire and Banbury in Oxfordshire, both thriving market centers in this period but without any illusions about their agrarian lifeblood, must have been as difficult for a contemporary royal official as it is for a modern historian.

As a starting point, then, the dividing line between possible regional hubs and lower-order marketing centers can be drawn between the group identified in all or all but one of the applicable indices and those absent from two or more. But even within the group of settlements consistently identified as urban are a number that were unlikely to have had much impact on regional commercial patterns. A number of the places that contemporaries consistently designated as urban settlements had remarkably modest levels of wealth; in some cases one might even describe them as impoverished. Our best reference point for comparing levels of wealth in different settlements in this period is furnished by the assessments made for the lay subsidies, among which the assessment made in 1334 is the most complete.[27] A comparison of the assessments of the 83 core towns with other settlements in the country results in a very uneven distribution. On the one hand, towns that were in the core group dominated the upper echelons of the assessment and, conversely, towns that were not rarely made an exceptional showing.[28] On the other hand, many of the core towns failed to reach the levels even of the wealthier villages in their counties. More than a third of the core towns (28 in total) had assessments indicative of total taxable wealth under £100, a level attained by hundreds of peasant villages. Most of these places thus should probably be classified as lower-order marketing centers rather than as regional hubs, even though they were consistently identified as towns in contemporary sources. Unfortunately, the subsidy data cannot be used as a straightforward guide to urban function or commercial importance, unless we were willing to accept that the village of Bampton in Oxfordshire, with an assessed wealth of £969 in 1334, was the eighth most important commercial hub in the country, ahead of such places as Norwich and Oxford and only slightly behind Lincoln and Yarmouth, a ludicrous proposition. Bampton is an extreme example, but several other sprawling manorial complexes were in the same league. Even if these wealthy villages were weeded out, it would still be difficult to establish a direct relationship between assessed wealth and commercial function. Many towns, including most of the wealthiest ones, had substantial arable holdings among their resources, and the flocks and fields held by the burgesses accounted for a substantial proportion of the wealth in these places. Other towns, though, were blessed with only minimal agrarian resources, and although they invariably tried to make up for their deficiency by investing in neighboring villages, they still found themselves more reliant on commerce and manufacturing for their livelihood than their better endowed peers.[29]

At the bottom end of the scale of potential core towns, though, even an impoverished agricultural base would not justify inclusion within the ranks of regional hubs. Even if every farthing in Okehampton were in the hands of ambitious merchants, its total assessed wealth of £17 would not have given it a commercial significance of much note. The same can probably be said with reasonable certainty for all of the places with assessments of less than £100, towns such as Appleby and Axbridge. Most of these threadbare boroughs were situated in the southwest, where centrifugal commercial, political and historical forces influenced the urban landscape much more than in other parts of the country, a regional distinction that will be considered in greater detail below.[30] The picture becomes a bit murkier, though, above this arbitrary floor. Setting the floor at £120 loses towns such as Dartmouth, Windsor, and Rochester, not yet towns with a credible regional scope, but no longer towns whose commercial impact was entirely local. Raising the floor another £20 loses towns such as Huntingdon, Portsmouth, Bath, Carlisle, and Stafford, towns for which a good case can be made as anchors of regional

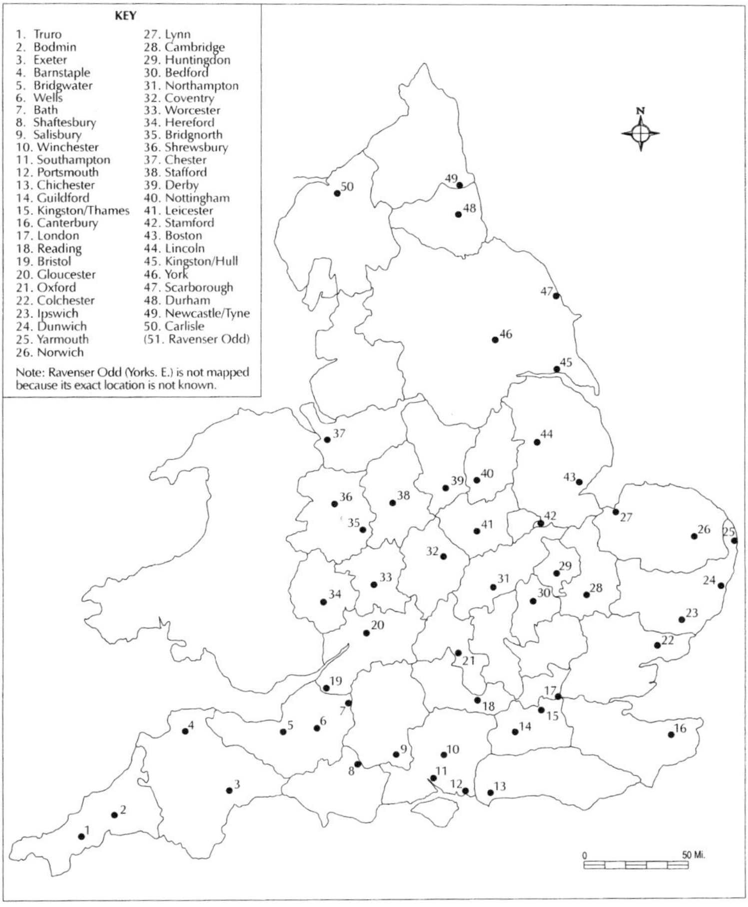

Map 4-1: The regional towns of medieval England, ca.1300

commercial networks; the case for Huntingdon will be set forward in greater detail in part 4 of this book. Setting the floor at £120 eliminates from contention 34 of the towns consistently identified by contemporaries as possible regional hubs, leaving 49 places in the category. The palatinate towns of Chester and Durham, neither of which contributed to the lay subsidies, should be added to the group, bringing the total to 51 towns. This select group, depicted on map 4-1, comprises the settlements that contemporaries repeatedly perceived as being economically distinct from all other settlements in the country and that had sufficient capital resources to influence commercial development within a regional environment.

This is still a substantial number of regional centers for a country as small as England, but it fits much better with an interpretation of regional marketing networks than does the total of all towns showing minimal signs of urban life. As is apparent on the map, very few parts of the country apart from some areas of the north were situated more than about 20 miles from a prominent regional town. In fact, the remarkable regularity in the spacing of these towns in many parts of the country strongly suggests that a radius of about 20 miles marked the effective limit of a town's regional influence, a point that will bear keeping in mind during chapter 9's look at modes of transportation. The pattern depicted on map 4-1 also readily lends itself to an interpretation of overlapping and interlocking regional systems. In many parts of the country villages had access not just to one but to several regional towns within a distance of 20 miles. By the same token, a burgess could expect to find one or perhaps several other major towns in view as he scanned the horizon from a local vantage point. More to the point, the burgess would have had to make economic decisions with an awareness of potential competitors dwelling in these points on the horizon, competitors who were just as eager to snap up the wool and barley and hides of the villages in between.

Emphasizing the core of regional commercial towns gives a clearer sense of how England's urban history compares with that of other parts of Europe. Because so many of the places described as towns in England were at best poor cousins of their continental counterparts, historians have traditionally described England as being relatively lightly urbanized.[31] While there are grounds for such an interpretation, the picture does need some modification. In most of England urbanization is best described as having occurred horizontally, resulting in greater equality between centers and a relative dearth of exceptionally large cities, unlike many parts of the continent, where major cities were more numerous and hence where the urban hierarchy tended to be more stratified. While London can be classed alongside the great Flemish and Italian towns, in most of England the pattern was, as Susan Reynolds has observed, one of smaller but more numerous towns.[32] In both Flanders and northern Italy, the big three—Ghent, Bruges, and Ypres in Flanders, Milan, Florence, and Venice in northern Italy—were clearly distinguished by their size, wealth, and political clout from the surrounding countryside and from other towns in their vicinity, a model that the Industrial Revolution would recreate 600 years later. Unlike these highly urbanized parts of the continent, and unlike its own subsequent history, England's urban path prior to industrialization depended less on the size than on the number of its towns.[33] Apart from London, the dividing line in England between town and country tended to be more muted than elsewhere, partly because the towns were smaller and retained their roots in the soil, but also because the country was repeatedly broken by the presence of one of these regional towns.

II

Although their commercial functions were more circumscribed than those of the leading towns, smaller market centers had a crucial role to play in the development of regional trade. In an integrated commercial system, these intermediate centers provided the contact points that allowed merchants in larger regional centers to gain access to local production zones without incurring inordinate search costs; simultaneously they provided markets capable of keeping the transactions costs of marketing low enough to entice smaller producers to participate. In a peasant economy, the success with which these intermediate centers managed to integrate the marketing activities of smaller producers with those of merchants based in regional towns was a critical measure of the viability of peasant involvement in producing for the market.

The intermediate centers of medieval England fell into two basic types—small towns and rural market villages—although problems of definition and categorization similar to those involving the selection of regional towns exist at this level as well. Not all places with minimal urban traits merit description as intermediate commercial nodes, nor can it be assumed that all rural markets had more restricted commercial horizons than the small towns; as chapter 3 revealed, some rural markets were able to attract trade over considerable distances. Understanding the internal dynamics of regional marketing systems requires us to determine which of the hundreds of small towns and thousands of rural markets managed to establish themselves in these intermediate positions. At first glance this seems like a daunting task, but it is not quite as unmanageable as it seems. A unique experiment in taxation in 1340-41 has provided a collection of sources that helps to identify which of the thousands of candidates best fit the bill as the leading intermediate commercial centers.

The collection of sources in question has come to be known among historians as the Nonae Rolls, because their chief purpose was to record the proceeds of a tax of one-ninth on the value of certain rural and urban goods. Pursuing an expensive and ill-advised policy of buying allies as part of his strategy in the first phases of the Hundred Years War, Edward III found himself desperately short of cash just as the war threatened to break out in earnest. Revenue generated by the lay subsidies, still lucrative but frozen at its 1334 level, could no longer cover the vastly augmented expenditures made in the initial phase of the war. To make up the deficit, Edward's advisers came up with several new tax plans, including one designed to mirror the tithes collected by the Church. In 1340, Parliament accepted the plan, under which the king would be entitled to every ninth sheaf of grain, fleece, and lamb produced during the following two years.[34] There was, however, one critical difference between Edward III's tax plan and the traditional tithes of the church. As a practical system of finance, tithing had developed in Catholic Europe only after the collapse of the Roman state and consequently was based on an economy given over almost entirely to agriculture. While agriculture was still the overwhelmingly predominant store of wealth in the fourteenth century, towns had by then long reached a level of prosperity that a revenue-hungry king like Edward III could ill afford to ignore. A good portion of the wealth in towns was still generated by standard agrarian pursuits, but beyond collecting tithes on such pursuits, the Church itself had reached no satisfactory solution to the problem of taxing urban wealth. Lacking a viable ecclesiastical precedent, Edward and his advisers decided to adapt the procedures used for taxing urban wealth in the lay subsidies. The resulting tax was thus effectively a hybrid of tithe and lay subsidy. Rural parishes were asked to contribute one-ninth of their agricultural production, or the equivalent value thereof, while towns were asked to contribute one-ninth of the value of their trade goods.

Even this arrangement was not entirely satisfactory from the king's point of view. For one thing, there were places that had not achieved formal recognition as chartered boroughs but that were towns in most other senses of the word, including the presence of merchants. Included among this group were settlements that are now referred to as monastic boroughs, places such as Bury St. Edmunds and St. Albans, where monastic overlords opposed the assumption of the independent legal status that characterized the franchised boroughs. Some of these were fish too big to let swim through the taxer's net. Additionally, there were many settlements that were more purely agrarian but nonetheless home to individuals whose capital would unfairly escape a tax imposed solely on grain, wool, and sheep. What Edward and his advisers had specifically in mind on this score were the thriving rural market centers that had sprung up over the course of the preceding couple of centuries. These comprised places such as Biggleswade in Bedfordshire and Blyth in Nottinghamshire, sites of long-established markets, each with a handful of resident traders nestled within settlements that from all other perspectives were the same as their neighboring villages. In order to broaden the tax base as much as possible, Edward included a provision in his instructions to the taxers that any trading stock in the country that was not in a town was to be taxed at the rate of one-fifteenth of its value. Thus, there were three tax brackets included in the parliamentary grant made in 1340, one for villages, one for towns, and one for places that fell somewhere in between the two.

Two generations before this attempt at secular tithing was undertaken, the Church had conducted its own examination of parochial revenues, and the record of this scrutiny, known as the *Taxatio Ecclesiastica,* was still extant when Edward III hit upon his new tax plan. In the eyes of the king and his officials, the beauty of emulating tithes as a form of secular taxation lay in the fact that, unlike most experiments in taxation, receipts could be more or less known in advance. Much to Edward's chagrin, however, the tax of one-ninth failed to produce the revenue anticipated on the basis of the returns in the *Taxatio Ecclesiastica.* Suspecting fraud, the king sent special inquisitors out into the shires to investigate why the returns had fallen so far short of expectations. Many places explained the shortfall by claiming that some of the arable land in the settlement had fallen out of production between the drawing up of the Taxatio and the new assessment on ninths.[35] A host of other explanations were put forward as well, attributing the blame to such things as adverse weather, murrain, and the debilitating taxation endured in previous years.

The record of a large number of these investigations was published in 1807 by the Record Commission, and this edition has formed the basis of all subsequent analyses of the tax.[36] Useful as it is, though, the volume published by the Record Commission is only a partial edition, omitting a large number of the returns generated in the course of these investigations, presumably for considerations of space.[37] For many counties, substantial parts of the record are still in manuscript in the Public Record Office. More significantly for present purposes, many of these manuscript sources include information about the collection of ninths from places assessed as towns and the collection of fifteenths from villages that were home to stocks of merchandise. These were often listed separately at the end of the returns concerned with the collection of rural ninths. Some of these lists found their way into the Record Commission edition, but many were passed over by the editors.[38] There is, in short, considerably more evidence about the collection of ninths and fifteenths in 1340-41 than is apparent in printed sources.

As in the lay subsidies, instructions about which places had to pay the ninth on their trade goods rather than their arable production were not explicitly formulated in the instructions to the assessors. It is clear from a comparison of the assessments in the Nonae Rolls with those in the lay subsidies, though, that the roster of towns is similar. A few of the smallest boroughs in Cornwall were not assessed as towns in 1340, and some of the others, such as some of the smaller boroughs in Somerset, were assessed as villages with trade goods rather than as towns, but apart from these few exceptions there were very few omissions or additions in the intervening period. James Willard was unaware of the manuscript portions of the Nonae Rolls, but their evidence corroborates his interpretation that assessors used a site's trading activities to guide their decisions about which places to assess as towns: As the Cornwall and Somerset returns demonstrate, the terms of the Nonae assessment made it possible to treat borderline towns as villages, and yet this option was only rarely chosen.

When it comes to revealing on a national scale the leading sites of commercial activity outside the towns, the Nonae Rolls are a source without parallel among contemporary records, and their contents deserve close scrutiny. The vast majority of settlements recorded in the Nonae Rolls were peasant villages that had neither merchants nor merchandise and thus did not contribute to the assessment apart from paying the ninth on agricultural produce. Nonetheless, in most counties villages were still expected to indicate this fact in their report to the royal inquisitors.[39] The most common response of a village jury explaining why the village did not collect any fifteenths on trade goods was simply to note that there were no merchants or merchant goods in the village. Some of the villages in Yorkshire, for example, reported that there were no merchants in the settlement, only people who lived "from agriculture or from their labor."[40] Numerous places stated that there were people in the village who did not live from agriculture but went on to add that they were common laborers rather than merchants. "There are no goods of city-dwellers, or burgesses, nor any merchants or other outsiders not living from agriculture in this parish," said the jurors of Millbrook in Bedfordshire, "except the poor cottars who live by the work of their hands."[41] A number of Sussex villages echoed the sentiment that all residents worked for their living. In Chithurst, for example, the response to the commissioners was that "there are no merchants in the parish, only those who live by the culture of their lands and by their great labors."[42] Occasionally, a village jury offered a slightly different interpretation of the directions for the tax on merchandise, implying that there was a market economy in the village but not one that involved any merchants. Bexhill in Sussex told the chief assessors that the village had no merchants "except for people living from the growth and profit of wool."[43] Acomb in Yorkshire made a similar response, stating that there were no merchants in the parish "except for those living from agriculture."[44] According to a jury reporting on the villages situated in the hundred of Thedwardistre in Suffolk, "there is no merchant in the hundred who lives more from his merchandise than from his agriculture."[45] Quasi-rural settlements that included assessments on mercantile goods tended to use similar language to describe their merchants. The jury in Luton in Bedfordshire explained that there were no burgesses in the community but that "some of the people of Luton are buyers and sellers of grain and malt and other chattels." The goods of these dealers were assessed for the fifteenth, but the jurors went on to note that they all lived in part from agriculture.[46] In Abingdon and several other market centers in Berkshire the jurors reported that the totals from the fifteenth were not as high as expected "because almost all the parishioners are landholders who pay the ninth."[47]

The language found in these descriptions of merchants and merchandise was, to some extent, inspired by the categories established in the original authorization of the tax and promulgated in the directions issued by the king to the overseers of the tax. Governments routinely attempt to define the ranks that make up society; our twentieth century experience has revealed how inadequate such attempts can be. But in the case of England in the mid-fourteenth century, the governmental categories did correspond reasonably well with at least one facet of society's own sense of itself. As the inquests in 1340 and 1341 reveal, a genuine merchant was considered to be someone who was not directly involved at any stage of the manufacture of a good. The merchant's concern was to buy what others had produced and sell it again without having put in any of his own labor to add value to the product. Any good that was capable of being bought and sold in this manner became known as merchandise and ordinarily would be traded at a wholesale as well as a retail level. We find the same distinction in many different contexts in this period. When, in 1315, toll collectors in Nottingham were sued for levying a distraint on someone wishing to cart firewood for personal use past one of the towns's toll bars they were told by the carter that "no merchandise was in the said wood."[48] The point bears some stressing, because one often finds references to merchandise in medieval sources without any fuller description of the goods involved, references that are indicative of a more complex level of trade than is often assumed because of historians' less precise understanding of the term. Even basic foodstuffs could be deemed merchandise if they were traded in this way: a Close Roll entry in 1231 makes mention of merchants of victuals, subsequently described as those "who buy . . . victuals to sell elsewhere."[49] As in the case of market tolls described in chapter 3, what mattered was not so much the good per se as the way it was handled in the process of exchange: Grain purchased by a baker became merchandise insofar as the baker intended to use it for profit; grain purchased by a cottar for domestic consumption—even if purchased from the same producer who sold to the baker—never became merchandise. As many of the juries suggested to the king's officials, trade involving merchandise was a step beyond simple marketing. The two were intimately related and mutually reinforcing, but they represented different branches of the commercial hierarchy. In most instances, assessments on merchandise in the villages applied to goods that had already passed from the hands of the producer to the hands of someone else who would not consume the goods. In other words, assessors in most villages were interested in holdings of merchandise, not in holdings of goods destined for the market.

There were no precedents for dividing property in the countryside into rural produce and merchandise in this sense of the term. Differential rates in the lay subsidies had depended entirely on the status of a community and not at all on the individual components of a community's or an individual's wealth. Now, for the first time, assessors were expected not just to inventory property but to classify it as well. There is little doubt that the property involved in both arrangements was similar; for contemporaries the principal difference was that some goods now had to pay at a different rate than others. It is not clear precisely how they went about doing this as a practical exercise. The grant of the tax enrolled on the rolls of Parliament stated that the fifteenth was to be collected from "merchants who do not live in cities or boroughs and others who live in forests or wastelands, and who do not live from their own produce *(lour gaignerie)* or stock of sheep."[50] A qualification was subsequently added that this was not intended to mean cottars or other manual laborers.[51] The language used to distinguish places in which the fifteenths on trade goods was collected suggests that the main criteria was personal rather than material, that villages identified merchants first and merchandise second. Thus in Hertfordshire, the list of fifteenths collected in the county is described as the payments made by "foreign merchants," by which was meant merchants living outside the boroughs; in Lincolnshire, payments were described as "the fifteenth of divers merchants" in the county; in Lancashire, the deanery jurors stated that there were no fifteenths to collect on trade goods because the only merchants in the county lived in the boroughs.[52] Thus although the tax was officially imposed on mercantile goods, assessors ordinarily had to be able to point to an individual who behaved like a merchant before they would make assessments on any goods.

Juries contemplating assessments on rural trade goods effectively had two criteria with which to define individuals behaving like merchants. One was spelled out in the terms of the parliamentary grant, namely, people living in the country who did not produce their own food, later modified to mean people who neither produced their own food nor lived from manual labor. The other criterion was implicit in the first, namely people who engaged in buying and selling commodities for a profit. The two were not mutually exclusive categories, and this left a fair bit of room for local interpretation. The return for Bridport in Dorset, assessed as a village even though it was a chartered borough and had no agrarian base, states emphatically that everyone in the settlement made their living from merchandise, but other places paying the fifteenth described their merchants as part-timers.[53] In Biggleswade, Bedfordshire, the assessors affirmed that there were merchants in the village but added that they "live in part from agriculture."[54] Assessors in Bury St. Edmunds used exactly the same language, recording the names of those "who live in part from their agriculture and from their chattels."[55] All of the places contributing to the fifteenth in Berkshire informed the king's inspectors that all or nearly all of the parishioners were landholders who paid tithable ninths.[56] The low values of some of the portfolios of goods attributed to individual merchants also suggest that other forms of income would have been needed to keep body and soul together. In Wheldrake, Yorkshire, for example, the three merchants in the town held between them goods worth only

15s., a sum that surely would have gone towards only a few loaves of bread and jugs of ale had there not been other sources of income available.

The indentures of assessment for parishes with merchant goods often recorded the names of the individuals holding merchandise and the value of their goods, but they rarely described the goods themselves beyond the generic labels of "goods" *(bona)* or "merchandise" *(mercandisa)*. Exceptions to the rule occur in only two instances. In the course of explaining why their contribution to the fifteenth fell below expectations, Cirencester's jurors explained that three of the local merchants had lost goods worth £50 in Southampton and that one merchant was completely bereft of goods liable for the fifteenth because the king had seized his entire stock of wool, valued at 200 marks (£133 6s. 8d.).[57] A more complete description of the stock assessed in the fifteenths occurs in the return from Alderton, Northamptonshire:

> Henry Mark has 40 marks (£26 13s. 4d.) in the merchandising of wool and wine. Gregory atte Personnes trades with half a sack of wool worth 33s. 4d. Richard le Poket trades with half a sack of wool worth 5 marks (£3 6s. 8d.). Laurence le Polet, chattel-holder *(catallar')* and distributor of merchandise *(percenar' mercandize)*, [goods] worth 100s. Henry son of Henry Walter, chattel-holder, [goods] worth 40s. Richard Thresher trades with half a sack of wool worth 33s. 4d.[58]

Wool and wine were particularly lucrative commodities conferring high prestige on merchants who could deal with them successfully, and it is not surprising that people trading either of these goods would be singled out for the fifteenth. Among the places with middling assessments to the fifteenth, Alderton was probably fairly typical. Unfortunately, no local rolls for the places paying the fifteenths exist, and apart from the two examples quoted above, the Nonae records do not describe the merchandise assessed. There are obvious candidates—hides, victuals, and cloth, among others—but no way to know for certain what goods attracted the assessors' attention.

The communities singled out as having resident merchants contributing to the fifteenth fall into three basic types. The first comprise what might be called *villes manquées,* places that were unquestionably urban from an economic point of view but which failed to acquire the panoply of legal perquisites conveyed by borough status. In this category are places like Boston, St. Albans, Bridport, and Whitby. The status of some of these communities is purely anomalous: Bridport, for example, was a chartered borough that sent representatives to Parliament and, as its jurors told the king's inquisitors, all of its wealth was mercantile.[59] In most cases, though, the assessment of such places as villages rather than as boroughs stems from the presence of a strong overlord unwilling to loosen manorial bonds. Such is patently the case in the assessment of St. Albans, where 166 individuals were assessed on merchandise worth £228, an assessment comparable to some of the regional towns.[60] Newark-on-Trent, Cirencester, and Bury St. Edmunds fall into the same category. Relations between secular lords and communities of a stature similar to places such as Cirencester are not as well recorded as for the ecclesiastical sites, but they may explain why places like Whitby and Richmond were assessed as villages rather than boroughs.

At the other end of the spectrum is the second type of rural mercantile location represented in the Nonae Rolls by a considerable number of assessments involving only a single merchant or a small handful of merchants and relatively small holdings of merchandise. Debenham in Suffolk typifies the communities in this position: Four individuals were assessed there as holders of merchandise, the total value of their stock amounting to a bit more than £5.[61] The value of the great tithes in the village amounted to £168, more than 30 times the value of the merchandise. Like the dwarf towns, these places undoubtedly had only a limited role to play in regional commercial activity, but their concentration in certain parts of the country may provide some useful clues about the structural dynamics of inland trade in different regions. Assessments of this type were particularly common in Sussex, Hampshire, and Yorkshire, a feature that will be discussed in more detail below.

Between these two extremes are a number of places that might be described as preeminent rural market sites, the third category of contributors to the fifteenth on merchandise. Although there was considerable variation within the group, most of these settlements had several traits in common. Typically, they were wealthy agrarian settlements, whose lay subsidy assessments were considerably higher than those of other villages in their county. The rural component of their assessment in the Nonae Rolls was similarly high relative to most other villages. In almost all instances, they were sites of long-established weekly markets. Most had merchant communities with at least a dozen members, and, in most of the cases in which a relationship can be established between the assessment on merchandise and the assessment on great tithes, the merchandise was worth somewhere around one-quarter of the value of the production of corn, wool, and lambs. This group comprises places such as Yaxley in Huntingdonshire, Biggleswade in Bedfordshire, and Banbury in Oxfordshire, places whose wealth and commercial importance were built through a combination of agrarian wealth and successful marketplaces. The difficulties in trying to find a meaningful boundary between these thriving rural market sites and equally thriving quasi-boroughs such as Bury St.Edmunds, or even official boroughs such as Bedford and Stafford—which relied as much on their fields to make a living as on their commercial acumen—indicate just how permeable the boundary was between different kinds of commercial sites. In commercial terms, these market sites were virtually indistinguishable from smaller towns: The absence of a borough charter was no more likely to inhibit merchants from dwelling among farmers than its acquisition was likely to transform a settlement's inhabitants from farmers into merchants.

III

Although some of the Nonae Rolls have perished over the centuries, those that are extant allow us to plot the location of merchants outside the towns in most parts of the country. As in the lay subsidies, Cheshire's and Durham's traditional exemptions from royal taxes kept the Nonae assessors out, and the same was true in the liberties of the Cinque Ports. All of the relevant records for three counties that were included in the assessment—Devon, Surrey, and Westmorland—have, unfortunately, perished. In several other counties, returns are less than complete. The records for Norfolk, Staffordshire and Cumberland are especially deficient: All three record the collection of urban ninths but, with one exception, none furnishes information about the collection of fifteenths. For Derbyshire and Kesteven in Lincolnshire, we know the total value of the fifteenths collected but not where they were paid. In sum, we lack usable data for eight entire counties and part of a ninth. There are minor lacunae or irregularities in a handful of other counties that are also worth noticing. The bottom of the list of fifteenths collected in Northamptonshire has rotted away, and it is possible that some data have been lost as a result.[62] Some parts of Somerset and Hampshire reported on rural merchants by hundred rather than by individual village, making its data complete as far as the assessors were concerned, but less than complete for the purposes of historical analysis. In a handful of other counties we have to rely principally on collections of individual parish indentures for data rather than the separate lists drawn up in most counties. These are normally small slips of parchment, a feature that greatly increases the chances that portions of the record will have been lost over time. On the whole, though, the losses in these files appear to have been minimal.[63]

In addition to casting a wistful glance at the Nonae material that has not survived, we must also consider the possibility of evasion and under-enumeration in the records we do possess. Instances of fraud and collusion can be found in virtually all medieval imposts, and it would be misguided to expect higher standards from the payers of the Nonae tax.[64] If anything, we might expect to find the opposite, since the Nonae tax came in the midst of a major political crisis closely linked with the crown's war finance. The Nonae experiment came hard on the heels of repeated lay subsidy assessments that Edward III had frittered away with little concrete advantage, and the country was reluctant to undergo yet another round of taxation.[65] Resentment of the tax, and the likelihood of successful resistance to it, was enhanced by procedural problems inherent in the design of the Nonae. This is not the place to rehearse the complicated administrative history of the tax, but the difficulties in implementing and collecting it need to be kept in mind when contemplating the reliability of the data conveyed by the source. To bring his plans for the Nonae assessment to fruition, the king had twice to alter the original commission issued to the chief taxers—each time making substantial procedural revisions—before the country accepted the novel form of taxation.[66] This alone made for a confused administrative exercise, but even when the third commission initiated a steady flow of revenue into the royal coffers, the king expressed dismay with its workings and demanded that his assessors investigate perceived shortfalls in addition to collecting the revenues owed.[67] These inquisitions could not have done much to boost the popularity of the tax, and it is not surprising that in light of its manifold problems, the king and Parliament decided to forego the planned second year of the Nonae, substituting a more straightforward levy on wool in its stead.[68]

Given the circumstances surrounding the collection of the tax, the Nonae Inquisitions can serve only as a limited reflection of the fourteenth-century economy. But the source's shortcomings should not be overstated. Collectors and assessors undoubtedly committed as many acts of petty evasion and fraud in the Nonae assessment as they did in all other financial exercises of the period, but they did not manifest a wholesale and egregious disregard for their duties once the king and his advisers had arrived at a suitable procedural arrangement. For present purposes, the most problematic flouting of the rules of assessment would have involved a covering up of all merchandise in a village rather than an understatement of its extent or value. In some instances, such as Henley-on-Thames in Oxfordshire and possibly Witham in Essex, other contemporary sources would lead one to expect an assessment on merchandise, yet one does not appear in the Nonae records.[69] But while a few instances of significant marketing sites omitted from the source can be found, such omissions were exceptional rather than common. Any attempt to cover up a significant mercantile location would have required the collusion of at least three distinct parties: the local juries asked to explain the contributions made in each parish; the receivers and collectors appointed to supervise the collection in each county; and the royal inquisitors responsible for investigating the discrepancies between the income anticipated by the king and the income actually gathered. In many counties, deanery jurors or hundred jurors also vetted local verdicts, adding a fourth procedural level to the collection process.

While collusion on this scale is certainly conceivable, it was probably not common, at least not for villages with significant concentrations of mercantile goods. The county collectors—men with intimate knowledge of local circumstances—were particularly unlikely to have allowed important concentrations of mercantile goods to escape their notice. The role of the county collectors in limiting evasion of the mercantile fifteenth can be seen in several ways. First of all, the collectors often drew up separate lists of the places contributing fifteenths, and while most of these were probably drawn up directly from the local returns, it is entirely possible that in some instances they designated such places on the basis of their knowledge of the local economy, much like the assessors of earlier subsidies used their own judgment when selecting places required to pay the urban rate rather than the lower rural rate.[70] Second, the fact that some juries felt compelled to explain why they failed to identify any contributors to the fifteenth also suggests that they were uneasy about brazenly disregarding the rules of assessment. A jury reporting on the contributions of a number of villages in Oxfordshire, for example, stated that Chipping Norton did have some resident merchants but went on to explain that these merchants did not contribute to the fifteenth because their merchandise was held by the king, presumably referring to the prises mentioned by a few of the towns in the Nonae returns.[71] Similar statements can be found in a few other counties, enough to suggest that local juries expected to be challenged if they flouted the assessment.[72] The third, and most direct, piece of evidence arguing against widespread whitewashing of the returns is provided by a contentious assessment in Banbury. Oxfordshire in general seems to have been less cooperative with the Nonae commissioners than other counties, perhaps because it had been particularly heavily burdened by earlier wool taxes and purveyances. Whatever the explanation, Banbury refused outright to make an evaluation of both its tithable ninths and its holdings of merchandise, but its resistance failed (administratively at least) even at the level of its deanery jury, which simply assessed its ninths at the value registered in the *Taxatio Ecclesiastica* and came up with an estimate of £10 to cover the value of its contentious merchandise.[73]

Thus, although the Nonae returns are not an infallible guide to the sites with rural merchandise, they do reveal the location of the vast majority of the country's leading market sites. A few villages undoubtedly managed to elude the notice of the crown's tax agents, but evasion was probably the exception rather than the rule. A much greater problem in interpreting the Nonae data than wholesale evasion is the likelihood of inconsistent understanding and application of the novel terms of the tax from one jurisdiction to the next. The assessment and inquest bodies that saw service in the course of the experiment were anything but uniform, and the same can be said of the types of document these bodies engendered. Some counties had contributed more heavily to purveyance and other taxes in the years leading up to the Nonae assessment, and thus it cannot be assumed that they were all equally willing to cooperate with the crown in implementing the tax. As will become apparent from the data marshalled from different parts of the country, some counties limited their attention to places with substantial holdings of merchandise in the hands of multiple merchants, while others extended theirs to piddling holdings worth a few shillings in the hands of a single individual. We will probably never know for certain the extent to which these differences reflect variation in administrative practice rather than real economic differences, but the uncertainty can be partially diminished by adopting a regional rather than a county perspective. When several contiguous counties display a similar and distinctive pattern of activity, odds are that this similarity derives from real differences in prevailing mercantile geography rather than from differences in administrative behavior. Furthermore, when these patterns concur with other distinctive elements in regional economic structures that can be established from other points of view, the odds are even greater that this is the case. Ultimately, the Nonae returns are more suggestive of contrasting regional patterns than probative, but their suggestions deserve serious consideration.

The location of places assessed for the fifteenth on merchant goods is depicted on map 4-2. The map records the location of three different kinds of commercial sites: the 51 regional towns discussed above, other towns that

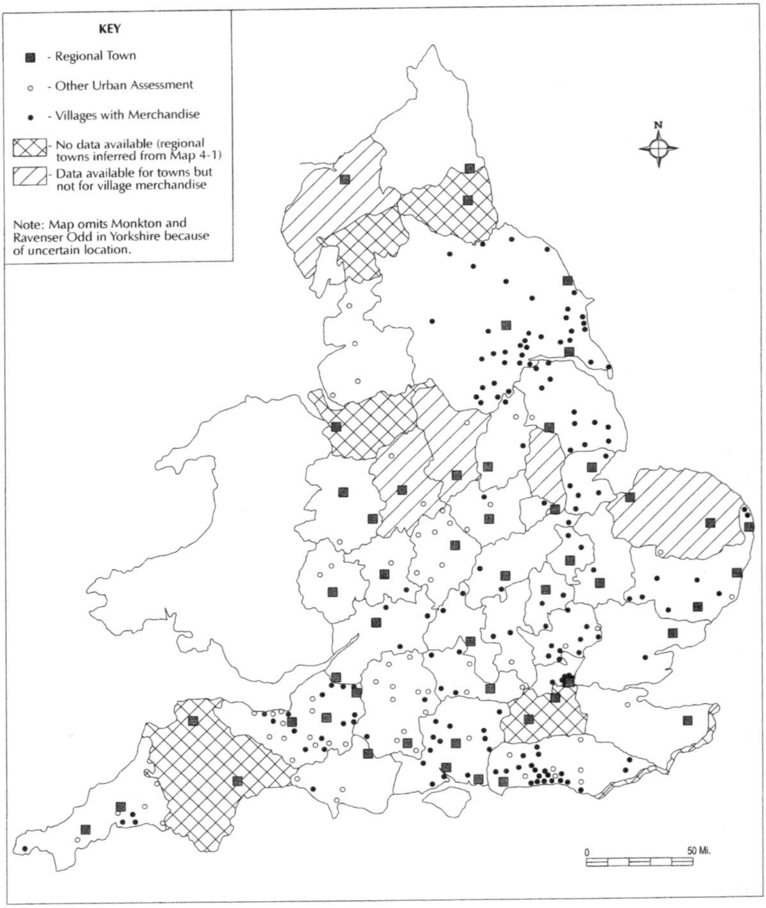

Map 4-2: Taxation boroughs and rural merchandise in the Nonae Rolls, 1340–41

paid the urban rate in the Nonae assessment, and villages that were assessed on merchandise. In the case of Somerset and Hampshire, where some of the fifteenths were collected by hundred, the wealthiest village in the hundred has been depicted as representative of the hundred; because the hundreds were fairly small, this gives a meaningful impression on a large-scale map, but the data need to be treated carefully in a local context.

Several interesting patterns can be detected on the map. Assimilating all the commercial sites on the map reveals two areas of the country with particularly dense distributions, one in the eastern riding of Yorkshire with an adjoining strip of the west riding, and one in the south. The latter area evokes the old kingdom of Wessex. It lies south of a line joining the mouth of the Severn to London and conforms both to the patterns documented for the locations of parliamentary and taxation boroughs as well as to the data about borough density compiled by Beresford and Finberg.[74] Though not recorded in the Nonae Rolls, Devon had a consistently large stock of taxation boroughs in the lay subsidies, and there is little doubt that it had a similarly dense distribution of mercantile sites, as Maryanne Kowaleski has recently documented in her study of the region's commercial development.[75] On the other end of the density spectrum are two areas of the country that seem to be particularly devoid of locations with merchant goods, one comprising the counties of Kent and Essex and the other comprising western Yorkshire, Lancashire, and Northumberland. Again, these patterns are similar to those described for the location of boroughs. Depredations in the Scottish war were a factor in reducing the stock of merchandise outside the major towns in the north, but even before cross-border raiding became a problem these areas had relatively few towns. Judging from earlier lay subsidy returns and the data available for neighboring counties, it is unlikely that the three northern counties that are not documented in the Nonae returns would have deviated much from the pattern. The final broad pattern apparent on map 4-2 is an intermediate and fairly consistent pattern covering the Midland plain and extending across Suffolk in the east and the vale of Hereford in the west, the implications of which will be dealt with more fully below.

While there is considerable overlap between the patterns that emerge from the data in the Nonae Rolls and the patterns that have been described solely on the basis of borough location, there are also noticeable discrepancies. One is the density of locations with merchandise in eastern Yorkshire, which finds no parallel in the borough evidence. There were no taxation boroughs in the triangle formed by York, Kingston upon Hull and the border with Staffordshire in the 1334 subsidy, nor were there any parliamentary boroughs situated there; even Beresford and Finberg's handlist of borough sites does not compare with the evidence of the Nonae Rolls. Yet there were a score of villages assessed with merchandise in this triangle in 1341. A second noticeable difference is the pattern in the West Midlands, where the evidence of both parliamentary representation and the absolute number of places with borough traits suggests a dense distribution, but where the Nonae Rolls, like the lay subsidies, show a pattern closer to the East Midlands than to the south. Consequently, differences in the commercial structures of the West and East Midlands are less noticeable than we have been led to expect. The small boroughs of the West Midlands find their peers in the important rural market sites of the East Midlands: In the west there were a number of smaller taxation boroughs and relatively few villages with merchandise; in the east the situation was reversed. In commercial terms, the difference between the two areas was largely one of semantics rather than any underlying economic reality.

This last conclusion helps to reformulate regional differences in some fairly important ways. What needs to be explained is not so much a discrepancy between eastern and western parts of the country, as has often been thought, but a contrast between the Midlands and other regions. These divergent patterns can be illustrated by taking Nottinghamshire as representative of the Midland pattern and Hampshire as representative of the non-Midland pattern. In Nottinghamshire, the county town was a relatively wealthy settlement, but not quite in the top rank: It had the eleventh highest assessment among all towns documented in the Nonae Rolls, but it did not make the top 25 in the 1334 lay subsidy.[76] The size of the merchant contingent recorded in the subsidy, though, was among the largest in the country, with 204 merchants contributing to the town's assessed wealth of £465. None of the other settlements in the county had anywhere near this level of wealth, although it is worth remembering that one of the very wealthiest towns in the country, Lincoln, lay only a few miles east of the county border. Only one other place in Nottinghamshire—Retford—paid the ninth on merchant goods. Its trade goods taxed in the assessment amounted to £103, shared between 35 individuals. Retford, though, was a settlement with pronounced agrarian traits. The deanery jurors reporting on Retford's goods included an addendum to their verdict on the value of merchant stock in the town, noting that four of the people they assessed "lived exclusively from agriculture." Their goods were said to be worth £6 of the total assessment. One suspects that a fair number of the other people in the assessment would have fit Biggleswade's description of its merchants as people living partly from agriculture, but there is nothing so explicit in the Retford verdict. Two places in the county merited attention from the deanery jurors reporting on the location of merchants dwelling in the countryside: Blyth, where 15 people paid the fifteenth on goods worth £73 and Newark, where assessors taxed 16 people holding merchandise worth £146. All other settlements were included in the blanket statements made by respective deaneries that there were no merchants apart from these four places.[77]

Hampshire reveals a much different pattern of commercial activity. The county was home to three important regional towns: Southampton, Portsmouth, and Winchester. The last occurs in the Nonae Rolls as one of the leading regional towns of the kingdom, with a stock of goods worth £654 and

315 named contributors.[78] Southampton ranked in most other sources from this period on a par with Winchester. Its prominence in the Nonae Rolls is, however, extremely muted, probably on account of the devastation wrought by the French, who sacked and burned the town in 1338 and threatened to return in 1342.[79] The assessed merchant community mentioned in the Nonae record of the town was limited to 76 people whose goods were evaluated at £81. A similar story needs to be told for Portsmouth. In 1334, Portsmouth's assessment was about one-quarter the size of Winchester's, but in the Nonae Rolls it was reduced to a rump settlement with eight assessed merchants and goods worth less than £5. One other place in Hampshire paid the ninth, New Alresford, whose 36 merchants and trade stock of about £25 accurately reflected its nature as a small town of intermediate commercial rank. Allowing Southampton and Portsmouth their peacetime wealth and importance leads to the conclusion that the urban sector of Hampshire's economy was somewhat more developed than its counterpart in Nottinghamshire, though not exceptionally so if Lincoln's role is acknowledged. A greater contrast emerges, though, from the ranks of communities paying fifteenths on their trade goods. In Hampshire, there were 14 places in this category.[80] Four of these were simply designated by hundred, leaving open the possibility that several places in the hundred were subsumed under a single entry. The ten places specifically identified as having resident merchants ranged in size and wealth from Mapledurwell and Petersfield, where 6 people held merchandise worth £5, to Romsey, where 56 people held merchandise worth almost £100. All told, then, Hampshire's assessors reported on stocks of merchandise in 17 separate communities, more than four times the number of places in Nottinghamshire.

How do we account for this contrast in the distribution of merchandise between Midland and other counties? Answering this question requires specifying as precisely as possible what is being investigated. The different patterns apparent on map 4-2 do not necessarily equate to a greater overall level of commercial activity; they simply indicate a greater dispersion of merchants and merchandise. The two are not the same. Although the Midlands had fewer sites of merchandise than other parts of the country, these few had higher assessments and greater numbers of merchants than other areas. In fact, a significant number of the villages with merchandise outside the Midlands had only meager assessment totals. In Sussex, assessors recorded merchandise in 21 different villages; in 17 of 19 instances where they recorded the number of individuals contributing to the fifteenth they entered the names of five or fewer individuals, and in these 17 places the combined stock of merchandise amounted to less than £10. In the county as a whole, merchandise in the villages was worth approximately £125. Similarly jejune totals are recorded in Cornwall and Somerset. Some of the assessments in Hampshire and Yorkshire were in the same league as places in the Midlands, but a considerable number in these counties were not cut from the same cloth. Small pockets of merchandise were not entirely absent from the Midlands, but they were exceptional. Much more common were the kinds of assessments made in Nottinghamshire, where there were only two villages contributing to the fifteenth, but where the two held £219 worth of merchandise, substantially more than the amount found in all 21 of the villages in Sussex. Thus, what needs to be explained is the geographical pattern of mercantile settlements, not an absolute orientation to commercial activity. In the Midlands, professional commercial agents resided in a relatively small number of sites, but these sites had a substantial stake in mercantile activity; in other parts of the country they resided in a greater number of places, but most of these places had relatively small pools of mercantile capital.

Even if the fundamental difference involves degrees of dispersion rather than degrees of overall activity, though, there is still a discrepancy in commercial life that merits further attention. Needless to say, explaining the pattern is a more difficult task than observing it. The only certainty is that there are no simple answers: The pattern results from combinations of influences rather than single causes, and so the best that can be hoped for is to narrow the range of possibilities and assign more weight to some causes than to others. A good place to begin is by isolating features that did not have a strong influence. One of these is density of population. The most densely settled parts of the country in this period were in East Anglia and the East Midlands, yet these areas had considerably fewer sites of merchandise than the south.[81] In other words, an area did not necessarily develop more towns or mercantile sites as a byproduct of a greater concentration of population. A second factor that can be ruled out is that the pattern was somehow connected to the production or trade of wool. According to extant price schedules from the period, Shropshire, Staffordshire, Leicestershire, and Lincolnshire produced the best quality wools.[82] Only two of these counties are documented completely in the Nonae Rolls, but neither showed an unusually dense pattern of merchandise. Conversely, wool in Somerset was valued at the identical price as wool in Northamptonshire, but their mercantile patterns bore little resemblance. A third factor that does not seem to have had much influence is the size of a dominant regional town. The distribution of towns and merchandise in the vicinity of London, for example, was very uneven: North of the city there were many villages with merchandise; east of the city there were none. Some parishes just outside the walls of the city were home to merchants; others were not. Nor is there any consistent pattern among towns in the next rank. In the lay subsidies, Bristol, York, and Newcastle upon Tyne ranked as the three wealthiest towns after London. Two of these—Bristol and York—showed significant dispersions of merchandise, but not in all directions, while the third stood alone as a commercial enclave. In some instances, the presence of a major town seems to have encouraged the dispersion of commerce, in others it seems to have hindered it.

On the other side of the ledger, there are some obvious candidates that explain at least part of the distribution patterns observable on map 4-2. One of these is the presence or absence of a coast. As can be seen on the map, a fair number of the locations that gave rise to merchants paying the fifteenth were strung out along the shoreline, a pattern that is particularly noticeable on the southern coast, but one which finds a parallel in Yorkshire and the northern coast of Somerset. Not surprisingly, the vast majority of these mercantile locations were small ports, with many of the southern ones active in cross-Channel trade as well as the domestic coastal trade.[83] The size and distribution of ports in these areas actually mirrors the distribution of merchandise in inland areas. Southern ports tended to be small and numerous, in contrast to much of the eastern coast, where ports were larger and further apart. In an extensive, and unusual, listing of customs revenues on overseas trade in the early thirteenth century, for example, the top nine ports in the country were all on the eastern coast, and they accounted for nearly 90 percent of all the customs revenue generated between 1203 and 1205.[84] There is still much to learn about regional and local variations in port activity, but one of the major differences between the eastern and southern ports appears to reside in their relationships with their hinterlands. Most of the major inland waterways in England flow to the east, making it easier for well-situated ports such as Boston or King's Lynn to draw large areas into their respective orbits.[85] Furthermore, the gentler terrain of eastern England allowed communities that were not directly adjacent to a river to reach an inland port with relative ease. Rivers in the south, on the other hand, generally did not permit the same kind of penetration into the interior, nor did the harsher terrain allow areas outside the river valleys to link up easily with existing waterways.[86] As a result, many ports found it difficult to develop extensive internal hinterlands, with the result that few were in a position to build commercial momentum by poaching trade from their rivals on neighboring stretches of coast.

Important as they were in determining the commercial nexus of a region, though, ports on their own do not entirely explain the divergence between the Midlands and other regions. Wiltshire, for example, had no coastline, yet conforms to the pattern of southern coastal counties much more than to the pattern of inland Midland counties. Ports are part of the explanation, but there are other candidates worthy of consideration. Chief among these is the diversity of settlement patterns and economic activity in different areas of the country. One of the distinguishing feature of social and economic life in the Midlands in the Middle Ages was its internal uniformity. While there were important variations in the precise mix of cereal crops and livestock raised in different parts of the Midlands, the range of variation was kept within fairly strict bounds. Some regions grew more barley and less wheat than others, but almost all parts of the Midlands devoted the lion's share of arable land to one of these two cereal crops. There was greater regional variation in the orientation toward livestock production, but because of the almost universal common-field arrangement, there were fairly narrow limits within which diversification in the pastoral economy could be pursued. The essence of the common-field system was communally established field locations and harvest times for particular crops, arrangements dictated by the need to pasture animals on the stubble after harvest.[87] Communal grazing practices inevitably entailed communal regulation of flock and herd size and exerted an unwitting pressure for conformity in livestock production. The Midland economy was not a monolith, but it was exceptionally uniform.

In contrast to the uniformity of the Midlands, other counties exhibited considerable diversity in their economic composition.[88] Areas of fertile plain tended to organize their social and economic life in ways that emulated the communities of the Midlands. But these areas were interwoven with significantly different patterns of land use, and the presence of clusters of open-field farming only served to heighten the variation found in other parts of these counties. In some areas, the endowment of a particular natural resource, such as tin in Cornwall, created a special economic niche. The coast itself created opportunities for diversification in such areas as salting and fishing. But the overriding factor in the economic diversity of most coastal counties was simply the diversity in soil and terrain. Fully blown common-field systems demanded soils of good tilth and fertility, not the kinds found on Bodmin Moor in Cornwall, or the Black Down Hills of Devon and Somerset, or the Downs of Sussex, or the North York Moors, or any other of half a dozen regions of thin soil separating the Midland counties from the sea. Areas of good soil were not wanting from coastal counties, but they were invariably interspersed with moors and downs. In the transition zones between loam and moor, and even on the inhospitable heaths and chalks of the moors and downs, agriculture was possible, but it was often not the kind of agriculture that would have been familiar to a villager in the Midlands.

The Nonae Rolls, in their more traditional guise as indicator of agrarian contraction in the decades before the Black Death, reveal some of these differences in economic orientation. In Midland counties, the explanations given to explain why cash yields fell below expectations typically involve statements about land falling out of use, or a poor lambing season, or weather that failed to cooperate with the year's crop. The presumption is that the parish's wealth depended on the production of the goods that were included in the assessment scheme. While such rationalizations are also encountered in the verdicts of the coastal counties, one is as likely to find there statements that the parish income is based on a greater variety of tithable production than is encompassed in the goods liable for the tax. Among other things, one often finds mentioned as part of tithe income such commodities as honey, flax, brushwood, and fish. Jurors in Graffham in Sussex even reported that the rector's income in the parish ordinarily included tithes paid by a group of potters and more than £1 annually paid as tithe on the produce of apple trees in the village.[89] Such items are not absent from the verdicts of Midland counties, but they assume greater importance in some of the coastal counties, reflecting the greater diversity to be found there. More study is needed to fill in the details of this picture, but the general outlines are clear. In essence, areas outside the Midlands made a virtue of necessity. Lacking the Midlands' option of adjusting to a growing population by intensifying production of the standard agricultural commodities, they bridged the gap by supplementing agriculture with the production of other commodities: Within two generations of the Nonae assessment, extant tax records (the ulnage accounts) reveal that Somerset and western Wiltshire were the leading woollen-producing regions of the country.[90] Wherever one of these commodities could be developed into a local economic specialty, merchants had scope to act, as the organizers of production, as the distributors of the good, as the suppliers of the staples of life, or, as was more often the case, all of these combined.

Diversity in production thus provided an impetus toward a more dispersed pattern of commercial activity outside the Midland belt. On its own, however, diversity in production need not necessarily call forth a greater dispersion of the merchant class. Uniformity in production, as in the Midlands, is after all not the same thing as subsistence agriculture, and it cannot be assumed that a more limited range of commodities prevented production for the market. Indeed, monocultures are invariably far more dependent on market conditions than are mixed-farming regimes. Europe's insatiable demand for England's wool actually rewarded areas that could consolidate around raising sheep rather than diversify in the production of other livestock. Indeed, one could argue that the emphasis on the staples of wool and grain would have left more commercial space for a dispersed merchant group to service, since, in addition to dispatching local wool, there would be a greater range of goods—salt, fish, metals, and so on—that would need importing into the villages. Conversely, one can imagine an economy in which production is relatively diversified but which nonetheless has a centralized merchant class. Villages routinely spun wool and wove textiles without generating any cloth merchants. As the textile trade demonstrates very clearly, there was no guarantee that production of a commodity would necessarily give a settlement a role in the exchange of that commodity. Textiles were particularly well-suited to putting-out, but there is no reason to assume that merchants from a centralized location would have been less interested in colonizing other commodities simply because they involved lower inputs of labor.

If we cannot assume that diversified production on its own led to a more dispersed merchant class, we still need to explain why dispersion occur more noticeably outside the Midlands. To do this we need to return to the diversity of the landscape to examine its more direct influence on commercial development. In his study of the markets of Derbyshire, Bryan Coates has noticed a strong correlation between the sites of markets and the boundaries of areas of contrasting physical environment: Markets were more often situated in transition zones between environments than in the middle of a particular zone.[91] Coates explains this phenomenon largely in terms of different modes of production in the contrasting zones. In the case of markets this is a compelling explanation, but in the case of merchants we are left with the colonization problem: The incentives for merchants of a central regional town to draw into their own hands the trade in forest products, for example, in addition to their other pursuits were little different from the incentives to monopolize the trade in wool or barley. Nonetheless, even if we want to modify the explanation behind the relationship between transition zones and merchant activity, we are still left with an important observation, one that finds broader application in the evidence derived from the Nonae Rolls. Four of the ten locations with rural merchants in Hampshire, for example, are located on or near the edge of the downs, and a fifth is situated where the River Avon bisects the New Forest. In neighboring Sussex, 4 of the 14 locatable places paying fifteenths are on the edge of the downs. Of the ten others, four are ports, and only six do not appear to be in a transition zone between areas of topographical contrast, although three are located on the edge of a modern forested area. In Yorkshire's North Riding, two of the nine rural merchant locations are on the edge of the moor, and a third is on the edge of the dales. One of the remaining places is a port, one cannot be positively located, and the remaining four are located more centrally within a particular terrain, one in the dales and three in the open country between the dales and the moors.

Almost by definition, areas of contrasting physical relief are areas that present physical barriers to human interaction. To a medieval merchant dwelling in a particular town and contemplating the hinterland of his place of business, the downs and moors seen on the horizon must often have been the effective limits of enterprise. There might have been valuable commodities on the downs or moors, and there might also have been valuable commodities on the other side, but they were not ones that were easily found and returned to a home base. All merchants were limited by the speed of their animals and boats, but animals and boats could cover a considerably greater distance on a plain than they could in rougher terrain. Put another way, a rough terrain created niches within which smaller local merchant communities could develop without coming into direct competition with the merchants of a major center. In fact, the roughness of the terrain, which often brought with it a different economic orientation, enhanced the likelihood that a merchant community would spring up to serve as the conduit through which the larger towns and ports gained access to areas that were not directly colonized.[92] Direct access was preferable to a merchant, but when direct access was difficult or impossible, indirect access through an intermediate commercial community was preferable to no access at all. In short, merchant communities were fewer and farther between in the Midlands than in areas of rough terrain because the reach of each Midland commercial center extended much further from home than was true of commercial centers situated in other regions. As long as there were market sites with fixed times in the countryside, it was possible for urban merchants in the Midlands to trade with a fairly extensive hinterland without any need for intermediate merchants. In areas of less hospitable terrain, orbits were more likely to be circumscribed by physical barriers, and the result was a more dispersed commercial structure.

There is little question that factors other than those described here also came into play. Lancashire and Northumberland, for example, stood apart from the pattern in most other areas of poor soils and dispersed settlement. In this part of the country, there probably was a substantially lower level of commercial activity and a degree of economic backwardness not found in places farther south. Kent and Essex also stood apart, in ways that defy ready explanation. Southern Yorkshire is another anomaly, this time in the other direction as an area of relatively fertile plain, with open fields and nucleated villages akin to those in the central Midlands, but with mercantile activity dispersed like the counties of the south. Like the south, many of the Yorkshire villages paying fifteenths had small numbers of merchants and correspondingly small amounts of merchandise, but like the Midlands there were important concentrations of mercantile wealth outside the towns. Some of the Yorkshire assessors counted capital invested in fishing as merchandise, adhering more strictly to the precise terms of the assessment, which specified that fifteenths be taken from people of substance who were not involved in agriculture, but the main cluster that needs to be explained lies inland. In all government projects in this period, local people had great latitude in interpreting the directives that originated with the central government, and it can be surmised, though it is not certain, that the assessors in Yorkshire included borderline goods and individuals that assessors elsewhere chose to overlook.

But the exceptions should not obscure the entire picture. In most parts of the country, upland regions exhibit a consistent pattern of dispersion and Midland counties a pattern of concentration of commercial capital. The precise mix of factors could vary significantly from one area to the next, and local features and tradition often had as much to do with patterns of trade as the more general features of economic orientation, settlement patterns, transportation opportunities, and physical relief. Urban merchants often succeeded in eliminating competitors by legal as well as economic factors, and consequently the commercial pattern in any part of the country cannot be explained simply by referring to landscape or land use. Nonetheless, the natural environment exerted a profound commercial influence in a culture that, unlike our own, believed that the physical world was there to be accepted rather than altered. Like settlement patterns and modes of land use, commercial networks adapted to their circumstances. In practical terms, this meant concentrating commercial functions in a select number of locations in areas of easy terrain and dispersing them in areas where nature was less cooperative.

IV

As all historians know, a document can say as much by its silence as by its explicit description, and the Nonae Rolls are a good case in point: In the final analysis their most significant contribution to our understanding of the commercial skeleton of medieval England may well be to serve as a kind of Ockham's razor. What they indicate on a national scale in a way few other sources can is how relatively few places were home to a permanent resident population of merchants. In every county for which there exists a reasonably complete record, there are, in addition to the places singled out for their merchants, dozens of places that were either chartered as a market or borough or in possession of some other trait that might suggest a commercial role. Most of these places were not only omitted from the lists of places with merchants and merchant goods, they were also omitted on the evidence of a jury explicitly stating in the midst of its appraisal of the value of the great tithes that the settlement had no merchants or merchandise. The importance of these negative indications is well illustrated in the case of Buckinghamshire, where Beresford and Finberg found evidence for ten boroughs, and Michael Reed for 29 rural markets founded before the Nonae juries made their statements.[93] Here is the typical fragmented commercial pattern described in most studies of local and regional marketing, replete with maps of theoretical marketing distances resembling the nightmares a logician might have about Venn diagrams. In the Nonae Rolls, however, there was only one place in the county, Wycombe, that was required to pay the urban ninth on trade goods, and only two places, Aylesbury and Brill, that had resident merchants assessed to the fifteenth. This does not mean that the other "towns" and markets in the county were commercially moribund; it simply means that they played a different role than the three principal commercial sites in the county. The county had a hierarchy of commercial sites, with most nodes serving to provide a basic level of marketing facilities and a select few giving rise to mercantile communities and concentrations of commercial capital.

In the end, we are not necessarily dealing with inherently contradictory sources when we compare the charter evidence documenting hundreds of towns and thousands of markets with the evidence described in this chapter. The simultaneous existence of a large number of commercial sites and a relatively small number of merchant sites makes perfect sense if we think in terms of larger commercial systems. Indeed, in any pre-industrial commercial system exhibiting well-developed links between town and country, one would expect to find exactly the pattern laid bare in the Nonae Rolls, a pattern featuring a concentration of merchant functions in a limited number of places co-existing with a dispersion of the sites of exchange. Postulating the existence of an integrated commercial system on the basis of the discrepancy between merchants and markets is not, of course, a substitute for concrete illustrations of the system in operation. These will be given in the following chapters. But the overview does suggest where some of the boundaries of different commercial networks lay in this period. In the areas of England characterized by dispersed settlement patterns and irregular terrain, mercantile systems tended to be irregular, with the characteristics of each mercantile network varying according to the mix of topography and commodity production in the region. In most instances, commercial horizons of individual places were less extensive than in lowland England, with networks displaying correspondingly lower levels of hierarchical integration between different sites. In areas of lowland England with nucleated villages and common fields, a more regular commercial pattern developed, with large merchant populations operating out of major towns with a commercial radius extending about 20 miles from the town. Within this radius—or as was often the case, within the overlapping radii of several towns—were a handful of places with smaller resident merchant populations and smaller commercial horizons. In all parts of the country, rural markets were at the base of the commercial system, each one linked with one or several of the larger market towns and regional centers. In these markets, peasants and merchants met face-to-face, each no doubt wary of the guile of the other, but each ready to strike a deal.

Part 3

Networks of Trade

5

Trade between Towns

In 1275, a group of royal justices travelled to Salisbury, one of the great towns of the country, as part of a series of national enquiries investigating usurpations of royal prerogatives and complaints against petty local tyrannies. When they reached their destination, the justices found themselves caught in the middle of a dispute between merchants in the town and those in one of its upstart neighbors, the borough of Wilton, located about three miles away. According to the burgesses of Salisbury, Wilton's bailiffs had for some time been forcing Salisbury's traders to make unscheduled stops as they journeyed with their merchandise to and from their native town: Wilton's bailiffs were said to "seize [Salisbury's] merchants with their merchandise and drive them by force to Wilton against the merchants' will."[1] This was not simply a case of organized highway robbery; in fact, Wilton's bailiffs did not so much as touch the merchandise belonging to Salisbury's merchants. Their only concern was to escort the merchants into their town, where they proceeded to force the merchants to put their goods up for sale in the town's market. One can imagine the perplexity of the justices asked to uphold Salisbury's rights *not* to have to sell its merchandise in Wilton, but, unfortunately the source does not record how, or even if, they managed to find an acceptable resolution to the problem. But we can at least reconstruct the motivations behind both the hijacking and the subsequent complaint. Towns relied heavily on the income generated from tolls on trade to underwrite their annual budgets, and the men who ruled the towns relied on their control of external trade to maintain their positions of authority and wealth within their home communities. If Salisbury's complaint is to be believed, Wilton's bailiffs went to exceptional lengths to enhance their town's market, but the motive was one that every bailiff in every town in the kingdom understood. Wilton was a moderately prosperous small town in this period, and at first glance it seems a bit surprising that any merchant would complain about finding a market for his wares.[2] One of the incidental remarks made in the presentment, though, helps to clarify the nature of Salisbury's displeasure: The inconvenienced traders were traveling along the king's roads to London, Oxford, and Wallingford when they were diverted to Wilton. The offending borough might very well have offered an attractive spot for localized retail trade from Salisbury, but it could not offer the concentrated demand and wholesale market of a major town. From Salisbury's perspective, Wilton's cardinal error was to confuse its proper place in the established trading hierarchy.

As this anecdote suggests, merchants were willing and able to travel considerable distances to trade with their peers in other towns: Oxford and Wallingford were about 50 miles distant from Salisbury and London about 80 miles. Confronting an economy with limited demand stamping one side of their coin and limited powers of production stamping the other, merchants by necessity developed market networks that took them both to the rural markets of their region and to the urban markets of other areas. The capital requirements and entrepreneurial skill needed to tap into these markets differed greatly from one level to the next, but the two levels of marketing—rural and local on the one hand and interurban and longer-distance on the other—were inextricably bound to each other as parts of interlocking networks built up by the endeavors of merchants in scores of provincial towns. Places that achieved commercial success did so by developing both levels of trade; indeed, developing contacts at both levels was the only way to avoid the Winchcombe syndrome of gentle decay into commercial insignificance. For analytical purposes it is necessary to view these different components of trade separately: This chapter will deal with trade between larger towns, and the following chapter will concentrate on trade relations between towns and their surrounding countrysides. But it should be kept in mind from the outset that analytical convenience is easily confused with historical reality. While the mechanics and scale of different branches of a town's trade did vary, interurban trade is best seen as an extension of the trade that occurred between towns and their regional markets rather than as something *sui generis.* The same commodities were traded in towns as in the countryside, and the same merchants were involved in transacting business in both kinds of markets. The essential difference between the two branches of trade was one of scale rather than kind: Towns were each other's "supermarkets," adding extra layers of activity and personnel to those ordinarily found in the countryside. Such concentrations of demand and supply attracted the attention of merchants in towns located at a considerable remove from each other, creating a dynamic that provides a useful boundary marker for other branches of the inland trade.

I

Much of our information about specific trade links between communities is derived from records of tolls and toll disputes. The use of tolls to finance public works grew considerably over the course of the thirteenth century, and with the general commercial expansion of the period, local market tolls assumed a similar importance in the revenues of towns and other corporations.[3] Collecting tolls in their own market was critical for the financial solvency of the boroughs—the problem many towns faced in paying their farms after the Plague was at least in part due to a fall in toll receipts related to the fall in population. But equally critical, as F. W. Maitland observed a century ago, was gaining immunities from toll in other places.[4] Burgesses and members of a guild merchant had free access to their own local market, but once they ventured to markets outside their town they were akin to geese laying golden eggs. To insulate themselves as much as possible from the proliferating collectors, towns and other corporations sought to have exemptions from toll included in royal or seigneurial charters of liberty. Inclusion of more specific clauses granting exemption from new tolls may, in fact, explain the willingness of so many towns and corporations to pay through the nose to have their charters "inspected" with each change in reign. As a result, there was a kind of symmetry between the increase in the use of tolls as sources of revenue and corporate efforts to secure exemptions from the tolls for members of the corporation, be it a town, monastery, or feudal estate. Almost inevitably, there were bound to be disputes between corporations vested with the right to collect tolls and those enjoying exemptions from toll. Because the arrangements made to deal with these disputes shed light on trade relationships in general, and because they provide a context for particular relationships dealt with in the following sections of this and the following chapter, they merit preliminary consideration in their own right.

The right to collect tolls was inherent in the creation of a borough and the grant of a market or fair.[5] Any individual wishing to trade at one of these sites did so with the presumption that toll would be collected as a matter of course. The precise arrangements varied from place to place. Ordinarily toll was charged on commodities when they entered a town or marketplace but sometimes it was collected only if and when goods were actually sold.[6] As discussed in chapter 3, the rates on individual transactions were generally fairly low, and individuals who purchased goods for personal consumption did not have to pay toll. Merchants, though, were fair game for toll collectors, and their involvement in multiple transactions made even low rates a financial concern. Consequently, they were eager to acquire exemptions from toll whenever and wherever possible. Grants of exemption were often made in the very same charters that established a borough's right to collect toll from others. Although Domesday Book records that Dover's merchants were free from toll throughout the kingdom, London's charter in 1131 was the first specifically to enumerate freedom from toll among the privileges of an urban corporation, and its dispensation in this regard served as a model for many other towns in later years.[7] By the end of the twelfth century at least 32 other towns had received charters containing similar exemptions of toll throughout the kingdom, and 5 others had received regional exemptions.[8] By the end of John's reign (1216), another 20 towns had won the same favor, and by the end of the thirteenth century almost all of the regional towns discussed in chapter 4 had been added to the list.

The co-existence of widespread rights of collection with almost equally widespread rights of exemption inevitably led to complications. If a merchant from a town with a royal charter granting its citizens freedom from toll throughout the kingdom traveled to another town with a royal charter granting it the right to collect tolls on all merchandise entering the town, only one of the privileged parties could receive the benefits conveyed by royal charter. Forced to decide such cases, royal courts established the principle that chronological priority of grant should decide which set of rights would take precedence in these cases.[9] Grants of toll exemption were thus chronologically contingent, valid only in places that acquired their collection rights at some point after the grant of exemption was made. As a result, the date at which a town acquired its first grant of toll exemption assumed great importance in determining the scope of the privilege. Because a large proportion of the rural markets in the country were founded after the main towns had won their toll privileges, much of the trade taking place in them bypassed the marketholders' collection pots and, incidentally, the scattered quantitative sources documenting market revenues. Among the larger towns themselves, the interval between a grant of collection and a grant of exemption might be only a few years, but those few years could assume great importance for the town with the earlier grant.

While disputes on these grounds happened fairly regularly (fortunately for historians of trade), they were less common than one might expect given the general litigiousness of the age. To reduce the likelihood of expensive and uncertain legal disputes between foreign merchants and local toll collectors, towns and other bodies developed procedures to deal with claims of exemption at an administrative level before they were dragged into the courts. To keep track of trading partners whose citizens were eligible for remission of toll, a number of towns kept a record of such places among their official muniments.[10] If a bailiff was in doubt about whether to recognize a claim of exemption, all he needed to do, in theory at least, was to consult the list to see if the claimant did in fact have a legitimate claim. This system of registration limited honest mistakes in toll collection, but bailiffs also had to be wary of unscrupulous individuals falsely claiming citizenship in a privileged town. Bailiffs and toll collectors undoubtedly used common sense measures, such as accents, clothing, and type of merchandise to identify fraudulent claims, and they probably also relied on a sense of familiarity with their town's most common trading partners. As an added safeguard, bailiffs could also ask to see some form of identification to corroborate a merchant's claim to exemption. In response to such requests, merchants often carried with them letters of citizenship or exemplifications of their town's charter to show to the bailiffs as proof that they really did deserve the privilege they were claiming.[11]

In spite of these precautions, however, the grounds for dispute over payments of toll remained fertile. Bailiffs and toll collectors had the mindset of law enforcers in all periods: It was better to act first and sort out the ambiguities later than not to act at all. A bailiff's power in such matters, usually spelled out in unambiguous terms in the charters vesting rights of toll collection, was to take a distraint from the merchant who refused to pay the customary toll. Much of the evidence about trading relationships in this period thus revolves around disputes between towns over seizure of property as distraint for toll. Once the distraint was made, the dispute ordinarily became corporate rather than individual. An illegal distraint was seen as a challenge to the rights of all members of the corporation. If left unchallenged it could very easily establish a precedent that would nullify the cherished privileges of the charter.

The preferred solution to an interurban trade dispute was one reached through ordinary diplomatic procedure. If the trading partner in question were an important one, a dispute could be handled by a high-level delegation, as in a dispute in 1312 over a distraint taken in London from a merchant from Andover.[12] In this case, the sheriff of London distrained for payment of toll on six bales of cumin, and the merchant responded by going with his town's bailiff and a fellow burgess to the mayor and aldermen of the city, to whom they showed their charter of exemption. Less picturesque but probably more common than high-level personal intervention of this sort were efforts to resolve a dispute by means of official correspondence. When a town was informed by one of its citizens about an inappropriate distraint for toll in another town, the standard response was to write a letter to the offending party, stating that the individual whose property was distrained was a legitimate citizen entitled to all of the town's privileges and asking that the seized property be returned.[13] If the offending party agreed to return the goods, the matter was dropped, so long as the offender did not persist in harassing other merchants in the same way. If the offender refused to comply with the first request, one or two more peremptory letters might be sent. If these failed, a town had several options open to it. One was to write to the king asking him to intervene with the offender. If the king agreed to get involved, he sent a writ to the offenders indicating that he expected them to return the distraint and henceforth to recognize the validity of the exemption.[14] A more dramatic alternative was to place an embargo on the offending town or market, as discussed in chapter 3. A third alternative was retaliation in kind, the seizure of property belonging to someone from the offending town, regardless of whether or not that person had any connection with the original distraint. If a trade dispute deteriorated this far, the parties almost invariably wound up in the king's court.

Although it represents only a fraction of the total volume of trade taking place, the litigation engendered by toll disputes demonstrates effectively the geographical range over which urban merchants operated. Table 5-1 presents a sampling of trade disputes encountered in a variety of sources from this period. Most of the entries in the table document quarrels arising from distraints for toll, although a few other kinds of distraint are included. The first column of the table records the towns that took distraints from foreign traders, and the second column the town in which the trader resided and, by extension, the town whose rights were brought into question. The third column records the distance between the two towns, given as the crow flies, or in one instance, as the seagull flies. The last column notes the date of the dispute and any particulars about the commodities that gave rise to contention. These data are nothing more than a representative sampling of the disputes occurring in this period; a more systematic search through the manuscript records of the central courts would unquestionably come up with significantly more cases. Even as a representative sample, though, they indicate that trading connections between towns located more than 20 miles apart were not uncommon.

TABLE 5-1:
Interurban Trade Disputes, 1200–1350

Distraint Taken in:	Merchant's Home Town:	Distance (miles)	Date and Particulars
Tamworth	Lichfield	7	1204; not stated
Worcester	Droitwich	6	1221; salt and food
Shrewsbury	Bridgnorth	18	1223; hides and cloth
Southampton	Marlborough	39	1239; not stated
Montgomery	Ludlow	23	1252; "all kinds of trading"
Bristol	Marlborough	40	1259; not stated
Basingstoke	Andover	17	1263; not stated
Cirencester	Bristol	32	1275; not stated
Bristol	Old Salisbury	42	1275; not stated
Southampton	Old Salisbury	20	1275; not stated
Oxford	Old Salisbury	50	1275; not stated
Nottingham	Derby	12	1279; livestock
Newcastle/Lyme	Stafford	15	1280; wool fells, cloth
Stafford	Newcastle/Lyme	15	1286; wool fells
York	Hedon	40	1294; not stated
London	Coventry	86	1299; copper, wool, wine
Northampton	London	61	1301; goods worth 20s.
London	Northampton	61	1301; 10 casks of wine
St.Albans	London	19	1302; not stated
Scarborough	Kingston/Hull	43	1305; not stated
London	Norwich	98	1307; not stated

London	Andover	65	1312; 6 bales of cumin
Leicester	Nottingham	24	1314; herring
Sandwich	London	63	1315; almonds, figs, raisins
Southwark	Cinque Ports	53	1316; not stated
York	Berwick	132	1318; not stated
Pontefract	Beverley	38	1325; not stated
Southampton	Salisbury	20	1329; various merchandise
Warwick	Coventry	10	1335; not stated
Chester	Leicester	81	uncertain; not stated
Shrewsbury	Leicester	69	uncertain; not stated

NOTES: Distance from Scarborough to Kingson-upon-Hull computed by sea rather than by land. Distance from Southwark is to nearest member of Cinque Ports.

SOURCES: Calendar of London Letterbooks, Letter Book D, ed. R. Sharpe; PRO C255/12/1; PRO C255/12/2; PRO C255/12/3; *Calendar of Miscellaneous Inquisitions;* C. Gross, *The Gild Merchant; Records of Leicester,* ed. M. Bateson; *Rotuli Hundredorum,* ed. W. Illingworth and J. Caley; *Tamworth Borough Records,* ed. H. Wood; *Records of Nottingham,* ed. W. H. Stevenson; *Calendar of Charter Rolls; Curia Regis Rolls; Calendar of Early Mayor's Court Rolls of London,* ed. A. H. Thomas; *Rolls of the Justices in Eyre for Lincolnshire and Worcestershire,* ed. D. Stenton, Selden Society, no. 53 (1934); *Southampton Oak Book,* ed. P. Studer.

A complex history of trade relations lay behind many, perhaps all, of the cases summarized in this table. To appreciate the circumstances of the trade disputes represented by this sample, it is helpful to consider a few examples in greater depth. Several are drawn from an archive of Chancery documents in the Public Record Office known as "Quiet Enjoyment of Privileges" (C255/12) which contains writs reprimanding individuals or corporate groups who came to the king's attention for disregarding various grants and franchises.[15] One such writ was directed to the bailiffs of the town of Scarborough, who were directed to stop demanding toll of traders from Kingston upon Hull, located more than 40 miles away. The bailiffs returned the writ to the king with a note on the back explaining that their town's right to collect toll predated Kingston upon Hull's exemption, "but if the king or his council orders us by law to stop, then we are prepared to obey his mandate."[16] In another use of this semiformal procedure in 1307, the mayor of London was directed to cease taking tolls from citizens of Norwich.[17] The mayor replied on the back of the writ that London did indeed recognize Norwich's exemption from pontage, murage, and pavage (in other words from specially granted public works tolls), but that his city was not obliged to exempt the East Anglian town from its customary tolls because its right to collect predated Norwich's grant of exemption. Unlike

Scarborough's bailiffs, the lord mayor gave no indication that he was ready to interfere with custom if the king so directed. In these as in many of the cases recorded in the table, one can see that a level of contact beyond the merely casual lay behind the dispute. Before the king acted, the town claiming exemption had to present its case, probably in the guise of an informal plaint; after the writ went out, there was likely to be further discussion of the issue when the recipient returned the writ with its version of the relationship. None of the parties involved in these triangles would have bothered to make an issue of tolls unless they were considered to involve more than isolated nuisances: Rates of toll on individual transactions were not high enough to warrant corporate action unless there was a meaningful volume of trade taking place.

II

As these examples involving Scarborough and London illustrate, conflicts over tolls and distraints were most likely to enter official records when they raised issues of concern to the broader merchant communities of the towns embroiled in the disputes. Even in situations where corporate interests were less directly implicated in a disagreement, individual merchants counted on their fellow burgesses to back up their claims and expected their local guild or town government to step in if needed. To some extent, guilds and local governments provided a kind of insurance for individual merchants by agreeing to take reprisals against towns that refused to accept the trading rights of their members. In 1301, for example, the city of London seized ten casks of wine belonging to a merchant from Northampton in retaliation for a distraint taken from one of the city's merchants who had gone to trade in that town's market.[18] Such distraints were, however, an awkward and indirect way of resolving trade disputes, dragging in people whose only connection with the original problem was one of common residence. Towns generally recognized that it was in their own best interests to minimize potential sources of conflict and to develop intermediate procedures between the outbreak of a dispute and the imposition of retaliatory reprisals. In most cases, these efforts required some form of written documentation, either of the general trading rights of particular communities or of the steps taken to bring a dispute to an early settlement. In a few instances records originating with these administrative steps have survived, providing a more expansive view of the trading interests of particular towns.

One of the ways a town could limit the possibility of conflict was to maintain a record of toll exemptions that it was willing to observe. (Presumably, a town would not have bothered to include trading partners whose privileges were of no practical significance.) In its simplest form, such a record was nothing more than a statement of places that had freedom from toll in the town. Torksey included such a list as part of its schedule of tolls, noting that merchants from London, Lincoln, Nottingham, York, and Beverley were exempt from the tolls outlined in the rest of the document.[19] More elaborate listings recorded the details of particular charters granting various communities their toll privileges. A particularly complete and comprehensive example of such a register can be found in Southampton's Oak Book.[20] The Oak Book was drawn up in the first part of the fourteenth century to record the customs of the town's guild merchant, as well as to record other matters of commercial interest, such as the text of the Laws of Oleron, used as an international law of the sea by maritime communities of the later Middle Ages.[21] Apart from a few miscellaneous notes added in the fifteenth century, the first section of the Oak Book is a list of various towns in England that had received grants of toll exemption, each town entered with the date of its charter.

The first item in the list is a summary note of the fact that Southampton acquired its charter as a borough in 1199, in return for agreeing to pay henceforth a farm (an annual contribution to the crown) of £200. This was undoubtedly included as the benchmark against which the liberties of other towns could be measured. Following this reminder is a list of 39 towns with charters granting exemptions from toll, and a second list of 14 towns described as having charters of uncertain date that needed to be investigated. Most of the leading towns in the country can be found among the 53 towns recorded in the Southampton register; indeed the list reads very much like the list of regional towns discussed in chapter 3.

It is not clear what such a list signifies in terms of volume or frequency of trade. Obviously, exemptions for places like London and Bristol were more significant than those for smaller and more distant places. A special agreement over toll rights with Salisbury in 1329 is recorded in a later section of the Oak Book, and the terms of the deal give some insight into the kinds of trade that could be involved between Southampton and the other places recorded in the list of toll exemptions.[22] Disagreements with Salisbury were an ongoing and almost inevitable feature of the commercial life of Southampton. Both were among the 20 wealthiest towns in the country, and although they were situated about 20 miles apart, their economies were closely intertwined: Salisbury was a leading textile producer, while Southampton was a major importer of dyestuffs. Salisbury's grant of toll exemption and the creation of its guild merchant date to early in the twelfth century, well before Southampton's creation of a guild merchant, incorporation as a borough, or grant of collection rights. In theory, Southampton had no right to exact any toll from the merchants at Salisbury. Nonetheless, as the agreement reached in 1329 reveals, practical issues came before legal precedent, and Salisbury accepted Southampton's right to collect tolls from its merchants as long as they stayed within specified boundaries. It is a bit surprising that Salisbury would agree to any compromise at all, considering the strength of its legal position; perhaps the town decided that a drawn-out court case would at best result in a Pyrrhic victory. The record of the settlement notes that Southampton had collected tolls from Salisbury's merchants and that this was likely to lead to "the gravest danger in times to come." To prevent the possibility of discord arising, "mutual friends" of the two towns had brought the two sides together to negotiate a compromise. The record does not reveal who these friends were, but the witness list at the end of the document includes the names of the sheriffs of Wiltshire and Southampton, the Steward of the King's Household, and a Baron of the Exchequer, among others.

The terms of the agreement specify that henceforth, Salisbury's citizens would be exempt from tolls, murage, pavage, quayage, and pontage on all merchandise bought and sold in Southampton and on all merchandise shipped or carted through the town. In return for their exemption, however, the merchants of Salisbury agreed to make certain payments, spelled out in a long list, to assist Southampton with its annual farm. In effect, the agreement preserved Salisbury's legal rights while at the same time recognizing Southampton's fiscal needs. The payments stipulated in the settlement amount to a private toll schedule for Salisbury's merchants. Included in the schedule are payments for wool, cloth, fish, leather, hides, spices, dyestuffs, and dozens of other commodities; more than 60 separate rates are given in the schedule. Salisbury even agreed to pay on any goods not mentioned in the schedule at rates set according to the total value of the goods.

We are fortunate to have a separate list of the standard tolls collected in Southampton from a slightly earlier date, preserved in another section of the Oak Book.[23] There is considerable overlap between the two lists, although the Salisbury schedule has fewer than half the items included in the standard list, and a number of the items on the Salisbury list are not mentioned in its generic counterpart. The greatest difference between the two, though, is in the rate of toll collected: The price of compromise for Southampton was to accept a rate of toll from Salisbury's merchants that was in many instances half or less of the rate collected from other merchants. Significantly, though, the reduction varies from one item to the next: on grain Salisbury paid one-half the standard rate, on salmon one-third, on wax one-quarter and so on. In other words, the omission of more than half of the items on the standard list and the variation in rates both suggest that the Salisbury list was based on item-by-item negotiation between the two towns and is thus a faithful reflection of the trade going on between them.

Another measure taken by some towns to prevent individual trade disputes from escalating into corporate challenges was to send formal warnings to offending towns, giving them an opportunity to resolve the dispute before retaliatory measures were imposed. A number of the larger towns made use of the formal procedure of correspondence known as withernam, by which a particular town would send out a series of letters, successively more peremptory, warning another town of a commercial grievance that would lead to indiscriminate seizure of its citizens' goods if left unresolved.[24] Relatively few bodies of municipal correspondence have survived from this period, but there are at least two good collections from Great Yarmouth and London. In both collections, disagreements over tolls and debt payments were the principal concerns leading to the use of withernam procedure, although demands for the return of fugitive apprentices also feature prominently in the London letters. The Yarmouth letters are recorded with other memoranda of the town on membranes attached to the town's court rolls, which probably explains their fortuitous survival. The letters begin with the earliest surviving court roll in 1290 and continue in sequence until 1312, with only two years missing (1307-1308 and 1308-1309).[25] During this period, Yarmouth sent out more than 90 letters to different towns in England, along with a substantial number of letters directed to places on the Continent.

As one might expect, Norwich was the leading recipient of Yarmouth withernam letters. In 1293, Yarmouth sent a letter attesting to the citizenship of one of its merchants and asking that Norwich respect his toll exemption.[26] Eight years later, Yarmouth asked that Norwich release a distraint taken from one of its citizens.[27] In five other years, letters were sent asking for the repayment of debts related to sales of iron, ginger, oysters, and tanning services, as well as other unspecified commodities.[28] Ipswich and Colchester were also common recipients of withernam letters, registering eight and five letters respectively.[29] The letters directed to Ipswich mention debts for herring and firewood, while the Colchester letters mention debts for wood and potash. One of the Colchester letters also asks that Colchester not distrain a Yarmouth citizen for payments of tallage and other taxes; for this to make any sense the Yarmouth burgess must have established at least a temporary residence in Colchester. More distant partners were naturally less prominent in Yarmouth's correspondence than towns in East Anglia, but they are in evidence. Newcastle upon Tyne, more than 200 miles up the coast, was asked in 1295 to release a pipe of lampreys that had been seized in a mistake of ownership (interestingly, the true owner from Yarmouth was a woman), and three years later the Northumbrian town was asked to enforce payment of a debt.[30] Even longer voyages were involved in the dealings with port towns on the southern coast: Portsmouth, Weymouth in Dorset, and Teignmouth in Devon each received two debt enforcement letters in the period covered by the withernam letters.[31] Unlike ports, distant inland places are relatively rare in the letters. Winchester was asked to help secure a debt in 1293, and Nottingham was asked in 1303 to compel delivery of 11 quarters of lead owed to a Yarmouth burgess.[32] Equally surprising as the fact that Yarmouth had trade connections with these distant places is the fact that it was willing and able to use withernam procedure to deal with them. The letters, which were probably sent along with whomever happened to be traveling to the relevant destination (itself an interesting comment on mobility), presupposed an opportunity to make a distraint if the other town failed to cooperate.

London's withernam letters have survived for a twenty-year period immediately after the Plague; earlier letters were, unfortunately, destroyed in the

Great Fire of 1666.[33] Like the Yarmouth letters, they often record the commodities at the center of a dispute as well as the names and locations of the parties involved in the dispute. A letter to Gloucester, for example, claimed that 19 sarplers of wool being carted to London had been mistakenly seized for a debt owed in the town. A letter to Stamford requested restitution of a bag, 11 kerchiefs of "Eipre" (Ypres), and 2 pieces of "Bokerham" (course cloth) seized from a London citizen on suspicion that the goods had been stolen. Huntingdon's bailiffs levied a distraint for toll from a merchant leading four carts laden with cloth through the town. The interests of city vintners found expression in letters to Colchester, Bristol, Cambridge, Winchelsea, Rye, and Northampton. In addition to the seizure in Gloucester, woolmongers' transactions can be traced in Bristol, Reading, Kyme, and Sleaford in Lincolnshire, Oxford, and Edington in Somerset. The Home Counties and the southeast are naturally represented most fully in the letters, but towns and markets in the Midlands are also regularly encountered. Apart from Newcastle, which was surprisingly prominent, contact with the north was relatively rare. Overall, the letters suggest that London's routine trading network in the fourteenth century extended to a distance of about 100 miles from the city.

III

While many of the sources available to describe mercantile trade are the result of corporate activity, the commercial dealings they describe were ordinarily based on individual initiatives. It is often difficult to visualize the dynamic and ongoing relationships that linked individual merchants with their peers in other parts of the country because legal and administrative sources inevitably concentrate on the immediate circumstances of the particular acts giving rise to corporate intervention. This difficulty is exacerbated by the way the sources emphasize the exceptions when trade relations became problematic rather than the norm when merchants returned from their expeditions without incident. Trade thus becomes a static moment frozen in time rather than part of an ongoing dynamic. In a few cases involving extraordinarily successful enterprises—the William de la Poles and Jacques Coeurs of high finance—individual careers can be mapped in some detail, but merchants of this ilk were in a league of their own. We can, however, occasionally descend deeper into merchant society than the ranks of these high financiers and still recover some of the private initiatives behind the interurban trading networks of the period. Two case histories—one involving a partnership between two merchants in London and one involving an individual based in Kingston upon Hull—will help to contextualize the relationship between individual urban traders and the world in which they operated.

The London trading partnership involved two prominent merchants, William de Flete and John Chigwell, both of whose families were influential in city government.[34] In 1304, the two men agreed to form a partnership in which each party would invest £40 for one year, at the end of which term each would accept an equal portion of profits or losses. Partway through the year, however, the two had a falling out and de Flete sued Chigwell for abusing the terms of their agreement. Ultimately, the suit found its way before the auditors of the Exchequer, who required as part of their effort to adjudicate a fair settlement that the partners furnish a description of the terms of the original contract, a description of the activities both men engaged in on behalf of the partnership, and an accounting of revenues and expenses derived from the original investments. On the basis of the Exchequer's summary of their evidence, the commercial horizons of the partnership can be reconstructed for a period of about eight months.

The two men began the partnership with their money tied up in woad in Picardy (ultimately the prime matter of contention between the two) and wine, beans, and salt in London. Chigwell was the active partner in the agreement, and his first trip on behalf of the partnership took him to Scotland, where the wine, beans, and salt were sold to the king and delivered to the royal garrisons in Berwick and Stirling. While overseeing this deal, Chigwell was invited by the Scottish magnate John Comyn to view a remarkable stash of 45 sacks of wool, 8 lasts of hides, and 1700 wool fells held in his castle of Lochindarb in Badenoch, not far from Inverness. An Italian was also invited to view the stash, and the two decided to pool their resources and purchase the wool and hides jointly. As soon as the terms of the purchase were settled, Chigwell—still acting on behalf of his partner in London—and his new Italian partner shipped the goods to St. Omer, near the border between Flanders and France, where both men travelled to look for customers. While Chigwell was parceling out the goods in St. Omer, de Flete raised questions about the woad in Picardy, which Chigwell claimed had been lost at sea at some point after the partnership was formed. De Flete's actions forced Chigwell to sell the remaining stock of hides short and return to London to answer allegations that he had misrepresented his assets and ultimately to present his version of the partnership and his accounting of receipts and expenses before the Exchequer auditors. This effectively signaled the end of the partnership, which in the short space of eight months saw the two men trading wine, salt, beans, wool, hides, and possibly woad in ventures stretching from London to the north of Scotland and extending across the Channel to Flanders, and, perhaps, to Picardy.

Like this pair from London, Hardelevus of Barton, a merchant from Kingston upon Hull, lived a remarkably peripatetic commercial life. We are vouchsafed a glimpse of his commercial horizons largely as a result of his involvement in the royal wool schemes of the 1330s and 1340s. His name suggests that he began his career in Barton-on-Humber in Lincolnshire, but by

1340, when he can first be traced in surviving records, he is described as a merchant of Kingston upon Hull, where he probably came under the tutelage of William de la Pole.[35] In 1340 he and a merchant from Beverley contracted with the king to purchase 500 sacks of wool collected for the royal wool monopoly in Derbyshire, giving an advance of £500 to seal the contract—a substantial sum even for a wealthy wool merchant.[36] The following year Hardelevus contracted to purchase the clip of Nottinghamshire as part of the king's cartel, and he continued his involvement in various royal wool schemes into the next year, being rewarded at one point with a safe conduct to ship his own wool from Hull to Flanders.[37] In 1343, though, he fell out of the king's favor and was indicted before the king's justices for various unspecified extortions committed in Yorkshire.[38] The writ authorizing his arrest describes him as "flying from that county" to become "a vagabond." His troubles were related to his activities in the wool syndicates, and two years later the king was still gathering information about his use of a remission of customs that had been granted in 1340.[39] His vagabond life came to a crude end when he was imprisoned in the Fleet; an order for his temporary release from the prison in 1346 notes that he had been incarcerated "for no small time" for arrears in debts owed to the king for wool.[40] The king agreed to the release in order to allow the once-wealthy merchant an opportunity to collect from various people letters that he claimed would acquit him of his debts, on the condition that he appear at the Exchequer two months later to answer for his deeds. As a precaution, the king had seven guarantors stand as surety for his reappearance, including individuals from London, Yorkshire, Norfolk, Buckinghamshire and Wales. Unfortunately, we do not know how this audit turned out, but within two years of his release Hardelevus was dead, leaving his executors to fret over the jagged fragments of his commercial world.[41]

What makes Hardelevus a particularly revealing case study is the survival of an undated document among the Exchequer Miscellanea in the Public Record Office listing his debtors.[42] Presumably the document was drawn up at some point between his release in 1346 and his death; perhaps it is the Exchequer's summary of the evidence Hardelevus presented as the condition of his release from the Fleet. Whatever the explanation, the document provides a compact overview of the commercial contacts made by Hardelevus. On the front of the document are listed the names of debtors in Yorkshire, and on the dorse the names of debtors in Nottinghamshire and Lincolnshire. Several of these can also be traced in other sources emanating from the towns with which they were associated in the list, and they prove to be wealthy and powerful merchants, as one would expect.[43] All together the document contains the names of 48 people, who owed amounts ranging from 6s. to £58, adding up to a total of £280 10s. 3d. Most are identified by compound locative surnames, such as Thomas de Lyndeseye de York, allowing for an unusually unambiguous determination of their places of residence. The Yorkshire section records 40 debtors, of which 32 have compound locative surnames. More than half of this number (17) hailed from Hardelevus's home town of Hull, while most of the rest lived in the other leading towns of the county: three in York, seven in Beverley, one in Pontefract, and one in Scarborough. Two of the remaining debtors lived in Holderness, and a third lived in the village of Snaith. Five of the debtors in Nottinghamshire and Lincolnshire can also be localized by their surnames: two came from Newark, one from Lincoln, one from Boston, and one from the village of Weston in Nottinghamshire. In short, Hardelevus's commercial contacts extended across at least three counties and involved him in credit arrangements with other merchants in at least eight major towns.

IV

Given the predominance of agrarian commodities in the urban economies of this period, one can legitimately wonder what compelled towns to engage in longer-distance trade with each other. Because of the reliance on rural producers for basic sustenance and for the raw materials of manufacturing, the interests of towns in developing commercial links with the countryside are easier to account for than are the incentives for interurban trade. To explain fully the dynamics behind interurban trade would require more knowledge than we currently possess about the commodities exchanged between towns, especially about the relative volumes and values of the goods exchanged. Unfortunately, extant sources simply do not offer comprehensive information of this sort, and efforts to devise surrogate measures are invariably hampered by the very nature of the merchant class.[44] Although merchants frequently oriented themselves towards a particular branch of trade, they had no qualms about involving themselves in trading other commodities if the right opportunities presented themselves. The case of the two London partners described above, John Chigwell and William de Flete, is instructive in this regard. Chigwell was ostensibly a fishmonger, while de Flete was known to his peers as a vintner, yet in their partnership we find them trading in a variety of unrelated goods.[45] In this they were typical of merchants in this period, who were defined by how they traded rather than what they traded. Consequently, even in the rare cases when the relevant sources distinguish merchants from other tradesmen, they are unlikely to use anything other than a generic description. Individuals are occasionally described as cornmongers or woolmongers or vintners, but even such seemingly precise designations were more likely to be used to denote someone's principal concern than his (or, in rare cases, her) exclusive specialization. Any attempt to delimit the main interests that led merchants to frequent markets in other towns thus depends more on impressions than on any kind of quantifiable basis. We do at least have a reasonably generous supply of evidence with which to develop impressions: chance references to the goods involved in trade disputes; allusions to commodities involved in debt agreements; the orientation of individual portfolios in local lay subsidy rolls; the volume of goods imported and exported by foreigners in the customs accounts; the requisitioning and purchasing of supplies by the king documented in Wardrobe journals and Liberate rolls; and the purchasing of goods by monasteries and nobles documented in their household account books, to name just some of Clio's bounty.

These sources suggest that in most towns, the main interests of merchants involved in longer-distance trade lay in a fairly restricted number of commodities. In the first rank both in terms of descriptions of merchants' prime orientations and the frequency with which the commodities can be detected are wool, cloth, and wine; in the second rank grain, fish, livestock and hides; and in the third rank metals, spices, dyestuffs, salt, and building materials, principally wood.[46] (It is important to remember that this framework applies only to trade between towns, and not necessarily to other branches of trade.) The gradation between the first and second ranks, however, is much finer than is the one between the second and third ranks. Trade in commodities in the first tier was concentrated in the larger towns, and even there the second tier did not lag far behind. Furthermore, as one moves down the urban hierarchy the relationship between goods in the first and second ranks begins to reverse itself. If one were to portray this relationship using the curves economists find so seductive, with the size and wealth of the town along one axis and the commodity emphasis along the other, the point at which goods in the second rank take precedence over goods in the first rank should be placed somewhere around the twentieth wealthiest town or, in more concrete terms, somewhere around a town the size of Cambridge. Location naturally also influenced the mix of commodities traded by urban merchants. Because of the stronger orientation toward pastoralism in their regional hinterlands, towns in the north and west such as Newcastle upon Tyne and Carlisle showed a stronger orientation toward livestock and hides than did their counterparts elsewhere in the country; conversely ports like Southampton and Bristol dealt more heavily in wine than did most other towns. But taking the country as a whole, and acknowledging that some towns developed a slightly different mix than others, this categorization reasonably captures the relative importance of the principal goods exchanged between towns.

The great attraction of the goods in the first rank, particularly wool and cloth, was their high value relative to weight, making it easy for merchants to absorb the transport costs involved in merchandising them elsewhere. All three were also in high demand, although for different reasons. Wine and cloth were intimately associated with gradations in status in medieval society and thus found a ready market among groups with higher incomes, primarily within the towns and among the aristocracy, gentry, and ecclesiastical establishment. Indeed, wine and cloth were as close as the Middle Ages ever came to developing broad consumer-oriented markets driven by fashion rather than need. Partly for this reason, the prominence of wine as an item of trade between towns bore little relationship with its importance in the economy as a whole. Trade in wine was entirely distributive: All of the wine consumed in England was imported, the vast majority of it coming from Gascony. It entered England in great quantities, averaging about 20,000 tuns a year in the early fourteenth century (more than 5,000,000 gallons, with an annual wholesale value of nearly £100,000 in some years), with most of the trade directed through a handful of nodes, principally Southampton, London, Bristol, and Sandwich.[47] From these few nodes it made its way to towns throughout the country, as is seen most directly in the presentments made under the assize of wine in the eyre courts. In the Wiltshire eyre of 1281, for example, 60 vintners in the county were fined for breaking the assize, with the bulk of the infractions committed by vintners in Salisbury, Wilton, and Marlborough and the remainder by merchants or taverners in other small towns; undoubtedly, all of these vintners were supplied from Southampton.[48]

In contrast to wine and cloth, wool was the great industrial commodity of the period, and its market was found among the merchants themselves rather than among consumers. Its desirability as an item of exchange is inseparable from the almost insatiable international demand for it, which created a large differential between the costs of production and the prices obtainable on the international market.[49] In some respects, the wool trade presents a mirror image of the distributive network formed in the wine trade, flowing from all points in the country into the ports in the south and east, particularly Hull, Boston, London, and Southampton. It could be profitably handled by several middlemen before it reached the hands of a draper: A merchant in Coventry could sell his stock to a merchant in London who could then sell it to a merchant in Bruges, and because of the high differential between prices in England and those in Flanders, each could realize a healthy profit on his transaction.

Looking at the commodities traded between urban merchants as a whole reveals two underlying dynamics behind their circulation. One is based on the merchants' activities as arbitrageurs, exploiting price differentials in different markets. Wool is the best example of a good traded on this basis. While the quality of the clip available in different markets in the country varied—as we can see in the variations in prices found in different price schedules—differences in quality within the country do not seem to have been at the heart of the trade.[50] What drove the trade was the fact that all wool of whatever quality could be sold internationally for far more than it was sold locally. Thus, there was a strong price incentive for merchants to travel to other towns and markets looking for wool, even if they lived in areas that were major producers. A merchant in Northampton, for example, was quite happy to travel to Leicester to buy wool from a merchant there, even though he was also able to buy wool produced locally. Whatever he purchased could be readily sold to the export trade. Strengthening this universal incentive were the particular geographical circumstances of production and distribution. A number of the best producing areas were situated in western parts of the country, while the highest-priced markets were located across the Channel; hence it was profitable for merchants to establish networks of exchange linking London, Southampton, and Hull on the one hand with Shrewsbury, Oxford, and Leicester on the other.

In addition to wool, the arbitraging incentive lay behind trade in other primary agricultural commodities, even fungibles such as wheat and barley. A limited export trade in grain and other foodstuffs suggests that even at this basic level merchants were sensitive to price differentials over long distances. England's role as an exporter of grain can be traced back at least as far as the 1170s, and by the fourteenth century the country was sending thousands of quarters abroad annually: In 1303-1304 exports by aliens—the only exports recorded—through the two ports of King's Lynn and Sandwich reached more than 10,500 quarters.[51] Much smaller price differentials were needed to sustain a domestic trade. David Farmer has recently argued that over the long haul, prices in the main agricultural commodities tended more toward standardization across regions than toward ongoing differentiation, leading him to conclude that by the fourteenth century at least prices were reasonably consistent over the entire country.[52] But in the short term, prices could show considerable regional variation, as Farmer's data reveal. In the first few years of the fourteenth century, for example, the price of barley in South Hampshire was nearly double the price in the Severn valley; at roughly the same time, the price of oxen in the upper Thames region was about a third higher than in Wiltshire.[53] Such regional differentials were not persistent; indeed, they were easily reversible from one year to the next, depending on the vagaries of weather and disease. One of the great weaknesses of the medieval economy was the ineffectiveness of long-term storage facilities. The surplus from a good year's harvest was sometimes able to tide people through a lean harvest in the following year, but it could not be stretched any further: a second consecutive lean year was potentially disastrous.[54] Fortunately, though, good years and bad years were often localized phenomena, and as prices rose in a less fortunate area, merchants could and did step in to shift surpluses from areas that were better supplied. With the exception of London and its suppliers, however, the opportunities and incentives for trading surplus agricultural produce over longer distances were inevitably intermittent and thus failed to generate the stable market incentives needed to shift producers and distributors strongly in any one direction. At the same time, though, they created the conditions in which arbitraging merchants could seek healthy profits, and it may very well be that the unpredictability of regional agricultural yields reinforced merchants' decisions to persist as diversified general traders rather than attempt to develop specialized market niches.

Alongside the strictly commercial incentives inherent in arbitraging price differences between markets, the second main dynamic behind trade between towns in this period was based on industrial or extractive local specializations. The basic features of any one town's economy were replicated in most if not all other towns in the country, but even under these circumstances there was room for specialized orientations to take root in different places. A list of English places and their associations, written probably in the mid-thirteenth century and possibly by a merchant, indicates that contemporaries themselves recognized the distinctive items produced in many different towns.[55] In fact, the document provides a remarkably accurate synopsis of urban and regional specializations in the period, right down to the places to go for schooling (Oxford) and pleasures of the flesh (Charing Cross). Among the associations between towns and specialized goods in this list one finds the following: the razors of Leicester, the iron of Gloucester, the herring of Yarmouth, the ale of Ely, the cord of Bridport, the pewter of Exeter, and numerous others. Several of these are demonstrably accurate descriptions. Gloucester was a regular and large-scale supplier of iron goods to the royal household and army in this period. In 1242, for example, Henry III ordered 10,000 horseshoes and 100,000 nails from the town, with delivery in Portsmouth set for 20 days after the order was issued.[56] The strength of Bridport's cord and rope industry is apparent in a letter in the town's archive recording debts owed for hemp and cord, as well as in local lay subsidy rolls for the town that features holdings of hemp and cord, stocks not typically found in other local subsidy rolls.[57] The herring fishery in Yarmouth, an industry of international significance in this period, is also well attested in both local and national records.[58] Even Ely's brewers can be found plying their wares in St. Ives and King's Lynn within a few generations of the composition of the list.[59] There is, in short, every reason to take the list at face value and to accept that most of the goods mentioned in it were part of the inland trade.

Specialized productive capacities could also arise within certain categories of goods that, on the surface at least, were interchangeable. Cloth is the obvious example of such specialization, although similar interests can be detected in clothing design and, to a lesser extent, in leather goods. The list of associations mentions a half-dozen types of cloth identified with specific towns in the mid-thirteenth century: the scarlet of Lincoln, the hauberge of Stamford, the blanket of Blyth, the burnet of Beverley, the russet of Colchester, and the linen cloth of Aylesham. Identification of particular towns with particular qualities and varieties of cloth is a well-known feature of the international market in cloth, and although England was not a prominent exporter before the second half of the fourteenth century, the same kind of identification found in the international market can be found in the domestic market. Richard Britnell found that the suggested association between Colchester and the production of russet cloths is well borne out in the town's records in the later thirteenth century and that the cloths were distributed throughout the country.[60] Public works toll lists likewise suggest that Aylesham linen was a familiar commodity in the period.[61] Lincoln scarlets and Beverley burnels feature prominently among the cloths sold in English fairs at the time the list was compiled.[62] All of these specialized cloths, as well as the better-known types imported from

Flanders and northern France, circulated through the country via interurban networks of exchange, supplemented by contacts made in fairs. Indeed, the fact that so few of the native types made a dent across the Channel is an indication of just how important domestic distribution networks were in making such industries feasible.

Many of the structural features of the networks that joined towns and merchants to each other in this period are irretrievably lost. Little is known about the frequency or duration of commercial expeditions between towns, about the role of servants and employees in representing the interests of their masters in other towns, about negotiating techniques, and a host of other practical matters. In spite of such limitations, though, there is no doubt that by the end of the thirteenth century, English merchants participated in networks of exchange involving regular and substantial trade between major towns in contiguous counties and that even longer-distance exchange was not unusual. Interurban trade was subject to theft and guile, encumbered with a multitude of legal and political restrictions, and potentially a source of financial ruin when circumstances ran amok, as it has been in all periods since. But it was also a source of personal and corporate wealth, at once reinforcing social divisions within the towns and reconstituting those in society as a whole. Moreover, its significance spread beyond the movement of goods to encompass the exchange of ideas and forms of political organization, evidenced locally in the filiations of borough customs and nationally in the experiments in government that for a time saw merchant representatives turned into a separate parliamentary estate.[63]

6

The Quest for Markets

As in all nonindustrialized societies, towns in medieval England were heavily dependent on rural producers for their basic sustenance and for their supplies of essential raw materials. Agricultural activity was by no means eschewed in an urban setting, but for towns in the upper ranks of the urban hierarchy at least, extending supply lines into the surrounding countryside was a matter of life or death and, as such, a moral imperative for mayors and aldermen as well as an economic imperative for artisans and laborers. The extent to which a town depended on the peasants of the vicinity for basic sustenance varied greatly from place to place, depending on both the size and the particular geography of the town; larger towns inevitably needed longer supply lines to support their dense settlements. In recent years, population estimates for London and Norwich before the Plague have been drastically revised upwards—London to around 80,000 and Norwich to 25,000—and it may very well be that similar revision will be needed in other leading towns.[1] Such population densities could only be achieved by means of an active trade in victuals between town and country.[2]

Many of the staples of life were brought directly to the towns' doorsteps by the primary producers of the goods, who viewed the concentration of demand in an urban environment as simply a larger-scale version of the markets operating throughout the countryside and hence as markets that potentially offered better prices and better prospects for sales.[3] But towns and their merchant communities could not afford to be only passive recipients of the surplus produce of the countryside. Towns were insatiably hungry for the raw materials that fueled manufacturing and gave employment to large numbers of their citizens, principally wool and hides. In the competition to control access to natural resources, urban merchants had to be willing to travel to the sources of supply, since Flemish, Italian, and French merchants, not to mention the merchants from other English towns, were perfectly happy to do so. To be successful in a world with severely limited powers of production, an individual merchant or an entire mercantile community had to be energetic in pursuing commodities at their point of origin. Eager to acquire access to the products of the countryside at the earliest possible stage in the commercial cycle, urban merchants inevitably developed regional contacts that drew them into the countryside to seek their sources of profit.

I

For an urban merchant, competition for natural resources was a simple fact of life, and control of the supply of natural resources an almost certain path to status and wealth. In a world in which severe dearth was only as distant as the next destructive storm, control of the supplies of foodstuffs could convey power of life and death to one able to act as an intermediary between producers and consumers. Even in less traumatic circumstances, those able to interpose themselves between the initial production of a commodity and its processing held the trump card in the scramble for power and prestige. In most economic systems middlemen are in an enviable position, but their precise role and wealth vary according to the forces of production and distribution prevalent in the economy. In the High Middle Ages, population growth and increasing urbanization and commercialization combined to augment the pivotal position held by middlemen. Production of natural resources was based preeminently on the peasant household, as discussed in chapter 2. In their first foray beyond the household, the commodities produced by the peasantry entered into circulation in small allotments, making individual producers pricetakers rather than pricemakers. At the same time, in the demographic conditions prevailing before the arrival of the Plague, the demand for these commodities was high, especially in the towns. In these circumstances, merchants could be amply rewarded simply for buying up the small bits of surplus generated by peasant households and reselling them at the opportune moment either to the artisans in their home town or to merchants from elsewhere. With some commodities, notably wool, merchants were inclined to venture beyond bulking and breaking to become the organizers of industrial production as well. Supplies of labor in the period were plentiful and therefore cheap, and the reward for capturing rural surplus could be magnified by arranging for the surplus to be transformed into higher-value manufactured goods. The incentive for doing so was especially high in an economy in which the laborers themselves were willing to absorb most of the costs of physical plant. Capital was by far the scarcest factor of production, and those in a position to invest on any kind of scale in commodities not required for immediate consumption found themselves in an enviable position.

Internally, guilds and oligarchic governments strictly regulated competition for raw materials among local merchants. In fact, one of the primary motivations for forming a guild merchant was the desire to control the flow of commodities into and out of the town. In many towns individual merchants even agreed to offer fellow merchants the same terms of sale as they had negotiated on their own private commercial dealings: If, for example, a merchant struck a deal with a shipowner to buy an entire shipload of wheat at 5s. per quarter, any of the merchant's fellow guild members wishing to do so could buy a share of the wheat at the same price.[4] In this corporate environment, the real source of competition lay beyond the walls. Guilds and local oligarchies sought as much as possible to restrict external competition, but the best they could do was to regulate the terms and conditions of sale within their own marketplace, and even there, merchants had to reckon with the privileges and interests of other groups. Outside their local market commercial life was a free-for-all. No matter how successfully particular guilds or towns managed to control the flow of resources internally, they all had to act on the knowledge that foodstuffs and industrial raw materials were produced in the surrounding countryside and that other groups were equally intent on gaining control of desirable commodities. Only by traveling to the point of production could merchants ensure that rural commodities would pass through their own hands.

The competition for rural commodities was not, however, solely an urban phenomenon. To the consternation of urban merchants, the same soil that produced the commodities also yielded entrepreneurs capable of engrossing the available surplus. Peasant producers were as happy to sell their produce to their fellow rural dwellers as they were to urban merchants, and the fear of being undercut by their rural neighbors was a significant motivation behind merchants' forays into the countryside. Hitherto, such homegrown competition has received relatively sparse attention from historians. To understand the context surrounding the quest for rural commodities by urban merchants, we need to begin by giving closer attention to this rural-based competition.

A particularly useful source revealing the relationship between rural engrossers and urban economies is supplied by the toll exemptions granted to ecclesiastical corporations, which were similar to those granted to towns. In fact, grants of toll immunity to religious houses may well have been the models upon which later urban exemptions were based. For the grantor (usually the king), gifts of toll exemption were a charitable and pious act that would merit spiritual rewards akin to those earned for grants of land and jurisdictional rights; for the recipient, they were useful additions to the armory of privileges that ensured the fiscal health of the house and the leisure its members needed to pursue less earthly aims.

In most cases, such exemptions were originally designed to encompass the purchase of basic supplies for the religious house: food, clothing, fuel, building materials, and so on.[5] But what began as a favor intended solely for the subsistence needs of the brethren of the house soon developed into a much more extensive privilege, covering other members of the corporation as well—notably the manorial tenants of the house—on the presumption that the welfare of the house was based in part on the welfare of its tenants: When a tenant purchased an ox as part of his plow team, the monastery that made use of the tenant's plowing services also benefited from the purchase.[6] Such exemptions are already evident in the reign of Henry I, and by the early years of the thirteenth century most large ecclesiastical corporations had acquired toll exemptions that were valid for their manorial tenants as well as for the more limited circle of brethren and servants in the house.

These grants were ordinarily couched in broad and general terms. In a typical grant, the king conveyed freedom from tolls for the house "and its men" throughout all of the king's dominions.[7] Such grants presumed that manorial tenants would use their privilege in similar ways and for similar reasons as the brethren of the religious house, namely to purchase subsistence needs and the working stock necessary for farming. It is also fairly clear from some of the disputes that eventually arose as a result of these grants that direct sales of surplus produce—necessary to allow tenants to meet the estate's rent demands—were meant to be included within the limits of the grant. In short, the intent of a royal grant of toll exemption was to insulate a religious house and its tenantry from the expense of participating in a commercial economy.

Ironically, these grants often yielded precisely the opposite result. Rather than insulating religious houses from commercial transactions, toll exemptions often led their members to participate more fully in the world of merchants and merchandise. By stretching the meaning of their exemptions, members of privileged estates found themselves on an equal commercial footing with guild members and burgesses, even on the latter's home turf, and thus able to open up the otherwise circumscribed trading monopoly in the towns. Combining unfettered access to urban markets with an intimate knowledge of the sources of rural supply, tenants of religious houses—and sometimes the brethren themselves—were able to usurp some of the merchant's role in bulking the produce of the countryside. Towns found themselves in an awkward spot, forced to choose between recognizing the words of a royal charter on the one hand and the health of their finances and well-being of their merchants on the other. Faced with such limited options, a number of towns either mounted court challenges or appealed directly to the king to prune back what they considered to be abuses of the original grants, in the process disclosing the kind of rural-based commercial sweeping that they saw as a direct threat to their economic well-being.

Typically, a dispute between a town and a religious corporation would begin like any other toll dispute with a complaint against the levying of a distraint for toll. In most cases the town acknowledged the corporation's exemption on purchases made for personal consumption but contested the exemptions claimed on transactions involving merchandise. In 1302, for example, the Templars sought the king's intervention on behalf of their tenants trading in Bridgnorth, who, the order claimed, were unjustly made to pay toll in the town.[8] The order persuaded the king to send a writ to the bailiffs of the town requiring them to stop collecting toll from their tenants, but the bailiffs responded by returning the writ with an explanation that they only took toll when the tenants traded "for the sake of profit." A virtually identical drama was played out between the Hospitallers and the town of Southampton in 1334.[9] Southampton's bailiffs, however, acted more decisively than their peers in Bridgnorth: They refused to comply with the king's demand because, they said, the tenants were "merchants who resell the things they have bought."

As these two examples suggest, the crusading orders and their tenants were particularly energetic in making use of their toll immunities. The most remarkable case of a crusading order's aggressiveness in this matter was presented to the king's itinerant justices engaged in the Hundred Roll inquiries. In the proceedings conducted in the borough of Totnes, the justices learned that the Hospitallers took their privilege a step beyond even the most liberal interpretation of their original charter.[10] According to the town's presentment, people without any legitimate connection to the order had been paying to join in order to make use of its toll exemption. Even more surprisingly, the town claimed that if anyone attempted to take toll from one of these pseudo-Hospitallers, the order would initiate litigation to ensure that their exemption was observed. Such charges suggest that the town faced something more serious than isolated instances of individual abuse; it faced an order with a calculated and determined policy of exploiting the commercial advantages inherent in its privileged position.

The Templars and Hospitallers were by no means the only orders making aggressive use of their toll exemption. Another complaint recorded in the Hundred Rolls reveals that the Cistercians and Gilbertines were equally adept at the practice. In a presentment by a jury in Lincoln, a number of Cistercian and Gilbertine houses in the county were said to have abused their toll privilege for the past 15 years by working as agents of Flemish and other overseas merchants.[11] According to the presentment, the brethren of the offending houses "buy wools and other merchandise for themselves throughout the county and carry the same wools and merchandise to markets and fairs in the county and there sell them to Flemish and other overseas merchants." In their summation, the jury claimed that these actions were not only prejudicial to the town and consequently to the king but also contrary to the rules of their own orders. Damages to the town as a result of this behavior were said to amount to 100 marks (£66 13s. 4d.) a year. What the jury found particularly galling about the whole affair was the fact that the brothers were not even taking the commercial risks on their own behalf but rather had reached agreement with the foreigners to accept cash in advance in return for their services. In effect, the brothers acted as hired agents, selling their knowledge of the area's economy and their skill in negotiating with local people to foreign merchants. In so doing, they effectively prevented the merchants in the county town from acquiring the wool and other merchandise for themselves. Sales to foreigners per se did not create problems for the town; indeed, the townsmen were perfectly happy to sell the wool to foreigners themselves or even to act as agents for foreigners. Their only concern was their ability to position themselves between the producers of the goods and the buyers. The townsmen knew that if anyone managed to usurp this position, as the Cistercians and Gilbertines now threatened to do, their wealth and power would be seriously jeopardized.

More traditional ecclesiastical corporations did not behave as audaciously as the newer religious orders in pursuing the commercial opportunities inherent in grants of toll exemption, but their tenants did sometimes behave in similar fashion. A dispute between the town of Norwich and tenants of the Bishop of Ely provides a particularly good example of how different interests aligned themselves in such cases. In the 1290s, Norwich was twice reprimanded by King Edward I for taking toll from Ely's tenants. In the first case, the bishop persuaded the king to write to the bailiffs of the town directing them to desist. The bailiffs responded by informing the king that they took toll from the bishop's tenants in Pulham, a manor located about 15 miles south of the town, because Henry III had done so when the town was in royal custody.[12] They also pointed out, as did bailiffs in many other towns caught in a similar predicament, that market tolls were necessary to help the town meet its annual farm.

When the bailiffs continued to collect toll in the aftermath of this correspondence, the bishop induced the king a few years later to act again on his behalf. Edward sent a stern rebuke to the bailiffs, who responded by suggesting that the bishop may not have given him the full story behind the conflict.[13] The bishop's tenants, it turns out, were not charged toll on sales of goods they themselves produced; they were charged toll only on goods they had purchased elsewhere to resell in the Norwich market. The bailiffs contended that Ely's tenants would come to the town leading carts laden with commodities combed from the countryside of Norfolk and Suffolk and demand recognition of their privileges upon arrival in the town. In other words, these enterprising tenants endeavored to turn the royal grant of immunity into a commercial windfall. How the issue was finally resolved remains unknown; the only record of it is the explanation sent by the bailiffs to the king, now lodged in the Public Record Office. The petititon does, however, reveal something indirectly about the social status of the tenants. It states explicitly where the tenants in question resided: Pulham (once again), Shipdham, Dereham, Bridgham, Feltwell, Brandon, and Northwold, all settlements located 15 to 35 miles south or east of the town. Such behavior by peasants dwelling at a considerable distance inland from the town is surprising in and of itself, but it is made even more striking when we realize that Ely's manors in these areas had virtually no freehold tenants.[14] In other words, these entrepreneurial tenants were almost certainly villeins, not the social class one would normally turn to in the historiographical literature for signs of commercial vigor.

Similar kinds of disputes broke out between towns and another privileged group of peasants-cum-entrepreneurs dwelling on the royal demesne, who enjoyed an exemption from toll that was customary rather than chartered. In these cases, the issue was again almost invariably the distinction between exemptions on personal goods, which towns and marketholders universally accepted, and exemptions on goods which tenants bought and sold as merchandise with the expectation of reaping a profit. In 1286, for example, tenants of the ancient demesne manor of South Tawton in Devon challenged the Bishop of Exeter's right to collect toll from them in his market in Crediton, located about 12 miles from the manor.[15] The bishop claimed that he only collected toll on goods purchased as merchandise, as he was allowed to do, and a jury backed him up on this point.

One of the clearest statements of the different interests involved was presented in 1309 in a case involving the market in Birmingham—at that time more akin to a village than a town—and the tenants on the ancient demesne manors of King's Norton and Bromsgrove, located four and twelve miles from the market, respectively.[16] The ancient demesne tenants sued the bailiffs responsible for the market in Birmingham for infringing their rights to be free from toll in all markets by virtue of their tenure. The bailiffs replied that they had done so for their lord, whose ancestors held the market by prescriptive right extending back to before the Norman Conquest. In the course of the pleading, the tenants claimed that they had used the market primarily for "small merchandise," such as victuals, and not as "common merchants trading merchandise." The bailiffs claimed that they had always collected toll from sales of victuals and other household necessities as well as from sales of merchandise and that they were within their rights to do so. Their protestations were set aside by the court, however, which found for the plaintiffs and imposed on the bailiffs a hefty damages payment of 20 marks (£13 6s. 8d.) and an order to desist from collecting toll from ancient demesne tenants in the future.

A certain monotony came to attend the pleading of such cases, with the privileged tenants insisting on their exemption as an unassailable right derived from their tenurial status and the town or marketholder claiming the right to collect tolls on goods purchased or sold for profit rather than for personal use.[17] We have relatively few verdicts in such cases, but those we do have suggest that the collectors of toll had the law on their side, as long as they acted before an exemption for trade in merchandise could be considered to be customary. A compromise reached between the town of Derby and tenants of the Priory of the Holy Sepulcher in Warwick is particularly revealing in this regard. In 1243, the bailiffs of Derby seized some millstones as a distraint because the prior's tenants were unwilling to swear that the millstones were not destined for resale. The prior sued the town to recover the millstones but agreed that his men should swear that the stones were not purchased as merchandise. In future, the prior agreed that his men should similarly swear that goods in their possession had not or would not circulate as merchandise if they expected their toll exemption to apply. When the men in charge of the millstones came forward to swear that they were not intended for resale, the bailiffs released them and the suit was dropped. Policing such exemptions must have been awkward and difficult for bailiffs and other toll collectors; probably privileges were contested only in egregious or recurring cases of abuse.

The willingness and ability of peasant tenants, even villein tenants, to turn toll immunities to commercial advantage illustrate the competitive context in which urban merchants operated in their quest to control the flow of rural commodities. From the perspective of an urban merchant, the activities of these entrepreneurial tenants were not necessarily threatening. If they could ensure that the commodities ended up in their town's marketplace, merchants might conceivably have welcomed outsiders' assumption of the search and transport costs involved in transferring rural goods into an urban environment. In most instances, major towns probably did continue to attract the great majority of rural commodities produced in their region, even in cases involving rural middlemen. Indeed, the incentives for peasant middlemen to scour the countryside would have been much reduced were it not for the demand represented by the urban markets as the endpoint of the scouring. But there was no way for any single town to ensure its continued supply of the right commodities at the right prices once outsiders succeeded in interposing themselves between local and regional producers and consumers. Middlemen based in the countryside had their own interests to pursue, and these interests could easily lead them to another town or market, or even into dealing with foreign merchants. What was true for the town was also true for the merchants inhabiting it: There was no way for urban middlemen to ensure that goods would continue to flow through their hands in the most profitable way once others came to occupy their niche. For the town as well as for the individual merchant, economic security in these circumstances could be found only by making direct inroads into the countryside.

II

The wool trade provides a particularly good example of the motives and methods of urban merchants in their forays into the countryside. In the thirteenth and fourteenth centuries, the demand for English wool was, and was perceived to be, almost unlimited; whatever could be produced was assured of finding a profitable market.[18] Every major town in Europe had a textile industry, and English wool had no rivals as the favored material of serious, high-quality producers. Because Flanders was the principal international market for wool, most of the trade in England passed through the eastern and southern ports, but even towns located well inland were deeply immersed in overseas trading: A royal enquiry in 1275 into unauthorized export of wool in the town of Northampton learned that five local merchants had, in recent years, sent more than 160 sacks (nearly 60,000 pounds) to Southampton and thence to the Continent, and that several foreign merchants had sent large amounts from the town to Southampton and Boston.[19] The number of merchants operating at this level in any one town was probably fairly small—probably countable in single digits in the vast majority of towns—but these small pockets of leading merchants were widely scattered throughout the country, and beneath each were much larger numbers of local agents and engrossers. The incentives for participation in the trade were powerful—in the 1330s, wool sold for twice as much in Flanders as in England, and even with high rates of taxation and the costs of collection and export, profit margins were high.[20]

The key to these high profits lay in getting hold of supplies before the competition did, and the only way to do this successfully was to travel to the points of production. High rollers usually managed to sew up private contracts with major individual producers, but as discussed in chapter 2, the principal source of supply in this period came from the aggregate production of myriad peasant households. The natural contact point between an urban merchant willing to travel into the countryside to acquire wool and the hundreds or thousands of peasant producers situated in the hinterland of any given town was in the markets sprinkled around the countryside. In the 1275 inquiry into unauthorized exports, a jury in the wapentake of Elloe in Holland reported that the district's wool had been sent abroad via the port in Boston but also mentioned in passing that all of it had been purchased in markets in the wapentake.[21] In the same inquiry, a merchant from Stamford was identified by separate juries in Peterborough and Rutland as an unauthorized exporter who sent wool from their respective areas to King's Lynn and Boston for export.[22] The Rutland jury also reported that a Londoner exported 10 sacks of wool he had purchased in the county. Lincoln's complaint about the involvement of the Cistercians and Gilbertines in rural wool purchases takes on added resonance when seen against the indictments encountered in these presentments. Indeed, Lincoln also fingered a foreign merchant who went around the countryside purchasing wool for export.[23] In the eyes of the Lincoln jury, the offense in this instance—committed by a woman and her son—was not unauthorized export, a ban that the town probably did not support in any case, nor even entrepreneurial forays into the countryside, which the town grudgingly had to recognize as legitimate competition, but rather the offender's gall in exporting the collected wool through the port in Boston without a stop in Lincoln.

Leicester's guild records provide some tantalizing glimpses into this urban quest for rural wool. The great advantage every town had over national and international rivals was intimate knowledge of production and marketing habits within its region. Merchants in Leicester expected to beat their competitors to the supplies of wool in the hinterland of the town because they knew where and when to go for the best markets, and they probably also counted on personal contacts and established reputations in their dealings within the region. To some extent, the guild engaged in a great conspiracy to keep crucial knowledge about the local wool trade to itself, its great fear being that individual merchants would break ranks and sell the guild's secrets to outsiders. Thus, the guild records contain a number of ordinances and disciplinary measures imposed to punish any members who let others in on the secrets of the guild. In 1260, for example, the guild passed a statute forbidding its members from assisting outside merchants in locating merchandise in the county, which suggests that this had probably been done in the past. The statute, though, failed to solve the guild's problem: In 1281, one of the members was brought to book for acting as an agent of Lombard merchants; in 1289, a guild member purportedly led foreigners to several places in the county where they could buy wool; in 1307 a guild member was accused of leading a merchant from Northampton around the region for the same purpose; in 1336 two guild members were confronted for taking foreign merchants to Hungarton, again in quest of wool.[24] Leicester was not alone in its anxiety to keep outsiders in the dark about local conditions: In 1275, five merchants in Scarborough were accused of collecting wool in the Yorkshire countryside as agents for foreign merchants, and a similar concern lay behind Lincoln's complaints in the Hundred Rolls.[25]

Much as it would have liked to make its policy stick, Leicester, like other towns, had to accept the reality of outside competition on its regional turf, even if it could enforce internal discipline. Indeed, Leicester's own guild records show the other side of the coin, with local merchants involved in trade in numerous places in neighboring counties.[26] In an attempt to find a compromise between its own interests and those of merchants from outside, the guild in 1274 formally acknowledged that outsiders had the right to purchase wool in the county but attempted to restrict the number of places where they could do so.[27] The guild statute recording this change in policy notes in passing that much of the wool foreigners bought eventually ended up in the town, suggesting that its concern was more the ability of guild members to get their hands on the wool at the point of production than it was concern about the supply of wool into the town. It goes on to designate Melton, Loughborough, Breedon on the Hill, Hinckley, Bosworth, Lutterworth, and Lilbourne as the places where foreign merchants could buy without hindrance in the county. It is clear from this list of places that the guild's goal was to force outsiders to make their purchases in formal markets within the county. Of the seven places designated, at least five had chartered markets (three of the five also had a fair) and a sixth had a fair but no market.[28] Local merchants were deeply concerned that outsiders might undercut them before supplies even entered into formal circulation. They took it for granted that competition would be found in the local markets and assumed that they would have to travel if they wanted to keep abreast of their competitors. If competition could be restricted to the formal markets, both would be satisfied that their own interests would be served.

III

Every town in the country developed links with its surrounding countryside akin to those apparent in the wool trade in Leicester. While we have few comprehensive sources documenting the origins of merchants engaged in trade in specific country markets, in a few instances we can reconstruct rural trade from the other side of the ledger by looking at the range of market contacts forged by specific towns.[29] The Hundred Rolls of 1275 lend themselves particularly well to this approach. Because the justices involved in the Hundred Roll inquiries heard plaints rather than formal legal challenges, it was relatively easy for towns to present a ragbag of commercial grievances in the hopes of winning favorable royal intervention on at least some of them. Grievances were, in fact, actively solicited by the justices, and a number of towns willingly complied, convinced that they need not worry about the expense and inconvenience inherent in more traditional legal challenges. Two prominent towns—Lincoln and Northampton—used the opportunity to present grievances about tolls collected from their merchants in surrounding markets, and their statements furnish unusually detailed depositions about their forays into the countryside.

Lincoln's deposition lists 11 different places where its merchants were made to pay toll, unjustly in the eyes of the presentment jury. Several of the places had a history of rancorous trade relations with Lincoln. Disputes with Horncaster, for example, had been going on for more than 40 years, ever since the Bishop of Lincoln, the holder of the market, quarreled with the town over the rights of his tenants trading in Lincoln and with the town's behavior in his market.[30] Two of the other purported offenders—Louth and Sleaford—had more recently found themselves in court quarreling with Lincoln over their respective trading rights within the county, and it is possible that this dispute was still *sub judice* when the Hundred Roll inquiry took place.[31] All three of these contentious trading partners were home to well-established markets, and the same is true of at least six of the eight other members of the group.[32] Two of the places—Newark and Stamford—can be characterized as small towns, though neither was a formal borough, but the remainder are best described as prominent rural market sites, exhibiting all the traits characteristic of such places, such as early dates of foundation, persistence through later centuries, and relatively high levels of taxable wealth.[33] As its presentment to

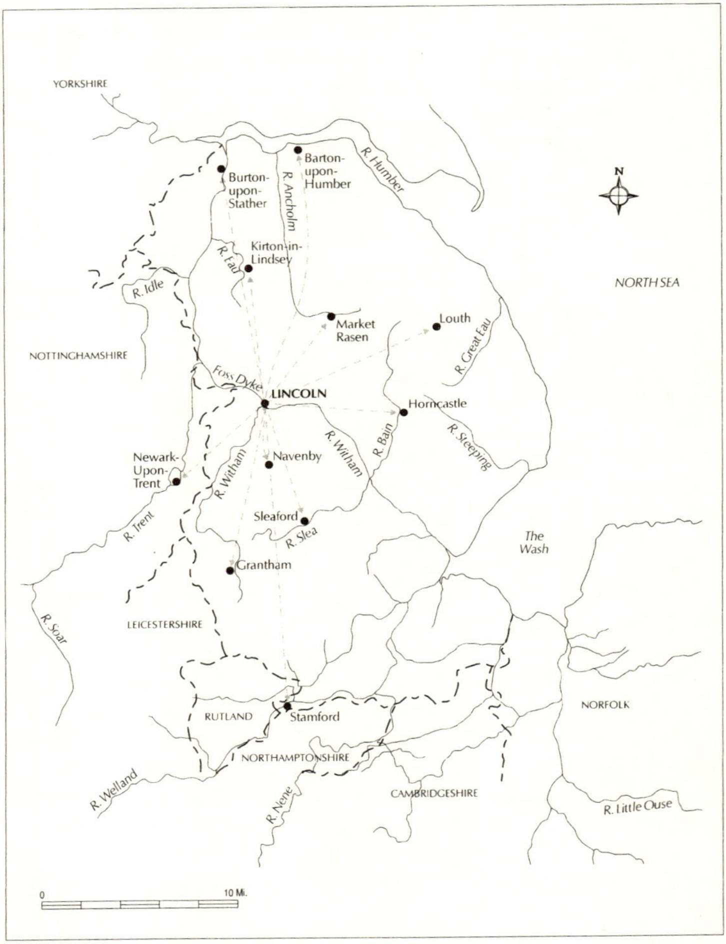

Map 6-1: Lincoln's toll disputes in 1275

the justices illustrates, Lincoln in 1275 clearly had trading relations with a network of prominent market centers distributed throughout the entire county.

The geographical distribution of these markets is shown on map 6-1. As can be seen on the map, almost all of the places with which Lincoln had trade relations were spread out in a semicircular area surrounding the town. Within this general area are two concentric arcs that may indicate the frontiers of the town's regular trading activity. The first has a radius of about 16 miles and includes Kirton-in-Lindsey (17 miles), Market Rasen (14 miles), Horncastle (17 miles), Sleaford (17 miles), and Newark (16 miles). The second arc comprises places located between about 25 and 30 miles from Lincoln, including Burton-upon-Stather (30 miles), Barton-upon-Humber (32 miles), Louth (24 miles), and Grantham (23 miles). Nottingham, to the west, is located at about this same distance away. Expressed in terms of travel time, a round trip to one of the places on the inner arc comes close to the maximum limit that could be traveled on horseback in a single day; likewise for a one-way trip to one of the places on the outer arc.[34] It would have been difficult to make either of these trips in a single day hauling a cartload of goods, but it would have been possible for a merchant to make one of these journeys with some cloth packed in saddlebags or simply to ride to the market and make other arrangements for the delivery of any bulky goods purchased. It is also possible that merchants did not return to Lincoln but instead traveled from market to market, in the manner anticipated by the creators of new markets described in chapter three and actually conducted by merchants from King's Lynn, whose deeds will be explored in chapter ten.

An even more expansive statement of problematic tolls was presented to the Hundred Roll justices when they arrived in Northampton. At the time of its presentment in 1275, Northampton could claim a level of wealth and political significance relative to the other towns of the kingdom that it would never again enjoy.[35] In its presentment, Northampton singled out no fewer than 22 places that, the town claimed, unjustly demanded toll from its merchants.[36] Included among their number were a few of the town's economic peers (Leicester, King's Lynn, Ipswich, and Winchester) and several smaller regional towns (Stamford, Newark, and Torksey; the overlap with Lincoln in the case of the former two is intriguing). The majority of places Northampton identified are, however, best described as important rural market centers, similar in stature to the markets found in Lincoln's presentment. Included in this group were Yaxley and St. Ives in Huntingdonshire, Ely in Cambridgeshire, Banbury in Oxfordshire, Melton Mowbray and Market Harborough in Leicestershire, Grantham and Spalding in Lincolnshire, Downham Market in Norfolk, and Towcester, Daventry, Higham Ferrers, and Rothwell in Northamptonshire.[37] (One other place indicated in the presentment, Deeping in Lincolnshire, might also belong in this group. East Deeping did not have a chartered market until 1304, but the place name and subsidy wealth of its sister settlement Market Deeping are suggestive of a much earlier and more significant market.)[38] The final place mentioned, Holm, could be any one of a dozen places known by that name, none of which can be identified as an important market town. The most likely candidate is Holme-next-the-Sea in Norfolk, which was a prosperous village and possibly a port on the Wash, although not the site of a documented market.

Map 6-2 illustrates the geographical distribution of the trading partners with which Northampton had disputed toll relations. These partners were located in nine different counties covering a substantial portion of central and eastern England. There is a strong orientation toward places that lay to the east of the town: A line drawn through Northampton on a north-south axis reveals only six places that were situated west of the town, and none of these was more than about 15 miles westward. The eastern pull is partly explicable by the flow of the nearest major waterway to the town, the Nene, which flowed into the Wash, but is also indicative of the greater commercialization of eastern parts of the country in this period.

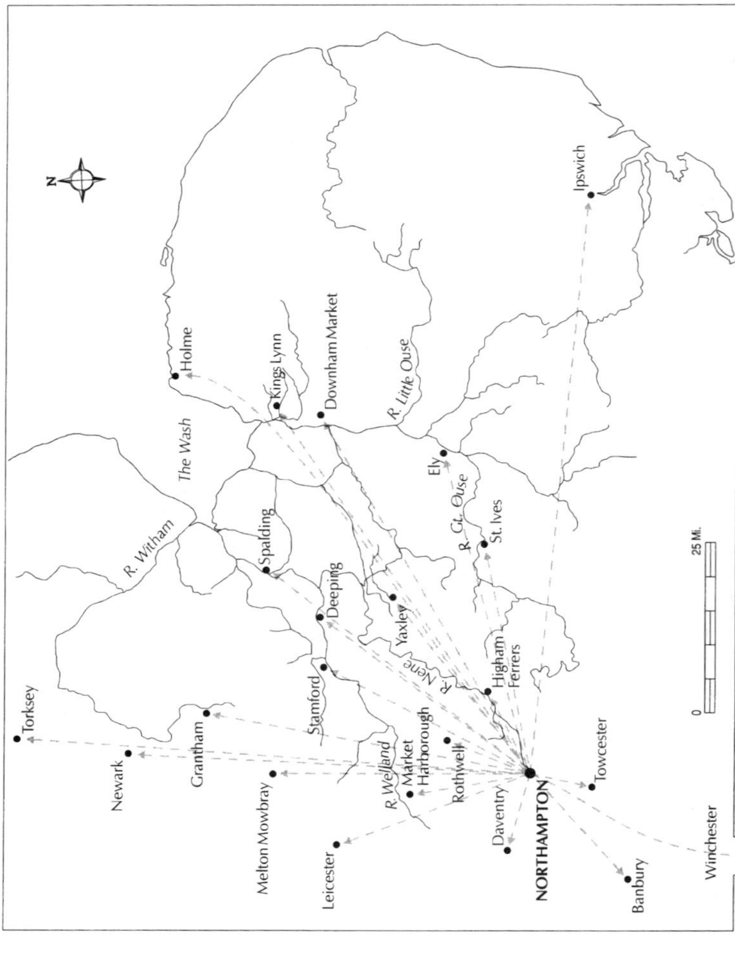

Map 6-2: Northampton toll disputes in 1275

Trading opportunities with these different settlements were probably as diverse as their territorial distribution. The presentment in the Hundred Rolls does not give any clues about the kind of trade behind the problematic tolls, but some general features in the list of settlements can be discerned. At least 15 of the places mentioned held fairs as well as weekly markets and at least four of them—St. Ives, Stamford, King's Lynn, and Winchester—held fairs of international significance in the thirteenth century.[39] The annual cycle of the great fairs in eastern England in this period began in Stamford during Lent and ended in Northampton in November and included gatherings in St.Ives over Easter, Boston in July, and Winchester in September. Of these places, only Boston was omitted from the presentment, and it may be significant that its fair was held around the same time as King's Lynn's, a town that was included. That Northampton's merchants were deeply immersed in this annual round of fairs is abundantly clear in surviving records, particularly those concerning trade in cloth.[40] Trade with ports also features in Northampton's presentment, specifically trade with the two most important ports lying east of the town, King's Lynn and Ipswich. The link with Ipswich is not well documented in surviving sources, but King's Lynn, the outport of the Nene, was clearly familiar territory for Northampton's merchants.[41] A third branch of trade involved other inland towns, including Leicester, Torksey, and Newark. Little is known about trade with the latter two places, but there are suggestions in the Leicester borough records that a mutual interest in wool and cloth gave rise to commercial contact between the two towns.[42]

In at least four of the cases recorded in the Hundred Rolls—Towcester, Daventry, Market Harborough, and Melton Mowbray—Northampton's trade almost certainly revolved around the weekly market, because all four were licensed to hold markets but not fairs. Not surprisingly, these four were located much closer to the town than the major fair sites and ports. Four other, nearer places—Yaxley, Banbury, Higham Ferrers, and Rothwell—had rights to fairs as well as markets, but their fairs were more extensions of their markets than significant trading venues in their own right. Seen in terms of distance from the town, these eight places show a level of concentric uniformity with surprising similarity to the situation in Lincoln. An inner circle of markets comprising Higham Ferrers, lying 14 miles in an easterly direction, Towcester, lying 8 miles almost due south, Daventry, lying 11 miles to the west, and Rothwell, lying 13 miles in a northerly direction ring the town almost like the points on a compass. In the outer circle are Yaxley, lying 33 miles to the northeast, Banbury, 22 miles to the southwest, and Melton Mowbray, lying 37 miles due north. Market Harborough, lying 17 miles almost due north falls into an intermediate position but perhaps fits best in the inner core of markets, as was true of markets located at a similar distance from Lincoln.

Although we have relatively few records documenting the kind of trade that went on between Lincoln and Northampton and their networks of surrounding markets, the Hundred Roll presentments suggest that the merchants in the two towns had more than a passing familiarity with the markets of their respective regions. Indeed, while the lack of a dispute with a particular place does not necessarily imply an absence of trade, the consistency with which both presentments single out the leading rural markets in their respective regions and ignore the lesser ones is a fact of considerable importance. The presentments suggest that urban merchants were likely to concentrate their efforts on the largest rural markets in their region, typically ones that were founded early and that would continue to form the core of rural marketing networks for many more centuries. These places tended to be more populated than the other market sites in the area, with a larger contingent of artisans than would be found in other villages. They also tended to be wealthier than their rivals, more centrally located on existing transportation routes, and ordinarily offered more substantial market facilities. Along with the towns, such places formed the core of the medieval marketing network, serving as a magnet for the produce of the surrounding countryside and as a focus for merchants based in the towns.

IV

As everyone knows from personal experience, the amount of time and effort expended on any one errand can be substantially reduced if it can be combined with other errands en route. The same principle guided an urban merchant's attitude toward his forays into the countryside: Commercial interests were much better served if trips to several different markets could be made in the course of the same journey than if each market had to be visited in isolation. This mercantile practice can be found in virtually all marketing systems in all parts of the globe.[43] Medieval English merchants have left only piecemeal evidence of such sequential peregrinations, but the pieces leave little doubt that they behaved in similar ways to maximize their marketing and minimize their traveling times.[44]

As noted in chapter three, when someone attempted to found a new market in the thirteenth century, the king required that the proposed foundation not be prejudicial to preexisting markets. Historians have tended to focus on the location of adjacent markets as the prime consideration in cases of market conflict, but the timing of a proposed market was ordinarily given equal consideration when assessing potential damages. Such conflicts typically required the courts to investigate how the day proposed for holding the new market fit into preexisting marketing cycles. In most cases, the issue of timing did not revolve around markets proposed for the same day, which would have been the biggest concern for local trade. Rather, the issue most commonly fought over was a market granted for the day before a preexisting market, which had the potential to cut the preexisting market out of the cycle of urban merchants. Local traders would not have been much affected by such jockeying for slots, but for traders coming from a town, possible a town more than a day's journey away, the slots in the cycle were of fundamental importance.

One such case involved a market granted in 1252 to the Archbishop of Canterbury to be held on Tuesdays on his manor in Wingham, a village located about six miles east of Canterbury and about the same distance west of Sandwich. When the sheriff convened a jury of inquiry to report on the damages that might result from the founding of a market in Wingham, the jurors informed him that not only would the new market not damage preexisting markets, it would actually strengthen them.[45] They went on to explain that both the market in Canterbury, which was not described in the verdict but probably convened on several days of the week as in most other large towns, and the market in Sandwich, which was held on Wednesdays, would benefit from a new market on Tuesdays. Their reasoning was that the proposed market had the potential to attract more merchants into the area, which could only benefit the markets held on other days. They did not specify where they expected the merchants to come from, but it is clear that they expected them to visit the market in Wingham while making the rounds of the markets in Canterbury and Sandwich. The nearest market held on Tuesdays, they noted, was in Lenham, said to be 20 leagues distant (a good approximation; it is, in fact, about 22 miles distant from Wingham), too far away to be damaged by the proposed market and too far away to help the markets in Canterbury and Sandwich. Based on this verdict, the market was allowed to proceed.

A suit heard a few years later involving markets in Gloucestershire and Wiltshire gives a more explicit identification of the relationship between the interests of merchants and marketholders than does the case from Kent. In this instance, the Abbot of Pershore was charged with founding a market in Hawkesbury, Gloucestershire, to the damage of Matthew de Bezill's market in Sherston, Wiltshire, four miles away.[46] Matthew explained to the justices hearing the case that he held a market in Sherston on Tuesdays and that the Abbot had begun to hold a market in Hawkesbury on Mondays. As a consequence, "the goods which should and are accustomed to be sold at his market at Sherston are now sold in the abbot's market and the tolls and stall-dues and other customary payments which should and are accustomed to be paid on the goods bought in his market in Sherston are now paid and levied in the abbot's market." The Abbot's attorney replied to the charge by arguing that the market in Hawkesbury actually benefited the market in Sherston, because it attracted merchants who would be willing to travel on to the neighboring market the next day. Furthermore, the merchants who traveled on to Sherston would be able to take along with them the goods they had purchased in Hawkesbury: not only would there be more merchants, but they would have more merchandise with them.

Because the two markets were in different counties, the jury that was assembled included eight people from each county. They were asked to look into which of the two descriptions of merchant activity best represented existing practice, and they ultimately sided with Matthew de Bezill, giving two reasons for their verdict. The first was that as soon as the abbot's men had a market in their own village, they began to sell all of their grain, meat, and other goods there rather than in the market in Sherston, which they had customarily patronized. The second reason put forward was that up until the founding of the market in Hawkesbury, merchants from Bristol had regularly traveled to Sherston to purchase grain to take back to their hometown, but they had stopped doing so recently because Hawkesbury was closer for them. Neither of the contending markets was what might be called a "local" market for Bristol: Sherston was 19 miles distant from the town, and Hawkesbury 15 miles. Bristol's merchants were keenly aware of the situation between these two markets, and they knew very well where their own interests lay. A few years before Matthew de Bezill took the case before the justices in eyre, where it was ultimately settled, the king ordered an inquiry in Bristol into potential damages if he allowed the abbot to have a market in Hawkesbury.[47] The burgesses, with an obvious eye to their own advantage, informed the king that he could go ahead with the grant because the market in Hawkesbury would not cause any damages to preexisting markets.

The assumptions that the different parties brought to the case are as striking as the practical details. The defendant, knowing that he was in jeopardy of losing his market, based his entire defense on the expectation that the justices and the jurors involved in the case would find it an eminently reasonable proposition that merchants would be happy to include a new market in their peregrinations through the countryside. The king assumed when he ordered Bristol to conduct a formal inquiry into the potential harm caused by his granting a market in Hawkesbury that the town's merchants would have a role to play in the new market. The bailiffs and burgesses of the town probably had the clearest sense of all about the commercial opportunities that would result from the founding of a new market, and they knew that they would benefit if it came to pass. The fact that merchants from a town located 15 miles away might be interested in a new rural market was taken for granted by all concerned; whether or not they actually were interested could be established only by looking into the particular circumstances of the market. Whether in Hawkesbury, where the jurors ultimately found that the new market should not be allowed, or in Wingham, where they found that it should, everyone involved accepted without comment the fact that urban merchants and rural markets were intimately associated with each other. In the face of unremitting competition to control access to economic resources, urban merchants could not afford to wait for the market to come to them.

7

Trade into Towns

While merchants from the country's regional towns scoured the countryside looking for wool, barley, and a market for the products of urban industry, residents of neighboring villages and market sites developed distribution networks that flowed in the opposite direction, from the country into the town. For a villager, towns offered especially "full" markets, where sales were likely to be brisker and prices higher than those found in rural markets. As long as towns agreed not to place too many legal or economic obstacles in the way of producers in their hinterlands, they could count on a steady stream of peasants passing through their gates with carts and packhorses loaded with goods destined for their marketplaces. The importance attributed to this traffic is well illustrated in an acrimonious dispute over toll collection that pitted St. Swithun's Priory against the bailiffs of Winchester in 1259.[1] For reasons that are not fully explained in the record of the dispute, the priory had recently erected roadblocks at three of the town's four gates as part of a protest against local toll collectors. According to the jury's verdict in the case, the priory's roadblocks closed the routes "by which men coming from the surrounding countryside with carts traditionally entered the marketplace." When, in the course of the ensuing controversy, several bailiffs and a group of workmen attempted to enforce a court order to tear down the obstruction, a number of monks "dressed in albs and stoles and carrying a cross, candelabras and lighted candles" excommunicated them and, for good measure, raised the hue and cry to alert local residents that a crime was being committed. The monks' defiance led to the seizure of the priory's lands and the arrest of all its lay adherents. Clearly, the issue of access to an urban marketplace for residents of the surrounding countryside was not one to be trifled with.

For peasants and other rural producers, town markets were enticing outlets for surplus output. By 1300, England's total urban population may well have exceeded one million people.[2] Many of these people lived in cramped quarters; English towns tended to be less densely populated than their continental counterparts, but at least some managed to reach densities exceeding 50 people per acre.[3] Such concentrations of population placed insupportable burdens on the agricultural lands attached to the towns—lands that were, in many cases, surprisingly limited, as James Tait observed more than 50 years ago in his discussion of Domesday boroughs.[4] Georges Duby has calculated that towns with 3,000 inhabitants—a population level reached by the end of the thirteenth century in most of the regional towns discussed in chapter 4—required the produce of about 9,000 acres of arable land, or an area of about 14 square miles, to ensure an adequate subsistence base.[5] Even relatively small towns such as Colchester and Godmanchester, both of which were well-endowed with arable land surrounding their respective cores, were necessarily immersed in exchange with their rural neighbors. Richard Britnell found that the supply lines of Colchester extended to about eight miles from the town, and J. A. Raftis coined the expression "greater agrarian zone" to refer to the same phenomenon in his study of Godmanchester.[6]

Suppliers of agricultural staples were, however, not the only residents of the hinterland attracted to urban markets by the heavy concentration of demand. Agricultural staples often reached the towns in processed rather than unprocessed form, conveyed by bakers, cooks, and a host of other victuallers.[7] Wood and other fuel sources must also have been conveyed into the towns in sizable quantities; even if medieval burgesses accepted cold and dark as unavoidable facts of life, they still wanted fuel for cooking, brewing, and a number of industrial pursuits.[8] Some types of manufactured goods were also commonly produced in the countryside and marketed in the towns. Pottery is a good example: Over the course of the twelfth and thirteenth centuries, potting migrated from its original home in the towns out into the countryside, and trade in pottery naturally began to flow in the opposite direction, from village production sites into the towns.[9] Tanned hides also commonly entered the larger towns as trade goods, typically from the smaller towns and market sites of the surrounding region; the unsavory process of production, with its urine and guano solutions and waste products of dried blood and rotted hair, placed limits on internal production within the larger towns, thereby creating opportunities for outsiders to make up shortfalls in supply.[10]

Traces of the relationship between towns and the residents of their hinterlands can be found in many contemporary sources. Many of the items included in contemporary lists of urban tolls deal with victuals and simple manufactured goods. The origin of these goods is seldom specified, but many of the entries are predicated on the presumption that the goods will enter the town in quantities characteristic of the production of peasants and artisans.[11] Descriptions of market regulations mirror toll lists in this respect, often referring specifically to the rights and obligations of victualers and other commodity sellers hailing from outside the town.[12] The concern exhibited by the governing bodies of even relatively modest boroughs to limit forestalling—the interception of foodstuffs en route to urban markets—likewise indicates the flow of goods from the hinterlands into the towns.[13] The very layout of most towns reveals the symbiosis between urban growth and rural suppliers characteristic of the period: Prior to the twelfth century towns typically oriented themselves around a castle or a church, but from the twelfth century their marketplaces became their central focus.[14]

In spite of its generally recognized importance, the use of urban markets by peasants and other producers residing in the hinterland of a town has proven difficult to reconstruct in any detail. Much progress has, however, been made in recent years, particularly through reconstructions of credit relationships recorded in urban court records. Several recent studies have illustrated that residents of the surrounding countryside were frequently involved as both creditors and debtors of towndwellers, often in circumstances that suggest regular and ongoing commercial relationships.[15] This chapter seeks to build on these foundations with the help of a rich but underutilized body of source material: the membership lists kept by various merchant guilds.[16] Like court records of credit relationships, guild membership lists can be used both to document the geographical range of commercial contact between a town and its hinterland and to shed light on the specific commercial interests that led outsiders to make use of urban markets. Thus, like pleas of debt, they offer a welcome opportunity to develop a more precise understanding of an important branch of the inland trade.

To appreciate the significance of these membership lists, it is helpful to know why and how they came to be written. Guild membership lists are analogous to the more familiar registers of freemen surviving from York and several other towns.[17] In practice, becoming a freeman and joining a guild merchant amounted to much the same thing. The primary economic rationale for both agencies was to guarantee privileged access to the local market to the members of the club. To keep track of those who possessed this privilege, and of those who had paid their membership dues, both towns and guilds compiled running lists of their members. There is, however, one crucial difference between surviving lists of guild merchant members and surviving lists of freemen: Guilds did not necessarily require that their members take up residence in the town.[18] In fact, some merchant guilds established two ranks of membership, distinguishing between members who resided in the town, termed "insiders" *(intrinseci)* and members who resided elsewhere, described as "foreigners" *(forinseci)*. As used by urban corporations of the thirteenth century, the term "foreigner" normally referred to an individual who resided outside the town but who had business in the town, or at least one who had business with townspeople. Incessantly preoccupied with asserting and protecting their independence, towns were wont to characterize the world as being divided into two groups of people: On the one hand, there were those who lived within the walls of the town and contributed to the upkeep of the same, those who were in scot and lot with each other as fellow taxpayers, those who settled disputes internally using their own courts and forms of action, those who enjoyed unrestricted rights of trade in the town; on the other hand, there were the foreigners, those who lived beyond the walls, and thus those who did not share the special privileges and obligations of the town.

Society, of course, often fails to adhere to the hermetic compartments that privileged groups pretend to delineate for it. Many towns, recognizing that their fortunes were inextricably linked with the world outside the walls, created the intermediate status of foreign guildsman, or in some instances foreign burgess, to foster the trading relationships upon which their prosperity depended. These foreigners typically received privileged access to the local market, akin to that enjoyed by resident merchants, without establishing permanent residency in the town. They are mentioned in passing in the records of numerous towns—Barnstaple, Leicester, King's Lynn, Derby, Wallingford, and Totnes, among others—and a select few of the surviving membership registers actually list insiders and outsiders separately.[19] Two towns—Ipswich and Shrewsbury—have particularly useful membership records, both beginning in the early thirteenth century. In both towns, surviving membership lists record not only who the foreigners were but also, in many instances, where they resided. Used carefully, these lists have much to say about the nature of urban trade in the country as a whole.

I

The Ipswich list survives as an addendum to the town's so-called Domesday Book, recording both the names of foreigners and the amount they paid for their membership rights.[20] The list was designed to be ongoing and open-ended, with the names of those newly acquiring the privileged status entered in chronological sequence after the name of the last recipient. The earliest entry was made in 1200 and the latest just over a century later. Virtually all of the foreigners buying their way into the guild were members of the East Anglian nobility. This group certainly did not exhaust the ranks of outside traders who were commercially active in the borough, and thus is not a complete register of Ipswich's commercial horizons. Nonetheless, this group of outsiders was important enough to merit recording in the principal document of the town's cherished privileges, and even as a partial register of outsiders, the list furnishes some valuable information. The lords of neighboring manors were an important constituency in the local market as both buyers and sellers.[21] But the town was probably more interested in the tenants of these lords, to whom the privileges extended. As in the case of ecclesiastical corporations who acquired toll rights, the rights inherent in foreign guild membership extended to all tenants in the lordship. Robert de Vaus, for example, purchased freedom from toll in Ipswich in 1200 or 1201 for himself and his villeins living in Wenham and elsewhere. Three years later, Hugh le Rus acquired privileges for himself and his villeins in Akenham, Hemingstone, Henley, Hasketon, and elsewhere. The list begins with a noteworthy description of what guild membership meant for these foreigners:

> he [the lord] and all his villeins are free henceforth from toll in the town, namely on all grains and all other things grown and raised on their own lands or on the demesne and on these alone, and on all things bought for their own sustenance, but not on anything else. . . . If his villeins are merchants, they should pay into the royal farm the just and customary toll, particularly on their merchandise.

The town's concern expressed in this passage is remarkably similar to the problems encountered by towns dealing with the toll exemptions of religious houses. At several points in the list of foreigners the record reiterates that the toll exemptions were not meant to extend to goods traded for profit; at one point the list expressly states that "all villeins, internal burgesses as well as foreign, will always pay toll on all their merchandise [goods traded for profit] as part of the town's farm."[22]

For the most part, these enigmatic villein entrepreneurs lived in villages within a radius of about ten miles of the town. The distribution of villagers granted special access to the town's market appears to be random, dependent no doubt as much on the willingness of a lord to foot the bill for membership as on the commercial aspirations of the tenants. Apart from the ongoing problem of distinguishing between goods that were self-produced and goods that were traded as merchandise, there is no indication in the list or in other parts of the town's written customs to show how these peasants made use of the privileges their lords acquired for them. Other formal statements of custom note the presence of individuals from the surrounding countryside in the town's markets, but apart from a reference to foreigners in the bread market, they do not distinguish between privileged foreigners and others. But the care that both lord and town exhibited in enumerating all of the villages involved as part of a membership grant and the regulatory headaches the status created for the town both suggest that trade into the town was more than just casual. Indeed, the fact that the town continued to offer foreign membership in the face of these problems is testimony to the significance that its officials attached to the maintenance of trading links with the surrounding countryside.

The surviving guild membership lists from Shrewsbury are much more comprehensive than the single list from Ipswich.[23] There are, in fact, several fundamental differences between the foreigners accorded special status in

Shrewsbury and their East Anglian counterparts. Ipswich did not create a special body for foreigners to join; the privileged status was granted either directly to individuals or through individuals who had no relationship with any of the other foreigners. Shrewsbury, on the other hand, created a special body, and individuals acquired their privileges as members of that special corporation. Nor did Shrewsbury concern itself with lordship; simple commercial involvement in the town determined the ranks of foreign members. These differences in structure are mirrored in the structure of the surviving records of membership. In Ipswich, the ad hoc grants of privilege were relatively limited in number and easily incorporated within a running list. In Shrewsbury, there were periodic sessions to admit and enumerate the membership, which resulted in a series of discrete lists amenable to analysis.

The key to understanding both the nature of these lists and the structure of the corporation is to recognize that a guild was considered to be an occasion as well as an organization. Approximately every 15 years in Shrewsbury—the precise interval varied—the entire body of the guild, natives as well as foreigners, convened to admit new members, update the membership lists, and conduct other business appropriate to such a gathering. The arrangement was similar to that adopted by the town of Preston, which also divided its members into natives and foreigners. Among the ordinances passed by Preston's guild in 1328 was a stipulation that the guild should be held every 20 years, or more often if need be, to confirm the charters and other privileges of the town.[24] There are no surviving lists of foreigners in Preston before the Plague (the earliest dates from 1397), but the practice was still being observed more than 400 years later.[25] In 1741, an official of the town described the guild as it then operated:

> There is and time out of mind hath been a Guild Merchant held every Twenty Years, in and for this Burrough. The Freemen or Burgesses are of two sorts, viz., the Foreign Burgesses and the Inn-Burgesses. The Foreign Burgesses are admitted at the Guild Merchant and at no other time; and they are exempt from payment of Toll for Goods that they buy in the Burrough for the use of themselves and their family.[26]

The description, which echoes the concern in Ipswich that trade in merchandise not be free from toll, goes on to add that the privileges of a foreigner did not extend into other realms of town life, such as holding municipal office or enjoying rights of common. Although there is no such explicit description of how Shrewsbury's guild conducted itself, internal evidence in the membership lists reveals that the town's guild was organized on similar principles.[27]

Prior to the Black Death, the Shrewsbury foreign guild met at least eight times: in 1209, 1232, 1252, 1268, 1281, 1304, 1319, and 1344. Internal evidence suggests that meetings were also held in 1220 and in either 1239 or

1242, but there are no extant membership lists from these other meetings. There are at least partial lists of members for all eight of the certain meetings of the foreigners before 1348; for five of the meetings (1209, 1232, 1252, 1268, and 1319) complete rosters of members exist. These five lists attest to rapid growth in the numbers of foreign guild members during the thirteenth century, particularly in the first half of the century. On the earliest membership list of 1209, there are 116 names; by 1232 the number had increased to 164, and by 1252 there were 312 members. Virtually all of the members in these and later lists were men.[28] The membership remained fairly stable during the next generation, with 321 foreigners attending the 1268 guild, but there was another substantial increase in the membership by 1319, when the foreign guild could boast of 456 members. In little more than a century, then, membership in the guild increased nearly fourfold.

TABLE 7-1:
Range of Shrewsbury Foreign Guild Members

Distance (miles)	**Identified Place Names**				
	1209	**1232**	**1252**	**1268**	**1319**
1-5	6 (29%)	14 (41%)	45 (40%)	39 (32%)	90 (31%)
6-10	5 (24%)	7 (21%)	23 (20%)	30 (25%)	56 (19%)
11-15	2 (10%)	1 (3%)	11 (10%)	18 (15%)	50 (17%)
16-20	2 (10%)	4 (12%)	10 (9%)	16 (13%)	35 (12%)
21-25	0 (0%)	1 (3%)	5 (4%)	3 (2%)	9 (3%)
26-30	2 (10%)	0 (0%)	0 (0%)	0 (0%)	6 (2%)
31-35	0 (0%)	3 (9%)	4 (4%)	4 (3%)	5 (2%)
36-40	0 (0%)	0 (0%)	0 (0%)	0 (0%)	5 (2%)
41-45	0 (0%)	0 (0%)	0 (0%)	0 (0%)	3 (1%)
46-50	3 (14%)	1 (3%)	6 (5%)	6 (5%)	8 (3%)
over 50	1 (5%)	3 (9%)	10 (9%)	5 (4%)	24 (8%)
Total Identified	21	34	114	121	291

NOTE: Percentages do not always total 100 because of rounding.
SOURCE: Transactions of the Shropshire Archaeological and Natural History Society.

The Shrewsbury lists do not intentionally identify the home communities of the foreigners joining the guild. A substantial proportion of the surnames occurring in these membership lists, however, are locative names. These occur both as simple locative names such as John de Ludlow and as compound locative names such as John Smith de Ludlow. There is a substantial body of evidence, both within the lists and in other records, to demonstrate that both forms of locative surname actually designate the home community of the individual acquiring foreign status.[29] In other words, the lists are a record of an ongoing relationship between individuals who retained their interests in their home community when they joined the guild; they are not simply a record of immigration into the town. Consequently, the surname evidence provided by the membership lists can be used to reconstruct in a very concrete fashion the spatial horizons of Shrewsbury's trading partners. Data yielded by an analysis of the home communities of the foreigners are presented in table 7-1, which records the distances that individuals traveled to acquire their status in the town.[30] These data are derived from all examples in the membership lists in which an individual is identified with a locative surname. In 1209, only about one out of five of the foreigners used a locative surname that can be confidently identified, but by 1319 the figure had risen to nearly two out of every three.

As the table illustrates, there is some increase over time in the range of members joining the guild. The data from 1209 and 1232 are based on a relatively small number of identifiable place names, a fact that probably explains why the 1209 data in particular deviate from the other data. Overall, the data show that Shrewsbury continued to forge new links with places in the immediate hinterland of the town throughout the thirteenth century, but they also show that links with more distant places, specifically places in the eleven-to-fifteen mile range, assumed greater relative importance in the town's trade as the century progressed. In addition, the data show some surprising consistency across the century. Most noticeable is how little change there was in the range of longer-distance members. With a dividing line for this group set arbitrarily at 20 miles, such members constituted 29 percent of all members in 1209, 24 percent in 1232, 22 percent in 1252, 14 percent in 1268, and 21 percent in 1319. Most likely, this is related to constraints in transportation, but it may also be related to the pull exerted by the other large towns of the West Midlands: 20 miles marks the approximate midpoint between Shrewsbury and several other important regional towns, notably Chester, Worcester, and Hereford.

II

Many of the names found in the Shrewsbury guild lists are based on occupational designations. It was common practice at the time, of course, for people to acquire their surnames from their occupations, and one finds many instances of this in the guild lists. In most of the Shrewsbury guild lists, as in most other prosopographical sources, occupation and location were competing wellsprings of surnames, precluding the possibility of making correlations between mobility and occupation. There is, however, one important exception to this rule among the Shrewsbury lists. In 1319, the scribes frequently recorded both an occupational and a locational designation for the members. Pooling the entries for these individuals allows unusually precise correlations to be established between mobility and occupation in a regional town of the early fourteenth century.

Information about occupation is presented in two different ways in the 1319 list. The first is the surname itself: Occupational surnames account for approximately one in ten (44 in total) of the names entered on the list. Almost three-quarters of these occupational names occur with the article 'le' as part of the name (such as Hugh le Chaluner de Ludlow), implying that the surname was truly occupational rather than simply inherited. The second, and more common, way that occupations are designated in the list is by a simple appositional description (such as John de Oswestry, tanner, or William Wakes de Astley, cook). Such designations, which do not seem to have served any administrative purpose, can only be described as extremely fortuitous for historians; they are given for 111 of the guild members. By combining the occupational surnames with these appositional designations, it is possible to establish occupations for a total of 155 of the members in 1319, or about one-third of all those who joined the guild in that year. Data derived from these occupational references are presented in table 7-2. In this table, specific occupations are grouped together into economic sectors, as in chapter 1.

TABLE 7-2:
Occupational Mobility of Shrewsbury Foreign Guild Members in 1319

Occupational Category	Number of Members	Number Localizable	Median Distance (miles)
Victualing	36 (23%)	20	9
Hide and Leather	28 (18%)	23	24
Mercantile	20 (13%)	14	17
Clergy	12 (8%)	9	7
Clothing/Textiles	10 (6%)	6	12/15
Building	6 (4%)	5	17
Servant	5 (3%)	0	n.a.
Other	38 (25%)	23	12
Total	155 (100%)	100	15

SOURCE: See Table 7-1.

As can be seen in the table, the victualing trades gave rise to the most numerous contingent of discernible tradesmen joining the guild, constituting slightly less than one-quarter of all members with designated occupations. Subsumed within this category are individuals designated as cooks (5 members), fishermen (6), bakers (17), taverners (3), butchers (4), and brewers (1). Given the importance of victualing in the economy as a whole and the reliance of large towns on food imports, it is not surprising that victualers took first rank as members of the guild. Bakers are particularly prominent in this contingent, a phenomenon that finds parallels in other large towns in this period. In Northampton in 1274, for example, bakers from more than two dozen surrounding villages agreed to pay an annual fee for access to the town's market.[31] Assuring a constant and reliable supply of foodstuffs was a universal concern of municipal authorities in this period, and the presence of so many victualers among the foreigners was probably regarded as a major benefit of the town's liberal guild policy.[32]

Individuals involved in the processing of hides and leather, who accounted for nearly one-fifth of all designated occupations in the list, formed the second largest contingent of members in the foreign guild. Eight discrete occupations are included in this category: tanners (16), glovers (1), saddlemakers (1), parchment makers (2), bagmakers (1), cordwainers (2), tawyers (1), and cobblers (4). Tanners were particularly prominent among those acquiring membership rights, nearly matching the number of bakers joining the guild. To some extent, this reflects the importance of the hide and leather industries in all large towns, a feature of economic life that is apparent in the urban employment data discussed in chapter 1. Shrewsbury was reputed to be one of the leading hide and leather centers of the thirteenth century, and areas of the town's hinterland were strongly oriented toward pastoralism.[33] The combination of these factors probably made it an exceptionally attractive market for tanners and other artisans with interests in the leather trades.

Mercantile occupations constituted the third largest contingent of distinguishable guild members in 1319. Particular occupations found within this group include mercers (12), spicers (3), merchants (1), mustarders (1), and chapmen (3). These were all peripatetic professions with goods that could bear transport costs with relative ease. Conspicuous by their absence from this list are woolmongers and vintners, two mercantile groups that one ordinarily finds involved in a major urban market. Considering the quality of the local wool and the importance of sheep in the region, the absence of woolmongers is especially problematic. Shrewsbury may have adopted a conscious policy of excluding wool merchants from the guild to limit competition in a particularly lucrative branch of trade. Such a policy had parallels in York, where the ruling families deliberately excluded weavers from entering the ranks of freemen.[34] Shrewsbury's wool merchants were a powerful group of national significance, and it may well be that they manipulated guild policy to protect their own narrow interests in the local market.[35]

A similar bias may also have been at work in grants of membership involving the clothing and textile trades, which were relatively poorly represented in the guild. Shrewsbury's local lay subsidy roll of 1306 records a number of assessments made on cloth, and though its wares were not well known in other parts of the country, the presence of a well-established textile industry in the town is suggested by several contemporary sources.[36] Nonetheless, only ten of the foreigners whose occupations can be determined worked in textile trades, considerably fewer than the number of members in victualing and leather trades. Seven of these ten were tailors, two were blanket-makers and one was a dyer. As with merchants, membership may have been denied to foreigners with interests in the most lucrative occupations in the textile trades.

The remaining categories in table 7-2 represent a diverse range of occupations that are not easily related to the leading economic interests of the town. Members of the clergy were surprisingly well represented among those with discernible occupations. There is no obvious explanation for the clergy's interest in acquiring guild membership; clerics could and often did participate in mundane economic endeavors, and these other interests were probably behind their decision to enter the guild. Six of the other members had interests in the building trades, four as carpenters, one as a lath-layer and one as a mason. Servants, like clerics, made up a group whose interests in the guild are not immediately evident from their assigned occupation. They were usually designated by their masters' names, and they may have had their names entered on the guild lists as proxies for their employers rather than in their own right. The 38 other members whose occupations can be established represent 23 different occupations, ranging from such common pursuits as smithery and milling to such uncommon ones as playing the crout, a musical instrument with a Welsh pedigree. Some of these professions were necessarily peripatetic, involving skills that were in limited demand in any single location. A large regional town was an attractive venue for individuals with such skills, offering longer and more consistent employment opportunities than were available in smaller centers.

The final two columns in table 7-2 record the numbers of individuals in each occupational category whose place of origin can be discovered and the median distance separating these places from Shrewsbury. As can be seen from the latter set of data, there is a substantial divergence in patterns of mobility from one occupational category to the next. Most of the victualers resided in places that were relatively close to the town, with the median for the group found at a distance of nine miles, a figure that corresponds with Derek Keene's findings for victualers involved in supplying Winchester and also Richard Britnell's findings for Colchester.[37] Bakers were particularly likely to hail from villages and liberties within a few miles of the town walls. In contrast to the victualers, tradesmen involved in the hide and leather industries hailed from places considerably farther away. The median distance traveled by hide and leather specialists to join the Shrewsbury foreign guild was 24 miles, beyond the range usually associated with the trade of an early-fourteenth-century provincial town but not out of line with the data derived from mercantile toll disputes presented in chapter 5. As noted above, Shrewsbury was known for its hides and leather, and its specialization probably made it a particularly attractive market for tanners and other leather craftsmen in the West

Midlands. Specialized markets inherently attract traders from larger catchment areas than unspecialized ones: An individual trader's willingness to travel is directly related to the rewards he or she expects to find at the end of the journey. To some extent, then, the mobility of the foreign tanners in Shrewsbury was unusual, predicated on the vitality of the town's concentration on a particular resource and industry. But Shrewsbury was only one among many regional towns, and its reputation as a specialized market had parallels in other places with other interests. We rarely see this relationship in other towns of similar stature, but this is due more to the vagaries of record survival than to the uniqueness of Shrewsbury's economy.

III

The presence of bakers, tailors, and carpenters in what is ostensibly the roster of a guild of merchants begs the question of how the commercial activity of this prominent regional town should be characterized. However broadly a "merchant" is defined in the context of foreign status, it is clear that members who might fit this description were distinctly in the minority. This is particularly relevant in light of the fact that those with stated occupations account for only one out of every three members in 1319. What about the others, those whose names were entered on the list without any clues about their occupation or commercial interests?

There are very few intimations in the guild lists to help answer this question. By process of elimination, however, some general observations can be made about the communities that fostered the foreigners. One certainty is that the majority of guild members were villagers from Shropshire. Of the 291 localizable members in 1319, 215—nearly three-quarters—came from within the county. Bridgnorth was the only one other full borough in the county, and, rather surprisingly, it was home to only two of the foreigners entering the guild. Seven other settlements had pretensions to borough status, but only one of these (Newport) was ever selected as a taxation or parliamentary borough.[38] These seven combined to account for 29 of the foreigners, a fairly significant concentration but one that still leaves the vast majority of the members unaccounted for. There were 43 other villages in the county that shared with Shrewsbury, Bridgnorth, and the seven quasi-boroughs the right to hold a market.[39] Only 16 of these settlements were represented in the guild membership, and these 16 were home to 27 of the foreigners in the guild. Combining all of the towns and market sites in Shropshire accounts for 58 of the foreigners in 1319, or about one of every four localizable members who resided in the county. To this group the foreigners who lived in Abbey Foregate and the other suburbs of the town, who made up 19 of the foreign members, should be added.[40] Thus, taking all of the towns, markets, and suburbs together accounts for 76 of the members from the county in 1319. This leaves

139 county residents still unaccounted for, members whose native communities can only be described as rural villages.

The presence of members of the gentry among the foreigners in the guild can be established with some certainty. Three members are explicitly named as lords: John, son of Thomas de Lee, lord of Berrington, Lord Roger Tromwine, and Lord Waterel. The location of Tromwine's and Waterel's estate is not recorded, and they may well have come from other counties. John de Lee, though, can be easily traced in Berrington's records.[41] A handful of other guild members can also be tied to the county's gentry families, though in most instances only by identifications involving simple locative surnames, such as Thomas de Cherrington and Thomas de Rosshall.[42] What proportion of the guild members in 1319 they constituted, however, can only be surmised. There were more than 500 manors in the county enumerated in Domesday, considerably more than the 139 foreigners in 1319 who were resident in villages in the county.[43] One's imagination would not have to stretch too much to visualize most of the guild members as coming from this class, but this is unlikely. By 1319 the familial names of gentry families had stabilized, and the familial names of men of this standing tend to be well represented in surviving sources. If most of the foreigners were drawn from the gentry of the county, we can reasonably expect to trace either the individuals or their families in the standard prosopographical sources of the period, especially since the toponyms in the guild list suggest where best to look. Manorial descents and genealogical synopses of the Shropshire gentry were painstakingly assembled by the remarkable nineteenth-century antiquarian, R. W. Eyton, whose 12-volume history of the county and its leading families is a model of its kind.[44] With monotonous regularity, the localizable foreigners fail to turn up in Eyton's accounts of their native villages. One would expect this to happen with social classes below the gentry, but one would not expect it at or above the level of families exercising even limited powers of lordship. Arguments from silence are never entirely satisfying, but they are nonetheless sometimes worth making.

By process of elimination, then, we can reasonably conclude that a significant number of the people who joined the foreigners' guild in 1319 were more humble residents of peasant villages. The membership of two individuals from the sleepy village of Cressage—John, son of Roger atte Cros, and Roger Crompe—provides a good case in point. Located on the Severn about eight miles southeast of Shrewsbury, Cressage was as typical a Shropshire village as one is likely to find.[45] It had a generous endowment of forest and its location along the Severn probably secured for it a healthy supply of meadow. The overlordship was vested in the earldom of Shrewsbury at the time of Domesday, passing to the earldom of March in the early fourteenth century and ultimately to the crown in 1461. Direct lordship also changed hands several times but was never divided, and in the twelfth century passed into the hands of the de Lacy family, who held a demesne of about 240 acres into the

1360s. Domesday Book shows the demesne being worked by 8 serfs, with 7 villeins, 11 bordars, and four cottars also dwelling on the manor. While more land was cleared at some point after the Domesday survey, there was only a small amount of freehold property in the village in later centuries, and there are no traces of freehold tenancies in the village, apart from a few smallholdings, until the sixteenth century. In the first half of the fourteenth century, the vast majority, possibly all, of the land in the village was in the hands of the de Lacys and their customary tenants. Like most villages in Shropshire, Cressage has no surviving manorial court rolls or full manorial extents to verify the tenurial situation and social position of the atte Cros and Crompe families, but there is nowhere else to look for them than among the ranks of the customary tenants of the manor.

IV

Shrewsbury's guild of foreigners was, in many respects, a mirror image of the town's native commercial population. Just as merchants and other traders from the town might travel across the country to trade in towns of comparable market influence elsewhere, residents of these other towns were active in Shrewsbury. Already in 1209, individuals from Hereford, Worcester, and Gloucester can be found in the membership lists. By 1252, there were a pair of merchants from London in the guild, along with others from Coventry, Bristol, Oxford, St. Albans, and York. In 1209, only a single member came from further than 50 miles away; by 1252 ten members fall into this category. But significant as Shrewsbury's long-distance trade connections might be as a sign of the sophistication of the town's commercial development, relations with these distant trading partners is not the best measure of the commercial changes occurring in this period. What stands out in the guild lists more than the membership of individuals from London and York is the predominance of members originating in the market centers and rural villages in the hinterland of the town. For regional towns like Shrewsbury, deepening the channels of trade with these nearer partners was of far greater consequence than building commercial links with regional hubs on the other side of the country.

The mercantile elites that governed towns like Ipswich and Shrewsbury had reservations about the wisdom of allowing outsiders to trade on their home turf, but in most cases their desire to augment the supply of rural commodities led them to accept what they saw as a necessary evil. In some ways, they had no choice. By the middle of the thirteenth century, the commercial opportunities inherent in the network of rural market sites had become sufficiently developed that no town could take for granted that the commodities produced nearby would automatically migrate into its own marketplace. Under these circumstances, neither town nor country could lay claim to the driver's seat. For rural producers, the attractions of highly concentrated urban demand had to be weighed against the restrictions imposed by guilds and mercantile oligarchies, and for the commercial classes in the town, the advantages of an augmented supply of commodities had to be weighed against the loss of control exercised over the market.

When their respective interests intersected, as they did in the institution of foreign guild membership, the results are a striking confirmation of the importance of regional trade for both parties. Ipswich's guild records reveal a regional market in which even lowly villeins could get involved in mercantile exchange. Shrewsbury's membership lists document a market that brought people together from a dozen different counties with a wide array of social and economic interests. Victuallers and artisans sat in the guild cheek-by-jowl with mercers and spicers; Londoners mingled with people from small rural marketplaces; and a cross-section of rural society, from the lords of manors down to peasant villagers, rubbed shoulders with the merchants of numerous regional towns. The foreign members took back with them to their towns and villages an intimate knowledge of the market prices and commercial practices of a regional hub, along with whatever goods they might have purchased from their fellows in the guild. They also imbibed a different way of looking at the world, developing the kind of human capital without which human society languishes. In the course of their buying and selling, and gossiping and feasting, they helped to establish the ever-deepening interdependency between town and country that was one of the principal achievements of the entire period.

Part 4

A Case Study: Huntingdonshire and its Environs

8

A Regional Market System

The county of Huntingdonshire offers several attractions as a case study of commercialization. In common with most areas of the Midland plain, the county was made up of nucleated villages nestled within a core of open fields, and its farming practices were similar to those found across the Midlands.[1] Village fields were devoted first and foremost to the production of grain, with wheat, barley, oats, and dredge (a mixture of oats and barley) constituting the principal cereal crops. Fields were generally sown in a three-course rotation, and sowing rates were relatively heavy, but the county's clay soils nonetheless managed to generate returns per seed that were a bit above average and returns per acre that compared favorably with all parts of England except the most fertile and intensively cropped. Sheep and cattle raising were also important pursuits, fostered by the fertility of the county's riverine meadows, and the plentiful supply of pasture in the fens in the eastern parts of the county. The fens, "such a country as a man would wish to see once for curiosity; but would never desire to visit a second time," created the most distinctive feature of the landscape and were a valuable local resource, exploited for fish, fowl, reeds and rushes, and especially for the peat used to ward off the chills of a fenland winter.[2] There were no major forested areas in the county, although there were dozens of *gravetta,* or small groves, sprinkled across the county, commonly owned by manorial lords but accessible to villagers and their pigs.[3] From this combination of arable, pasture, fen, and woodland, inhabitants of the county produced a level of wealth per square mile comparable to other parts of the East Midlands and East Anglia, with the wealthiest villages being situated along the routes of the two main rivers flowing through the county, the Ouse and the Nene.[4]

As in all parts of England, there was great diversity in the tenurial composition of local villages. Villages within the royal demesne, villages of fragmented lordship, and villages of ecclesiastical estates nestled cheek-by-jowl with each other. A few of the great secular baronies held manors in the county, but with the partitioning of the honor of Huntingdon in the 1230s, none of the baronies was based in the county, and their presence was relatively muted.[5] By contrast, the great ecclesiastical estates were deeply engrained in the county's soil. Pride of place went to Ramsey Abbey, lord or major proprietor in 22 villages.[6] Other ecclesiastical establishments well represented in Huntingdonshire included the abbeys of Peterborough, Thorney and Crowland, and the bishoprics of Lincoln and Ely. Partly because of its restricted area and partly because of the predominance of monastic estates, the county's contingent of knights and gentry landholders was relatively small. When Edward I called upon his knights to attend his daughter's wedding in Bristol in 1293, summons went out to only 18 men from Huntingdonshire.[7] Inquests connected with the same king's campaigns to distrain wealthy landholders to take up knighthood survive for two of the four hundreds of the county and record the names of 20 secular individuals with holdings worth £40 or more.[8]

As its estate structure implies, the county's land was largely in the hands of the peasantry. The dominance of large ecclesiastical estates, characterized by their early formation and inherently conservative management structures, gave the county a greater orientation toward villein tenure than most other parts of the country. E. A. Kosminsky found that nearly half of the land included in the detailed extents in the county's Hundred Rolls in 1279 was in the hands of villein tenants.[9] Virgates averaging about 30 acres were the largest villein holdings, but by the time of the Hundred Roll inquiries these were more likely to be found broken up into half-virgates and quarter-virgates. Possession of a full virgate was a sign of considerable wealth and status within a village. In some places, generally those held by secular lords, the virgate structure had largely broken down by the third quarter of the thirteenth century, and individual holdings were smaller and less uniform than on the more traditional ecclesiastical manors.[10] As a consequence of twelfth- and thirteenth-century population growth, all villages had substantial bodies of cotlanders and other smallholders, who eked out an existence from their garden plots and the wages earned as day laborers. Freehold tenures varied substantially from one village to the next, in some places accounting for almost all land in the village, while in others accounting for next to none. Across the county as a whole, freeholders made up a bit less than one-quarter of the recorded landholding population in 1279.[11] Very few freeholders were in possession of more than 30 acres, and the majority held fewer than 10 acres.

Urban life in the county was relatively limited. Huntingdon, the only place to send local representatives to Parliament, was the sole formal borough in the county. It ranked as one of the regional towns described in chapter 4, but it was one of the poorer members of the club. Apart from the market villages, which will be described below, only two other settlements in the county showed any distinctively urban characteristics: the self-governing semi-borough of Godmanchester, located across the river from Huntingdon, and the planted settlement of Holme, which had 18 burgage tenants in 1318 harbored within the much larger rural manor of Glatton.[12] Two major towns were located within easy reach in neighboring counties: Cambridge, situated about 10 miles from the southeastern border of the county, and Northampton, located about 20 miles from the northeastern border. Bedford was situated within 10 miles of the southwestern border of the county, but it was a relatively modest town, more like Huntingdon than either Cambridge or Northampton. The settlements that grew up in the shadow of the two great abbeys in or near the county—Ramsey and Peterborough—round out this overview of the urban geography of the area. Both might be described as small towns rather than villages, but in many respects they had more in common with the prosperous market villages of the region than with places like Huntingdon or Cambridge.

I

Evidence can be found for 18 different markets in the county established prior to 1348, as documented in Appendix 2. Combining all these places yields a density of one market for every 20 square miles by the early decades of the fourteenth century, a somewhat higher figure than the ones calculated for most other counties.[13] But this figure should be seen more as a theoretical maximum than as a practical reality. Knowledge of the location and foundation chronology of these markets derives chiefly from the testimony of market charters granted by the crown. Useful as this testimony is, it needs careful cross-examination. Charters say a good deal about a founder's hopes to create a profitable venture, but they are completely silent about whether or not the venture bore fruit. Many chartered markets, in fact, did not live up to their founder's hopes.[14] To examine the network of markets actually in use in the county we need to expand our investigation beyond the familiar boundaries of the charter evidence. An important first step in this regard is simply to determine whether all of the sites licensed to hold a market actually succeeded in establishing themselves as active trading ventures. If a significant number failed to do so, we might see the county's commercial network in a different way than we would if all chartered sites proved to be viable.

While the failure of a venture, unlike its founding, was seldom formally registered in official documents, the likelihood of failure can sometimes be established indirectly. In Huntingdonshire prior to 1348, two opportunities to observe the relationship between markets that failed and markets that managed to establish themselves as ongoing, functioning concerns present themselves. The first is provided by the claims for franchisal rights, which included the right to hold a market, submitted as part of the Quo Warranto investigations conducted in the reign of Edward I.[15] These Quo Warranto enquiries formed part of the king's policy of asserting royal authority by pruning back the proliferation of private rights and jurisdictions in the kingdom, including the rights inherent in the holding of markets and fairs. Franchise-holders typically laid claim to their privileges either by virtue of a royal charter or by virtue of long usage, referred to as holding by prescription—"the poetical word for cool, impudent presumption," according to Charles Bradlaugh, the MP who inspired a Royal Commission on market rights in the 1880s.[16] Theoretically, those who could neither proffer a charter nor prove long usage forfeited their franchise to the king, but in most cases they simply paid a fine for belated royal confirmation of their privileges. Pleas of Quo Warranto were ordinarily held as part of a general eyre, and in Huntingdonshire the most complete set of returns comes from the eyre of 1286.[17] By this time, ten markets had been founded. Claims for markets, though, were registered only in seven places in the county, to which the town of Huntingdon, whose franchisal right to hold a market was tacitly accepted by the justices, can be added. Thus, on the basis of this source, we can establish that two of the markets chartered before 1286 (in Somersham and Chesterton) failed to find a niche within the county's market system.

The second opportunity to identify markets that failed to live up to the expectations of their founders is provided by the fines imposed by the Clerk of the Market.[18] The Clerk of the Market was a royal official attached to the king's household who was responsible for regulating weights, measures, and certain commercial practices conducted within the "verge" of the royal household, defined as the space within 12 miles of the king's residence. Medieval kings moved about a great deal, and in some years virtually every part of the country became a temporary part of the verge and thus subject to the attention of the king's household officials. A number of rolls listing the fines imposed in the course of these itinerations survive in the Public Record Office, recording the names of the towns and markets visited by the Clerk.[19] Records of visits to Huntingdonshire survive for three years in the late 1320s and early 1330s and for three other years in the 1350s.[20] The number of markets paying a common fine in these visitations varied from year to year: In 1328 fines are recorded for seven markets; in 1331 for four markets; in 1332 for ten markets; in 1354 for five markets; in 1355 for four markets; in 1356 again for four markets. Data drawn from these visitations are presented in table 8-1.

As the data in table 8-1 reveal, none of the markets in the county was fined in every visitation of the Clerk. Five of the markets, though, were fined in at least four of the six visits: Huntingdon, Yaxley, St. Neots, Kimbolton, and Buckworth. With the possible exception of Buckworth, these were all prominent regional markets. Four other markets were visited on at least two occasions, and two of these—Ramsey and St. Ives—were also regionally important foundations. The infrequency of visits by the Clerk of the Market to Ramsey was probably due to the exceptional immunities the abbey enjoyed within its banlieu: In 1355, the king granted the abbey any amercements the Clerk might make within the monastery's banlieu, which explains why Ramsey's market was omitted in the last two visitations noted in table 8-1.[21]

TABLE 8-1:
Huntingdonshire Markets Fined by the Clerk of the Market, 1328–1356

Market	**1328**	**1331**	**1332**	**1354**	**1355**	**1356**
Huntingdon	yes	yes	yes	yes	no	no
Yaxley	yes	yes	yes	yes	yes	no
St. Neots	yes	no	yes	yes	yes	yes
Kimbolton	yes	no	yes	no	yes	yes
Buckworth	yes	no	yes	yes	yes	yes
Gt. Gidding	yes	yes	yes	no	no	no
Alconbury W.	yes	no	yes	no	no	yes
Ramsey	no	no	yes	yes	no	no
St. Ives	no	yes	yes	no	no	no
Fenstanton	no	no	yes	no	no	no
Alwalton	no	no	no	no	no	no
Holme	no	no	no	no	no	no
Woodston	no	no	no	no	no	no
Chesterton	no	no	no	no	no	no
Somersham	no	no	no	no	no	no
Earith	no	no	no	no	no	no
Keyston	n.a.	n.a	n.a	no	no	no
Everton	no	no	no	no	no	no

SOURCES: PRO E101/256/6; PRO E101/256/9; PRO E101/256/14.

The omission of St. Ives in four of the six visitations is more difficult to explain. Although its weekly market was slow getting off the ground, by the time the Clerk of the Market made his rounds it had become an important trading site in the county, as is apparent from its inclusion in the Nonae Rolls as a village with a resident merchant population.[22] Possibly, the Abbot of Ramsey, the holder of the market rights, managed to secure exemption from some of the later visitations, although it seems unlikely that St. Ives would have enjoyed such a privilege in 1354 when the market in Ramsey did not. In any event, its considerable wealth and resident commercial population suggest that it too acquired a regional status, though its prominence is not as transparent as is that of the county's other leading markets.

The same cannot be said, however, about the other two sites that were visited on at least two separate occasions, Alconbury Weston and Great Gidding. Both were founded early in the fourteenth century, and their appearance among the markets paying fines in the 1330s is confirmation that they managed to establish themselves as functioning trading venues. Although Alconbury Weston was still worth noticing when the Clerk of the Market made his rounds in the 1350s, Great Gidding was not, and neither of them was destined to survive into the sixteenth century. Fen Stanton was likewise a market with a limited lifespan. It was chartered in 1315 and visited by the Clerk of the Market in 1332, indicating that it did at least get off the ground, but it did not occur in any of the visitations of the 1350s and had ceased to operate by the sixteenth century, possibly even by the 1350s. The poorly documented market in Holme was never visited by the Clerk, although it may have been given special treatment because its rights belonged directly to the king.[23] It, too, was moribund by the sixteenth century, and it is unlikely ever to have been a prominent commercial center.

In an analysis of the county's marketing grid, places that failed to pay any fines to the Clerk of the Market are as worthy of notice as those that did. A number of the markets founded well before the Clerk made his rounds of the county failed to attract any notice at all. Somersham and Chesterton were already moribund by 1286, and the Quo Warranto evidence of their failure is corroborated by the lack of Clerk's fines. Along with the two early failures, two other markets claimed in 1286, Alwalton and Woodston, failed to make an appearance in any of the records produced by the Clerk of the Market. Both were founded in 1268, and although they apparently managed to survive for a generation or two, both had failed by the 1330s. The list of unsuccessful ventures needs to be further extended to include two markets chartered in the early fourteenth century (Everton in 1307 and Earith in 1318). As the lists of fines indicate, neither of these places fulfilled the hopes of their founders. The same can also be said for an even later attempt made in Keyston in 1341, which did not leave an imprint in the Clerk's visits in the following decade.

All told, then, seven of the eighteen attempts to found markets prior to 1348 proved to be unsuccessful over the longer haul, and at least two others (Fen Stanton and Holme) were shadowy at best. These data, which are in line with recent findings made in other parts of the country, indicate the presence of an ongoing core of markets in the county in place by the early thirteenth century and continuing on into later centuries.[24] They also suggest a companion process by which the enduring markets were supplemented at various times by more tenuous establishments that sought but almost invariably failed to fit into the core structure. These lesser markets were seldom more than peripheral forces in regional commercial activity, and they typically fizzled out within a generation or two of their foundations, giving way to other ventures of similar ilk with a similar fate in store.

The inability of these peripheral creations to fulfill their founder's ambitions is further borne out by other types of evidence. The level of prosperity attained by the host settlement is an obvious measure of the success or failure of a particular market. Successful markets were typically situated in communities that were relatively wealthy according to the standards of the region, whereas unsuccessful ones were often (though not always) associated with places that had more modest levels of wealth. In Huntingdonshire, this was certainly the case. Lay subsidy records reveal that successful market sites had much higher assessments than nonmarket villages in the county, and they also reveal that the sites of failed markets held taxable wealth below the county average.[25] In fact, the taxable wealth in the 1334 lay subsidy of the nine villages that drew the attention of the Clerk of the Market in 1332 was about £150 per community, nearly twice that of the county average. In contrast, the five markets that were chartered at some point prior to 1332 but which did not draw the attention of the Clerk as he traveled through the county had an average wealth of only £56, well below the county average and barely above one-third that of the successful markets. It is impossible to identify the extent to which any given market contributed to the overall prosperity of a particular settlement, but it is clear that the two were related. Markets tended to succeed when established in wealthier settlements, and, conversely, wealth tended to accumulate in sites that had successful markets.

Further corroboration of the divergent paths followed by different market sites in Huntingdonshire is supplied by the physical evidence of village morphology. Throughout most parts of England, the perduring topography of local settlements, particularly urban and quasi-urban settlements, was firmly in place by about 1300. By that time, enough houses had been built in stone, even in peasant villages, that the core housing stock could not be easily restructured, and the basic pattern of local streets and interconnecting roads was likewise firmly in place.[26] As a community's internal space took on the forms desired by local inhabitants and allowed by vested interests, successful marketplaces had an incontestable claim to special attention and care.

In Huntingdonshire, a county that was largely bypassed by the Industrial Revolution and one that has even managed thus far to escape most of late twentieth-century suburbanization, it is still possible to visualize the spatial imprint successful markets made in their first centuries of existence. In Huntingdon borough, for example, Market Hill, an open space of about 500 square feet located in the heart of the town along High Street, bears witness to a market that predates the Normans.[27] The High Street in Kimbolton, one of the county's early and lasting markets, enters the settlement as a regular road, then expands to a width of about 30 yards for a length of about 150 yards (giving it a potential market area of 4,500 square yards) before reverting back to regular width.[28] Ramsey's marketplace has been built over, but it formerly occupied the space between High Street and Little Whyte, a space of roughly 2,000 square yards.[29] The best example of the physical stamp a successful market could make on a village's layout occurs in St. Neots, whose market was founded by the local priory early in the twelfth century. Showing exemplary foresight, the prior, the sole lord of the settlement, laid out Market Square at the western end of the town, abutting the River Ouse, along which many of the commodities traded in the market would travel. To the west of the marketplace lay a bridge that linked the market site with the road leading to Bedford. The High Street led out of the market on the east, joining Cambridge Street at its intersection with Huntingdon Street.[30] The marketplace originally comprised about 10,500 square yards and still contains about 7,500 square yards, making it one of the largest market squares in all of England.[31] Map 8-1 offers a sketch drawing of the layout of the settlement.

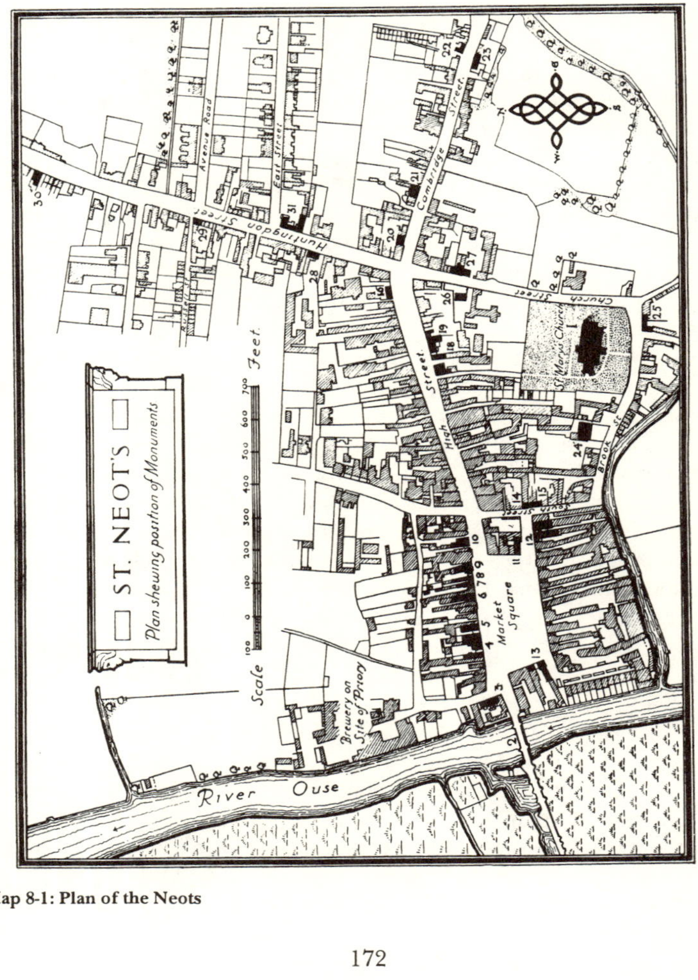

Map 8-1: Plan of the Neots

St. Neots had a particularly successful market, with all the attributes one expects of such sites: early foundation date, survival into later centuries, and high lay subsidy assessments. As with the other successful markets in Huntingdonshire, its market left a topographical imprint that can still be read nearly 900 years after its creation. The same cannot be said for the peripheral or failed markets in the county. As every lawyer knows, it is difficult to prove a negative; as every historian knows, it is even more difficult to prove a negative embedded many centuries in the past. What can be said with certainty in this instance is that none of the unsuccessful market sites left imprints on local land use patterns that can be discerned in the twentieth century; the kinds of morphological formations evident in the sites of successful markets do not find parallels in other settlements in the county. Every village had communal open spaces: churchyards, greens, and the interstices created by a haphazard arrangement of property lots. Successful market sites had their share of these lesser spaces, but they also had larger areas reserved for the weekly market; sites of marginal or failed markets did not.

II

As discussed in chapter 3, the goal of founders of new markets in this period was to secure a niche in existing patterns of regional trade. As numerous studies of nonindustrial marketing systems have shown, the temporal and geographical relationships among individual market sites are crucial variables in the integration of local economies into larger economic systems.[32] A well-integrated regional system features markets located and conducted in such a way as to facilitate the movement of goods and people from one market to the next, with the two main variables determining the level of integration being the spatial and temporal relationships between markets potentially or actually within the same marketing system. Certain relationships advance the integration of individual markets into regional systems; other relationships consign markets to operating in virtual isolation from each other. If all the markets in an area are held on the same day, for example (as is generally true of the lower-order markets of contemporary highland Ecuador, where more than 70 percent of rural markets are held on Sunday), then there is obviously little chance that an individual market will find a role as part of a larger integrated system.[33] If, on the other hand, there is a meaningful sequence to market periodicity that takes account of the spatial relationship between individual markets, then it is likely that the markets will integrate themselves into larger regional systems. As the commercial orientation of a region increases, new marketing venues will be created to fill the temporal and locational spaces between preexisting markets. Propitious spacing and timing of markets do not by themselves ensure that a region's markets will coalesce into an integrated system, but they certainly lend themselves to it.

The attempt to relate the marketing system of medieval England to those found in other pre- or nonindustrialized economies has long been bedeviled by the difficulty in separating important regional markets from marginal or nonfunctioning chartered markets. Several previous studies of markets in medieval England have, in fact, questioned the existence of a meaningful pattern in the temporal arrangement of markets. The market cycle in Buckinghamshire, for example, has been described as "very nebulous" in the south of the county and nonexistent in the north.[34] That of Oxfordshire is said to conform "to some extent" to a discernible pattern, but only in the relation of Oxford to other markets, not in the relations between local markets themselves.[35] The most thorough analysis of the temporal and spatial patterning of a county market system is Tim Unwin's study of the markets of Nottinghamshire.[36] Unwin identified four distinct groupings of markets in the county and suggested a possible fifth, although his conclusions were couched in tentative terms, and he took pains to draw attention to anomalies that could not be explained. Judging from previous work on the subject, one would have to conclude that while there was some contact between traders dwelling in different commercial sites, there was little in the way of a broader systematic structure to facilitate the integration of rural markets into larger commercial systems. None of these studies, though, has attempted to discriminate between successful and failed markets, let alone between important regional markets and marginal local ones. Previous studies of markets have invariably assumed that all the markets for which charter or other evidence exists have somehow to be fit within the particular regional commercial system. Inevitably, this has led historians to conclude that regional commercial systems were haphazard affairs, more likely to be ignored than observed by both the founders of markets and the people who made use of them.

The evidence for the founding of markets in Huntingdonshire reveals how readily the configuration of a regional system can be distorted by treating all markets culled from available sources as equally important commercial venues. Looking at the complete harvest of Huntingdonshire markets documented in official sources prior to 1348, one is hard pressed to discern any structured relationship between the different markets in the county.[37] Map 8-2 presents graphically the location and timing of markets in the county predicated on the assumption that all markets documented in sources prior to 1348 were successful ventures. If, however, one removes those markets which did not succeed, as documented in the Quo Warranto inquiries and the records of the Clerk of the Market or physical presence in village layout, the picture is quite different. Maps 8-3 and 8-4 show just how substantial the difference is. Map 8-3 documents the location and timing of markets functioning in the county as recorded in the Quo Warranto inquiries in 1286 and map 8-4 the markets listed in the records of the Clerk of the Market in his most thorough visitation of the county in 1332.

On these maps, a refinement of the distinction between successful and failed markets is introduced. Failed markets were obviously insignificant in the development of regional commercial systems, but even markets that endured for several generations sometimes remained in the shadows cast by their better favored peers. Unfortunately, there is no simple way to distinguish categorically between the two, but it is possible to develop some criteria that are at least suggestive of a market's importance relative to its peers. Two such criteria—frequency of notice by the Clerk of the Market and level of taxable wealth—have already been discussed. Two other criteria that lend themselves to comparison are related to the longevity of commercial activity. The first is the date of foundation: The earlier it was founded, the more likely a market was to become prominent in regional commerce. Throughout the country, markets founded before 1200 were very likely to have enjoyed prominence, while those founded after 1250 were very unlikely to have done so. Between those two dates, the likelihood of significant success declined with each passing decade. The second criterion related to longevity is the long term viability of the venue. Because they were hardier to begin with, markets that had acquired regional prominence before the Black Death ordinarily fared better than their less well articulated counterparts in the depopulated and dislocated economy of the later Middle Ages. Thus, for analytical purposes, survival into the early modern period can be used as another surrogate measure of the relative importance of a particular market.

In addition to the county town, five of Huntingdonshire's markets merit attention as venues enjoying special prominence: Yaxley, Kimbolton, St. Neots, Ramsey and St. Ives. All had high lay subsidy assessments, all survived into the early modern period, and all except St. Ives had been founded by 1200. (St. Ives' unusual status will be discussed later in the chapter.) This group is depicted on the maps in uppercase type. Markets that did not share these attributes are depicted in lowercase type. A few of them had high subsidy assessments, but none survived into the early modern period, none except Somersham was an early foundation (and it died an early death), and none except Buckworth was fined consistently by the Clerk of the Market. As with the distinction between functioning and non-functioning markets, the distinction between prominent markets (or core markets as they will be called in the remainder of this chapter) and less prominent markets (called local markets henceforth) is designed to clarify the actual working structure of the county's commercial network.

Unlike map 8-2, with its seemingly random hodgepodge of all possible market sites in Huntingdonshire, the arrangement of markets in 1286 presents little difficulty in finding a single marketing cycle that covered most of the county. On two days of the week, there was only a single market held in the county, in Buckworth on Tuesdays, and in the county town on Saturdays. As in all parts of the country, no markets were held on Sundays following the Church's campaign in the early thirteenth century to ban Sunday trading.[38]

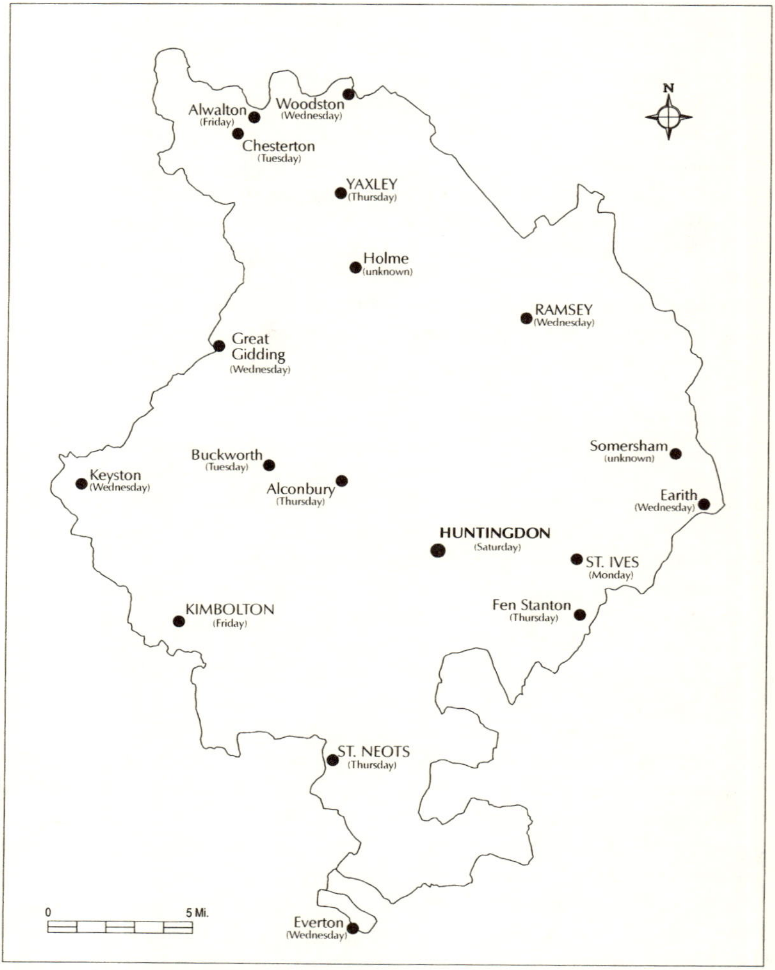

Map 8-2: Markets in Huntingdonshire chartered or claimed prior to 1348

Nor were any markets held on Mondays, an anomaly that was removed within a few years of the Quo Warranto proceedings by the founding of a weekly market in St. Ives on that day. On the other three days of the week, there were potentially two markets functioning on the same day, although only one of these was likely to have caused any difficult decisions for regional traders interested in following a cycle of markets in the county. Two of the conflicts involve markets located at the extreme northern end of the county (Alwalton and Woodston). Even if they had been important markets, the venues with

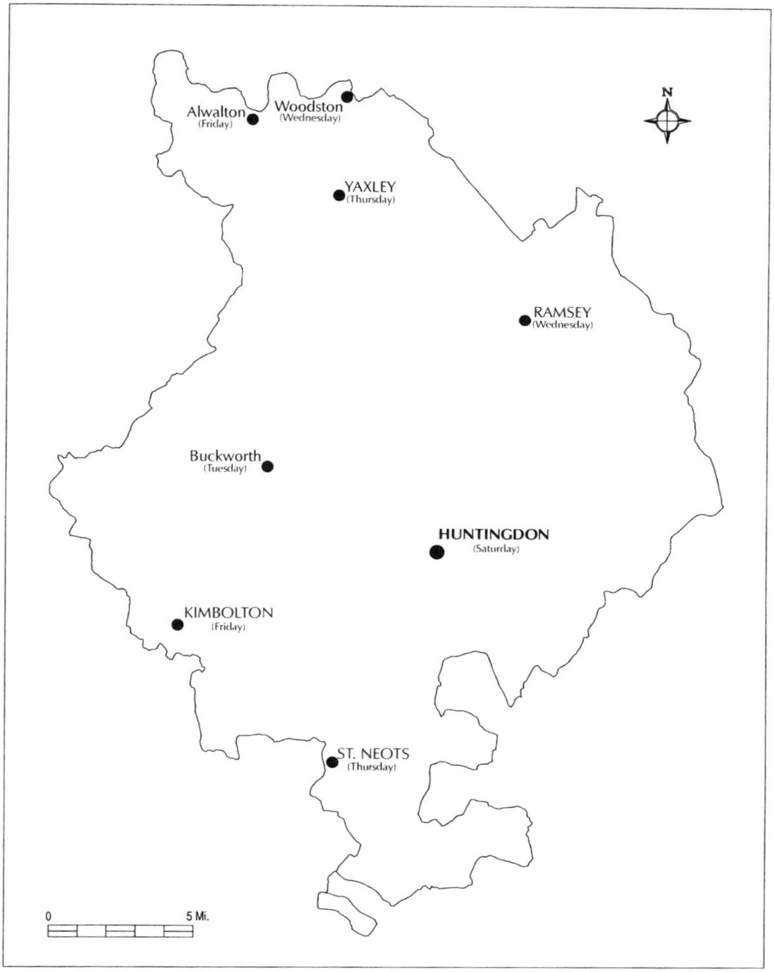

Map 8-3: Markets functioning in Huntingdonshire in 1286

which they conflicted were better situated to form part of an internal marketing cycle based on the county town. The fact that both had disappeared by the time the Clerk of the Market visited the county suggests that neither achieved noteworthy success during its life. Unlike their competitors, the markets in Ramsey and Kimbolton were both core sites, and there is little doubt that these two were integral parts of the county's marketing system.

Accepting Ramsey's as the principal Wednesday market and Kimbolton's as the principal Friday market in the county leaves us with only one certain

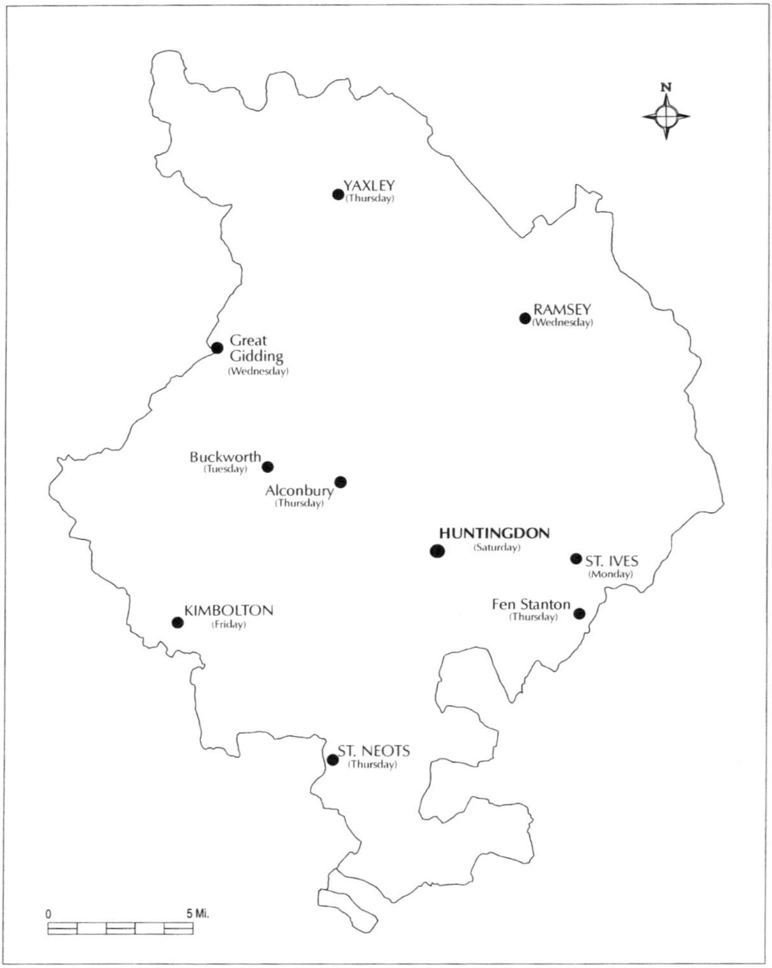

Map 8-4: Markets functioning in Huntingdonshire in 1332

example of conflict in the county, between the markets in Yaxley and St. Neots, both held on Thursdays. As will be developed further below, both were transitional markets between the network based in Huntingdonshire and networks based in neighboring counties, but their conflict appears to have been irreconcilable. The exception should not, however, define the rule: Apart from the Thursday conflict, the weekly cycle presented by the markets functioning in the third quarter of the thirteenth century is remarkably well-suited to operating as a regional network. A merchant in the county town, for example, could have followed a cycle which took him or her to Buckworth on Tuesday, to Ramsey on Wednesday, to Yaxley or St. Neots on Thursday, and to Kimbolton on Friday, returning to Huntingdon each day and never having to travel more than about 18 miles in one day. The pattern was similarly advantageous for those wishing to market agricultural produce from a village.

The fundamental constituents of the network apparent in 1286 were still in place in 1332 when the Clerk of the Market visited the county. By that time, the conflicting markets in Woodston and Alwalton had disappeared, and the Monday slot had been taken by the Abbot of Ramsey for his market in St. Ives, making for a complete cycle through the week. Three more markets had also been established, a Wednesday market in Great Gidding and Thursday markets in Alconbury and Fen Stanton. All of these were in direct conflict with core markets in the county. Of the three, the Wednesday market in Great Gidding seems to have had the greatest chance of survival. It conflicted with the market in Ramsey, but was located on the other side of the county. Ramsey's market was somewhat isolated from the rest of the county by inhospitable surrounding terrain, and a rival venue probably had a legitimate chance of success. The Thursday markets in Fen Stanton and Alconbury, though, seem to have been too poorly established to develop into regional trading sites. The region's Thursday slot was already double-booked with two core markets, and the prospects for newcomers to find a niche in this slot must have been very slight. Why they were founded in the first place is a difficult question to answer. Both places were large and wealthy manors, and it is possible that their owners hoped that their size and wealth might make them effective competitors of the established markets. If so, the owners must have been disappointed because neither ever became anything more than an outlet for local trade, as their repeated neglect by the Clerk of the Market in his other visitations suggests.

The evidence derived from the location and timing of functioning markets in Huntingdonshire suggests that most of the county participated in a single regional constellation of markets based on the county town. This constellation covered an area of about 200 square miles, with individual nodes situated between 5 and 10 miles of each other, and with all nodes located within 15 miles of the central hub of the system. Central-place theory holds that the best-integrated market systems consist of interlocking series of hexagonal lattices with a core market at the center of the lattice and intermediate markets at each of the points of the hexagon.[39] While the constellation formed by the principal markets of Huntingdonshire does not fully meet the geographer's geometric ideal, its basic configuration does show a number of characteristics that are typically associated with the mature market systems of other societies. In theory, at least, the markets of Huntingdonshire were well suited to operate as one of the basic cells constituting the honeycomb of inland trading networks.

III

In an integrated market system, each market functions as part of several adjoining constellations, just as each vertex of a honeycomb forms part of several adjacent cells. Thus, in order to see more clearly where the boundaries of Huntingdonshire's regional market network were situated, we need to visualize how the network's nodes fit into surrounding constellations. Huntingdonshire is surrounded by three counties, Bedfordshire to the south, Northamptonshire to the west and north, and Cambridgeshire to the east. The medieval markets in two of these counties (Northamptonshire and Bedfordshire) have been the subject of modern study, while their counterparts in Cambridgeshire were investigated by a pair of nineteenth-century antiquarians.[40] None of these studies has attempted to discriminate systematically between different levels of markets, but it is possible to do so with the same methods and sources used to differentiate the markets in Huntingdonshire. Map 8-5 depicts graphically the results of such an inquiry, recording the location and timing of markets founded in the four counties by 1250. These markets are divided into two types: core or regional markets, represented by bold, uppercase type, and intermediate or local markets, represented by lowercase type. The rationale for making this division is similar to that outlined for Huntingdonshire: To qualify for the former category, a market had to show two of the essential traits associated with such markets in Huntingdonshire—survival into later centuries and exceptionally high lay subsidy assessments, defined here as more than 50 percent higher than the other settlements in their hundred in the 1334 subsidy.[41]

In each county in the middle of the thirteenth century there is a consistent pattern in the relationship between the county town and surrounding rural markets, featuring a dearth of markets situated within a radius of between eight and ten miles of the towns. In Huntingdonshire, this meant that most rural markets were situated near the county borders. But the evidence derived from neighboring counties suggests that this overlap between commercial and administrative boundaries was essentially coincidental: In all counties in this part of England, structural economic forces rewarded markets situated eight to ten miles from a primary regional center; in Huntingdonshire, this distance from the county town just so happened to correspond with the location of the county's borders. Political factors may well have played a role in shaping the commercial geography of the period. There is little doubt that towns perceived other nearby markets primarily as threats rather than opportunities and that the monopoly they enjoyed in their immediate hinterlands was due at least in part to their political clout.[42] But the exclusion of markets within these zones was probably principally rooted in more mundane commercial forces: The attraction of a large urban market may well have been so great that smaller proximate markets simply could not compete as trading venues. These exclusionary zones probably mark the limits of simple agrarian marketing, as they would continue to do for many centuries to come.

Map 8-5: Markets founded in four counties prior to 1250

Marketing in these county towns was also alike in that markets met on Saturdays, a marketing rhythm that persists in our own malls and Main Streets. (The markets in three of the four county towns certainly met on Saturday, and the fourth probably did.)[43] This correlation between Saturday markets and county towns can be observed in some other counties as well and suggests that such markets typically served as the anchors around which other markets revolved.[44] This in turn suggests that Saturday markets may well indicate the central focal points of neighboring market networks and that even when held outside the county towns they had a special role to play. In the four counties considered here, for example, Saturday markets were held in five places other than the county towns. Of these other places, four were particularly prosperous and successful market centers: Peterborough, Oundle, and Rothwell in Northamptonshire, and Dunstable in Bedfordshire. Only Potton failed to establish itself as a core market, although one can readily understand the attempt to found a Saturday market midway between Bedford and Cambridge. Two other candidates—Ely and Wisbech in Cambridgeshire, both with unknown medieval market days but with Saturday markets documented in later centuries—probably deserve to be fit into this pattern as well. The inclusion of the Saturday markets held outside the county towns yields a noteworthy pattern. Looking from the perspective of Huntingdon, and accepting Bedford and Ely as Saturday markets, one can find five prominent and approximately equidistant Saturday markets—Cambridge, Ely, Peterborough, Oundle, and Bedford—located within 15 to 20 miles of the town. Each of these sites almost certainly served as the anchor of a local marketing network, the basic building blocks of inland trade in the period.

Other patterns discernible by 1250 provide the flip side to the pattern of county towns and Saturday markets. Competing with the anchor markets was a recipe for failure, and consequently the holders of other markets sought room for their ventures within the parameters defined by their anchors. As a result, there was a certain crowding of markets situated on the peripheries of the exclusionary zones surrounding the principal market sites. Within these crowds, however, it is possible to detect patterns consistent with a strategy of finding niches within a marketing cycle. Markets held on the same day of the week tend to be located on opposite sides of their Saturday markets. In Huntingdonshire, the Thursday markets of Yaxley and St. Neots form such a pair; in Cambridgeshire, the Tuesday markets of Linton and Swavesey; in Northamptonshire, the Wednesday markets of Wellingborough and Brackley; in Bedfordshire, the Thursday market in Toddington finds its partner in St. Neots in Huntingdonshire. While there are other pairings involving smaller markets, all of those just cited involve core markets. Part of this can be attributed to the desire to position these markets both geographically and temporally at the midpoints between the Saturday markets: Holders of core markets anticipated workers in industrial societies by avoiding activity on Mondays and Fridays. Only two of the markets depicted on map 8-5 met on Mondays, one of which (Rothwell) also met on Saturdays, and only one met on Fridays; by contrast, there were three markets that met on Thursdays and four each that met on Tuesdays and Wednesdays. Only a conscious policy of holding markets at or near the midpoints of the region's main markets would produce such results. Midweek markets maximize the opportunities to service accumulated demand in a system in which the weekend serves as the primary release of demand. Such markets are held long enough after the primary market that demand has begun to return, but long enough before the primary market that consumers have several days to wait before the next session of the primary market.

By about 1220, both the Saturday and the coveted midweek spots had largely been sewn up, leaving markets founded after that date to fill the increasingly scarce niches left in the weekly cycles. The timing of local markets is, consequently, almost the mirror image of the core markets. Wednesday was the least popular day for such markets in the four counties, being chosen by only two founders between 1220 and 1250, whereas Mondays, Tuesdays and Fridays were the most popular, with five markets meeting on each of these days. Latecomers had to make the most of the opportunities available to them, and it made more sense to try to fill the temporal space between the core markets than it did to compete with them, even if this meant meeting on a less desirable day in terms of the regional cycle. Temporal and spatial niches were still available to complete more localized marketing cycles, but even these were well on their way to reaching saturation point.

Freezing the picture of markets operating in the four counties in 1250 shows a number of interlocking systems similar to the one suggested for Huntingdonshire. A cycle based on Cambridge, for example, included the Monday-Tuesday pairs of Caxton and Swavesey to the northwest and Balsham and Linton to the southeast, with Thursdays being spoken for in Ickleton, and possibly St. Neots in Huntingdonshire. Wednesdays and Fridays were still open, although the market in Fowlmere, whose market day is not recorded in surviving sources, probably met on one of those two days, most likely on Wednesday, if the founder of the market had any wisdom. Similar networks can be detected surrounding Oundle, Bedford, Dunstable, Rothwell, and Northampton. Peterborough probably anchored another network, although only its southern portion can be seen in the counties depicted on map 8-5. Each of these hypothetical cycles constituted a marketing system stretching about 20 miles from one end to the other, or about the same distance as separated one regional town from the next across the Midland plain, as documented in chapter 4.

Like urban contacts, none of the rural marketing networks was hermetically sealed from neighboring networks. In addition to securing a median temporal position relative to the anchor markets, most other core markets also found themselves with a median geographical position, literally occupying the middle ground between anchors. Yaxley, for example, was an important player in at least three cycles, being situated between anchor markets in Peterborough, Oundle, and Huntingdon. The St. Neots market was likewise situated near the middle of a triangle comprised by Huntingdon, Bedford, and Cambridge. The desire to find this middle ground undoubtedly explains the seeming conflict between the pairs mentioned above, in which core markets on opposite sides of an anchor market met on the same day. Yaxley and St. Neots, for example, inevitably competed to some extent for the loyalty of the traders in their shared county town, but this competition was probably considered to be sustainable for the sake of securing a prominent niche at the mediate point between other anchor markets. Similar comments can be made about the core markets in Swavesey and Wellingborough and, extending the analysis into neighboring counties, probably also about Linton, Daventry, Brackley, and Towcester.

IV

As the preceding analysis suggests, markets in the four counties were already plentiful enough by 1250 that the founder of a new site had to give careful thought to preexisting patterns of trade when selecting a day for trading. The core markets were firmly ensconced in the favored slots in regional cycles, and many of the lower-order niches had already been taken as well. Nonetheless, the following couple of generations saw the height of the craze for founding new markets, in these counties as elsewhere.[45] How consciously, and how successfully, did these later founders manage to integrate their creations into preexisting marketing cycles? To answer this question requires a look at the data presented on map 8-6, which depicts the location and timing of all markets founded by the early 1330s that appear in Quo Warranto pleas and in the records of fines imposed by the Clerk of the Market. By that time, the enthusiasm for founding markets had almost vanished, and with good reason, since the four counties had become thoroughly saturated with markets, as can be readily seen on the map.[46]

Map 8-6 maintains the distinctions between core and local markets used on map 8-5. As on map 8-5, core markets appear on the map in bold uppercase letters, while local markets appear in plain lowercase letters. Unlike its earlier template, though, map 8-6 distinguishes between two types of local markets: those whose existence can be verified from Quo Warranto pleas and Clerk of the Market records and those that were either moribund or so marginal as not to find record in either source.[47] Moribund markets are depicted on the map with unshaded circles. These distinctions help to isolate at least some of the thinking behind the plethora of new markets founded in the interval between map 8-5 and map 8-6 and some of the reasons for their viability.

As the map illustrates, the only market founded after 1250 in these counties that meets the requirements for a core market—high subsidy assessment and ongoing activity in later centuries—was St. Ives in Huntingdonshire, founded by the Abbot of Ramsey in 1292.[48] Considering the number of markets that were chartered earlier in the century, it may seem odd that such a likely candidate for a weekly market was overlooked for so long. Its tardiness was, however, not due to want of effort: The Abbot of Ramsey had attempted

Map 8-6: Markets founded in four counties prior to 1330

to found a market there well before 1292 but ran into a legal quagmire in obtaining a franchise, a situation that will be described more fully in chapter 10. Apart from St. Ives, none of the other markets founded in this period enjoyed much success. The vast majority failed to survive into later centuries and of the handful that did manage to survive, none achieved notable prosperity in its early days. Even surviving into the 1330s was problematic for many of the markets. In Bedfordshire, two markets founded before 1250 had failed by the

1330s, as had two of the markets founded in the first part of the fourteenth century, leaving 16 successful ventures, 11 of which were founded before 1250. In Northamptonshire, more than a third of all the markets founded in the county had failed by the 1330s, including six founded before and nine founded after the middle of the thirteenth century. Cambridgeshire's markets fared even worse than those in Northamptonshire, with 11 of 26 failing at some point prior to the 1330s, all of which were founded after 1250. Of 55 new markets founded in the four counties between 1250 and the early 1330s, only about half (29 in total) managed to keep their heads above water until the latter date.

Why were so many new ventures attempted? One explanation is that market charters were given out on easier terms after mid-century than in preceding decades.[49] Even so, however, founders still had to give serious thought to how they wanted to take advantage of the king's largess. The strategic options open to the founders of new markets after 1250 were greatly limited by the existence of a large and ever-growing cohort of previously established markets. Since most days of the week were already spoken for, there was less virgin territory left to be exploited than there had been for the founders of markets before 1250. Thus, new markets in these counties were spread fairly evenly throughout the week, ranging from 9 new foundations held on both Tuesdays and Wednesdays to 13 on Thursdays. The one exception to this pattern of dispersion was the policy of avoiding competition with anchor markets: Saturdays were eschewed by all but two founders. Understandably, if a founder had to choose a day that was already taken by one or more other markets, he or she preferred to choose one belonging to a lower-order market than to an anchor market.

On other days of the week, competition was unavoidable. There is, however, some evidence in the patterns found on map 8-6 to suggest that holders were mindful of the extent of same-day competition in the region. There was, for example, a particularly dense concentration of Wednesday markets by 1250 in eastern Northamptonshire, including Northampton itself and the core markets in Wellingborough, Daventry, and Brackley. By 1330, however, only one of the new Wednesday markets founded in the four counties (Yardley Hastings) ventured near this saturated zone. By contrast, the most highly saturated area of Thursday markets in 1250 was around the town of Bedford, with two core markets and two local markets in existence. By 1330, no one had thought it wise to attempt another Thursday market there, even though new Thursday markets were fairly plentiful in other parts of the four counties.

A corollary of this regional policy was the filling in of local niches throughout the four counties. A good example of this can be seen in the space between Huntingdon and Oundle, which had no markets in 1250. By 1330, five new seedlings had been planted in this soil, but as the decades passed, they found little nourishment. Two of the five markets had failed entirely by 1330, and only one, the Tuesday market in Buckworth, can be described as a successful venture. Not surprisingly, Buckworth also happened to be the one with the best position in a larger regional cycle incorporating Ramsey, Yaxley, and Kimbolton.

The causes of failure in these counties are more difficult to discern than the strategies of foundation; unlike the creation of a new market, the decay and death of a site is difficult to pinpoint. The data on map 8-6 suggest several possible impediments to a market's prosperity and longevity. One involves markets that trespassed on the exclusionary zones of the anchor markets, a transgression that often put them out of business. Among this group we can place Milton, situated too close to Northampton to be viable, Blunham and Warden near Bedford, Fen Ditton and Impington near Cambridge, Woodston (and possibly Alwalton and Chesterton) near Peterborough, and Barnwell near Oundle. Even though the founders of such markets obtained viable temporal slots, they were undermined by spatial considerations and possibly by legal challenges. With the exception of Huntingdon, near which Alconbury did succeed in finding a viable niche, the exclusionary zones observable in 1250 were still largely intact in 1330 in spite of numerous efforts to infringe them.

Another pattern that may explain the failure of so many markets is suggested by the clustering of unsuccessful venues. Failed markets were not distributed randomly across the four counties; some areas provided good fallow for the planted seeds while others proved to be almost barren. One such cluster of sterility can be detected south and west of Oundle, a relatively compact area with five failed markets. Another cluster occurs north and east of Cambridge, where six failures surrounded the only successful venture in Reach. By contrast, there are other parts of these counties with equally dense market saturation but without a correspondingly high rate of failure. The area to the east of Northampton, for example, stretching across to Huntingdon and toward Bedford, gave rise to at least eight successful markets without a single failure. Southern Bedfordshire was likewise supportive of the hopes of market founders: In the triangle formed by Bedford, Luton, and Leighton Buzzard there was only a single failed market among the dozen venues founded there. The explanation for this clustering doubtlessly involves a variety of economic causes, including such factors as topography, transport, population density, and variations in agricultural practices.

Finally, the weight of the past undoubtedly had a large role to play in determining the success of new markets. Later foundations faced an uphill struggle from the very beginning because the prime spatial and temporal spots in regional trading networks had already been spoken for; later founders did not get to play on a level playing field. This handicap was exacerbated by the ingrained traditions of merchants and other traders whose behavioral patterns had to be altered to bring a new commercial site into the fold. Humans, even entrepreneurial representatives of the species, are creatures of habit and prone to stick to what they know unless they are given good reason to change.

In spite of their founders' best efforts to integrate them into existing networks of trade, many markets simply failed to redirect interest away from previously established venues and thus withered away over time. A good example is the Tuesday market in Warden, Bedfordshire, founded in 1218. It managed to hang on for more than a century, but when asked to verify the holder's claim to the franchise in 1330, a jury reported to the justices that "it often happened that no one came to transact any business."[50] Without doubt, many other markets, particularly those that were founded after the middle of the thirteenth century, shared Warden's fate. Often they managed to eke out an existence by meeting local needs for basic supplies, as population growth increased the numbers of people without land. Only rarely, though, did they reward their founders' hopes of reorienting regional trading patterns.

V

At any given moment in the later thirteenth and early fourteenth centuries, merchants, lords, and peasants interested in participating in the commercial economy needed to make a number of decisions about when and where to go to market. Was it best to use the nearest local market in order to keep transport costs down? Or did the advantage of a larger market with greater demand for goods and a greater selection of consumables offset the added time and expense of a longer journey? If so, which of several possible core markets within reach offered the greatest potential for profitable exchange? At what point did a longer journey outweigh the attractions of a better market? Among contemporary peasantries, activity in markets is a perennial topic of conversation: "Two of the most absorbing subjects for conversation among most people in the area of the Oaxaca market system," writes the anthropologist Ralph Beals, "are prices and *movimento,* that is, the numbers of people or the amount of activity at *plazas.*"[51] Similar conversations are a staple in rural communities in the First World as well. We will never be able to recover all of the motivations that led people in the thirteenth and fourteenth centuries to favor one market site over another. But such decisions, multiplied thousands of times over, are the best way to explain the varied fates of markets in the period. People of the time spoke of the "fullness" of particular markets, as, for example, in a three-way dispute in the middle of the twelfth century over the market in Abingdon: Abingdon claimed that its market had long been "as full as possible"; Wallingford that it had traditionally sold only bread and ale; and Oxford that it was "fuller" than Wallingford allowed but not as full as Abingdon claimed, because it did not involve merchandise brought in boats or wagons.[52] The handful of anchor and core markets in Huntingdonshire and surrounding counties were, to borrow the language then current, full markets, and they are the ones that need to be investigated more closely to understand the dynamics of inland trade in the county.

9

A Regional Transportation System

The importance of an adequate transport infrastructure to the development of an economy is so readily apparent in the modern world that it hardly needs to be mentioned. Improvements to transport facilities have long been at the heart of development schemes for Third World economies, and the expenses incurred therein have played a major role in the international debt crises of recent years.[1] Historians, too, have given the question of transport considerable attention, as the many studies of railroads, canals, and turnpike roads evince.[2] Until fairly recently, though, historical interest has been confined largely to periods subsequent to the rise of turnpikes and canals, that is, roughly from the seventeenth century to the present. The rationale for studying transport history as an element of economic history is, however, as valid for earlier periods as it is for later ones. Transport efficiency determined which commodities could be traded and how widely they could circulate; it determined the level of integration between separate communities and regions; and it condemned some towns and villages to neglect while making others into meccas of opportunity and wealth.

The primary goal of this chapter is to describe the transportation infrastructure used by residents of Huntingdonshire in the thirteenth and fourteenth centuries. This involves four related tasks: exploring the networks of waterways and roads that residents of the county used to transport their goods within the local area and into other regions; examining the methods used to ensure that transportation networks successfully served the needs of the people likely to use them; investigating contemporary evidence documenting how people actually used the roads and waterways available to them; and, finally, determining the effectiveness of the network by calculating the relative costs of land transport and water transport. Historians commonly assume that transportation facilities in this period were unequal to the task of facilitating a commercial economy. Each of the topics dealt with in this chapter suggests that this assumption needs some rethinking.

I

By the standards of other English counties, Huntingdonshire was relatively well served by major transportation routes in this period, both riverine and overland. As H. C. Darby and others have shown, the entire fenland was interlaced with a series of rivers and navigable channels that stretched well into the county.[3] Two of the four main rivers of the watershed feeding into the Wash—the Great Ouse and the Nene—pass through Huntingdonshire, a natural endowment that gave the county cheap and easy access to one of the country's leading medieval ports in King's Lynn. The routes of all of the fenland waterways have been drastically reconfigured over the centuries by silting and reclamation projects, and it is only with some difficulty that the path of the main channels prior to the age of improvement can be reconstructed. Today, the Great Ouse and the Nene are distinct channels with separate outlets into the Wash, but in the thirteenth and fourteenth centuries, the two joined their courses via Well Creek, about ten miles inland from the port.[4] Within Huntingdonshire, the two rivers were joined by a series of channels and inland lakes running between Earith on the Ouse and Peterborough on the Nene. Elizabethan cartographers drew this linkage as a fairly substantial waterway running via Ramsey Mere—then a substantial inland lake situated to the north and west of the town of Ramsey—and Whittlesea Mere—then the largest inland lake in the country.[5] Feeding into these two lakes and their connecting channel were numerous smaller channels, some natural and some constructed. Many villages that appear on a modern map as being situated at a considerable remove from a navigable waterway were in fact well integrated into medieval riverine routes via these smaller channels. The village of Sawtry, for example, which modern maps depict as being situated almost ten miles from any navigable waterway was directly connected to both the Ouse and the Nene in the twelfth century, thanks to a channel leading into Whittlesea Mere that the local monastery built to facilitate the transport of stone and other building material.[6]

Two of Huntingdonshire's principal market sites, Yaxley and St. Ives, served as the effective navigational heads of the Nene and Ouse in this period and thus had direct and unobstructed access to King's Lynn.[7] St. Ives usurped its role as inland port from the county town, which was cut off from direct access to King's Lynn by the construction of mills on the stretch of river between the two settlements.[8] In a dispute in 1227, Huntingdon claimed that these obstructions made it as expensive for a ship from King's Lynn to navigate the few extra miles to Huntingdon as to make the entire voyage to St.

Ives.[9] Yaxley's emergence as the inland head of the Nene is well attested in contemporary sources. When provisioning his estates in Northamptonshire in 1228, for example, Henry III sent wine purchased in Boston by ship to Yaxley and then by cart to the manors and towns he intended to visit.[10] Later in the century, sheriffs of Northamptonshire reversed these arrangements when sending grain and other goods down the river to King's Lynn.[11] On a modern map, Yaxley is situated well off the main course of the Nene, but the path of the river has changed dramatically since the days when Yaxley was a prominent inland port. In the thirteenth and fourteenth centuries, the main branch of the Nene probably flowed via Well Creek and led directly to Yaxley rather than to places further north, as is the case with the modern river.[12]

As the example of Sawtry illustrates, other settlements in the county also sought to take advantage of the transportation possibilities offered by the presence of fenland waterways. Both Ramsey and Alwalton had access to branches of the Nene, and the presence of vessels carrying merchandise can be documented in both places in the thirteenth century.[13] Ramsey's cartulary also refers to ships being loaded and unloaded in the village of Warboys in this period, indicating that the branch of the Nene that led to Ramsey continued even further inland.[14] Local navigation along the Ouse between Huntingdon and Bedford was also feasible throughout most of the thirteenth century: In 1279, a jury complained that a mill built by the Bishop of Lincoln in Offord Cluny restricted navigation between the two towns.[15] Estate-holders in the area sometimes included carriage by water among the work services expected of customary tenants. Ramsey's tenants on the Cambridgeshire manor of Chatteris, for example, had to carry their lord's goods by water four times a year to St. Ives or Ramsey.[16] In 1342, the Abbot of Ramsey adjudicated a dispute involving the villages of Walton, Sawtry, and Conington, the record of which mentions various ditches used by ships and boats to carry "grain, turves and other goods of certain men to various places within and beyond the county."[17] As these references indicate, villages with access to navigable waterways did not hesitate to make the most of them.

For most settlements in the county, though, land routes were a more viable transportation option, particularly for journeys involving shorter distances. Roads in this period were seldom more than dirt tracks relieved by occasional stretches of level stonework in and around the towns, but even so they formed a surprisingly intricate and integrated system of routes, both at the national and the regional level.[18] The mid-fourteenth-century Gough Map shows Huntingdonshire situated on one of the most prominent roads of the period, a road whose importance as a national artery dates back to the Roman occupation.[19] In Roman times, when it was known as Ermine Street, the road ran between London and York, but by the time the Gough Map was drawn, it had undergone modifications on parts of its northern stretch, causing it to terminate in Carlisle rather than York.[20] With the advent of regular war in Scotland, the route took on added significance as a military conduit, illustrated by

Edward III's decision to rebuild the bridge over the Ouse between Godmanchester and Huntingdon at a cost of more than £600 to the royal treasury.[21]

The fate of the other main roads built by the Romans in the area that was to become Huntingdonshire is less certain.[22] None of them attracted the attention of the author of the Gough Map, but there is no doubt that some of them persisted through the medieval period. One of them, the *via Devana,* continued in use well past the medieval period. The road was known in the Middle Ages by several different names, with reference either to its construction—Stanstraete (1012) or Stonwey (1467)—or to its route—Huntedonstret (1251 and later parallels) and Cambridge Waye (1595).[23] In Roman times the *via Devana* also led from Godmanchester into Bedfordshire. The continuity of this stretch of the road is less well documented, but it probably formed the basis of the medieval road between Huntingdon and St. Neots. Another main Roman road ran from Godmanchester to Leicester, sharing the first few miles out of Godmanchester with Ermine Street. It too is poorly documented, but it probably laid the basis for the medieval road joining Huntingdon and Oundle.

By the thirteenth century at the latest, these major roads came to be supplemented by other identifiable roads designed to service more localized needs. It is difficult to pinpoint exactly when such local routes came to be seen as dedicated and inviolable stretches of ground, but some of them probably date back to before the Norman Conquest; W. G. Hoskins felt that most of the roads used in Leicestershire in later centuries dated back to the period of Anglo-Saxon and Scandinavian occupation.[24] In most cases, though, the earliest documentary evidence of the roads in use for local and regional travel and trade dates to the thirteenth century, when the number of local records referring to such mundane things as paths and roads exploded as part of the revolution in recordkeeping associated with the rising sophistication of the English state.[25]

These roads can be located primarily by relying on incidental references in property conveyances and other sources that describe topographical features. Even the most diligent search will fail to uncover all of the roads in use, but a surprising amount about the pattern of regional and local roads can be learned from the patient accumulation of isolated references. By the thirteenth century, most of the principal commercial sites of the region were joined into an integrated network of roads.[26] St. Neots was linked to both Huntingdon and Cambridge, as is apparent from the existence of a Huntingdon Street and a Cambridge Street in the market village. Rentals from St. Ives reveal street names indicative of links to Ramsey and Ely. The Bishop of Lincoln was granted a charter by King John giving him the right to alter slightly a road described as running between Kimbolton and Huntingdon. From the fourteenth century, again describing what was likely an ancient situation, comes a reference to a road joining Huntingdon to Ramsey passing through Abbots Ripton. A "Huntingdon Weye" is recorded in a Wistow court roll in 1320, possibly forming part of this Ramsey-to-Huntingdon road. Another "Huntingdon Weye" occurs in a court record in Woodhurst in 1332. Finally, a property conveyance in Elton in 1297 refers to the "high road to Yaxley" as one of the boundaries of the property.

Combining these roads with the principal thoroughfares running through the county yields a network of roads that approximates a hub-and-spoke pattern, with the county town serving as the hub and the spokes radiating out to the other principal market sites in the county. This is illustrated on map 9-1, which depicts the roads outlined in the preceding paragraphs as well as others passing through Great Gidding that will be discussed below. As can be seen on the map, all of the leading markets in the county—St. Neots, Kimbolton, St. Ives, Ramsey, and Yaxley—were either on or near one of the roads recorded in contemporary sources, a situation that finds parallels in other counties.[27] The map also illustrates how some of the major commercial sites of the county fit into the larger regional network described in chapter 8. Principal roads led from the county to Cambridge, Lincoln, and London, and these connections were, in some cases, important enough to influence local toponymy: Mention has already been made of Cambridge Street in St. Neots, and a further example occurs in the London Street of thirteenth-century Godmanchester.[28] As is apparent on the Gough Map, the choice of road and street names reveals a great deal about contemporary senses of spatial orientation. In all of the places noted here, people used important regional centers as their points of reference rather than neighboring villages. Furthermore, their points of reference were, on the whole, commercial rather than manorial or administrative. In the case of Cambridge, such orientation was reciprocal, for we find references in that town to roads leading to Huntingdon and St. Neots.[29] People of the time were, in short, well aware of the regional context in which they lived their lives.

Since Huntingdonshire was first and foremost a county of peasant villages, it is appropriate to return to one of the villages to illustrate how the roads and bridges described in these pages influenced a local community. The village of Great Gidding, immortalized in the poetry of T. S. Eliot, was a large and relatively prosperous village in the thirteenth and fourteenth centuries, with a mix of peasant tenures, some free and some customary.[30] Although it was a bit larger than most of its neighbors, Great Gidding was in most respects a typical Huntingdonshire village. In 1541, someone familiar with the settlement decided, for unknown reasons, to draw a detailed map of the place, depicting the layout of the village and the roads running through it.[31] There is no reason to believe that either the village layout or the names given to the streets underwent any marked change after the thirteenth century, and thus it can be assumed that the map approximates local conditions in preceding centuries as well as at the time it was drawn up.

The map records the names of four of the roads that passed through or alongside the village. Forming the boundary with the village of Sawtry to the east was a road marked "the waye to Huntingeton." Dissecting the fields was

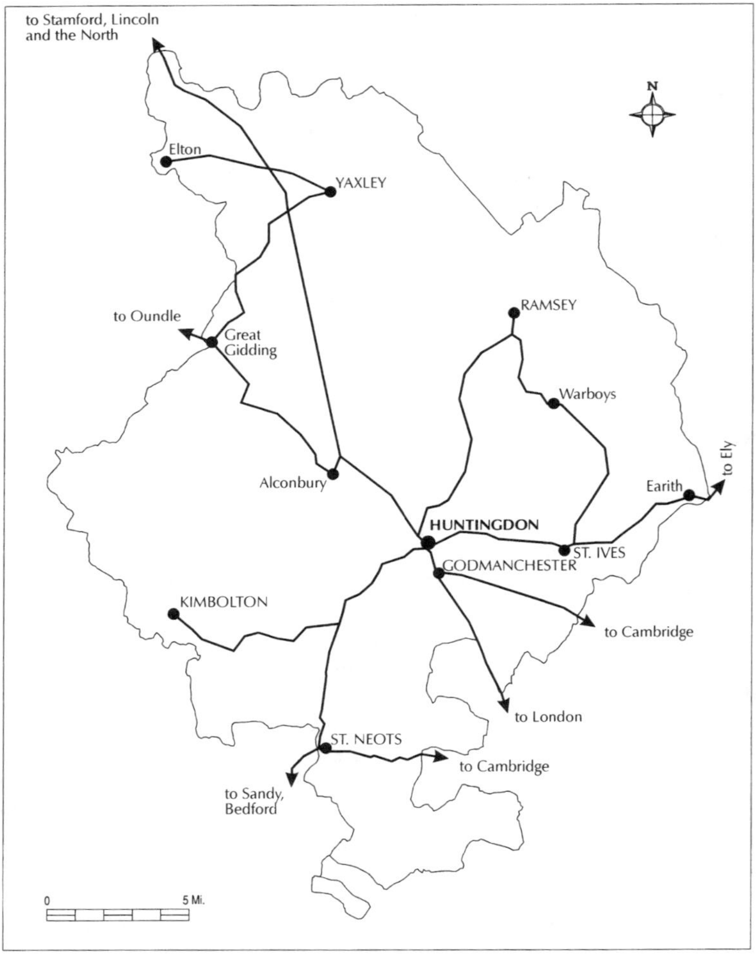

Map 9-1: Medieval roads in Huntingdonshire

the "waye from Stamforde." Branching off to the northeast from this route was the "waye from Yaxley." Completing the network, and apparently merging with the Yaxley route, was "Oundle Waye." The nomenclature of these roads is a fascinating example of the influence commercial concerns exerted over contemporary sensibilities, since all of the places giving rise to road names in Great Gidding were important regional markets. This village of virgaters and cottage-holders was nestled in a transportation network with horizons stretching almost 25 miles from south to north and with one of the region's leading market centers ready to welcome the villagers and their goods no matter which road they followed out of the village.

II

To function effectively, even a transportation network consisting of rivers and hardened earth needs regular maintenance. Rivers silt up and can be blocked by dams, weirs, and other obstructions, and earthen roads develop vitiating cavities and can be plowed up, obstructed, or otherwise rendered impassable. While such problems were endemic to the period, people did not simply resign themselves to a perpetual state of disrepair. Under the watchful eyes of royal administrators, local jurisdictions accorded a very real and ongoing vigilance to the maintenance of the transportation infrastructure, an example of what A. B. White so aptly described as "self-government at the king's command."[32] To appreciate the scope of this vigilance requires a close look at the measures taken both to safeguard the system from harm and to offset the decay inevitably suffered by routes in common use.

Care of the country's waterways in this period was exercised through a combination of local supervision and ad hoc panels commissioned by the king. Formal commissions of sewers received statutory recognition only in 1427, but their jurisdiction and administrative practices drew on at least two centuries of experimentation with similar bodies.[33] Both the ad hoc commissions of the thirteenth and fourteenth centuries and the more formalized bodies of later periods essentially sought to supervise and enforce a preexisting set of customary regulations operating at the local level.[34] Local authorities, though, were normally concerned with local problems and generally lacked the clout to deal with issues of broader scope, particularly those involving regional navigation rights. Thus, the crown found itself involved on a regular basis in conflicts involving riverine obstructions and other issues related to the use of waterways for navigation.

Such involvement is well illustrated by a commission set up by the king in 1334 to survey the condition of various water routes leading to Peterborough, Yaxley, and Spalding.[35] In the writ authorizing this investigation, the king noted that people from surrounding counties used these channels to travel back and forth to King's Lynn and that they were particularly important during winter months, when water levels would have been higher and roads less reliable. The panel was authorized to determine who should bear responsibility for the maintenance of the channels it inspected and to compel those responsible to effect repairs wherever needed. On other occasions, the king commissioned inquiries to deal with more specific problems. Several commissions in the early fourteenth century, for example, explored the problems resulting from a dam built on Well Creek that obstructed the passage of boats and ships traveling to and from King's Lynn.[36] The resulting dispute over the respective rights of the dam builder and the shipowners dragged on for almost 30 years; the dam was ultimately torn down to allow ships to make their accustomed journeys without impediment.[37] In the 1340s, a similar investigation scrutinized the navigational problems caused by Crowland Abbey's interference with the course of a waterway known as "Shepeau Currere," which, the presentment notes, gave people from Cambridgeshire, Northamptonshire, Lincolnshire, and Huntingdonshire access to the Welland.[38]

The balance of power in cases involving alternate river uses did not invariably favor shipowners over those with other interests. In spite of Huntingdon's repeated protests about the mills that limited ships' access to the town, mill owners continued to enjoy priority on that stretch of the river. The town's complaints, first voiced in 1227, came to the attention of justices on eyre in 1286, but though the king's justices lent a sympathetic ear, they did not bring the problem to a resolution favorable to the town.[39] A century later, burgesses in the town were still trying to win royal support to restore navigation, but their efforts met with no greater success than those of their forebears, even though their case was supported by merchants from as far away as Leicestershire and Derbyshire.[40] The dispute dragged on into the sixteenth century; the town may not have been fortunate, but it certainly was persistent.[41]

Land transport involved equally sticky problems, but the theory and procedures designed to deal with them were better formulated and more consistently applied. Most historians have accepted C. T. Flower's dictum that medieval roads "made and maintained themselves," but Flower did not do justice to the methods that the crown and local authorities developed to ensure the integrity of overland routes.[42] To appreciate the scope of contemporary concern for the upkeep of inland transport, we need to look more closely at the process by which kings and lawyers developed the concept of the king's highway *(via regia)*. The effort to exercise jurisdiction over roads has a long history in England, stretching back well before the Norman Conquest. In Anglo-Saxon times, privileged status involving royal oversight was originally restricted to the four great national routes—Watling Street, Ermine Street, the Foss Way, and Icknield Way—and was intimately connected with the territory over which the King's Peace extended.[43] Any abuse committed on or to one of these roads was considered to be an offence against the king himself and therefore one that deserved particularly harsh punishment. Gradually, this privileged status was extended to other main routes, and by the eleventh century a fundamental definition had been established. The *Leges Henrici Primi,* a post-Conquest compilation of Anglo-Saxon laws, defined the king's highway as that which "is always open, which no one can enclose or divert [and] which leads to a city, town, castle, or port."[44] The same set of laws also notes that a *via regia* should be wide enough to permit two carts to pass abreast.[45] Over the course of the following centuries, the concept continued to expand, eventually encompassing the idea that a royal road was not necessarily dependent on crown property and that the royal prerogative could include public right to passage even over private property.[46] Thus, what began as a definition applied to a small, readily identifiable number of roads was broadened first by increasing the number of routes and then by adding the notion of rights to through passage.

Defining the parameters according to which routes either could or could not be considered as king's highways was more than an academic exercise: At the same time as they expanded the theoretical definition, the king and his legal advisers also aimed to develop practical procedures to safeguard the integrity of the road network. Misuse of the royal road had to be guarded against, and court records reveal that this protection was more than a dead letter. The thirteenth-century legal text ascribed to Henry Bracton remarks on two occasions that anyone who narrowed or otherwise infringed the integrity of a royal road committed an offence against the king and that legal action on the matter could be sought by the crown.[47] As a practical concern, such legal action almost invariably took place at the local level in the "view" of frankpledge, a local court that in theory came under the jurisdiction of the sheriff but that in many parts of the country came to be appropriated by manorial lords. The use of frankpledge courts to deal with matters involving the king's highways is readily apparent in the lists of articles of inquiry written for use by the stewards holding the courts of frankpledge. Roads and bridges appear among the oldest known list of such articles, the *De Placitis et Curiis Tenendis* from about 1269, and similar articles appear in most other such lists.[48] A frankpledge formulary written in the middle of the fourteenth century specifies the types of problems to be dealt with. One model entry refers to an obstruction of the highway caused by a dungheap placed in the road "to the damage of the surrounding countryside"; a second to encroachment by plowing from the road "against the interests of the king and to the damage of the surrounding countryside."[49] Lists occurring in the legal texts Fleta and Britton contain similar articles, and many others could be added to their number.[50]

Presentments involving the king's highway are a common feature in manorial court records. The rolls from the Huntingdonshire holdings of Ramsey Abbey, for example, contain numerous cases of damage to the royal roads. Offenders were regularly brought into the abbey's courts for setting up dungheaps that obstructed the road.[51] Almost as common were malefactors who dug up portions of the road, presumably to use as landfill or to shore up a wall or ditch.[52] But by far the most common presentments in Ramsey's courts involved problems associated with drainage, no surprise in an area that lies below the 100-foot contour level and dips below sea level in some parts. In Broughton in 1316, seven villagers were fined for failing to clean their drainage ditches, which led to the flooding of the king's highway.[53] In the same year, nine people were presented for the same offense in Ramsey.[54] The court of the abbey town also records 25 presentments in 1309 made against people encroaching on the royal road by enlarging the ditches in front of their property at the expense of the road rather than their own property.[55] Similar presentments dealing with ditches occur in many of the other villages under Ramsey's jurisdiction.[56] Fines for all types of damage to the king's highway were normally set at 6d. per infraction, an amount consistent with that levied on the other infractions that formed the routine business of these courts. The court record often adds that the problem had to be rectified by the next session of the court, and in some cases explicitly mentions that the repairs were to be made at the expense of the negligent party.[57] Such cases suggest that maintenance of the road network was a responsibility that courts and presentment juries took seriously.

The same concern for maintaining roads can also be found for the maintenance of bridges, which were as critical to the viability of land transport as the quality of the roads. As D. F. Harrison has recently shown, the later Middle Ages was the most active period of bridge building in English history by a considerable margin.[58] Harrison found that the stock of bridges in existence by 1530, much of which comprised substantial structures built in stone and much of which had already been built by the early fourteenth century, underwent little addition until the nineteenth century, and he concluded that the supply of medieval bridges only makes sense in the context of a well-developed medieval transportation system.

Data derived from Huntingdonshire bear out Harrison's findings. By the twelfth century at the latest residents of the county had built at least three bridges across the Ouse: The river between Huntingdon and Godmanchester was spanned before the arrival of the Normans, and twelfth-century references can be found to bridges in St. Ives (1107) and St. Neots (1180).[59] A fourth bridge at Earith had been built by the thirteenth century.[60] There was, in short, one bridge for about every five miles of the Ouse's route through the county. Nor was the Ouse the only river in the county to be spanned in the Middle Ages. The Nene, forming the county boundary with Northamptonshire, was crossed by a bridge between Orton Longueville and Peterborough and by a second major structure at Wansford, carrying Ermine Street out of the county.[61] Lesser rivers in the county were also spanned: Alconbury Brook was crossed by a bridge at Alconbury Weston; Ellington Brook was bridged at Spaldwick; and the Kym was crossed at Staughton.[62] The locations of these bridges are illustrated on map 9-2. As with the evidence for roads, the data comes mainly from chance references in miscellaneous documents. Undoubtedly there were more bridges in use; the most thorough search for local bridges undertaken to date, Peter Goodfellow's study of bridges in Northamptonshire, found evidence for more than 90 bridges in that county.[63] But even considering only the bridges mentioned here, it is apparent that any waterway that might have created an insuperable obstacle to land traffic could have been crossed by traveling no more than several miles to the nearest bridge.

A variety of means were employed to finance the construction and maintenance of bridges. Testators often left bequests for local bridges in their wills as an act of charity.[64] It would be difficult to quantify the importance of such bequests, but their frequency suggests that they were more than incidental sources of funding. Important bridges were often funded by royal grants of pontage, which were capable of generating significant sums of money. Pontage grants authorized local authorities to collect specified tolls on goods passing over the bridge; in effect, they established a user fee designed to pay for repairs to the fabric of the structure. In the period from 1220 to 1350, about 150 pontage grants were given to local communities in England to defray the costs of repairing bridges, the vast majority going to support major structures that were

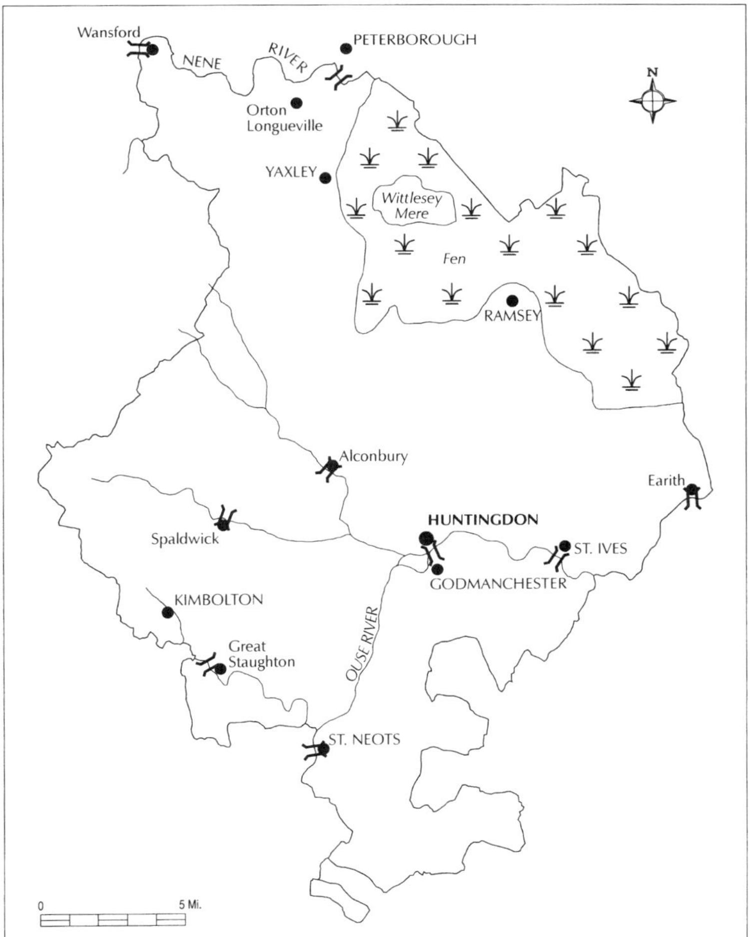

Map 9-2: Medieval bridges in Huntingdonshire

key components of national transportation routes.[65] But as with the upkeep of roads, most bridge maintenance was ultimately a private responsibility, overseen by the crown when necessary but ordinarily administered locally. Wherever possible—and it was usually possible—responsibility for bridge repairs fell to local landholders, for whom contributing to the local bridge was often a condition of tenure.[66] In practice, the application of the tenurial rule was flexible: It could fall on the lord of the manor, or on those who possessed land in the vicinity, or on a corporate group such as a town, parish, or hundred. The methods by which these groups raised the money to meet their obligations were similarly flexible. Some places established local assessment rates, with the collected money earmarked for the maintenance of the local bridge, while others favored a system of local user fees.

Not surprisingly, there were frequent difficulties with ensuring proper maintenance. But although it might have been a nuisance to contemporaries, the parsimony of those responsible for the upkeep of bridges is a boon for historians, because it often led to court cases to determine who was obliged to pay for the repair of decrepit structures. The bridge over the Ouse between Huntingdon and Godmanchester furnishes a particularly good example of this. In the late 1250s a complaint reached King Henry III from "the entire county of Huntingdon" to the effect that the burgesses of the county town were shirking their responsibility to maintain the bridge in good repair.[67] According to the "entire county" the burgesses were doubly to blame for the disrepair of the bridge. First of all, they had caused much of the actual damage by carting their manure over it to their lands in Godmanchester and elsewhere across the river and by carting their grain and hay back to their barns in Huntingdon. In response to these allegations, the burgesses claimed that they had always had the right to use the bridge for these purposes. The county, however, declared that the burgesses had always had the right to drive their cattle across the bridge and to cart their merchandise across it but not to use it to transport manure and grain between Godmanchester and Huntingdon. The county's position is entirely understandable: Constant carting of heavy goods would inevitably cause a great deal of wear and tear, and if the burgesses were allowed to do this at their will the county would, in effect, have to subsidize the town's local transportation needs.

Settling the squabble about who had damaged the bridge was not, however, the crux of the matter; the crux was who was going to pay for the repairs. Here lay the second complaint of the county against the townsmen. The town claimed that it had reached an agreement with the rest of the county that exempted residents of the county from all tolls in the town in return for their contributing to the upkeep of the bridge. In the town's opinion, this meant that it no longer had to contribute to the bridge, even when it used the span to cart produce from the fields of Godmanchester. The court, though, thought otherwise. It decided that the county had a legitimate grievance and ordered the sheriff to see that henceforth anyone who carted grain or manure across it pay a fair share of the bridge's upkeep.

As this case reveals, responsibility for the bridge lay with the county as well as the town. Insight into how this translated into a practical system of finance is furnished by a pronouncement made at the county eyre session in 1286. At that session the justices learned that the bridge was once again in need of repairs and once again the subject of local dispute. In order to resolve any existing differences of opinion and to preclude future disagreements, the justices took the unusual step of instructing each hundred of the county to assume responsibility for a specific portion of the structure. The resulting arrangement was formally entered in the record of the court. This apparently created a new momentum for the enterprise, for several years after the eyre session serious work on the bridge was well underway. Problems of a different sort afflicted the bridge a few years later when thieves made off with the supplies of wood, stone, and "certain instruments" that had been assembled for the repairs (calling forth in 1294 a threat of excommunication of the guilty parties by Bishop Sutton if not rectified).[68] The bridge's condition continued to be a concern in the fourteenth century, and calls for repairs were made in 1329, 1364, 1370, and 1377.[69] Liability in these instances was distributed across the county, apparently because the bridge was "acknowledged to be to the common advantage and its disrepair to the common hurt of the whole people."[70] On at least one occasion, though, the king contributed to the project from his own resources, opening the royal coffers to pay for stone, masons' wages, and other miscellaneous goods and services needed in the course of repairs.[71]

Other bridges in the county saw less use than this span across the Ouse on one of the country's principal national arteries, but they too required ongoing capital investment to remain serviceable. The bridge at Earith was in need of repair in 1346, as was the bridge at St. Neots in 1293 and again in 1388.[72] The seemingly endless litany of complaints about the state of the county's bridges might suggest a generalized state of neglect, but it might also suggest continued heavy usage; as in modern America, complaints about the condition of transportation facilities probably reveal more about people's unwillingness to be taxed than about the importance of the facility needing repair. There is no reason to think that Huntingdonshire's bridges were flimsier than those in other parts of the country. Like the roads, both their number and the concern exhibited for their maintenance testify to the impressive extent of the transportation infrastructure that was in place by the end of the thirteenth century. Each of the county's bridges was built to service a very real demand for improved transportation facilities. A bridge acts like a magnet, drawing people and goods to its location, but, like a magnet, it only exerts an influence when other, quite specific, elements are near.

III

As John Langdon has documented, the twelfth and thirteenth centuries saw a fundamental transformation in the modes of haulage in England, with the wholesale substitution of horse power for ox power in most parts of the country.[73] Though weaker and less durable than oxen, horses are able to cover ground more quickly, and Langdon has suggested that a concern with reaching markets rather than simply working the soil lay behind this great change. Most of Langdon's sources dealt with changes in manorial practices, but he also found evidence to document the ownership of horses and carts among the peasantry. In fact, Langdon argued that peasants were more likely than their lords to abandon oxen entirely in favor of horses.[74] Manorial lords had the luxury of being able to employ both oxen and horses for the tasks for which they were best suited, whereas peasants often had to rely on a single animal for both plowing and carting; in the vast majority of cases, they chose the speed of horses over the strength of oxen.

Both carts and packhorses were in common use in Huntingdonshire and throughout the country in this period. Boats and barges were also used to haul goods back and forth along the rivers and channels of the county, but, unlike horses and carts, their use was restricted to a small and relatively specialized group of carriers. Extant lists of tolls from this period suggest that packhorses were generally favored for goods that were relatively light, such as cloth or spices, or goods that were perishable and needed to be transported as fast and as far as possible, such as fish.[75] Their use required less investment in road surfaces and bridges, their mobility and speed were greater, and their associated capital requirements were smaller. Such advantages made them well suited for the periodic marketing of small amounts of agricultural produce. Carts, on the other hand, were preferred for goods that were heavy and bulky, such as stone, metal and other building supplies. Agricultural produce was carried by both means, with the prime determinant being the amount that needed to be carried. Packhorses had a maximum capacity of about four bushels of grain, whereas a fully loaded cart could carry 10 or 11 times as much: In 1345, the sheriff of Northamptonshire noted that a cart loaded with 44 bushels of grain purveyed for the king took longer than expected to reach its destination because it was "loaded to the utmost."[76] Teams of horses were used for larger loads hauled over longer distances, usually one horse per quarter of grain in the cart, so that a fully loaded cart would use a team of four or five horses.

In all periods of history, owning a horse has been an expensive proposition, and the thirteenth and fourteenth centuries were no exception. Purchase prices of horses varied enormously, depending on the type and condition of the beast, with market values ranging from as low as 2s. for a worn-out nag to 30s. for a top-of-the-line carthorse; most peasant horses probably fell somewhere between the bottom and the middle of this range.[77] Lacking antibiotics and modern veterinary services, the owner of a horse in the Middle Ages probably thought himself or herself fortunate to get ten working years out of an animal. Since the initial investment could be spread over this term, the actual purchase price would seldom have amounted to more than a few shillings a year, more than a negligible amount but certainly not an impediment to widespread ownership. Maintenance costs, though, were another matter. Langdon has calculated that manors spent about 25s. per year for feed and maintenance for each of their horses, and other sources bear out this reckoning.[78]

In spite of the expenses involved, though, a substantial proportion of peasants did own at least one horse. Manorial carrying services, which will be described more fully below, were predicated on the assumption that at least the principal tenants on the manor would possess their own horses. Our best source to document the extent of horse ownership among the peasantry is provided by local lay subsidy rolls.[79] In spite of the fact that a peasant's basic working stock was ordinarily exempt from taxation, considerable numbers of horses still appear in some local assessment rolls. In an assessment in the Huntingdonshire village of Wistow in 1290, for example, 37 people were assessed for the tax and of these, 31 owned at least one horse.[80] Many of the taxpayers in Wistow actually owned several horses: The number of horses included in the assessment was more than twice as high as the number of taxpayers. The neighboring village of Great Raveley shows comparable numbers of horses in the same assessment: 34 of 46 villagers owned at least one horse, and many owned several.[81] Assessments in other villages in other parts of the country reveal similar profiles. In Cuxham, Oxfordshire, for example, all but 3 of the 16 people taxed in 1304 had horses in their portfolios.[82] At least among the wealthier peasants in a village, ownership of a horse was the rule rather than the exception.

The distances that these beasts were able to cover in a single day depended, of course, on the nature of the terrain and the conditions of the road. As an outer limit, a horse and rider in this period could cover about 40 miles in a long day of riding in favorable conditions.[83] In America today, endurance racers can cover up to 100 miles in a day, but they do so using specially-bred horses that are highly trained for the task. Some useful illustrations of the speed of unencumbered journeys in medieval England are provided by the royal justices who traveled around the country hearing pleas in different venues in the course of their regional circuits.[84] On February 27, 1329, for example, a pair of justices began their morning by hearing a number of cases in Bedford and then traveled 20 miles to Huntingdon. They reached the town early enough to begin hearing cases before the sun went down, no mean feat considering the daylight available on a winter's day. A few days later, the same pair ended their session in Huntingdon and began a session 15 miles away in Cambridge on the same day. In the same year, a different set of justices heard cases in Shrewsbury and Stafford on the same day, two towns that are about 30 miles apart. But even they were outdone a few years later by colleagues who began their working day in session in St. Albans and ended it in Guildford, towns located nearly 40 miles apart. In addition to knowing the law, royal justices must have been exceptionally good horsemen.

Carters had to content themselves with daily journeys that were considerably shorter than those made by unencumbered riders. Purveyance records suggest that in favorable circumstances, a fully loaded cart could travel a maximum of about 25 miles in a single day. In 1347, the sheriff of Bedfordshire sent 17 carts loaded with barrels of flour from Holme Mill on the River Ivel to the royal household in London and paid expenses for the carters for three days for the round trip of 72 miles.[85] Forty years earlier, Bedfordshire's sheriff sent three carts loaded with grain from Bedford to Carlisle, a trip that took 10 days to complete, yielding an average of about 22 miles per day.[86] Carters from Cambridgeshire were paid two day's wages to cart wheat from Cambridge to London, a distance of 50 miles.[87] The longest distance covered for a single day's wage in surviving accounts was 31 miles, the distance that carters from Northamptonshire covered to carry grain from Spelho hundred to Yaxley.[88] While such distances were feasible, sheriffs more commonly paid daily wages for trips of about 20 miles, which they probably saw as a good day's work for a carter with a full load.

The descriptions of carrying services performed by manorial tenants as part of their rent obligations provide a good opportunity to observe the role horses played in meeting transportation needs. Provision of carrying services was an extremely widespread feature of customary tenure in the twelfth and thirteenth centuries.[89] As with so many elements of customary tenure, the precise terms of carriage that the tenant owed to his lord were carefully delineated and are often noted in manorial extents alongside the other services regularly owed by tenants. Our most extensive evidence about carrying services in Huntingdonshire is provided in the Hundred Rolls of 1279, which cover the entire county and a variety of landlord and manorial types. Many of the villages included in the Hundred Rolls, of whatever type of lordship, are recorded as owing carrying services. Often these are summarized by the uninformative statement that such services are owed "at the will of the lord" without any further specification, but in a number of villages either the distance or the destination of the carriage is specified. The virgater tenants of the prior of Huntingdon and of John Engayne in Great Gidding, for example, were required to carry their lord's goods once a week to Huntingdon, a round trip of 22 miles, probably using the "waye to Huntingeton" appearing on the 1541 map of the village.[90] Virgaters in Abbotsley had to make Saturday journeys to Huntingdon, 20 miles round trip, and Cambridge, 28 miles round trip.[91] From Alwalton on the Nene the destinations were Peterborough and Yaxley; from Fletton, a few miles upstream, they were Peterborough, Stanground, and Farcet.[92] In total, the carrying services of 19 locations in the county are specified, and these have been summarized in table 9-1.

Such carrying services ostensibly describe the requirements of the manor, but in many ways they tell us more about the importance peasants attached to transportation than about the demands of their lords. Tenants did not purchase horses and feed and shoe them throughout the year in order to meet their lords' requirements for carriage; they did so first and foremost for their own advantage and accepted provision of carriage as a tenurial obligation because they already owned the capital equipment necessary for the task. By including carrying services in the tenurial contract, lords were, in effect, trying to tap their tenants' resources, much as a modern government taps its citizens' resources through income tax. The same horses and carts that carried manorial produce on an intermittent basis served their peasant owner on a full-time basis. Even as a pale reflection of the investments peasants made for their own ends, though, manorial carrying services indicate some of the ways local people used the existing transportation infrastructure. They suggest that villein peasants—the regular providers of carrying services—had the resources to carry loads of agricultural produce to disparate parts of the county and even beyond the county.

TABLE 9-1:
Huntingdonshire Carrying Services Recorded in the Hundred Rolls (1279)

Location	Destinations
Spaldwick	anywhere within a radius of four leagues
Leighton	thrice yearly to Lincoln or London
Hamerton	anywhere within the county
Gidding Engayne	anywhere within the county
Great Gidding	to Huntingdon once a week
Wooley	all markets in the county
Weston	Ramsey, elseshere within the county
Ellington	Huntingdon, St.Ives, Ramsey, Yaxley
Steeple Gidding	Huntingdon, Yaxley, Ramsey
Alwalton	Peterborough, Yaxley
Fletton	Peterborough, Stanground, Farcet
Yaxley	no farther than Bolnhurst (22 miles) or Thorney
Woodston	Thorney
Stanground	Thorney, by water
Water Newton	Thorney, by water
Conington	anywhere within one day's journey
Chesterton	Yaxley, Peterborough, within county
Elton	Ramsey once a week
Abbotsley	Cambridge or Huntingdon, on Saturdays.

SOURCE: Rotuli Hundredorum, ed. W. Illingworth and J. Caley, vol. 2.

The actual distances tenants covered while carrying their lord's goods varied considerably, depending on the needs of the lord and the evolution of custom, but many of the services involved distances that would have put any village in the county in contact with several core market centers and several more local markets. In some cases, journeys to market are explicitly described.[93] Even when carriage to markets was not explicitly mentioned, transport to market sites is implicit in the destinations mentioned in the extents.

Huntingdon and Yaxley, for example, both feature prominently as destinations for tenant carters: Villagers in at least five different settlements in the county had to carry their lord's produce to each of these markets. Map 9-3 depicts the spatial relationship recorded in manorial extents between these peasant villages and the two core markets.

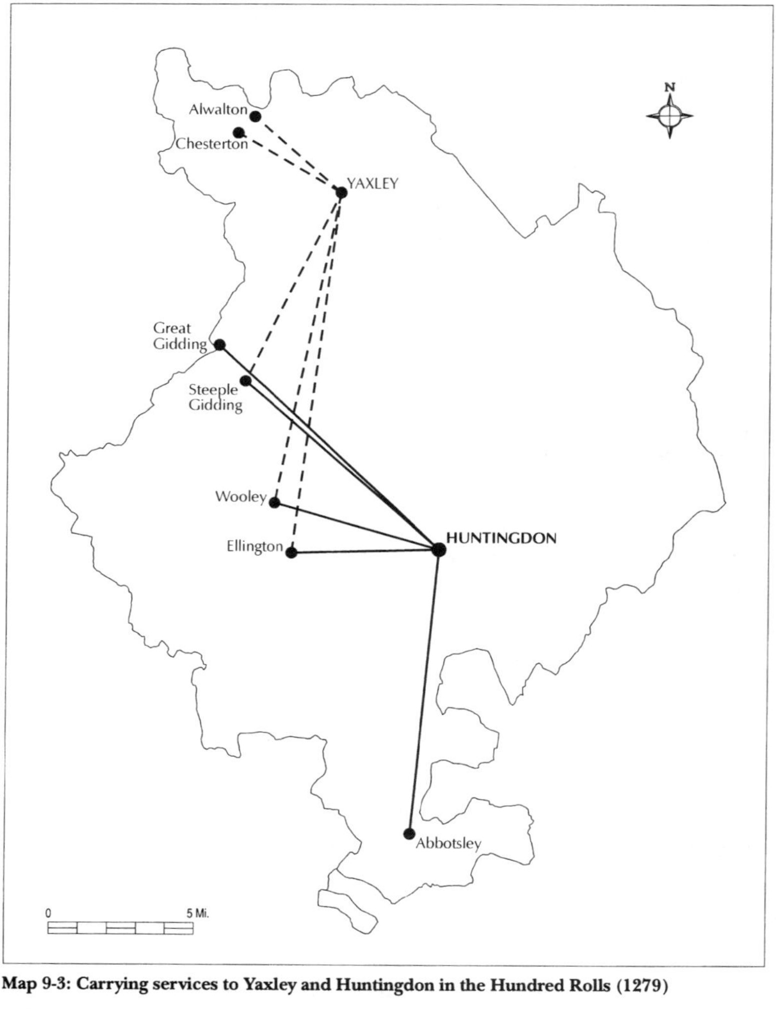

Map 9-3: Carrying services to Yaxley and Huntingdon in the Hundred Rolls (1279)

Undoubtedly, many other villagers whose carrying obligations are not explicitly mentioned in the extents also found themselves headed for regional markets loaded up with their lord's grain. When they made these trips for their lords, villagers temporarily reassigned the resources and transferred the knowledge and skills that they used on their own behalf through the rest of the week. They may even have managed to combine the two, filling part of a cart with manorial produce and part with their own. If the virgaters of Great Gidding could be expected to travel into Huntingdon once a week, then it is apparent that villagers in almost all other parts of the county could do the same. If the virgaters of Elton could be expected to carry once a week to Ramsey—a round trip, skirting the fen, of nearly 30 miles—then it appears that only at the extreme ends of the county would it be impossible to travel to any other point in the county and back in a single day. As the carrying services clearly reveal, Huntingdonshire's villagers were capable of making regular trips to any or all of the county's markets.

IV

In addition to indicating the distances carters could travel, the accounts kept by sheriffs to record the expenses they incurred in purveying foodstuffs for the king contain an abundance of detail about the cost of transporting goods around the county. Sheriffs' accounts often record details about the distance traveled by vehicles carrying purveyed goods, the size of load they carried, and the price paid for each trip. These data allow us to measure the actual cost of carriage in the period, both in terms of the value of the loads carried and in absolute terms using the standard unit favored by transport historians, pence per ton-mile. A recent study of these costs in all regions of the country involved in purveyance campaigns suggests that transport was relatively cheap, both in terms of the price of other commodities and in terms of the costs of transporting similar goods in other periods prior to the Industrial Revolution.[94]

The accounts show that in the country as a whole land transport was significantly more expensive than water transport, but even on land goods could be transported at an average rate of 1.5d. per ton-mile. A meaningful way to express what this average figure meant in terms of marketing opportunities is to compare it with the price of a staple agricultural commodity such as wheat. In accounts that include both the costs of carriage and the actual prices paid for the wheat that was in the carts, the carriage cost amounted to about 0.4 percent of the value of the wheat for every mile of carriage.[95] Thus, a trip of ten miles would cost about 4 percent of the value of the grain. These figures involved hired carriage at fairly generous rates, and a producer who owned his or her own cart and horses probably could have carried goods to market more cheaply than the sheriffs who had tight deadlines to meet.

The accounts surviving for the twinned bailiwick of Huntingdonshire and Cambridgeshire indicate that carters there carried out their duties with exemplary efficiency. The fruits of their labors can be seen in table 9-2, which records data derived from the carriage of purveyed wheat in the two counties. The table records the origin and destination of all loads itemized separately in a sheriff's account, the year, the distances covered, the amount carried (in quarters), the total spent on carriage, and the resulting cost per ton-mile calculable for each trip.[96] Weighted for the total amount of grain carried, the mean of all the trips recorded in this table is 1.2d. per ton-mile, with actual costs varying between 0.5d. and 1.9d. per ton-mile. As in most other counties, carters were ordinarily required to carry four quarters of grain as a condition of employment. Apart from the trips to London, costs were calculated as flat rates between destinations, presumably because all of the trips could be made in less than a single day.

TABLE 9-2:
Land Carriage Costs in Cambridgeshire and Huntingdonshire, 1305–1346

Origin	Terminus	Year	Miles	Qrs.	Total expense	Cost per ton-mile
Huntingdon	London	1305	57	40	50s.	1.5d.
Cambridge	London	1305	50	61	35s. 7d.	0.8d.
St. Ives	Cambridge	1305	12	10	1s. 8d.	1.0d.
Swavesey	Cambridge	1305	8	10	1s. 3d.	1.1d.
Caxton	Cambridge	1305	9	6	1s.	1.3d.
Royston	Ware	1305	17	15	3s. 6d.	1.0d.
Swavesey	Babraham	1305	15	20	2s.	0.5d.
Horseheath	Babraham	1305	7	20	1s. 8d.	0.8d.
Caxton	Royston	1305	11	18	1s. 6d.	0.5d.
Swavesey	Cambridge	1327	8	126	21s.	1.5d.
Kingston	Cambridge	1327	6	30	5s.	1.9d.
Linton	Cambridge	1327	10	10	2s. 6d.	1.8d.
Hatley	Cambridge	1327	12	10	2s. 6d.	1.5d.
Shingay	Cambridge	1327	11	10	2s. 6d.	1.6d.
Babraham	Cambridge	1346	7	42	5s.	1.2d.

NOTE: All entries involve carriage of wheat.
SOURCES: PRO E101/552/7; PRO E101/552/13; PRO E101/552/51.

The arrangements to send grain from Swavesey to Cambridge in 1327 were typical of those made in the sheriff's other dealings.[97] Swavesey, situated about halfway between Huntingdon and Cambridge, was one of the region's core markets, and the sheriff managed to acquire 126 quarters of wheat there at the exceptionally low price of 3s. 4d. per quarter, a price suggestive of a bumper harvest that year. To have the wheat carried the eight miles from Swavesey to Cambridge, the sheriff agreed to pay 2d. per quarter. This amounted to 5 percent of the price of the grain, more than a negligible amount to be sure, but certainly not high enough to preclude the possibility of trade if price differentials between the two markets arose. In years of higher prices—the national average in the decade from 1320 to 1330 was almost 7s. per quarter, more than twice that in 1327—the cost of transporting wheat over a comparable distance would have been correspondingly lower. Feeding costs would have gone up as grain prices rose, so we cannot assume a constant cost for transport, but even allowing that half of the cost of transport resided in the cost of oats and fodder, the share of transport in a year of normal prices would have been lower, no more than about 3 percent of the price of the grain for an eight mile trip.[98] And since producers who owned their own means of transportation could have moved goods more cheaply, the cost of transport relative to the price of the goods would have been even lower.

TABLE 9-3:
Riverine Carriage Costs in Cambridgeshire and Huntingdonshire, 1305–1347

Origin	Terminus	Year	Miles	Qrs.	Total expense	Cost per ton-mile
Wisbech	Lynn	1305	12	60	15s.	1.5d.
Yaxley	Lynn	1325	33	181	26s.	0.3d.
Yaxley	Lynn	1334	33	492	176s. 8d.	0.8d.
Yaxley	Lynn	1335	33	196	34s. 2d.	0.4d.
Yaxley	Lynn	1336	33	880	169s. 2d.	0.4d.
Alwalton	Lynn	1336	33	1014	232s. 5d.	0.5d.
St. Ives	Lynn	1336	37	380	87s. 1d.	0.4d.
St. Ives	Cambridge	1339	12	99	19s. 8d.	1.2d.
Cambridge	Ely	1347	15	42	7s. 1d.	0.8d.

NOTE: All entries involve carriage of wheat.
SOURCES: PRO E101/574/17; PRO E101/577/7; PRO E101/577/8; PRO E101/577/9;PRO E101/19/2; PRO E101/552/17; PRO E101/552/51.

These accounts also allow us to compare the effectiveness of land transport and water transport, since the sheriffs ordinarily hired boats and barges to send the accumulated grain to King's Lynn. Data derived from the costs incurred to send wheat along rivers running through Huntingdonshire and Cambridgeshire are presented in table 9-3. These data have been assembled and calculated in the same manner as those involving land transport in the two counties, with the exception that loading and unloading costs, which are not itemized among the expenses for land transport, are included in table 9-3 as part of the expense of water carriage. Weighted for the total amount carried, the mean for all the voyages included in the table amounts to 0.5d. per ton-mile, less than half the weighted mean for land transport in the same counties. The cost of transporting goods by water, then, would have been even less of an impediment to trade than the cost of transport by land.

On three occasions, sheriffs' accounts allow us to compare prices actually paid for wheat with the costs incurred to transport it: In 1334, the sheriff bought wheat for 5s. per quarter and paid 4d. per quarter to ship it to King's Lynn; four years later, he bought wheat for 4s. per quarter and paid 3.5d. per quarter for the same voyage; and in 1339, he acquired wheat at the exceptionally low price of 2s. 6d. per quarter and paid 2.25d. to send it from St. Ives to Cambridge.[99] In all three cases, the price of carriage amounted to about 7 percent of the purchase price of the grain. Wheat prices were often higher than those cited here, which would have dropped the relative cost of transport even further; in many years, the cost of transporting wheat from Huntingdonshire to King's Lynn would not have amounted to more than 5 percent of the value of the grain. An example of even lower transport costs relative to the value of the commodity transported is provided in a sheriff's account from 1352, which records both the purchase price of meat in Cambridgeshire and the costs of sending it to King's Lynn.[100] In that year, the sheriff procured 21 slaughtered ox carcasses, some at 4s. and some at 4s. 8d., and 71 hog carcasses, some at 2s. and some at 1s. 8d. To send the carcasses by boat from Cambridge, Ely, and Wisbech to King's Lynn, the sheriff paid 1d. for each ox and 1/4d. for each hog. Thus, carriage costs in this instance ranged between 1 and 2 percent of the value of the good being shipped.

V

In Huntingdonshire and across the entire country, carters and shippers managed to keep the costs of transport reasonably low because they had access to an infrastructure that allowed them to reach their destinations quickly and efficiently. The carters who hauled purveyed grain from Huntingdon to London could expect that the roads they took would be clear of obstructions and that there would be bridges to use when needed. These carters also had intangible knowledge about what such a trip entailed: how their carts would bear up with a heavy load over scores of miles, how they ought to equip themselves and their horses for the trip, how to pace their animals, and so on. Their deeds help us to visualize some of the possibilities and opportunities available in a more strictly commercial environment. After all, both the infrastructure and the human capital employed for such a trip arose in a commercial environment, an environment in which it made economic sense to invest in such things as bridges and teams of carthorses.

For the merchants in Huntingdon, who knew that, in the right circumstances, they could expect to cover up to 25 miles with a fully loaded cart in a single day, a vast array of commercial opportunities was available. Even if their interest extended only 12 miles out from the town—half the maximum distance feasible in a day's journey with a cart—they would have been able to visit every one of the core markets in the county and still return to their own beds at night, with only the trip to Yaxley testing the limits of their horses' endurance. Of course, these merchants would have needed time in their chosen destination to transact business, but even if they limited themselves to journeys of 10 miles in each direction, only the trip to Yaxley would have required more than a day's effort. By spending just a single night on the road, Huntingdon's merchants could have made round trips to Bedford, Cambridge, Oundle, Peterborough, Stamford, Ely, and even Northampton. Of course, merchants in all of these towns were capable of making the reverse trip, bringing their wares to Huntingdon in a day's journey. Perhaps merchants from both ends sometimes even found themselves together looking over the merchandise in one of the rural markets en route as they traveled in opposite directions. Whichever direction the merchants took, they could expect to find other merchants who had traveled to the same town from an equal but opposite distance. Thus, when they reached Northampton, they might find themselves negotiating with merchants from Coventry or Leicester. As will become evident in the next chapter, such trips and such commercial contacts in Huntingdonshire and surrounding counties are more than exercises of imagination.

A town's position at the heart of a regional transportation network gave its commercially minded residents a head start over people dwelling in the countryside, but the latter were nonetheless capable of similar kinds of mobility. In a well-documented study of northeastern Huntingdonshire, for example, Anne DeWindt has shown that many peasants had economic interests in multiple villages and markets situated up to 10 miles apart.[101] As outlined in chapter 8, by the middle of the thirteenth century, a 10-mile trip from any village in the county would have sufficed to reach at least three core markets. Villagers in Great Gidding, whose roads were described in an earlier part of this chapter, could have traveled to Huntingdon, Kimbolton, Yaxley, and Oundle with a cartload of grain and returned home the same day: It was no coincidence that three of these market sites gave rise to the names of roads in the village.

Given the size of the carts in use, we need not imagine any one villager making such trips more than a handful of times in any given year. For a peasant producer, a single cartload probably represented a substantial portion of a year's marketable surplus. Christopher Dyer has estimated that a typical virgater in the west Midlands probably sent about 100 bushels of grain to market in an average year; in Huntingdonshire, where yields were somewhat higher, the figure was probably closer to 150 bushels.[102] Marketable surpluses in this range could easily be handled in four or five trips with a fully loaded cart. Of course, peasants may have preferred to spread their market income more evenly through the year by marketing in smaller quantities. On the other hand, the ability to carry a substantial portion of the year's marketable surplus in a single trip also made it easier for a producer to bypass a nearby local market in the hope of getting a better price in a larger regional market.

Mobility on this scale was a major factor in determining a market's fate in the Darwinian world of thirteenth-century commercial life. A wealthy villager or a manorial lord did not have to settle for the nearest venue when deciding where to market the fruits of the year's harvest. He or she owned a horse and cart, had access to a network of roads and bridges leading to different market sites, and, with a modicum of wisdom, developed a sense of which markets had the most buyers, the highest prices, and the best consumer goods for sale. If that market happened to be situated a few miles further than the nearest available site, so be it: A trip to market was not a daily event. In all likelihood, the only ones consigned to using the nearest market were those at the bottom end of the social scale, who probably could not afford to feed a horse throughout the year and who would not have had much to put in a cart even if they owned one. For such people, a few extra miles made a big difference in their ability to market. Even in important towns people sometimes brought victuals to market slung across their backs.[103] In all periods of history, the spatial horizons of different groups have expanded in accordance with their level of income; in the modern world, slums trap poor people as much because of undernourished mental horizons as undernourished stomachs. Contrary to what many historians have said and thought, markets that found their clientele chiefly among the poorer peasants living within a few miles of the site do not typify the commercial economy of the period. They formed part of it, but that part needs to be understood in the same context as the villagers of Gidding who yoked up their horses, loaded their carts, and set off down the king's highway to the county town.

10

A Regional Economy in Action

Unlike the numerous local markets whose facilities were of interest only to the residents of a handful of neighboring villages, if they were of interest to anyone at all, the more limited number of core markets outlined in chapter 8 attracted merchants and other traders from towns and market sites well removed from the local economy. Several of Huntingdonshire's trading venues fell into this category and developed into important regional centers with horizons stretching dozens of miles from their market squares. With an identification of the core markets and principal transportation routes of the county under our belts, it is time to turn our attention more directly to the merchants and local traders, as well as to the kings and soldiers, who took advantage of the opportunities provided by this commercial infrastructure. To do so we need to look at the ability of the county's markets to entice outsiders into their midst and at the reciprocal involvement of residents of the principal markets engaged in commercial transactions elsewhere. We also need to take a short detour into military history, because our most vivid record of how the county's markets, roads, and commercial personnel worked together to form an integrated regional network is provided by the logistical demands of the king and his purveyors, who tapped into the structures created in times of peace to assemble desperately needed supplies of foodstuffs. Different sources show different parts of the network, but all of the sources discussed in this chapter reinforce the view that Huntingdonshire was part of a regional economic network.

I

Merchants from surrounding counties were no strangers to the markets of Huntingdonshire. As is so often the case with medieval commerce, they appear more frequently in circumstances of conflict than of routine contact, but given the historical distance, it is fortuitous that they appear under any circumstances at all. Two particularly revealing sets of circumstances are available to reconstruct their role in the county's markets: disputes over payments of toll and disputes over rights of access. The core markets of Yaxley and St. Neots were involved in a number of these disputes and furnish particularly instructive case studies.

The market in Yaxley was an extraordinarily successful venture in the thirteenth and fourteenth centuries, and indeed for many succeeding centuries. Devoid of any distinctive traits at the time of Domesday that might suggest its future orientation, it had become by the late thirteenth century a thriving entrepôt for traders in several counties, a textbook example of the commercial transformation of the rural world this book seeks to explain.[1] The first intimate view of the village after the Domesday inquiry is provided by a tenurial survey made in 1279.[2] By that time the market had been active for a little less than two centuries, and its imprint on the village is readily apparent. As both Richard Britnell and Richard Smith have observed, successful markets typically created economic opportunities that allowed their host villages to harbor unusually large populations of landless and land-poor tenants.[3] This was certainly the case in Yaxley, which had well over 100 tenants endowed with negligible agricultural property in 1279, more than half of all the tenants described in the survey. Many of these tenants had occupational surnames; a number of these were named after lucrative trades more commonly found in towns, including a glover, a wool merchant and two other merchants. The village's commercial orientation in 1279 is also suggested by the presence of a number of permanent shops, a form of real estate seldom associated with rural market sites. This profile of Yaxley as a village greatly influenced by its market is borne out a few generations later in the Nonae assessment, in which Yaxley was one of only two market sites in the county assessed for the fifteenth on merchandise (the other was St. Ives).[4] With its 11 merchants and £45 worth of assessed merchandise, Yaxley typifies the group of thriving rural markets found in select villages across the Midlands, as discussed in chapter 4.

The earliest reference to Yaxley's position as a hub of regional commerce comes in the course of a legal challenge over tolls mounted in the king's court by the burgesses of Northampton.[5] In 1201, the burgesses directed several charges against the abbot of Thorney, the holder of the market. They complained that the abbot took toll from them contrary to their borough's chartered exemption, that he took toll from them in Woodston where he had no right to collect any toll at all, and that he had recently begun taking twice as much toll from them as he had in previous years. In the course of the pleading, the burgesses quietly dropped their claim not to have to pay any toll at all and concentrated instead on how it should be paid. It turned out that the tolls in Woodston were imposed because the burgesses had begun landing their merchandise there before carrying it to the market in Yaxley (indicating, incidentally, that the River Nene was suitable for local traffic between Northampton and Yaxley). The abbot told the court that it was simpler to enforce payment at the point of unloading than at the point of sale in the marketplace in Yaxley, but since he lacked a charter expressly granting him the right to do so, the court found in favor of the burgesses and forbade him from continuing the practice. On the issue of the rate of toll in the market, the merchants claimed that traditionally they had paid 1d. per cartload of goods, 1/2d. per load on a packhorse, and 1/4d. per load carried on a man's back. The abbot, though, claimed that he had collected twice these rates for a number of years; the court accepted his avowal and let the higher rates stand. Thus, both sides came away with something from the settlement. Northampton's discontent with the abbot of Thorney was, however, to persist into future generations: as noted in chapter 6, Yaxley was one of the places Northampton complained about for collecting tolls in its presentment in the Hundred Rolls in 1275.

A quarter-century later, in 1226, the abbot of Thorney again found himself in court facing a challenge over tolls in his market in Yaxley, this time in a suit brought by merchants from Bedford.[6] Bedford's merchants denied entirely the abbot's right to collect toll from them, claiming that they had been granted freedom from toll in the reign of Henry II. They added that originally the abbot had respected this exemption, but that he had changed his course following a siege of the castle in Bedford, in which their charters had been burned.[7] The abbot's attorney replied, as did most marketholders in similar circumstances, that his client's right to collect tolls predated Bedford's right of exemption and that he had always exercised this right. The burgesses countered with the claim that their exemption actually went back to the reign of William the Conqueror, a convenient argument to make when the original charter no longer existed. The abbot's attorney, however, was shrewder than the burgesses in this case. He pointed out that Bedford's customs were modeled on those of Oxford and that the merchants from the university town had always paid toll in Yaxley. Furthermore, at some earlier date a royal official who had been ordered to liberate distraints that the abbot had taken in Yaxley from various burgesses of Huntingdon and Bedford chose not to do so after seeing the abbot's charter granting him the right to collect tolls. The case was postponed for judgment, but it shows unequivocally that merchants from at least three regional towns—Bedford, Oxford, and Huntingdon—were making use of the abbot's market.

In the same year as their challenge to the abbot of Thorney, Bedford's merchants also began proceedings against the prior of St. Neots over his demands for toll in the market there.[8] Though perhaps not as successful as its counterpart in Yaxley, the market in St. Neots had also managed to establish itself as one of the region's core commercial venues over the course of the twelfth and thirteenth centuries. Along with the remarkable market square illustrated in chapter 8, St. Neots, like Yaxley, had a significant concentration of tenants with little or no agricultural land, many of whom can be found in a partial rental of the village in 1286 with names indicative of artisanal specializations.[9] Its failure to attract notice in the Nonae assessment of rural merchandise suggests that it was a second- rather than a first-tier market site, but even so, its commercial significance extended well beyond its immediate environs.

The dispute with the burgesses of Bedford is a case in point. Improving on their performance in the dispute with the market in Yaxley, Bedford's burgesses managed in their dispute with St. Neots to come up with a charter ostensibly proving their right to an exemption, presenting the court with a document supposedly drawn up in the reign of Henry I (1100-1135), confirming an even earlier grant of exemption. Once again, they claimed that traditional observance of the exemption ended as a result of political circumstances, in this case informing the court that the prior had begun to take toll from them in the midst of the war between King John and his barons. And once again, the case was postponed without record of a verdict. But in the initial pleading, the prior noted that his right to the market and the right to collect tolls had been proclaimed by the king's sheriffs throughout both Huntingdonshire and Bedfordshire as well as throughout Cambridgeshire and Buckinghamshire.

Bedford's plaint does not specify any details of the trade with St. Neots, but other sources suggest that it probably took advantage of the riverine link provided by the River Ouse, which linked both places with Huntingdon, St. Ives, and places further downstream. A complaint made in the Hundred Rolls about a mill constructed on the stretch of the river between Bedford and Huntingdon states explicitly that the mill impeded boats plying the river between the two towns.[10] While in the market in St. Neots, Bedford's merchants may very well have rubbed shoulders with merchants from London. In 1338, the king sent one of his Marshalsea clerks from the Tower of London to the market in St. Neots (as well as to the markets in Abingdon and St. Ives) to buy horses for his household, suggesting that the market was well known in the metropolis. A generation later the market was stated to be the ultimate destination of a London merchant whose goods were seized for suspected theft.[11]

Residents of Huntingdonshire's principal market sites frequently reciprocated the commercial interest exhibited by the regional towns of central and eastern England. Henry Ponteys, a merchant from Yaxley, was well enough known in Northampton in 1275, to be singled out by name in the town's litany of toll problems recited before the justices conducting the Hundred Roll inquiries.[12] Great Yarmouth's herring attracted the interest of traders from Yaxley, St. Neots, St. Ives, and Huntingdon, all of which were home to merchants who contracted sizable debts in the Norfolk town.[13] Even London was probably familiar commercial terrain by the early fourteenth century. Eilert Ekwall traced 53 of the city's immigrants in this period to Huntingdonshire, the vast majority of whom came from the county's leading commercial centers: Huntingdon, origin of 19 immigrants, St. Ives of 11, and St. Neots of 10.[14] It comes as no surprise, then, to find a merchant from St. Neots, who also had commercial interests in St. Ives, registering a debt in London's recognizance rolls in 1285.[15]

While the residents of Huntingdonshire's leading market sites clearly had dealings with a number of regional towns, their primary conduit to more distant commercial opportunities was undoubtedly provided by the riverine routes linking the county to King's Lynn. By the early thirteenth century, King's Lynn was one of the leading ports in the country, surpassed in wealth only by London, Southampton, Boston, and possibly Bristol.[16] Its wealth was due principally to trade, both with an extensive interior and with foreign merchants who came from all parts of Europe.[17] The earliest documentary evidence of contact between the port and Huntingdonshire dates to the middle of the twelfth century, when a Lynn saltmaker settled in Yaxley.[18] Evidence exists of shipments of grain from the county to the port for export by Flemish merchants in 1170, and within two generations of this merchants from Yaxley and St. Neots registered as members of the town's guild merchant.[19]

A particularly detailed description of the trade links between King's Lynn, Huntingdonshire, and neighboring counties is furnished by what must have been something of a cause célèbre in the early part of the fourteenth century. In 1329, a plaint was made before justices itinerant in Northamptonshire that Walter Langton, former bishop of Coventry and Lichfield, royal treasurer, and crook extraordinaire, had built a dam as part of a drainage project on land he owned near the village of Wells in Norfolk and in so doing had obstructed the flow of the River Nene.[20] The presentment jury stated that formerly it had been possible to go directly from Peterborough to King's Lynn with grain, wool, and other merchandise and to return with victuals and other necessities. To assess the validity of the charge, the court ordered juries to be empaneled in all of the counties with an interest in the Nene navigation.

The ensuing commissions in both Huntingdonshire and Norfolk reported that Langton's obstructions were indeed a serious hindrance to commercial traffic between the two counties. The Norfolk jury stated that prior to the building of the dam people took their goods from Yaxley and parts further on directly to King's Lynn. Following construction of the dam, people could still travel back and forth but only by circumnavigating the dam, making the journey considerably longer. Because of these navigational difficulties, the jury said, "grain, timber, sedge, reeds, turves, stone, and other merchandise is more expensive, and fish, herrings, and other victuals are both more expensive and of lower quality."[21] Huntingdonshire's jury echoed the Norfolk presentment, stating that before the obstruction people could travel directly to King's Lynn from Yaxley and elsewhere in the county with grain and other saleable goods and that merchants from the port could travel easily in the other direction with victuals and merchandise. Based on such overwhelming evidence of the harm done by Langton's dam, the king ordered the sheriff of Norfolk to tear it down so that the Nene could be returned to use as an artery of commerce.

A century before the resolution of this case involving trade along the Nene, another case involving riverine trade relations between Huntingdonshire and King's Lynn was heard in the king's courts. This time the river involved was the Ouse, and the quarrel was not about transportation per se but about the relationship between different markets in the county and the routes that merchants from King's Lynn used in their trading ventures. The case furnishes a vivid example of the connection between rural market cycles and urban mercantile interests in the period. In 1227, the abbot of Ramsey acquired a royal charter granting him the right to establish a Tuesday market in St. Ives.[22] Possession of such a franchise was eminently practical for the wealthy monastery: For over a century Ramsey had held an Easter fair in St. Ives, and by the early thirteenth century annual profit from it was as high as £180.[23] The trading facilities, administrative knowledge, and habitual usage developed by the fair were all well suited to the holding of a weekly market.

The burgesses of Huntingdon were, however, not impressed by Ramsey's pragmatism. They contended that if a market were held in St. Ives their town would suffer because ships coming from King's Lynn would put in at St. Ives rather than continue downstream the five extra miles to Huntingdon. The burgesses explained that there were three dams between St. Ives and Huntingdon, making navigation so difficult that it was more expensive to rent a ship between the two locations than it was to rent a ship to travel all the way between St. Ives and King's Lynn. If St. Ives had a market, it, rather than the county town, would become the entrepôt linking the county to coastal and international trade routes. Furthermore, the townsmen complained that Ramsey's role as a major landholder in the county gave it an unfair competitive advantage, since the inhabitants of its numerous manors in the area would attend the abbot's market more willingly than they would the market in Huntingdon. The juxtaposition of these two complaints is striking: The proposed market is unequivocally portrayed as a venue where outside traders and local peasants would come together to exchange goods.

Ramsey's fellow abbot in Thorney also entered the dispute, claiming that a market in St. Ives would be detrimental to his market in Yaxley. Thorney's argument was likewise based on the trade with King's Lynn. The preferred route of merchants from King's Lynn involved in trade with markets in Huntingdonshire was the River Ouse, described as a waterway that was "good and alive," unlike the Nene, which Thorney described as a slow-moving river. If a market were established in St. Ives, ships from King's Lynn would invariably take the Ouse, and although Yaxley and St. Ives were linked by local water ways, the connection was not good enough to permit ships to make it to the Thursday market in Yaxley if they went to a Tuesday market in St. Ives.

The presence of a county marketing cycle is as apparent in Ramsey's defense of its newly acquired privilege as in the challenge made on behalf of the market in Yaxley. Rather than harm the trade of Huntingdon, the abbot contended, a market in St. Ives would actually improve it: Tuesday was not a market day in Huntingdon, and whatever was left unsold in St. Ives could be taken for sale in the town. The townsmen feared that a market in St. Ives would leave them with a smaller slice of a fixed pie of trade; the abbot argued that his market would create a bigger pie, with correspondingly bigger slices. The defense against Thorney's claim is an even clearer indication of the existence of a trading cycle. Contrary to the claim that ships could not reach Yaxley in time for a Thursday market, Ramsey maintained that such a trip would pose no trouble, that both by water and by land goods could reach Yaxley in time for its market. Both parties assumed that Lynn's merchants would travel from one market to the next if given the right opportunity; presumably this assumption was based on concrete knowledge of prevailing practices rather than on imagined optimism of a possible future.

No decision in the case is recorded; the margin of the Curia Regis Roll has the simple note "Loquendum"—to be discussed. Ramsey must have lost the case, though, because later in the century it failed to register a claim for the market with the justices involved in Quo Warranto proceedings, and in 1293 the abbot again sought a charter from the king to allow him to establish a market in St. Ives.[24] This second attempt proved to be successful, although the market day was changed from Tuesdays to Mondays, a less desirable slot in the weekly cycle. In the inquest convened by the sheriff to hear objections to this second attempt, a jury, drawn from all quarters of the county, pronounced that the market was not harmful, primarily because the abbot had agreed to assign revenue from the tolls in the market to the town of Huntingdon.[25] Having thus bought off his fiercest potential opponents, the abbot was allowed to have the franchise. Later fines imposed by the Clerk of the Market indicate that it developed into a functioning concern that would outlive the monastery by many centuries. Even without the sweetener, a Monday market was less of a threat to the markets in Huntingdon and Yaxley, and it may well be that by then the holders of other markets in the county accepted that St. Ives might do more good by increasing the county's attractions than harm by siphoning off the trade of other markets.

II

Like many parts of the country, Huntingdonshire's commercial infrastructure was severely tested under the duress of war provisioning. As a county with a productive agrarian base and good transportation links with eastern ports,

Huntingdonshire regularly found itself called upon to provide much-needed provisions for the English armies sent to fight in Scotland and France. Behind each of these recurring mobilizations lay a sophisticated economic structure capable of transferring supplies of arms and victuals with efficiency and speed from the centers of production to the centers of consumption, a structure that the king and his administrators took for granted as they devised strategies to ensure the flow of supplies. In this regard, the state was an imitator rather than a creator; it did not create an infrastructure but instead assumed one that was already in place, built up by generations of commercial endeavor. Thus, the expedients used by royal officials to provision the armies are, in effect, a mirror of the inner dynamics of a co-existing commercial world.

As discussed in chapter 2, direct purveyance from peasant producers was the principal means used to provision armies in the field; in some counties, including Huntingdonshire, purveyance campaigns became almost an annual ritual in the first half of the fourteenth century.[26] When the king needed foodstuffs for his troops, he ordinarily issued a writ to the sheriff of a targeted county specifying the type and quantity of goods required and the destination to which the goods were to be sent. Typically, these instructions were couched in broad and general terms, leaving most of the practical arrangements in the hands of the sheriff, who drew on his familiarity with local conditions to carry out his duties. Significant amounts of money were disbursed in the course of a purveyance drive: wages for people hired to move supplies to mills or docks, rent for storage facilities, contracts with boat owners to ship the supplies, payments for miscellaneous items such as rope, bushels, measures, and shovels, and a host of other related expenses. Sheriffs had wide latitude when making these arrangements, but they knew that their expenditures would be scrutinized carefully when the campaign was over; thus, most of them knew that it was in their own best interest to keep itemized records of what they had done and to pass this information along to the auditors when presenting their accounts. Fortunately, a large number of these accounts have survived, including a relatively good sample from Huntingdonshire. By working through these accounts, we can recreate the steps by which grain and livestock produced in the county's peasant villages ended up in the bellies of English soldiers fighting their king's enemies in Scotland and France.

The supplies demanded from Huntingdonshire varied from one purveyance to the next, but usually involved at least 1,000 quarters of grain and sometimes more than 2,000 quarters.[27] As noted in chapter 2, most requisitions involved combinations of cereals, usually wheat, barley or malt, oats, and sometimes peas. Meats were also occasionally demanded, typically in the range of 100 to 200 carcasses. In reality, the sheriffs seldom managed to meet their quotas, largely because in most campaigns concerns about speed outweighed concerns about quantity. Rather than delay shipment in order to gather more supplies, sheriffs simply sent whatever they had managed to collect by the specified date. In an environment of war, this made perfect sense.

And even though they routinely fell short of their official targets, sheriffs in Huntingdonshire handled significant quantities of grain and stock.[28]

The time allotted to the sheriff to carry out the king's orders seldom extended beyond a few months. The Huntingdonshire campaign of 1301 provides a good example of the speed expected of the sheriff and his staff.[29] On April 3 of that year the king sent a writ to the sheriff ordering him to proclaim publicly the king's need of supplies and his intention to pay for any purveyed goods from the proceeds of an upcoming lay subsidy. Because of discontent with previous campaigns, the king directed the sheriff to negotiate with the villages about how the county's quota should be met before any goods were actually taken. On April 27, the king sent another writ to the sheriff, directing him to send the supplies he collected to Berwick by June 24. The sheriff failed to meet the deadline but managed to come reasonably close: On July 16, nearly 400 quarters of wheat and malt, collected from 71 different villages in the county, were freighted in King's Lynn for the journey northward. A little over three months had passed since Chancery clerks had drawn up the first writ, during which time the sheriff first had to come to an agreement with the villages about their respective contributions before he could even begin to assemble the requested foodstuffs. All sheriffs involved in purveyance worked under similar kinds of deadlines, and most of them managed similar levels of performance. By the standards of the day, the collection of thousands of bushels of grain and their transfer from central England to Scotland or France in a matter of months was a tremendous administrative achievement.

How were sheriffs able to carry out such complex tasks in such a short amount of time? To answer this question, we need to look at what the sheriff actually did over the course of the few months he was allotted. The surviving purveyance accounts for Huntingdonshire allow us to do so in some detail. A major part of the sheriff's responsibility in a purveyance campaign was to organize the logistics of transmitting the supplies acquired in his county to the destination specified by the king. This task was broken down into three parts. First of all, supplies from the individual villages in the county were gathered together and stored in one or two central depots until the collection was completed. In Huntingdonshire, the standard storage site was St. Ives. Once the victuals were assembled, they were sent by boat to King's Lynn, the second stage in the process. In King's Lynn the victuals were transferred to larger ships for transport to Berwick, Newcastle, Calais, or elsewhere. St. Ives was a logical choice for use as a storage depot, given that the victuals were to be sent to King's Lynn. The navigational difficulties between Huntingdon and St. Ives, mentioned above, made the latter a much more practical choice. In addition to a good location, though, an intermediate storage site such as St. Ives also had to meet other requirements. First of all, it had to nurture reliable and experienced agents capable of handling a major influx of grain in a short period of time—in other words, it needed human expertise dealing in large volumes of goods. The names of a few of the agents employed in this capacity in

St. Ives are recorded, and in every case they were prominent members of the local commercial and political elite.[30]

Along with the human capital used to oversee the collection of the purveyance, the sheriff had certain physical requirements of the chosen depot. One of these, about which very little is said in the accounts, was reliable transportation access from other parts of the county: All parties took it for granted that the existing roads, bridges, and streets were up to the task of conveying hundreds of cartloads to the designated site. Another requirement was the availability of storage facilities in the village to hold the grain as it accumulated. In 1323, for example, the sheriff had to rent three granaries in St. Ives for five weeks to hold the 620 quarters purveyed in the county; similar arrangements had to made in other years.[31] As in the other parts of the operation, the sheriff found himself on these occasions working with leading members of the local community, who happened to have storage space available as long as the price was right. But the infrequency and unpredictability of purveyance campaigns meant that none of these people could have relied on purveyance-related rents as part of their regular income. Such short-term rents were nothing more than opportunistic windfalls: The granaries used to store the collected grain were not specially tailored for the sheriff's needs. They were structures existing prior to the sheriff's demand for them, and they served other, commercial, purposes for most of the year.

St. Ives was not the only village in the county to serve as a storage depot in purveyance campaigns. The same reasons that made St. Ives attractive—efficient riverine transport to a major port, human capital, storage infrastructure, and so on—also applied to Yaxley. Because it was located more centrally, St. Ives was the sheriff's preferred site, but occasionally the county was divided into northern and southern districts, with villages in the former part sending their goods to Yaxley to be pooled and transported.[32] In addition to its occasional role in Huntingdonshire's purveyances, though, Yaxley invariably played a large role as a favored storage depot in all purveyance campaigns undertaken in neighboring Northamptonshire. In most campaigns in that county, intermediate storage depots were set up to collect supplies locally, but these supplies were usually sent on to Yaxley to be loaded for the trip to King's Lynn. The volumes shipped in this fashion were comparable to those sent from Huntingdonshire via St. Ives.[33] Detailed local records for Yaxley have not survived, but there can be little doubt that the subcontractors there were cut from the same cloth as their better-documented counterparts in St. Ives.

While most purveyed grain left the county in unprocessed form, on some occasions the sheriff made arrangements to have it milled before shipment. These instances furnish yet further evidence of the versatility and responsiveness of regional commercial facilities. Shipments of flour not only necessitated additional labor in the process of milling, but also raised problems in the shipping because of the increased potential for spoilage. This meant that greater care had to be taken in packing the flour, requiring the purchase of large wooden barrels (dolia) for use as storage vessels. To ship the flour milled from 244 quarters of wheat in 1323, for example, the sheriff purchased 29 empty barrels, 19 in Huntingdon and St. Neots and the other 10 in St. Ives. Similar arrangements were made in a number of other years.[34] There is no indication in any of the accounts of the prior contents of these barrels; perhaps they were recycled from the wine trade. Each barrel held about 7 quarters of flour and thus would likely stand 5 or 6 feet off the ground with a circumference of about 20 feet.[35] Whatever they contained in their earlier incarnations must have been traded in wholesale quantities. But what is significant about these barrels is not so much their size as their origin. When he needed commercial containers, the sheriff inevitably turned to the leading market sites in the county to obtain them. Their presence in places like St. Ives and St. Neots indicates the role such market villages had in the regional economy as bulking centers for goods exported from the county or as distribution centers for goods sent from the bulking centers of other areas.

All of the goods assembled in St. Ives and Yaxley were ultimately shipped from their places of storage to King's Lynn. To transport the supplies from the storage depots, the sheriff procured the services of numerous boats *(batelli)* to send the goods to the port. The owners of these boats are seldom named, but details about how they carried out their tasks are sometimes recorded. In 1334, for example, 383 quarters of wheat, peas, and oats were sent from St. Ives to King's Lynn in eight boats, yielding an average cargo of 48 quarters—more than eight tons—per boat.[36] These boats, which plied the rivers with commercial goods when not filled with purveyed grain, must have been fairly substantial vessels, probably more than 30 feet long from bow to stern. Eight men were hired to go with the boats in 1334, each receiving wages for five days for the voyage to King's Lynn and back, described as being 60 leagues one way. In King's Lynn the grain was either loaded directly from these smaller boats onto larger ships for the coastal or cross-Channel voyage, or, if a ship were not immediately available, offloaded into storage facilities on or near the town's quay. Maneuvering a loaded barrel of flour onto these boats in the years the king requested that the milling be done locally must have been quite a job. As with all other steps in a purveyance campaign, these journeys simply replicated countless others that were routine events for those with commercial interests.

In spite of the complexity inherent in moving large quantities of bulky goods from villages in the middle of England to armies fighting hundreds of miles away, purveyance proved to be a remarkably efficient arrangement, and when Edward III agreed to scale back his reliance on the system in 1362, he did so because of domestic resentment of arbitrary requisitions, not because of any doubts about the reliability of provisioning.[37] The sheriffs and their staffs deserve much of the credit for this efficiency, but their success was ultimately due to the infrastructure already in place. Sheriffs made virtually no expenditures on capital equipment or infrastructure; they simply rented what they needed for the few months it took to carry out the king's orders. The sheriff did not provide the facilities to permit villagers to carry their grain to St. Ives; he did not build granaries or mills to store and grind the wheat; he did not hire carpenters to build the barges and boats needed for the goods he had assembled; he did not create the transportation network that allowed him to transport hundreds of quarters of grain and scores of animal carcasses to King's Lynn and thence to Scotland and France. All of these facilities were already in existence, and the sheriff's task was simply to organize them as best he could for his own purposes and to come up with the cash to secure their use. Shrieval efficiency in mobilizing these resources is a testament to their administrative ability, but it is also a tribute to the structures created by local people, who were, in the final analysis, the ones who made the system work by putting their skills, knowledge, and equipment at the sheriff's disposal.

III

In his classic study of the Hundred Years War, Édouard Perroy began by drawing up a balance sheet of the political and economic situations in England and France on the eve of the war.[38] England, with perhaps a fifth of the population of France, a far lower degree of urbanization, and a less-developed agrarian economy, could not have hoped for much success in a protracted struggle with her continental rival. In a different context, R. H. Hilton grappled with a very similar question, asking in a recent article the intriguing question, "Was medieval England a backward society on the periphery of Europe?"[39] Perroy's main concern was to account for England's ability to wage war so successfully; Hilton's to explain how a seemingly underdeveloped economy could ultimately give rise to the greatest economic transformation in history, the Industrial Revolution. Both men offer explanations worthy of consideration. Perroy contended that what England lacked in total resources was compensated for by more effective administration, while Hilton argued that though England lacked an urban economy as concentrated as that existing in other parts of Europe, the country's grid of rural markets gave an important commercial vigor to the rural economy that offset the reduced level of urbanization. Aspects of both of these phenomena are apparent in the networks of trade and purveyance discussed in this chapter. The king and his officials were well aware of the sophistication of these networks when they adapted them for military provisioning; indeed, purveyance on the scale practiced in this period would have been inconceivable without the economic infrastructure and human capital that had been built up in preceding generations.

By the end of the thirteenth century, most regions of England had developed into integrated entities comparable to the one in Huntingdonshire and its environs. Huntingdon had its counterparts in the Andovers, Colchesters, and Chichesters of the country; King's Lynn in the Ipswiches, Gloucesters, and Yarmouths; Yaxley in the Abingdons, Banburys, and Doncasters; the Ouse in the Severns, Thameses, and Trents; and the lower-order markets of the county in literally hundreds of other places. Huntingdonshire was not commercially precocious; it was a county with minimal urbanization and a high incidence of villein tenure, dominated by conservative Benedictine monasteries. It was not particularly wealthy; its agriculture was not uniquely productive or unusually oriented towards producing commercial goods. Yet it was clearly a county with an economy in which peasant villages, rural markets, and towns were linked together into a complementary network. Equally clearly, this network formed part of a larger regional constellation stretching into neighboring counties. Like other parts of the country, Huntingdonshire was a county of peasant farmers, and like other parts of the country, it was simultaneously part of a regional, national, and even an international economy.

Conclusion

By the end of the thirteenth century, England had developed a sophisticated commercial economy that embraced all levels of society, from the kings whose charters and courts helped to establish new marketing sites to the peasants whose crops and flocks turned them into perduring fixtures of social and economic life. As with most transformations in society and economy, there is no single group or single generation that served as the sole or even the predominant agent for change. Commercialization was a process that necessarily required the collective enterprise of succeeding generations, each one adding to the institutions and habits inherited from its predecessor. It was also a process that displayed great diversity in its formative influences and outcomes, a diversity that explains much of its intrinsic interest to historians. Some of its formative influences, such as the itinerancy of urban merchants, can be traced into the mists of time, while others, such as the development of a precise legal formula to protect the rights of market founders, can be dated to a specific year. Similarly, some of its outcomes, such as the sequential temporal ordering of market cycles, can be observed through many succeeding centuries, while others, such as the reliance on "earnest" money and tally sticks to document contractual obligations have faded into an obscurity that only medievalists can relish. It is, in short, a wonderfully complex phenomenon, much of which still awaits detailed investigation.

Among its many formative influences, pride of place should probably go to the underlying population growth that characterized the period covered in this book, details of which have been grist for historians' mills for several generations. Without the stimulus of a rising population in both town and countryside, medieval England probably would not have adopted commercial exchange as a central element of economic life. In all pre- and nonindustrialized societies, both past and present, the principal hindrance to economic growth is the weakness of effective demand. Without demand, there is little incentive to innovate or to intensify production levels, and households have no reason to concern themselves with anything other than the production of goods required for their reproduction. By stimulating the overall level of demand in the economy, a rise in population can, if other conditions are propitious, steer a society toward increasing reliance on the market.

Population growth alone, however, does not automatically lead a society to commercialize. If land and capital are not distributed in ways that allow demand to broaden at society's base, then creeping poverty rather than commercialization will result. Clifford Geertz has presented a powerful example of this in his study of the traditional Indonesian economy.[1] Geertz argues that as population increased and individual holdings of land correspondingly dwindled, Indonesian peasants simply intensified production techniques to make up for what they had lost in holding size, a process he described as "agricultural involution." Excess labor did not migrate into other sectors of the economy, and hence the society did not undergo any significant commercial reorientation. Medieval England traveled part of the way along this path in the centuries before the Black Death, but unlike Indonesia, its intensification of land use was accompanied by a release of labor into the towns and a gradual reorientation of the economy toward commercial exchange between town and country.

How can one explain the divergent paths that different peasant societies take in ostensibly similar circumstances of demographic growth? This question has been asked in many contexts by historians, geographers, economists, and economic anthropologists over the past 30 years without yielding anything remotely resembling a consensus of opinion. Unfortunately—but not surprisingly—historians of medieval England do not have a sword with which to cut this Gordian knot. They do, however, have a contribution to make to the debate, particularly on the subject of peasant differentiation. In some peasantries, the splintering of household endowments of land closely parallels the expansion of population; pauperization proceeds as the companion of equality. Splintering induced by population growth certainly occurred in medieval England, but even in densely populated areas it did not lead to a leveling of household resources. Even in such densely populated areas as East Anglia in the early fourteenth century, some peasants managed to resist the pressure to subdivide their lands, retaining holdings that were significantly larger—and more commercially oriented—than those of their neighbors.[2] At the other end of the spectrum, of course, this meant that other peasants were denied access to holdings amenable to subsistence farming. Thus, a dynamic was set up within the peasant economy that simultaneously expanded the labor pool, the internal demand for subsistence goods, and the incentives for a privileged tier of producers to intensify production. The growth of towns occurred in conjunction with this process, much like a shot of adrenaline speeding up processes that were proceeding more gradually at the village level.

Along with a propitious regime of property rights, commercialization also requires other favorable conditions if it is to insinuate itself into a society. Political circumstances, for example, must be favorable. Without peace and internal security, humans are justifiably reticent to expand their economic horizons beyond their local community. Even with its famous episodes of internal strife, the "long" thirteenth century was a period of unusual tranquility in England, as it was in many other parts of Europe. Auspicious institutional circumstances also existed, including a state capable of providing a relatively stable currency and a reasonably effective mechanism to arbitrate commercial disputes. Individual initiative and resourcefulness in making use of the opportunities presented by society also played a part, as did the cultural values and standards that made the accumulation of material wealth a significant measure of individual or community status.[3] Peasants and merchants shared this value, with all of the expectations, hopes, and fears that went with it.

As important as the complex ways in which population growth influenced commercialization is the reverse relationship: the relationship between commercialization and standards of living in a period of prolonged demographic growth. Most current work in the field maintains that commercialization facilitated a rise in absolute levels of national wealth and human capital during the twelfth and thirteenth centuries, and though there is no consensus that growth in real per capita incomes occurred at the same time, it is fair to say that dissenting voices on this point are in the minority. But questions about the details of the relationship bring forth a cacophony rather than a harmonious chorus. Was growth in incomes vigorous, as Graeme Snooks insists, or was it moderate, as Nicholas Mayhew posits?[4] Did market relations provide a way for at least some parts of England to develop specialized local resources and thereby escape the jaws of Malthus's trap, as Mark Bailey has suggested in his study of the Suffolk Breckland?[5] Or did they serve essentially as a palliative rather than as a remedy, easing the symptoms of Malthusian pressure but failing to cure the disease, as Richard Britnell has recently maintained?[6]

Few historians would now argue for a return to the strict Malthusianism prevalent a generation ago, which held that medieval society suffered unalterably and ineluctably from an imbalance between population and productivity. Equally few would argue that the period's commercial development created a momentum that was not impeded by the dead weight of increasing numbers. Ultimately, historians need to recognize that changes in population levels and commercial behavior are relative concepts rather than absolutes. Their significance resides primarily in their ability to influence allocations of wealth and power between and within social groups rather than across all social boundaries. In other words, there is no simple, unidirectional relationship between demography and commercialization, because both are immersed in complex social contexts that defy easy generalization. If historians lose sight of this fact, they risk consigning themselves to a sterile debate that has relatively little to do with the real experiences of the society they profess to be studying. The benefits of commercialization were not akin to Portia's sense of mercy, raining down on all alike: Some groups benefited more than others, and the challenge that lies ahead resides chiefly in clarifying who these groups were and how they used their opportunities to enhance their social positions.

The lower levels of the social pyramid deserves particularly close attention. The privileged social groups who were accustomed to dominating medieval society certainly took full advantage of the opportunities presented by commercialization, but they did not create the economic infrastructure described in this book, nor were they its principal beneficiaries. Credit for this creation must go to the merchants, peasants, and artisans of the period, groups that had previously flitted through history's shadows. These were the people who turned dirt paths and winding rivers into commercial thoroughfares; they were the ones whose patronage determined the success or failure of a newly established market; and they were ultimately the ones whose economic initiative supported the state and the nobility. Lords and gentry were caught up in the changes affecting the rest of society, but primarily because they understood how to ride coattails. The privileged social orders were economic imitators, not initiators. Even at the level of deciding what commodities to produce and how to produce them, many estate holders were content to leave matters in the hands of their peasant tenants.[7] Of course, the elites of society succeeded in reproducing their privileged position generation after generation throughout this period, but it is all too easy to overlook how much society had changed around them.

Among these changes, two stand out as particularly worthy of notice. The first is the penetration of commercial activity into the countryside and particularly into the ranks of the peasantry. Up until the second half of the twelfth century, village agriculture in England was little touched by market transactions. Markets were urban affairs, and the commercial activity they inspired had relatively little to do with the inhabitants of the countryside, apart from the furnishing of a few status goods to privileged elites and, perhaps, the purchasing of a few staples from contiguous villages. Economic contacts between burgesses and peasants were, in other words, infrequent and inconsequential. Trade was effectively limited to simple redistribution, comprising the movement of imported luxury goods between towns and the movement of a limited number of necessary or useful commodities with geographically limited production zones, such as salt and metals. In this environment, towns persevered more as isolated mercantile colonies than as hubs of regional trading networks; they were islands of commercial activity, and the countryside was the intervening ocean.

Starting in the twelfth century, though, the water covering the countryside began to recede, first exposing new patches of commercial earth where the core markets of later centuries, such as Yaxley and St. Neots in Huntingdonshire, came to be located. By the end of the thirteenth century, there was far more dry land than water, and only in a few remote areas did the ocean continue to impede inland commercial traffic. By that time, the economies of towns and villages had become closely integrated. Towns now relied on their regional hinterlands to supply the necessities of life and most of their industrial raw materials, while the residents of those hinterlands, including the peasantry, planned and managed their crops and flocks to take advantage of the new commercial environment. Peasants and merchants were no longer strangers: Merchants had learned that an integrated network of rural markets gave them cheap and efficient access to village producers, while peasants had learned that the goods they produced were highly coveted beyond the confines of the village. The result was the bustling commercial world described in this book, a world in which merchants penetrated the countryside in their quest for rural produce and peasants likewise sought their own best markets, sometimes in nearby villages and sometimes in the towns themselves.

The second great commercial change to occur in the period was the coalescence of towns and rural markets into a series of integrated regional networks of trade. These networks formed around the country's largest and wealthiest towns, which served both as the main focal points for exchange within the confines of the region and as the transfer points for goods that circulated nationally and internationally. In both capacities, though, towns established their positions only by making use of surrounding networks of rural markets, which came to serve as the principal points of articulation between the towns and their regional hinterlands. This new partnership between towns and rural markets involved a lengthy process of negotiation, one that began in earnest in the second half of the twelfth century and was still in progress in the fourteenth century. But the critical terms of the relationship had been hammered out by about 1250, by which time the basic configuration of most of the country's regional systems had assumed an outline that would be recognizable for many centuries to come. After 1250, succeeding generations continually revised the blueprint they had inherited from the founding century, but up until the Industrial Revolution their revisions seldom strayed far from the original lines.

The first period of revision extended from the 1250s into the 1320s. These generations—the immediate heirs of the founders—strengthened and deepened the commercial channels that had just recently been dug, but their embanking and dredging had to be accompanied by damming. As the vitality of the early rural markets became evident, a veritable frenzy to found new markets began, one that lasted through the 1320s. Between 1250 and 1330, far more markets were founded than were ever likely to find room within existing regional commercial systems. Peasants and merchants found themselves in the enviable position of being able to choose their venues from among a bevy of options. This period of experimentation proved the resiliency of the original regional structures, for even when given the chance, the users of trading places seldom traded places. Indeed, the formation of a subordinate tier of markets actually enhanced the position of the core rural markets. By the end of the period of experimentation, many of the core markets had sprouted resident mercantile and artisanal populations, tapping into the potential inherent in a regional economic base saturated with commercial outlets. Regional systems now had several tiers of markets: an upper echelon of primary towns; an intermediate echelon of quasi-urban markets, some formally situated in villages, others in smaller towns; and a lower echelon of simple rural markets, the survivors of the Darwinian struggle waged among the latecomers to the regional marketing scene.

Peasant involvement in the commercial economy and the development of regional marketing systems were intimately related to each other. As long as the commercial world revolved solely around the redistribution of precious and scarce commodities from town to town, peasants lacked incentives sufficiently powerful to persuade them to direct their attention consistently toward the market. This is not to say that the economy was entirely oriented to subsistence. Long before merchants engaged them in regional markets, peasants had participated in simple exchange between households within their own villages. Such household transfers can be found in virtually all peasant societies. Even after the creation of formalized institutions for trade between villages, or between villages and towns, this local exchange tends to persist as a central feature of village life. In her study of a number of West African villages—an area with a well-developed peasant market economy—Polly Hill discovered that private transactions between households accounted for the bulk of exchange in grain and prepared foodstuffs. Hill also found that villagers living in places without formal markets and exchange facilities nonetheless engaged in frequent and substantial dealings with each other and that most of these dealings were negotiated by women, whose "market is in continuous session."[8] Formal markets are used principally to bring outside merchants into contact with local peasant producers and consumers; their role is not so much to persuade peasants to engage in trade where none has previously existed as to persuade peasants to engage in trade with the world beyond the village. Peasants, merchants, and markets are, in other words, mutually necessary elements of commercialization; subtract one element from the mix and the other two will fail to solidify.

This book has explored some of the ways in which this trio first came to be bound together in England in the two centuries before the Black Death. Part of the story has involved an examination of the growing urban appetite for the produce of the countryside, stemming partly from demographic changes that yielded increasing numbers of mouths to feed, and partly from changes in economic orientation that enhanced the importance of such raw materials as wool and leather in urban manufacturing. Another part of the story has involved an examination of peasant responses to these stimuli, expressed in decisions to produce the kinds and quantities of goods that the towns so avidly coveted. But the bulk of the story has revolved around the conjunction of the two. Peasants and merchants came face-to-face in markets, and it was there that they assessed the current viability and future potential of their relationship. On the whole, these assessments proved to be positive, and as the number of positive assessments multiplied, the role of the market as a central institution of social and economic life was firmly entrenched, transforming both town and village in the process.

Appendices

***Appendix 1:** Deriving Commodity Values from Local Subsidy Rolls*

The local assessment rolls discussed in chapter 1 provide a particularly thorough record of the values of single commodities in each individual's possession. The data presented in tables 1-2 through 1-5 render these values as aggregated total sums of all of the individual stocks recorded and evaluated in each location. For the purposes of analysis, several related commodities were combined to create a single category. The amalgamated categories represented in the tables involve the following combinations: wood (comprising wood, timber, fuel, and boards); wool (wool and woolfells); horses and carts (horses of various description, carts, and wagons); grain (wheat, rye, oats, peas, but not barley); hides and leather (hides, skins, shoes, contents of a tannery, and bark); household (jewelry, silver spoons, goblets, cooking utensils, bowls, brassware, clothing, beds and linens, and generic household goods described as *usticia*); and livestock (pigs, cows, oxen, sheep, geese, but not horses). Miscellaneous goods are described at the feet of the relevant tables.

Deriving these aggregates involves several methodological challenges. The most troublesome interpretive problem in assigning goods to categories results from the problem of distinguishing between cloth and clothing in Ipswich and Shrewsbury. Scribes typically recorded both with the same word, *pannum* (commonly used in the form *in pannis* in Ipswich), or with the same abbreviation, *pann'*. In their analysis of the Shrewsbury lay subsidies, D. Cromarty and R. Cromarty have suggested that *pannum* refers to cloth when it occurs at the beginning of an individual's portfolio of goods (or when it occurs immediately after horses, money, or both at the beginning of a portfolio) and that it refers to clothing when it occurs elsewhere in an entry.[1] Their suggestion has been accepted in assembling the tables in chapter 1, although the assigned values, and in rare instances the language of the entry, suggest that the scribes might have designated cloth rather than clothing in entries occurring part of the way through a portfolio. The holdings of cloth in Ipswich and Shrewsbury may thus be slightly larger than is shown in the relevant tables, although probably not by more than a few percent.

A second challenge is presented by entries that record a single value for two or more goods. In most instances such entries were simply excluded from the tables, as discussed in the chapter, with two exceptions. When a multiple entry involved combinations of household goods (most frequently in entries for utensils and clothing in Ipswich) the assessed value was included in the table. A more difficult problem involved joint assessments of leather and utensils in Colchester. Unlike other joint assessments across categories, these entries were common enough and consistent enough that their exclusion would have noticeably skewed the comparative value of the Colchester data. To deal with these cases, the relative values of leather and utensils were averaged in assessments when the two are listed separately; the combination assessments were then divided into leather and household components using this average. (Leather constituted a mean value of 84 percent of the total in these cases.)

Finally, the categorization of the ubiquitous utensils found in the subsidy rolls is also problematic, because medieval people did not ordinarily distinguish between home and workplace. Consequently, many of the items generically described as *utensiles* more likely served primarily as tools for a trade than as household utensils, as was probably the case with the joint leather and utensil entries in Colchester just noted. In other instances, utensils probably served in both capacities, particularly in the case of the vessels and andirons used by alebrewers. Since there is no satisfactory method to distinguish consistently between tools and household implements in the rolls, all utensils have been included in the category of household goods.

Appendix 2: *Markets Founded in Huntingdonshire before 1348*

Alconbury Weston: Thursday market held by John de Segrave, 1304. Calendar of Charter Rolls, 1300-1326, p. 49.

Alwalton: Friday market held by Peterborough Abbey, 1268. Calendar of Charter Rolls, 1257-1300, p. 101.

Buckworth: Tuesday market held by Simon, son of Richard, 1256. Placita de Quo Warranto, ed. W. Illingworth and J. Caley (London, 1818), p. 299.

Chesterton: Tuesday market held by Priory of Royston, 1254. Calendar of Patent Rolls, 1247-1258, p. 378.

Earith: Wednesday market held by Bishop of Ely, 1318. Calendar of Charter Rolls, 1300-1326, p. 391.

Everton: Wednesday market held by Bishop of Coventry and Lichfield, 1307. Calendar of Charter Rolls, 1300-1326, p. 81.

Fen stanton: Thursday market held by John de Segrave, 1315. Calendar of Charter Rolls, 1300-1326, p. 289.

Great Gidding: Wednesday market held by John Engayne, 1303. Calendar of Charter Rolls, 1300-1326, p. 37.

Holme: Day unknown, royal market, by 1314. Calendar of Patent Rolls, 1313-1317, p. 242.

Huntingdon: Saturday market, by 963. The Anglo-Saxon Chronicle, trans. and ed. M. Swanton (London, 1996), p. 116.

Keyston: Wednesday market held by Robert de Ferariis, 1341. Calendar of Charter Rolls, 1341-1417, p. 5.

Kimbolton: Friday market held by the Earl of Hereford and Essex, 1199. Calendarium Rotulorum Chartarum [John-Edward IV] et Inquisitionem ad quod Damnum [1 Edward II-38 Henry VI], ed. J. Caley and R. Lemon (London, 1803), p. 6.

Ramsey: Wednesday market held by Ramsey Abbey, 1200. Calendarium Rotulorum Chartarum et Inquisitionem ad quod Damnum, p. 13.

St. Ives: Monday market held by Ramsey Abbey, 1292. Calendar of Charter Rolls, 1257-1300, p. 427.

St. Neots: Thursday market held by St. Neots Priory, 1100 X 1135. Regesta Regum Anglo-Normannorum 1066-1154, ed. H. A. Cronne, R. H. C. Davis, and H. W. C. Davis (Oxford, 1913-1968), vol. 2, p. 300

Somersham: Thursday market held by Bishop of Ely, 1199. Rotuli Chartarum in Turri Londinensi asservati, ed. T. D. Hardy (London, 1837), p. 12a.

Woodston: Wednesday market held by Thorney Abbey, 1268. Calendar of Charter Rolls, 1257-1300, p. 101.

Yaxley: Thursday market held by Thorney Abbey, 1094 X 1100. Regesta Regum Anglo-Normannorum, vol. 1, p. 115.

NOTES

Introduction

1. *The Charters of the Borough of Cambridge*, ed. F. W. Maitland and M. Bateson (Cambridge, 1901), p. 2.
2. *Die Gesetze der Angelsachsen*, ed. F. Lieberman (Halle, 1898), p. 139, cited in *British Borough Charters, 1042-1216*, ed. A. Ballard (Cambridge, 1913), p. lxvi. For a recent discussion of this policy, see H. R. Loyn, *Anglo-Saxon England and the Norman Conquest*, 2nd ed. (London and New York, 1991), pp. 148-49.
3. *British Borough Charters, 1216-1307*, ed. A. Ballard and J. Tait (Cambridge, 1923), p. 245.
4. See chapter 4 for a description of this tax.
5. R. H. Britnell, *The Commercialisation of English Society 1000-1500* (Cambridge, 1993), p. 102.
6. E. Rutledge, "Immigration and Population Growth in Early Fourteenth-Century Norwich: Evidence from the Tithing Roll," *Urban History Yearbook 1988* (Leicester, 1988): 15-30.
7. E. Lipson, *The Economic History of England*, vol. 1, *The Middle Ages*, 5th ed. (London, 1929); L. F. Salzman, *English Trade in the Middle Ages* (Oxford, 1931).
8. R. H. Britnell, "King John's Early Grants of Markets and Fairs," *English Historical Review* 94 (1979): 90-96; idem, "The Proliferation of Markets in England, 1200-1349," *Economic History Review*, 2nd ser., 34 (1981): 209-221; idem, "Burghal Characteristics of Market Towns in Medieval England," *Durham University Journal*, n.s., 42 (1981): 147-51; R. H. Hilton, "Small Town Society in England before the Black Death," *Past & Present* 105 (1984): 53-78; idem, "Medieval Market Towns and Simple Commodity Production," *Past & Present* 109 (1985): 3-23; J. A. Raftis, *A Small Town in Late Medieval England: Godmanchester, 1278-1400* (Toronto, 1982); J. Langdon, *Horses, Oxen and Technological Innovation* (Cambridge, 1986); C. Dyer, *Standards of Living in the Later Middle Ages: Social Change in England, c.1200-1520* (Cambridge, 1989); K. Biddick, "Medieval English Peasants and Market Involvement," *Journal of Economic History* 45 (1985): 823-31; idem, "Missing Links: Taxable Wealth, Markets and Stratification among Medieval English Peasants," *Journal of Interdisciplinary History* 18 (1987): 277-98; B. M. S. Campbell, "Agricultural Progress in Medieval England: Some Evidence from Eastern Norfolk," *Economic History Review*, 2nd ser., 36 (1983): 26-46; idem, "Arable Productivity in Medieval England: Some Evidence from Norfolk," *Journal of Economic History* 43 (1983): 379-404.
9. B. M. S. Campbell et al., *A Medieval Capital and Its Grain Supply*, Historical Geography Research Series, no. 30 (n. p., 1993).
10. Britnell, *Commercialisation.*
11. R. H. Britnell and B. M. S. Campbell, eds., *A Commercialising Economy* (Manchester, 1995); E. Miller and J. Hatcher, *Medieval England: Towns, Commerce and Crafts 1086-1348* (London and New York, 1995); M. Kowaleski, *Local Markets and Regional Trade in Medieval Exeter* (Cambridge, 1995).
12. A notable departure from this approach, though, is offered in Kowaleski, *Local Markets and Regional Trade*, which resolutely sets the commercial history of Exeter in the context of the regional economy of the southwest.
13. The literature on central-place theory is vast. A useful introductory survey from a geographer's perspective is L. King, *Central Place Theory* (Beverly Hills, CA, 1984). An excellent summary of the model is offered in the introduction to C. A. Smith, ed., *Regional Analysis*, 2 vols.

(New York, 1976). Other representative works include R. Beals, *The Peasant Marketing System of Oaxaca, Mexico* (Berkeley and Los Angeles, 1975); and S. Plattner, ed., *Markets and Marketing* (Lanham, MD, 1985).

14. G. W. Skinner, "Marketing and Social Structure in Rural China," *Journal of Asian Studies* 24 (1964-65): 3-43, 195-228, 363-400.

15. Skinner included two other types of markets, one below the standard and one above the central, but did not deal with either in detail.

16. Examples of explicit adoption of central-place theory by historians are R. Hodges, *Dark Age Economics: The Origins of Towns and Trade A.D. 600-1000.* (London, 1982), and P. M. Hohenberg and L. H. Lees, *The Making of Urban Europe 1000-1950* (Cambridge, MA, 1985).

17. T. Unwin, "Rural Marketing in Medieval Nottinghamshire," *Journal of Historical Geography* 7 (1981): 231-51.

18. E. Fournial, *Les villes et l'économie d'échange en Forez aux XIIIe et XIVe siècles* (Paris, 1967).

19. Winnie Lem, for example, states categorically that production of commodities for exchange, even at the household level (a form of production often referred to by Marxists as "petty commodity production") is "a form of production that has emerged with the development of capitalism in agriculture." W. Lem, "Household Production and Reproduction in Rural Languedoc: Social Relations of Petty Commodity Production in Murveil-lès-Béziers," *Journal of Peasant Studies* 15 (1988), p. 500.

20. E. W. Moore, *The Fairs of Medieval England: An Introductory Study* (Toronto, 1985).

21. *Curia Regis Rolls,* vol. 13, p. 110.

22. S. R. Epstein, "Regional Fairs, Institutional Innovation, and Economic Growth in Late Medieval Europe," *Economic History Review,* 2nd ser., 47 (1994): 459-82.

23. R. H. Britnell, "*Advantagium mercatoris:* A Custom in Medieval English Trade," *Nottingham Medieval Studies* 24 (1980): 37-50; E. B. Fryde, *Studies in Medieval Trade and Finance* (London, 1983); J. Munro, "The International Law Merchant and the Evolution of Negotiable Credit in Late-Medieval England and the Low Countries," in *Banchi pubblici, banchi privati e monti di pietà nell'Europa preindustriale,* ed. D. Puncuh (Genoa, 1991), pp. 49-80; Kowaleski, *Local Markets and Regional Trade,* pp. 179-221; P. Schofield, "Endettement et crédit dans la campagne anglaise au moyen âge," in *Endettement et crédit dans les campagnes d'Europe au Moyen Age et à l'Epoque Moderne,* ed. M. Berthe and F. Brumont (Toulouse, forthcoming, 1997). I am grateful to Dr. Schofield for allowing me to read a copy of his paper in advance of publication.

Chapter 1

1. M. Kowaleski, *Local Markets and Regional Trade in Medieval Exeter* (Cambridge, 1995), pp. 120-78; H. Swanson, *Medieval Artisans* (Oxford, 1989), *passim;* E. Miller and J. Hatcher, *Medieval England: Towns, Commerce and Crafts 1086-1348* (London and New York, 1995), pp. 325-30.

2. P. D. A. Harvey, "Non-Agrarian Activities in Twelfth-Century English Estate Surveys," in *England in the Twelfth Century,* ed. D. Williams (Woodbridge, Suffolk, 1990), pp. 101-11.

3. G. Fransson, "Middle English Surnames of Occupation, 1100-1350," *Lund Studies in English,* no. 3 (Lund, 1935), p. 30.

4. M. Carver, *Underneath English Towns* (London, 1987), p. 81.

5. Swanson, *Medieval Artisans,* pp. 4-6, 117-18; Kowaleski, *Local Markets and Regional Trade,* pp. 123-26.

6. G. Williams, *Medieval London* (London, 1963), pp. 157-95; Miller and Hatcher, *Medieval England: Towns, Commerce and Crafts,* pp. 361-75.

7. P. J. P. Goldberg, *Women, Work, and Life Cycle in a Medieval Economy* (Oxford, 1992), pp. 158-64.

8. For a similar comparative effort (with a different breakdown of sectors), see Miller and Hatcher, *Medieval England: Towns, Commerce and Crafts,* pp. 324-30.

9. S. Kelly, "The Economic Topography and Structure of Norwich, c. 1300" in *Men of Property,* ed. U. Priestly (Norwich, 1983), p. 16; D. Keene, *Survey of Medieval Winchester* (Oxford, 1985), pp. 252, 352-65; J. Lancaster, "Crafts and Industries," in *Victoria History of the County of Warwick,* vol. 8, ed. W. B. Stephens (London, 1969), p. 153.

10. *Sixth Report of the Royal Commission on Historical Manuscripts,* part 1 (London, 1877), pp. 576-79.

11. In Keene's arrangement, mercers are included in the clothing category rather than in the mercantile. Lancaster counted the mercers among the merchants and did not provide a breakdown of the group, so the merchants and clothing categories for Coventry are not strictly comparable with the other towns. The percentages for each category in Kelly, Keene, and Lancaster have been recalculated to take into account the excluded occupations, such as clerics. On the 1227 Wallingford tallage roll, there is a group of 29 names without occupation at the beginning of the roll. Later tallage rolls suggest that this group comprised cornmongers and other merchants. Butchers are not recorded separately on the 1227 roll, but it is clear from comparing this roll with the 1230 roll (the next surviving roll in the series), on which butchers are distinguished, that the butchers were included with the merchants at the head of the list in 1227. There were 12 butchers in 1230, and presumably the same number in 1227. Thus, 17 of the names without occupation are assigned to the mercantile category, and the 12 butchers to the victualing category. The list of fishsellers is incomplete in 1227 but complete in 1230 and thus the 1230 number has been assigned to the 1227 victualing category. For Coventry, the two glovers from the leather category were moved to the clothing category.

12. Kowaleski, *Local Markets and Regional Trade,* pp. 120-75.

13. See especially ibid., p. 125 (Table 4-1).

14. N. S. B. Gras, *The Early English Customs System* (Cambridge, MA, 1918), pp. 59-66.

15. J. Willard, *Parliamentary Taxes on Personal Property, 1290-1334* (Cambridge, MA, 1934); G. L. Harriss, *King, Parliament and Public Finance in Medieval England to 1369* (Oxford, 1975).

16. Willard, *Parliamentary Taxes,* pp. 54-72; J. A. Raftis, *A Small Town in Late Medieval England: Godmanchester, 1278-1400* (Toronto, 1982), pp. 95-101; *The Wealth of Shrewsbury in the Early Fourteenth Century,* ed. D. Cromarty and R. Cromarty (Shrewsbury, 1993), pp. 20-27.

17. Willard, *Parliamentary Taxes,* pp. 73-128.

18. Ibid. , pp. 81-85; *The Lay Subsidy of 1334,* ed. R. Glasscock, Records of Social and Economic History, no. 2 (London, 1975), p. xxv.

19. *Patent Rolls of the Reign of Henry III, 1216-25* (London, 1901), p. 560.

20. For an overview of extant assessments, see J. F. Hadwin, "Evidence on the Possession of 'Treasure' from the Lay Subsidy Rolls," in *Edwardian Monetary Affairs (1279-1344),* ed. N. Mayhew, British Archaeological Reports 36 (Oxford, 1977), pp. 148-55.

21. E. Powell, "The Taxation of Ipswich for the Welsh War in 1282," *Proceedings of the Suffolk Institute of Archaeology* 12 (1906): 137-57; *Wealth of Shrewsbury,* ed. Cromarty and Cromarty, pp. 89-99; *Rotuli Parliamentorum* (London, 1783), vol. 1, pp. 243-65. The Cromartys have recently shown in their analysis of the exceptionally rich corpus of local subsidy rolls surviving for Shrewsbury that "customary" allowances and the care exercised in making the inventories varied noticeably from one subsidy to the next. *Wealth of Shrewsbury,* pp. 21-24.

22. *Lay Subsidy of 1334,* ed. R. Glasscock, pp. 88, 257, 294; R. Glasscock, "England *circa* 1334," in *A New Historical Geography of England,* ed. H. C. Darby (Cambridge, 1973), p. 184.

23. M. J. Stanley, "Medieval Tax Returns as Source Material," in *Field and Forest: An Historical Geography of Warwickshire and Worcestershire,* ed. T. Slater and P. J. Jarvis (Norwich, 1982), pp. 231-56; S. Rigby, "Urban Society in Early Fourteenth-Century England: The Evidence of the Lay Subsidies," *Bulletin of the John Rylands Library* 72 (1990): 169-84.

24. On the controversy surrounding the reliability of the subsidies as registers of total wealth, see A. R. Bridbury, *Economic Growth* (London, 1962), pp. 70-82; R. B. Dobson, "Urban Decline in Late Medieval England," *Transactions of the Royal Historical Society,* 5th ser. , 27 (1977): 19; S. H. Rigby, "Urban Decline in the Later Middle Ages: Some Problems in Interpreting the Statistical Data," *Urban History Yearbook 1979* (Leicester, 1979), pp. 46-59; J. F. Hadwin, "The Medieval Lay Subsidies and Economic History," *Economic History Review,* 2nd ser. , 36 (1983): 200-17; S. H. Rigby, "Late Medieval Urban Prosperity: The Evidence of the Lay Subsidies," *Economic History Review,* 2nd ser. , 39 (1986): 411-16; A. R. Bridbury, "Dr. Rigby's Comment: A Reply," *Economic History Review,* 2nd ser. , 39 (1986): 417-22.

25. J. F. Hadwin, "From Dissonance to Harmony on the Late Medieval Town," *Economic History Review,* 2nd ser. , 39 (1986): 424.

26. Powell, "Taxation of Ipswich," pp. 137-57.

27. R. H. Britnell, "The Occupation of the Land: Eastern England," in *The Agrarian History of England and Wales,* vol. 3, 1348-1500, ed. E. Miller (Cambridge, 1991), pp. 63-64.

28. *The Black Book of the Admiralty,* ed. T. Twiss, Rolls Series, no. 55 (London, 1871-76), vol. 2, p. 188.

29. Arnald Pelliparius held £50 of a total stock assessed at just over £87. Powell, "Taxation of Ipswich," p. 146.

30. *Wealth of Shrewsbury,* ed. Cromarty and Cromarty, pp. 5, 89-99. The membrane for the town's liberty is missing, and there is no final sum on the document, but there is no doubt that the record is essentially complete.

31. The form of taxation and related writs can be found in *Lancashire Lay Subsidies,* ed. J. Vincent, The Record Society for the Publication of Original Documents Relating to Lancashire and Cheshire, no. 27 (London, 1893), pp. 256-60.

32. Glasscock, "England *circa* 1334," p. 184; D. Palliser, "Urban Decay Revisited," in *Towns and Townspeople in the Fifteenth Century,* ed. J. A. F. Thomas (Gloucester, 1988), p. 9.

33. *Wealth of Shrewsbury,* ed. Cromarty and Cromarty, pp. 5, 23.

34. Ibid., p. 37; T. H. Lloyd, *The English Wool Trade in the Middle Ages* (Cambridge, 1977), pp. 55, 132-33.

35. *Rotuli Parliamentorum,* vol. 1, pp. 228-36, 243-65; G. Rickwood, "Taxations of Colchester, A.D. 1296 and 1301," *Transactions of the Essex Archaeological Society,* n. s. , 9 (1906): 126-55. In making the quantitative aggregations of commodities in Colchester, Table 1-4 uses the data supplied by Rickwood, with a few exceptions. Rickwood included horses with other livestock, and he also aggregated all commercial goods into a category of "trade stock," by which he meant principally leather, cloth, mercery, wool, wood, and associated tools. To make this data comparable with the other towns, I returned to the original assessment in the Rolls of Parliament and established the relative values of horses and other livestock and the relative values of each of the different commodities described as trade stock.

36. *Lancashire Lay Subsidies,* ed. Vincent, pp. 237-38.

37. R. H. Britnell, *Growth and Decline in Colchester, 1300-1525* (Cambridge, 1986), p. 16.

38. K. Biddick, "Missing Links: Taxable Wealth, Markets and Stratification among Medieval English Peasants," *Journal of Interdisciplinary History* 18 (1987): 282-91; Rigby, "Urban society," p. 183.

39. F. W. Maitland, *Township and Borough* (Cambridge, 1898), p. 4.

40. Britnell, *Colchester,* pp. 41-47.

41. Public Record Office E101/505/24.

42. *Wealth of Shrewsbury,* ed. Cromarty and Cromarty, pp. 40, 80.

Chapter 2

1. A. V. Chayanov, *The Theory of Peasant Economy,* ed. D. Thorner, B. Kerblay and R. E. F. Smith (Homewood, IL, 1966). Although first published in 1925, this work was translated into English only in 1966. A useful summary of Chayanov's main arguments can be found in E. P. Durrenberger, "Introduction," in *Chayanov, Peasants and Economic Anthropology,* ed. idem, (Orlando, FL, 1984), pp. 1-25. For an appraisal of how Chayanov's views have influenced English medievalists see R. M. Smith, "Some Issues Concerning Families and Their Property in Rural England 1250-1800," in *Land, Kinship and Life Cycle,* ed. idem (Cambridge, 1984), pp. 6-38.

2. J. Ennew, P. Hirst, and K. Tribe, " 'Peasantry' as an Economic Category," *Journal of Peasant Studies* 4 (1976-1977): 295-322; G. Smith, "Reflections on the Social Relations of Simple Commodity Production," *Journal of Peasant Studies* 13 (1985): 99-108.

3. D. Thorner, "Peasant Economy as a Category in Economic History," *Papers Presented to the Second International Conference on Economic History at Aix-en-Provence, 1962,* vol. 2 (Paris, 1965), p. 291.

4. R. H. Hilton, *The English Peasantry in the Later Middle Ages* (Oxford, 1975), pp. 43-45.

5. M. Bailey, *A Marginal Economy? East Anglian Breckland in the Later Middle Ages* (Cambridge, 1989), pp. 159-91; E. Clark, "Debt Litigation in a Late Medieval English Vill," in *Pathways to Medieval Peasants,* ed. J. A. Raftis (Toronto, 1981), pp. 253-61; M. McIntosh, *Autonomy and Community* (Cambridge, 1986), pp. 136-78; J. Langdon, "Hand Tools," in *The Countryside of Medieval England,* ed. G. Astill and A. Grant (Oxford, 1988), pp. 86-107; P. Harvey, "Non-Agrarian Activities in Twelfth-Century English Estate Surveys," in *England in the Twelfth Century,* ed. D. Williams (Woodbridge, Suffolk, 1990), pp. 101-11.

6. R. H. Hilton, "Women Traders in Medieval England," in idem, *Class Conflict and the Crisis of Feudalism* (London, 1985), pp. 205-16.

7. *Nonarum Inquisitiones in Curia Scacarii,* ed. G. Vanderzee (London, 1807), *passim; The Rolls and Register of Bishop Oliver Sutton, 1280-1299,* vol. 1, ed. R. Hill, Lincoln Record Society, no. 39 (Hereford, 1948), pp. 31-33; C. Dyer, *Everyday Life in Medieval England* (London, 1994), pp. 119-20.

8. M. Prestwich, *War, Politics and Finance under Edward I* (Totowa, NJ, 1972), pp. 114-36; H. J. Hewitt, *The Organization of War under Edward III, 1338-62* (Manchester, 1966), pp. 50-74.

9. *The Political Songs of England,* ed. T. Wright, Camden Society, first series, no. 6 (London, 1839), p. 186.

10. J. R. Maddicott, "The English Peasantry and the Demands of the Crown," *Past & Present Supplement* no. 1 (1975).

11. In 1319-20, for example, three magnates with substantial properties in Kent—the Archbishop of Canterbury, the Earl of Pembroke, and Bartholomew Badlesmere—contributed nearly 3,000 quarters of grain from their estates to support the war in Scotland. Public Record Office (PRO) E101/371/8 no.51.

12. Maddicott, *English Peasantry,* p. 30.

13. M. Prestwich, *War, Politics and Finance,* pp. 122-23.

14. Maddicott, *English Peasantry,* p. 31. The acreage figure for Kent (970,000 acres) is taken from M. Beresford and H. P. R. Finberg, *English Medieval Boroughs: A Handlist* (Newton Abbot, Devon, 1973), p. 50.

15. PRO E101/552/4 (account of 1301); PRO E101/552/5 (account of 1303); PRO E101/552/26 (account of 1348); PRO E101/170/1 (account of 1351).

16. PRO E101/552/4; PRO E101/552/5.

17. J. Masschaele, "Transport Costs in Medieval England," *Economic History Review*, 2nd ser., 46 (1993): 277-78; C. Dyer, *Standards of Living in the Later Middle Ages: Social Change in England, c.1200-1520* (Cambridge, 1989), p. 153.

18. Modern relief agencies reckon that a pound of bread per day, representing an intake of about 1,100 calories, will keep a person's body and soul together. Dyer, *Standards of Living*, p. 153.

19. *Rotuli Hundredorum*, ed. W. Illingworth and J. Caley (London, 1812-18), vol. 2, pp. 591-687.

20. Ibid., p. 659.

21. Ibid., p. 642.

22. Ibid., p. 657.

23. Ibid., pp. 656-67.

24. All data about these individuals are derived from *Elton Manorial Records, 1279-1351*, ed. S. C. Radcliffe, trans. D. M. Gregory (Cambridge, 1946), passim.

25. PRO E101/552/26; PRO E101/170/1.

26. The structure of the records, though, is significantly different. Unlike the two earlier lists, the list of 1348 is arranged by commodity rather than by individual or place of residence, and the same individual can thus occur in several different places. The number of contributors is considerably lower than a cursory glance at the document might suggest, since most contributors supplied more than one commodity. The record of contributors in 1351 is not a list at all but a series of indentures in French made in each village to record the sheriff's debts.

27. The £10 of wheat from the estate of John Offord is not included in this total.

28. The one possible exception to this is a Robert Fox, who gave £1 15s. 2d. worth of produce in Buckworth in 1348 and 10s. 6d. in Coppingford in 1351.

29. The writ is in *Calendar of Fine Rolls, 1347-1356*, p. 274. The king requested 400 quarters of wheat, 100 of peas, 500 of barley, 100 oxen, and 600 pigs from Huntingdonshire alone. In February, these demands were reduced by more than half. Ibid., p. 289.

30. D. Arnold, *Famine: Social Crisis and Historical Change* (Oxford, 1988), pp. 54-55.

31. British Library Add. R. 39583.

32. *Early Huntingdonshire Lay Subsidy Rolls*, ed. J. A. Raftis and M. P. Hogan (Toronto, 1976), p. 93; E. Britton, *The Community of the Vill* (Toronto, 1977), p. 80.

33. *Elton Manorial Records*, ed. Radcliffe, pp. 360, 364, 390. The jurors were Nicholas Richard, Henry de Theynton, Walter Buk, and John Aylton. Adam de Framelington was the bailiff.

34. J. Thirsk, "The Common Fields," *Past & Present* 29 (1964): 3-25; A. C. Chibnall, *Sherington, Fiefs and Fields of a Buckinghamshire Village* (Cambridge, 1965); C. Dahlman, *The Open Field System and Beyond* (Cambridge, 1980); E. Kerridge, *The Common Fields of England* (Manchester and New York, 1992). The secondary literature on common fields is extensive. The works cited here address most directly the relationship between arable and pastoral uses of the fields, only one of the elements explaining the persistence of this particular agrarian practice.

35. K. Biddick, *The Other Economy* (Berkeley, 1989); B. M. S. Campbell and J. Power, "Mapping the Agricultural Geography of Medieval England," *Journal of Historical Geography* 15 (1989): 24-39; B. M. S. Campbell, "Land, Labor, Livestock, and Productivity Trends in English Seignorial Agriculture, 1208-1450" in *Land, Labour and Livestock: Historical Studies in European Agricultural Productivity*, ed. idem and M. Overton (Manchester, 1991), pp. 144-82; M. Kowaleski, "Town and Country in Late Medieval England: The Hide and Leather Trade," in *Work in Towns, 850-1850*, ed. P. J. Corfield and D. Keene (Leicester, 1990), pp. 57-73; idem, *Local Markets and Regional Trade in Medieval Exeter* (Cambridge, 1995), pp. 293-307.

36. M. Postan, "Village Livestock in the Thirteenth Century," *Economic History Review*, 2nd ser., 15 (1962): 219-49, reprt. in idem, *Essays on Medieval Agriculture and General Problems of the*

Medieval Economy (Cambridge, 1973), pp. 214-48. Subsequent references here are to the reprint version.

37. Ibid., pp. 233, 247.

38. The theme of "soil exhaustion" is treated more explicitly in idem, "The Economic Foundations of Medieval Society" in ibid., pp. 3-27.

39. J. Langdon, *Horses, Oxen and Technological Innovation* (Cambridge, 1986), pp. 184-85; A. R. Bridbury, *The English Economy from Bede to the Reformation* (Woodbridge, Suffolk, 1992), p. 17 n. 19. Langdon and Bridbury both draw attention to the deficiencies of the 1283 Suffolk subsidy, which Postan relied on heavily. Bridbury also asserts that the 1225 Wiltshire subsidy is flawed by the omission of the property of free tenants, although he offers no evidence to support this unorthodox view.

40. Postan, "Village Livestock," pp. 234-35. A revealing indication of Postan's dismissal of peasant agriculture is in the index to *Medieval Agriculture and General Problems of the Medieval Economy*, where the only entry for "village" or "villagers" is "villagers without."

41. Postan made no mention of J. Willard's *Parliamentary Taxes on Personal Property, 1290-1334* (Cambridge, MA, 1934), the standard reference work on the subsidies, published nearly thirty years earlier with a section devoted explicitly to this very question.

42. Postan, "Village Livestock," p. 239. In the 1283 Suffolk return, which was the centerpiece of Postan's analysis in this context, holdings of horses and oxen accounted for about 12 percent of all assessed property, as can be calculated from data given in *A Suffolk Hundred in the Year 1283*, ed. E. Powell (Cambridge, 1910), pp. xx-xxv, xxx, supplemented in a few instances with averages derived from the tables of individual villages.

43. Postan, "Village Livestock," pp. 240-41.

44. Animals constituted approximately 85 percent of all assessed wealth in the Wiltshire subsidy. This figure has been calculated using the data on holdings summarized by Postan in "Village Livestock," Table 11.1, p. 227 with the data on prices provided in *Rolls of the Fifteenth of the Ninth Year of the Reign of Henry III for Cambridgeshire, Lincolnshire and Wiltshire and Rolls of the Fortieth of the Seventeenth Year of the Reign of Henry III for Kent*, ed. F. Cazel and A. Cazel, The Publications of the Pipe Roll Society, no. 83, n. s., no. 45 (London, 1976-77), p. ix. These calculations use the low end of the price range for livestock and the high end for cereals.

45. Postan, "Village Livestock," p. 227 (Table 11.1).

46. J. Langdon, "Horse Hauling: A Revolution in Vehicle Transport in Twelfth- and Thirteenth-Century England?," *Past & Present* 103 (1984): 37-66; idem, *Horses, Oxen, and Technological Innovation.*

47. M. Mate, "The Agrarian Economy of South-East England Before the Black Death: Depressed or Buoyant," in *Before the Black Death*, ed. B. M. S. Campbell (Manchester, 1991), pp. 86-87. In this same article, however, Mate argues for deficiencies in peasant livestock holdings by the 1340s, citing problematic heriot payments as evidence.

48. J. Ravensdale, *Liable to Floods* (Cambridge, 1974), p. 75; J. A. Raftis, *Tenure and Mobility* (Toronto, 1964), pp. 23-25; Bailey, *Marginal Economy*, pp. 55-56; Mate, "Agrarian Economy of South-East England," p. 87; J. Hatcher, *Rural Economy and Society in the Duchy of Cornwall 1300-1500* (Cambridge, 1970), p. 15.

49. Bailey, *Marginal Economy*, pp. 65-76.

50. Sources for this paragraph include: *Rotuli Hundredorum*, vol. 2, pp. 757-58; E. Power, *The Wool Trade in Medieval English History* (Oxford, 1941), p. 29; Raftis, *Tenure and Mobility*, p. 24; E. Miller, "Farming Techniques: Northern England," in *The Agrarian History of England and Wales*, vol. 2, 1042-1350, ed. H.E. Hallam (Cambridge, 1988), p. 408; *Victoria History of the County of Wiltshire*, vol. 4, ed. E. Crittall (London, 1959), pp. 26-27; *Victoria History of the County of Leicestershire*, vol. 2, ed. W. G. Hoskins (London, 1954), pp. 164-65; *Thirteen Customals of the Sussex Manors of the Bishop of Chichester*, ed. W. Peckham, Sussex Record Society, no. 31 (Lewes, Sussex, 1925), pp. 25, 73, 79. See *Thirteen Customals*, p. 77 for an approximate date for the Ferring customal.

51. Powell, *A Suffolk Hundred,* pp. 78-82, 88-89.

52. Postan also dealt with this issue in "Village Livestock," pp. 242-46.

53. J. A. Raftis, *A Small Town in Late Medieval England: Godmanchester, 1278-1400* (Toronto, 1982), pp. 100-16.

54. Ibid., p. 101. Raftis argues for an association with the lay subsidy of 1334 for the earlier document. Since neither of these documents can be positively dated, the association with a particular tax assessment is conjectural. The exclusion of property traditionally assessed in lay subsidies is the principal argument in favor of linking the documents to the Nonae assessment, a position that is corroborated by the otherwise problematic references to tithes in both documents.

55. PRO E101/457/12; PRO E179/378/1; PRO E179/242/8. On the families of the two Needingworth villeins (Nicholas Scott and Reginald Lawman), see E. B. DeWindt, *Land and People in Holywell-cum-Needingworth* (Toronto, 1972), p. 199.

56. E. A. Kosminsky, *Studies in the Agrarian History of England in the Thirteenth Century,* trans. R. Kisch (Oxford, 1956), pp. 89-94.

57. N. Mayhew, "Modelling Medieval Monetisation," in *A Commercialising Economy,* ed. R. H. Britnell and B. M. S. Campbell (Manchester, 1995), pp. 57-60.

58. Notably G. Snooks, "The Dynamic Role of the Market in the Anglo-Norman Economy and Beyond 1086-1300," in *A Commercialising Economy,* ed. Britnell and Campbell, pp. 27-54.

59. The tax data will be discussed below. The division between urban and rural wealth in tax records is significantly different, but this can be attributed to different modes of assessment. Bruce Campbell has recently adopted Mayhew's estimates as a benchmark for comparison with his work on manorial marketing. B. M. S. Campbell, "Measuring the Commercialisation of Seigneurial Agriculture c.1300," in *A Commercialising Economy,* ed. Britnell and Campbell, p. 140.

60. Mayhew, "Modelling Monetisation," p. 59.

61. G. Duby, *Rural Economy and Country Life in the Medieval West,* trans. C. Postan (Columbia, SC, 1968), p. 261; G. Holmes, *The Estates of the Higher Nobility in XIV Century England* (Cambridge, 1957), p. 89; C. Dyer, *Lords and Peasants in a Changing Society* (Cambridge, 1980), p. 74; E. Miller, *The Abbey and Bishopric of Ely* (Cambridge, 1951), p. 94.

62. K. Biddick, *The Other Economy,* (Berkeley, 1989), pp. 129-33.

63. Campbell, "Measuring Commercialisation," p. 174.

64. R. H. Hilton, *The English Peasantry in the Later Middle Ages* (Oxford, 1975), pp. 184-96.

65. J. A. Raftis, *Peasant Economic Development within the English Manorial System* (Montreal, 1996).

66. M. Mate, "Medieval Agrarian Practices: The Determining Factors," *Agricultural History Review* 33 (1985): 22-31.

67. Kosminsky, *Studies in Agrarian History,* pp. 84-151.

68. Ibid., pp. 256-82. For an assessment of Kosminsky's position see R. H. Britnell, "Minor Landlords and Medieval Agrarian Capitalism," *Past & Present* 89 (1980): 3-22.

69. Kosminsky, *Studies in Agrarian History,* pp. 95-98. As Kosminsky pointed out, regional variations in manorial structure were enormous, making generalizations difficult.

70. Britnell, "Minor Landlords," pp. 3-22.

71. N. Denholm-Young, *Collected Papers on Medieval Subjects* (Cardiff, 1969), pp. 83-94; J. Quick, "The Number and Distribution of Knights in Thirteenth Century England: The Evidence of the Grand Assize Lists," in *Thirteenth Century England I,* ed. P. Coss and S. Lloyd (Woodbridge, Suffolk, 1986), pp. 114-23.

72. C. Dyer, *Standards of Living in the Later Middle Ages* (Cambridge, 1989), p. 30.

73. Kosminsky, *Studies in Agrarian History,* pp. 230-37; Dyer, *Standards of Living,* p. 115.

74. Kosminsky, *Studies in Agrarian History,* p. 228; M. Postan, *The Medieval Economy and Society* (London, 1972), p. 130; E. Miller and J. Hatcher, *Medieval England: Rural Society and Economic Change 1086-1348* (London and New York, 1978), p. 150.

75. Mayhew, "Modelling Monetisation," p. 57.

76. Z. Razi, *Life, Marriage and Death in a Medieval Parish* (Cambridge, 1980), pp. 83-86.

77. H. C. Darby, *Domesday England* (Cambridge, 1977), p. 14; *The Lay Subsidy of 1334,* ed. R. Glasscock, Records of Social and Economic History, no. 2 (London, 1975), calculated from index listings. Kent was included in the assessment but did not arrange its records by vill, so the number of settlements in the latter source was probably closer to 14,500.

78. Razi, *Life, Marriage and Death,* p. 75; DeWindt, *Land and People,* p. 35; McIntosh, *Autonomy and Community,* p. 97; J. A. Raftis, *Warboys: Two Hundred Years in the Life of an English Medieval Village* (Toronto, 1974), pp. 156-57.

79. E. M. Carus-Wilson and O. Coleman, *England's Export Trade 1275-1547* (Oxford, 1963), p. 122.

80. As, for example, in R. H. Britnell, *The Commercialisation of English Society 1000-1500* (Cambridge, 1993), p. 119.

81. Power, *Medieval English Wool Trade,* pp. 20-31; Bridbury, *The English Economy from Bede to the Reformation,* pp. 185-87.

82. Biddick, *Other Economy,* p. 100; J. A. Raftis, *The Estates of Ramsey Abbey* (Toronto, 1957), p. 152; B. Harvey, *Westminster Abbey and Its Estates in the Middle Ages* (Oxford, 1977), p. 137 (assuming an average price of £5 per sack).

83. *Francisco Balducci Pegolotti: La Pratica della Mercatura,* ed. A. Evans (Cambridge, MA, 1936), pp. 258-69.

84. Dyer, *Lords and Peasants,* p. 70.

85. Campbell, "Measuring Commercialisation," Table 7.3, p. 149.

86. Mayhew, "Modelling Monetisation," p. 58.

87. *Rolls of the Fifteenth,* ed. Cazel and Cazel, p. x.

88. Calculated from Bailey, *Marginal Economy,* p. 193.

89. *The Taxation of 1297,* ed. A. T. Gaydon, The Publications of the Bedfordshire Historical Record Society, no. 39 (Streatley, Bedfordshire, 1959), p. 105.

90. Power, *Medieval English Wool Trade,* pp. 41-51.

91. A similar point about the social horizons of consumption is made in C. Dyer, "The Consumer and the Market in the Later Middle Ages," *Economic History Review,* 2nd ser., 42 (1989): 305-27.

Chapter 3

1. R. Hodges, *Dark Age Economics: The Origins of Towns and Trade A.D. 600-1000* (London, 1982), pp. 67-74; idem, *Primitive and Peasant Markets* (Oxford, 1988), especially pp. 85-95.

2. Hodges, *Primitive and Peasant Markets,* pp. 89-90; idem, *The Anglo-Saxon Achievement* (London, 1989), p. 166.

3. H. C. Darby, *Domesday England* (Cambridge, 1977), pp. 369-70; P. Sawyer, "Early Fairs and Markets in England and Scandinavia," in *The Market in History,* ed. B. L. Anderson and A. J. H. Latham (London, 1986), p. 64.

4. P. Huvelin, *Essai historique sur le droit des marchés et des foires* (Paris, 1897).

5. H. R. Loyn, *Anglo-Saxon England and the Norman Conquest,* 2nd ed. (London and New York, 1991), pp. 148-49.

6. L. F. Salzman, "The Legal Status of Markets," *The Cambridge Historical Journal* 2 (1928): 205-07.

7. J. Masschaele, "Market Rights in Thirteenth-Century England," *English Historical Review* 107 (1992): 78-89.

8. *Placita de Quo Warranto,* ed. W. Illingworth and J. Caley (London, 1818), p. 115; L. F. Salzman, "Legal Status of Markets," pp. 205-12.

9. R. H. Britnell, "King John's Early Grants of Markets and Fairs," *English Historical Review* 370 (1979): 92.

10. *Curia Regis Rolls,* vol. 2, p. 136. For Ely's charter see *Rotuli Chartarum in Turri Londinensi Asservati,* ed. T. Hardy (London, 1837), p. 91b. This case is also discussed in Britnell, "King John's Early Grants," p. 90.

11. *Curia Regis Rolls,* vol. 2, p. 136.

12. *The Chronicle of Jocelin of Brakelond,* ed. H. E. Butler (London, 1949), pp. 133-34.

13. *Bracton's Notebook,* ed. F. W. Maitland (London, 1887), vol. 2, pp. 291-92; *Calendar of Miscellaneous Inquisitions, 1219-1307,* pp. 428-29; *Calendar of Miscellaneous Inquisitions, 1307-1349,* pp. 2-3, 151-52.

14. *Bracton On the Laws and Customs of England,* ed. G. E. Woodbine, trans. and rev. S. Thorne (Cambridge, MA and London, 1968-77), vol. 3, pp. 198-99.

15. Ibid., pp. 198-99.

16. *Britton. An English Translation and Notes,* trans. F. M. Nichols (Washington, DC, 1901), p. 327.

17. *Curia Regis Rolls,* vol. 9, pp. 305-06; *Dictionary of National Biography,* vol. 6, ed. L. Stephen (London, 1886), s. v. "Breauté, Falkes de."

18. Public Record Office (PRO) C143/5, no. 5.

19. *Curia Regis Rolls,* vol. 11, p. 564; vol. 12, pp. 7-8

20. The Clerk of the Market imposed a fine of 60s. on the market in Great Dunmow in 1305. PRO E101/256/4.

21. *Curia Regis Rolls,* vol. 16, pp. 490-91.

22. *Rotuli Parliamentorum* (London, 1783), vol. 1, p. 197.

23. *Curia Regis Rolls,* vol. 8, pp. 267-68.

24. *Calendar of Close Rolls, 1279-1288,* p. 278.

25. Britnell, "King John's Early Grants," p. 96.

26. Masschaele, "Market Rights," pp. 84-88.

27. *Rotuli Litterarum Clausarum in Turri Londinensis Asservati,* ed. T. D. Hardy (London, 1833), vol. 1, p. 42b.

28. Ibid., pp. 82b, 207a-b.

29. Ibid., vol. 2, p. 183a.

30. *Calendar of Patent Rolls, 1343-1345,* p. 141.

31. *Rotuli Litterarum Clausarum,* vol. 1, pp. 175a, 499b; vol. 2, p. 16; *Close Rolls of the Reign of Henry III, 1234-1237,* pp. 90, 152; *Close Rolls of the Reign of Henry III, 1254-1256,* p. 86.

32. *Rotuli Litterarum Clausarum,* vol. 1, p. 499b.

33. *Calendar of Charter Rolls, 1226-1257,* p. 247.

34. *Curia Regis Rolls,* vol. 16, no. 2477.

35. The Longespées' attorney presumably raised Gilbert de Gaunt's earlier silence at this juncture to suggest that de Gaunt found nothing objectionable when first alerted about the proposed market in Swaton.

36. *Rotuli Litterarum Clausarum,* vol. 1, p. 499b.

37. Ibid., vol. 2, p. 26b.

38. *Rotuli Litterarum Patentium in Turri Londinensi Asservati, 1201-1216,* ed. T. D. Hardy (London, 1835), p. 54b.

39. For examples, see PRO C143/1, nos. 13, 21, 22; PRO C143/3, no. 33; PRO C143/4, no. 22.

40. M. Kowaleski, *Local Markets and Regional Trade in Medieval Exeter* (Cambridge, 1995), pp. 193-95.

41. On the low rates of toll see ibid., p. 194. For examples of contemporary toll rates see *Calendar of Patent Rolls, 1327-1330,* pp. 3-4; *Placita de Quo Warranto,* p. 302; C. Fraser, "The Pattern of Trade in the North-East of England, 1265-1350," *Northern History* 4 (1969): 47-48, and appendix.

42. *Curia Regis Rolls,* vol. 1, pp. 449-50; *Placita de Quo Warranto,* p. 140.

43. *Statutes of the Realm,* ed. A. Luders et al. (London, 1810-28), vol. 1, p. 52.

44. *Rotuli Hundredorum,* ed. W. Illingworth and J. Caley (London, 1812-18), vol. 1, p. 106.

45. R. S. Gottfried, *Bury St. Edmunds and the Urban Crisis: 1290-1539* (Princeton, NJ, 1982), p. 85.

46. *Curia Regis Rolls,* vol. 15, pp. 364-65.

47. *Rotuli Hundredorum,* vol. 1, p. 320.

48. E. W. Moore argues a similar position in the case of holders of the major fairs in the period. See Moore, *The Fairs of Medieval England: An Introductory Study* (Toronto, 1985), p. 199.

49. *Close Rolls of the Reign of Henry III, 1242-1247,* p. 421.

50. *Calendar of Close Rolls, 1279-1288,* p. 344.

51. *Curia Regis Rolls,* vol. 16, no. 1547.

52. *Rotuli Hundredorum,* vol. 1, p. 239.

53. Ibid., p. 12.

54. Ibid., p. 185.

55. Ibid., p. 543. The reference may involve a through-toll on the river rather than market-toll, but this would not alter the principle.

56. Ibid., p. 356.

57. Ibid., p. 280.

58. *The Records of the Borough of Northampton,* ed. C. A. Markham and J. C. Cox (London and Northampton, 1898), vol. 1, p. 62.

59. *Rotuli Hundredorum,* vol. 2, p. 26.

60. The record of this dispute is translated in Salzman, "Legal Status of Markets," pp. 211-12.

61. Ibid., p. 211.

62. J. Masschaele, "The Multiplicity of Medieval Markets Reconsidered," *Journal of Historical Geography* 20 (1994): 255-71.

Chapter 4

1. C. Dyer, "The Hidden Trade of the Middle Ages: Evidence from the West Midlands of England," *Journal of Historical Geography* 18 (1992): 141-57.

2. M. Beresford and H. P. R. Finberg, *English Medieval Boroughs: A Handlist* (Newton Abbot, Devon, 1973).

3. *The Gild Merchant,* ed. C. Gross, 2 vols. (Oxford, 1890); *British Borough Charters, 1042-1216,* ed. A. Ballard (Cambridge, 1913); *British Borough Charters, 1216-1307,* ed. A. Ballard and J. Tait (Cambridge, 1923).

4. M. McKisack, *The Parliamentary Representation of the English Boroughs during the Middle Ages* (Oxford, 1932), pp. 1-24.

5. Ibid., p. 16: "The interpretation which the sheriff put upon the words 'every city and borough within your bailiwick' depended upon himself."

6. R. B. Dobson, "Urban Decline in Late Medieval England," *Transactions of the Royal Historical Society,* 5th ser., 27 (1977): 18-19; J. F. Hadwin, "The Medieval Lay Subsidies and Economic History," *Economic History Review,* 2nd ser., 36 (1983): 204, 210-11; S. H. Rigby, "Urban Decline in the Later Middle Ages: Some Problems in Interpreting the Statistical Data," *Urban History Yearbook 1979* (Leicester, 1979), p. 47.

7. J. Willard, "Taxation Boroughs and Parliamentary Boroughs, 1294-1336," in *Historical Essays in Honour of James Tait,* ed. J. G. Edwards, V. H. Galbraith, and E. F. Jacob (Manchester, 1933), p. 424.

8. Ibid., p. 427.

9. This number is derived from the list in *Gild Merchant,* ed. Gross, vol. 1, pp. 9-16.

10. Willard, "Taxation Boroughs," p. 427; *British Borough Charters, 1042-1216,* ed. Ballard, pp. cxxxviii-cxlv; *British Borough Charters, 1216-1307,* ed. Ballard and Tait, pp. xc-ci.

11. Beresford and Finberg, *English Medieval Boroughs.*

12. Numerous places that paid an urban rate of tax in the lay subsidies, thus earning them a place in the handlist, did so as ancient demesne rather than as boroughs, as the editors themselves pointed out. In the case of Huntingdonshire, five of the eight alleged boroughs are supported solely by their occurrence in the lay subsidy of 1319. All five were ancient demesne. *The Lay Subsidy of 1334,* ed. R. Glasscock, Records of Social and Economic History, no. 2 (London, 1975), p. 136.

13. M. Beresford, *New Towns of the Middle Ages* (New York, 1967), pp. 69-70.

14. Willard, "Taxation Boroughs," pp. 427, 430-35.

15. McKisack, *Parliamentary Representation,* p. 11.

16. Willard, "Taxation Boroughs," pp. 429-35.

17. Axbridge; Bamburgh; Barnstaple; Bath; Bedford; Bodmin; Bridgwater; Bristol; Cambridge; Carlisle; Derby; Devizes; Dunwich; Gloucester; Guildford; Hereford; Ipswich; King's Lynn; Lancaster; Launceston; Liskeard; Liverpool; Lostwithiel; Lyme Regis; Marlborough; Newcastle-upon-Tyne; Nottingham; Portsmouth; Preston; Reading; Rochester; Salisbury; Scarborough; Shrewsbury; Totnes; Wigan; Wilton; Winchester; Windsor; Worcester; Yarmouth.

18. Appleby; Bridgnorth; Calne; Canterbury; Chesterfield; Chichester; Colchester; Exeter; Grimsby; Hedon; Helston; Horsham; Hull; Huntingdon; Kingston (Surrey); Leicester; Lewes; Lincoln; London; Malmesbury; Morpeth; Northampton; Norwich; Okehampton; Old Sarum; Orford; Oxford; Plympton; Ravenser Odd; Shaftesbury; Southampton; Stafford; Stamford; Truro; Wallingford; Wells; Wycombe; York. Willard failed to recognize that Yorkshire East Riding and all parts of Lincolnshire other than Lindsey were unrecorded or incompletely recorded in the Nonae Inquisitions. Thus, Hedon, Hull, Ravenser Odd, Stamford, and York should properly be included in the group of towns omitted only in a single source, although they do not appear as such in Willard's table. He also neglected the manuscript return for Somerset (Public Record Office [PRO] E179/169/14), which adds Wells to the list of towns recorded in five of six sources.

19. *British Borough Charters, 1042-1216,* ed. Ballard, pp. cxxxix, cxl; *Gild Merchant,* ed. Gross, vol. 1, pp. 10, 12.

20. Willard, "Taxation Boroughs," p. 420.

21. E. M. Carus-Wilson and O. Coleman, *England's Export Trade 1275-1547* (Oxford, 1963), pp. 34-38; Glasscock, "England *circa* 1334," in *A New Historical Geography of England,* ed. H. C.

Darby (Cambridge, 1973), p. 184; S. H. Rigby, "Boston and Urban Decline in the Later Middle Ages," *Midland History* 10 (1985): 47-61.

22. *Gild Merchant,* ed. Gross, vol. 2, p. 10; *British Borough Charters, 1307-1660,* ed. M. Weinbaum (Cambridge, 1943), p. xxxii.

23. House of Commons, *Return of the Names of Every Member Returned to Serve in Each Parliament* (London, 1878; Kraus Reprint, 1980), Part 1, *passim; Inquisitions and Assessments Relating to Feudal Aids,* vol. 3, p. 184; *Lay Subsidy of 1334,* ed. Glasscock, pp. 167-68.

24. J. W. F. Hill, *Medieval Lincoln* (Cambridge, 1948), pp. 314-20.

25. Andover; Arundel; Ashburton; Bedwyn; Bishop's Stortford; Bradninch; Bramber; Burford; Chippenham; Crediton; Cricklade; Dartmouth; Downton; Droitwich; East Grinstead; Hinckley; Leominster; Ludgershall; Lydford; Melcombe; Midhurst; Newcastle-under-Lyme; Newport; Penryn; Reigate; Retford; Richmond; Shoreham; South Molton; Southwark; Steyning; Sutton Prior; Tavistock; Torrington; Warwick; Wells; Weobley; Woodstock.

26. *Gild Merchant,* ed. Gross, vol. 2, pp. 289-351.

27. Glasscock, " England *circa* 1334," pp. 179-85; *Lay Subsidy of 1334,* ed. idem, passim.

28. The only towns that did not find record in two or more of the indices and yet still revealed substantial wealth in the 1334 subsidy were Plymouth and Lichfield. In Plymouth's case, the high ranking was due partly to the inclusion of extramural sources of wealth as part of the town's tax base. M. Kowaleski, *Local Markets and Regional Trade in Medieval Exeter* (Cambridge, 1995), p. 71.

29. J. Tait, *The Medieval English Borough* (Manchester, 1936), pp. 68-77.

30. Kowaleski, *Local Markets and Regional Trade,* pp. 41-77.

31. J. C. Russell, *Medieval Regions and their Cities* (Indiana, 1972), pp. 126-29; C. Platt, *The English Medieval Town* (New York, 1976), pp. 15-16.

32. S. Reynolds, *An Introduction to the History of English Medieval Towns* (Oxford, 1977), pp. 60-65.

33. R. H. Hilton, "Medieval Market Towns and Simple Commodity Production," *Past & Present* 109 (1985): 3-23; R. H. Britnell, "England and Northern Italy in the Early Fourteenth Century: The Economic Contrasts," *Transactions of the Royal Historical Society,* 5th ser., 39 (1989): 167-83; idem, "The Towns of England and Northern Italy in the Early Fourteenth Century," *Economic History Review,* 2nd ser., 44 (1991): 21-35.

34. *Rotuli Parliamentorum* (London, 1783), vol. 2, pp. 112-13; *Statutes of the Realm,* ed. A. Luders et al. (London, 1810-28), vol. 1, p. 290. For the political background of the grant, see G. L. Harriss, *King, Parliament and Public Finance in Medieval England to 1369* (Oxford, 1975), pp. 259, 276-89.

35. A. R. H. Baker, "Evidence in the "Nonarum Inquisitiones" of Contracting Arable Lands in England During the Early Fourteenth Century," *Economic History Review,* 2nd ser., 19 (1966): 518-32.

36. *Nonarum Inquisitiones in Curia Scacarii,* ed. G. Vanderzee (London, 1807).

37. *Annual Reports of the Deputy Keeper of the Public Records,* vol. 2, Appendix 2, in *House of Commons Parliamentary Papers,* 1841, session 2 (London, 1841).

38. For example, those in *Nonarum Inquisitiones,* pp. 340, 349, 429-30.

39. The returns suggest that the inquisitors had a set list of questions which they required each village to answer, a procedure analagous to that used by the sheriff as he made his tourn holding sessions of frankpledge.

40. *Nonarum Inquisitiones,* pp. 223-24.

41. Ibid., p. 14.

42. Ibid., p. 351.

43. Ibid., p. 352.

44. Ibid., p. 229.

45. Ibid., p. 84.

46. Ibid., p. 14.

47. PRO E179/73/16.

48. *Records of the Borough of Nottingham,* ed. W. Stevenson (London, 1882), vol. 1, pp. 82-83.

49. *Close Rolls of the Reign of Henry III, 1227-1231,* p. 598.

50. *Rotuli Parliamentorum,* vol. 2, pp. 112-13.

51. *Calendar of Patent Rolls, 1338-1340,* p. 499.

52. PRO E179/120/24; PRO E179/135/27; *Nonarum Inquisitiones,* p. 41.

53. *Nonarum Inquisitiones,* p. 61.

54. Ibid., p. 16.

55. Ibid., p. 81.

56. PRO E179/73/16.

57. *Nonarum Inquisitiones,* p. 419.

58. Ibid., p. 34.

59. Willard, "Taxation Boroughs," p. 431; *Nonarum Inquisitiones,* p. 61.

60. PRO E179/120/24.

61. PRO E179/180/12.

62. PRO E179/155/14. Oundle is a likely candidate here. Judging from the continuation on the dorse, the beginning of the assessment on the town of Northampton has also been lost.

63. The counties in this category are: Essex, Kent, Leicestershire, Oxfordshire, Rutland, Staffordshire, and Yorkshire East Riding. Some parish returns are certainly missing from the Oxfordshire file, but there are indentures for all but one of the leading market sites in the county (Woodstock) and thus it is unlikely that any data about rural fifteenths are missing.

64. J. Willard, *Parliamentary Taxes on Personal Property, 1290-1334* (Cambridge, MA, 1934), pp. 219-29.

65. D. Hughes, *Social and Constitutional Tendencies in the Reign of Edward III* (London, 1915), pp. 141-42; Harriss, *King, Parliament and Public Finance,* pp. 274-76.

66. *Calendar of Patent Rolls, 1338-1340,* p. 112; *Calendar of Close Rolls, 1339-1341,* pp. 434-35; *Calendar of Patent Rolls, 1340-1343,* pp. 124-25.

67. These inquests make up the bulk of the surviving Nonae documents in both manuscript and printed form.

68. *Rotuli Parliamentorum,* vol. 2, pp. 131-33; *Calendar of Close Rolls, 1341-1343,* p. 255; *Calendar of Patent Rolls, 1340-1343,* p. 261.

69. On Henley see B. M. S. Campbell et al., *A Medieval Capital and Its Grain Supply,* Historical Geography Research Series, no. 30 (n.p., 1993), pp. 47-49; *Nonarum Inquisitiones,* p. 136. On Witham see R. Britnell, "The Making of Witham," *History Studies* 1 (1968): 13-21; *Nonarum Inquisitiones,* p. 323. I am grateful to Bruce Campbell and Richard Britnell for drawing these cases to my attention.

70. See, for example, *Nonarum Inquisitiones,* pp. 340, 418-19, 430-31. On the selection of taxation boroughs, see Willard, "Taxation Boroughs."

71. PRO E179/161/16.

72. PRO E179/202/41 (Ferriby, Yorkshire); PRO E179/177/10 (Tamworth, Staffordshire); PRO E179/158/14 (Northumberland); PRO E179/81/17 (Downham, Cambridgeshire).

73. *Nonarum Inquisitiones,* p. 139.

74. R. A. Pelham, "Fourteenth-Century England," in *An Historical Geography of England before 1800,* ed. H. C. Darby (Cambridge, 1936), p. 234; Glasscock, "England *circa* 1334," p. 178;

Beresford and Finberg, *English Medieval Boroughs,* p. 48. Data from the latter source are mapped in R. A. Dodgshon, "The Early Middle Ages, 1066-1350," in *An Historical Geography of England and Wales,* ed. R. A. Dodgshon and R. A. Butlin (London, 1978), p. 107.

75. Kowaleski, *Local Markets and Regional Trade,* pp. 41-81.

76. *Nonarum Inquisitiones,* pp. 287, 290; Glasscock, "England *circa* 1334," p. 184.

77. *Nonarum Inquisitiones,* pp. 283-93.

78. PRO E179/173/13. The totals include the assessments made in the Soke (£118 from 95 people). On the Soke, see D. Keene, *Survey of Medieval Winchester* (Oxford, 1985), pp. 70-75.

79. H. J. Hewitt, *The Organization of War under Edward III, 1338-62* (Manchester, 1966), pp. 156-57.

80. PRO E179/173/13.

81. Pelham, "Fourteenth-century England," pp. 233-35.

82. J. Munro, "Wool-Price Schedules and the Qualities of English Wools in the Later Middle Ages, c. 1270-1499," *Textile History* 9 (1978): 118-169; Pelham, "Fourteenth-century England," p. 245.

83. R. A. Pelham, "The Foreign Trade of Sussex, 1300-1350," *Sussex Archaeological Collections* 70 (1929): 98, 104; *The Local Customs Accounts of the Port of Exeter 1266-1321,* ed. M. Kowaleski, Devon and Cornwall Record Society, n. s., no. 36 (Exeter, 1993), pp. 14-16.

84. N. S. B. Gras, *The Early English Customs System* (Cambridge, MA, 1918), pp. 221-22.

85. J. Langdon, "Inland Water Transport in Medieval England," *Journal of Historical Geography* 19 (1993): 1-11.

86. R. A. Pelham, "Some Medieval Sources for the Study of Historical Geography," *Geography* 17 (1932): 33-34.

87. J. Thirsk, "The Common Fields," *Past & Present* 29 (1964): 3-25; A. C. Chibnall, *Sherington, Fiefs and Fields of a Buckinghamshire Village* (Cambridge, 1965); C. Dahlman, *The Open Field System and Beyond* (Cambridge, 1980); E. Kerridge, *The Common Fields of England* (Manchester, 1992).

88. J. Hatcher, *Rural Economy and Society in the Duchy of Cornwall 1300-1500* (Cambridge, 1970); Kowaleski, *Local Markets and Regional Trade*, M. Bailey, *A Marginal Economy? East Anglian Breckland in the Later Middle Ages* (Cambridge, 1989).

89. *Nonarum Inquisitiones,* p. 361. Tithes on orchards were, in fact, fairly common in Sussex, as were tithes on cider production.

90. Pelham, "Fourteenth-century England," p. 250.

91. B. Coates, "Markets and Fairs in Medieval Derbyshire," *Derbyshire Archaeological Journal* 85 (1965): 104-05. Kowaleski notes a similar correspondence between transition zones and marketing in Devon in *Local Markets and Regional Trade,* pp. 46-47.

92. Kowaleski, *Local Markets and Regional Trade,* chapter 2, passim.

93. Beresford and Finberg, *English Medieval Boroughs,* pp. 70-72; M. Reed, "Markets and Fairs in Medieval Buckinghamshire," *Records of Buckinghamshire* 20 (1978): 563-85.

Chapter 5

1. *Rotuli Hundredorum,* ed. W. Illingworth and J. Caley (London, 1812-18), vol. 2, p. 267.

2. The town ranked fourth among the twelve places assessed as boroughs in 1334. *The Lay Subsidy of 1334,* ed. R. Glasscock, Records of Social and Economic History, no. 2 (London, 1975), p. 333.

3. H. Turner, *Town Defences in England and Wales* (London, 1971); M. Kowaleski, *Local Markets and Regional Trade in Medieval Exeter* (Cambridge, 1995), pp. 192-202.

4. F. Pollock and F. W. Maitland, *The History of English Law before the Time of Edward I,* 2nd ed. (Cambridge, 1968), vol. 1, p. 650.

5. *First Report of the Royal Commission on Market Rights and Tolls* (London, 1889), pp. 1-29; *British Borough Charters, 1042-1216,* ed. A. Ballard (Cambridge, 1913), p. lxix.

6. Kowaleski, *Local Markets and Regional Trade,* pp. 192-202; *The Black Book of the Admiralty,* ed. T. Twiss, Rolls Series, no. 55 (London, 1871-76), vol. 2, pp. 184-207; *Liber Albus: The White Book of the City of London,* trans. H. Riley (London, 1861), pp. 196-217; R. H. Morris, *Chester in the Plantagenet and Tudor Reigns* (Chester, n. d.), pp. 554-58; *The Oath Book or Red Parchment Book of Colchester,* ed. W. G. Benham (Colchester, 1907), pp. 6-10.

7. E. Lipson, *The Economic History of England,* 5th ed. (London, 1929), vol. 1, p. 252.

8. *British Borough Charters, 1042-1216,* ed. Ballard, pp. cxxxviii-ccxlv.

9. *Year Books of Edward II,* vol. 17, ed. W. C. Bolland, Selden Society, no. 41 (London, 1924), p. 200.

10. Lipson, *Economic History,* vol. 1, p. 285; *The Red Register of King's Lynn,* ed. H. Ingleby (King's Lynn, 1919-22), vol. 1, pp. 68-69; Kowaleski, *Local Markets and Regional Trade,* pp. 196-201; Public Record Office (PRO) C255/12/1 (no.13).

11. A good example of this can be found in the letters of Great Yarmouth appended to the town's court rolls. For examples see Norfolk Record Office Y/C4/14 (exemption for Thorney Abbey) and Y/C4/26 (exemption for Spalding priory and an unidentified house of friars).

12. *Calendar of Letter Books Preserved Among the Archives of the City of London at the Guildhall, Letter Book D,* ed. R. L. Sharpe (London, 1902), pp. 299-300.

13. *Calendar of Letters from the Mayor and Corporation of the City of London,* ed. R. L. Sharpe (London, 1885); *Red Register of King's Lynn,* vol. 1, p. 26; Norfolk Record Office Y/C4/17 (Great Yarmouth).

14. PRO C255/12/1; PRO C255/12/2; PRO C255/12/3.

15. The archive is summarily described in *Chancery Files, Class List,* List and Index Society, vol. 130 (London, 1966), p. 136.

16. PRO C255/12/1, no.19.

17. PRO C255/12/2 no.2.

18. *Calendar of Early Mayor's Court Rolls,* ed. A. Thomas (Cambridge, 1924), p.115.

19. N. S. B. Gras, *The Early English Customs System* (Cambridge, MA, 1918), pp. 155-58.

20. *The Oak Book of Southampton,* ed. P. Studer, Publications of the Southampton Record Society, nos. 10 and 11 (Southampton, 1910-11), vol. 1, pp. 7-21.

21. Although the editor of the Oak Book dates the compilation to ca. 1300, there are indications that the toll list was compiled at a slightly later date, probably in the late 1320s. The latest date given is for a charter to Dunwich said to have been granted in 1324, but the entry is confused and cannot be corroborated in other sources. Another late, but verifiable, grant is recorded for Harwich in 1319, which speaks of the "recent" Edward II. Considering that an agreement over toll rights with Salisbury in 1329 is recorded in a later part of the document but not included among this list of towns with recognized exemptions, we should probably conclude that the list was drawn up in the first year or two of Edward III's reign. There are, however, indications that the list in the Oak Book was based on an earlier list, probably drawn up in the 1250s. After the first 16 towns the scribe copied a note to the effect that all of the previous charters were confirmed by Henry III, the current king. The charter for Shrewsbury included in the 16 is, however, said to have been granted by the "recent" *(nuper)* King Henry III, suggesting that the list may also have been revised between its original compilation and its entry in the Oak Book.

22. *Oak Book,* ed. Studer, vol. 2, pp. 19-27.

23. Ibid., pp. 3-17; see also Studer's comparison of the two lists in the introduction to the volume, pp. xvi-xxi.

24. On withernam procedure, see K. Murray, *The Constitutional History of the Cinque Ports* (Manchester, 1935), pp. 52-53.

25. Norfolk Record Office Y/C4/12 through 35.

26. Norfolk Record Office Y/C4/14.

27. Norfolk Record Office Y/C4/22.

28. Norfolk Record Office Y/C4/15, 21, 23, 24, 25.

29. For debts involving residents of Ipswich, see Norfolk Record Office Y/C4/16, 19, 21, 22, 23, 25, 27, 32; for Colchester, see Norfolk Record Office Y/C4/19, 20, 22, 24, 32.

30. Norfolk Record Office Y/C4/16, 17.

31. For Portsmouth, see Norfolk Record Office Y/C4/21, 22; for Weymouth, see Y/C4/15; for Teignmouth, see Y/C4/19, 26.

32. For Winchester, see Norfolk Record Office Y/C4/14; for Nottingham, see Y/C4/24.

33. *Calendar of Letters from the Mayor of London*, ed. Sharpe.

34. Details of the partnership are based on PRO E101/506/1. This documents is described in G. Williams, *Medieval London* (London, 1963), pp. 122-23, and more fully in J. Masschaele, "The Trials of Partnership in Medieval England: A Case History, 1304," in *The Salt of Common Life: Individuality and Choice in the Medieval Town, Countryside, and Church*, ed. E. B. DeWindt (Kalamazoo, MI, 1995), pp. 157-80.

35. *Calendar of Patent Rolls, 1338-1340*, p. 388; *Calendar of Patent Rolls, 1340-1343*, p. 103.

36. *Calendar of Patent Rolls, 1340-1343*, p. 103.

37. Ibid., pp. 271, 290, 435.

38. *Calendar of Patent Rolls, 1343-1345*, p. 100.

39. Ibid., p. 450.

40. *Calendar of Close Rolls, 1346-1349*, p. 146.

41. Ibid., p. 543.

42. PRO E163/4/20.

43. Examples include John de Barton of Hull (*Victoria History of the County of Yorkshire East*, vol. 1, ed. K. J. Allison (Oxford, 1969), pp. 39, 45, 81); Thomas Butler of Lincoln (*The 1341 Royal Inquest in Lincolnshire*, ed. B. McLane, Lincoln Record Society, no. 78 (Woodbridge, Suffolk, 1988), p. 39); Thomas Gra of York (E. B. Fryde, *Studies in Medieval Trade and Finance* (London, 1983), ch. 11, pp. 22-23).

44. D. Keene, *Survey of Medieval Winchester* (Oxford, 1985), p. 308.

45. Williams, *Medieval London*, p. 122; *Calendar of Letter Books Preserved Among the Archives of the City of London at the Guildhall, Letter Book B*, ed. R. L. Sharpe (London, 1900), p. 179.

46. Williams, *Medieval London*, pp. 106-33; Keene, *Survey of Medieval Winchester*, pp. 308-15, 324-32; H. Swanson, *Medieval Artisans* (Oxford, 1989), chaps. 10 and 11; M. Kowaleski, "Town and Country in Late Medieval England: The Hide and Leather Trade," in *Work in Towns, 850-1850*, ed. P. J. Corfield and D. Keene (Leicester, 1990), pp. 57-73; and R. H. Britnell, *Growth and Decline in Colchester, 1300-1525* (Cambridge, 1986), pp. 9-22.

47. M. K. James, *Studies in the Medieval Wine Trade* (Oxford, 1971), pp. 10, 18, 37; T. H. Lloyd, *Alien Merchants in England in the High Middle Ages* (Sussex, 1982), p. 90. For the conversion to gallons see R. Zupko, *British Weights and Measures* (Madison, WI, 1977), p. 149.

48. *Crown Pleas of the Wiltshire Eyre, 1249*, ed. C. A. F. Meekings, Wiltshire Archaeological and Natural History Society Records Branch, no. 16 (Devizes, 1961), p. 41.

49. In 1336-37, for example, wool prices in Flanders were twice as high as those in England. Fryde, *Studies in Medieval Trade and Finance*, ch. 9, p. 9.

50. On price differentials, see J. Munro, "Wool-Price Schedules and the Qualities of English Wools in the Later Middle Ages, c. 1270-1499," *Textile History* 9 (1978): 118-69.

51. *The Making of King's Lynn,* ed. D. M. Owen, Records of Social and Economic History, n. s., no. 9 (London, 1984), p. 42; N. S. B. Gras, *The Evolution of the English Corn Market* (Cambridge, MA, 1915), pp. 110-11.

52. D. Farmer, "Prices and Wages," in *The Agrarian History of England and Wales,* vol. 2, 1042-1350, ed. H. Hallam (Cambridge, 1988), p. 742.

53. Ibid., pp. 744, 751.

54. W. C. Jordan, *The Great Famine. Northern Europe in the Early Fourteenth Century* (Princeton, NJ, 1996), pp. 14-15.

55. *English Historical Documents,* vol. 3, 1189-1327, ed. H. Rothwell (New York, 1975), pp. 881-84.

56. *Victoria History of the County of Gloucestershire,* vol. 4, ed. N. M. Herbert (Oxford, 1988), pp. 25-26.

57. *Sixth Report of the Royal Commission on Historical Manuscripts,* part 1, Report and Appendix (London, 1877; Kraus Rprt., 1979), pp. 489, 491-92.

58. A. Saul, "The Herring Industry at Gt. Yarmouth, c. 1280-c. 1400," *Norfolk Archaeology* 38 (1983): 33-42.

59. E. W. Moore, *The Fairs of Medieval England* (Toronto, 1985), p. 86; *Calendar of Patent Rolls, 1317-1321,* p. 311; *Calendar of Close Rolls, 1318-1323,* pp. 160, 165, 175.

60. Britnell, *Colchester,* p. 13.

61. C. Fraser, "The Pattern of Trade in the North-East of England, 1265-1350," *Northern History* 4 (1969), non-paginated appendix.

62. Moore, *Fairs of Medieval England,* p. 38.

63. C. Stephenson, *Borough and Town* (Cambridge, MA, 1933), pp. 128-38; G. Unwin, "The Estate of Merchants, 1336-1365" in *Finance and Trade under Edward III,* ed. idem (Manchester, 1918), pp. 179-255.

Chapter 6

1. D. Keene, "Continuity and Development in Urban Trades" in *Work in Towns, 850-1850,* ed. P. Corfield and idem (Leicester, 1990), p. 7; E. Rutledge, "Immigration and Population Growth in Early Fourteenth-Century Norwich," *Urban History Yearbook 1988* (Leicester, 1988), pp. 26-27.

2. B. M. S. Campbell et al., *A Medieval Capital and Its Grain Supply,* Historical Geography Research Series, no. 30 (n.p., 1993), p. 76.

3. A more thorough discussion of this aspect of inland trade can be found in chapter 7.

4. R. H. Britnell, *Growth and Decline in Colchester, 1300-1525* (Cambridge, 1986), p. 36.

5. *Regesta Regum Anglo-Normannorum 1066-1154,* ed. H. A. Cronne, R. H. C. Davis, and H. W. C. Davis (Oxford, 1913-1968), vol. 1, pp. 54, 76, 102.

6. Ibid., vol. 1, p. 76; vol. 3, pp. 250-51.

7. See, for example, *Calendar of Charter Rolls, 1257-1300,* pp. 237-38.

8. Public Record Office (PRO) C255/12/1, no.15a.

9. PRO C255/12/3.

10. *Rotuli Hundredorum,* ed. W. Illingworth and J. Caley (London, 1812-18), vol. 1, p. 83.
11. Ibid., vol. 1, p. 317.
12. PRO C255/12/1 no.12.
13. PRO C255/12/1 no.14.
14. E. Miller, *The Abbey and Bishopric of Ely* (Cambridge, 1951), *passim.*
15. *Select Cases Concerning the Law Merchant,* ed. C. Gross and H. Hall, vol. 3, Selden Society, no. 49 (London, 1932), pp. 147-48.
16. *Abbreviatio Placitorum. Richard I - Edward II,* ed. G. Rose and W. Illingworth (London, 1811), p. 305.
17. See, for example, *Rotuli Hundredorum,* vol. 1, p. 185; PRO C255/12/1, nos. 3 and 6.
18. T. H. Lloyd, *The English Wool Trade in the Middle Ages* (Cambridge, 1977); idem, *The Movement of Wool Prices in Medieval England,* Economic History Review Supplement, no. 6 (Cambridge, 1973).
19. *Rotuli Hundredorum,* vol. 2, p. 4.
20. M. Ormrod, *The Reign of Edward III* (New Haven, 1990), p. 182.
21. *Rotuli Hundredorum,* vol. 1
22. Ibid., vol. 2, pp. 14, 54 (Gilbert de Chesterton).
23. Ibid., vol. 1, p. 314.
24. *Records of the Borough of Leicester,* ed. M. Bateson, (London, 1899), vol. 1, pp. 92, 187, 205-07, 262, 275; vol. 2, p. 31.
25. *Rotuli Hundredorum,* pp. 107-08, 115, 131-32.
26. For examples, see *Records of Leicester,* ed. Bateson, vol. 1, p. 275; vol. 2, p. 31; Lloyd, *English Wool Trade,* p. 304.
27. *Records of Leicester,* ed. Bateson, vol. 1, p. 123; Lloyd, *Wool Trade,* p. 304.
28. Leicestershire markets and fairs are identified and mapped in *Victoria History of the County of Leicestershire,* vol. 2, ed. W. G. Hoskins (London, 1954), pp. 175-76.
29. See, for example, M. Kowaleski, *Local Markets and Regional Trade in Medieval Exeter* (Cambridge, 1995), pp. 222-324.
30. *Curia Regis Rolls,* vol. 15, pp. 364-65.
31. *The Gild Merchant,* ed. C. Gross (Oxford, 1890), vol. 2, pp. 378-79.
32. G. Platts, *Land and People in Medieval Lincolnshire* (Lincoln, 1985), Appendix 1, supplemented by PRO E101/256/6 and PRO E101/256/7; T. Unwin, "Rural Marketing in Medieval Nottinghamshire," *Journal of Historical Geography* 7 (1981): 238, 246. I include Market Rasen (East Rasen) in this number, although according to Platts the market was actually chartered in West Rasen.
33. *The Lay Subsidy of 1334,* ed. R. Glasscock, Records of Social and Economic History, no. 2 (London, 1975); A. Everitt, "The Marketing of Agricultural Produce," in *The Agrarian History of England and Wales,* vol. 4, 1500-1640, ed. J. Thirsk (Cambridge, 1967), reprinted in *Agricultural Markets and Trade 1500-1700,* ed. J. Chartres (Cambridge, 1990), p. 23; Platts, *Land and People,* Unwin, "Rural Marketing in Nottinghamshire." For dates of foundation, see Platt's discussion of some of these relationships in *Land and People* as well as J. Masschaele, "The Multiplicity of Medieval Markets Reconsidered," *Journal of Historical Geography* 20 (1994): 255-71.
34. G. H. Martin, "Road Travel in the Middle Ages," *Journal of Transport History* 3 (1976): 167, 172; J. Masschaele, "Transport Costs in Medieval England," *Economic History Review,* 2nd ser., 46 (1993): 269-70.
35. *Victoria History of the County of Northamptonshire,* vol. 3, ed. W. Page (London, 1930), pp. 1-33.
36. *Rotuli Hundredorum,* vol. 2, p. 4.

37. Sources used to identify markets in these counties are summarized in Masschaele, "Multiplicity of Medieval Markets," p. 270 n.13. For Ely, see *Victoria History of the County of Cambridgeshire and the Isle of Ely,* vol. 4, ed. R. B. Pugh (London, 1953), p. 36.

38. Platts, *Land and People, Lay Subsidy of 1334,* ed. Glasscock, p. 169.

39. E. W. Moore, *The Fairs of Medieval England: An Introductory Study* (Toronto, 1985), p. 8 and passim.

40. Ibid., pp. 25, 67, 78.

41. *The Making of King's Lynn,* ed. D. M. Owen, Records of Social and Economic History, n. s., no. 9 (London, 1984), pp. 115, 304, 307, 383; *Calendar of Liberate Rolls, 1226-1240,* pp. 89, 91, 107-08; E. M. Carus-Wilson, "La guède française en Angleterre," *Revue du Nord* 35 (1953): 98; PRO E101/577/7; PRO E101/577/8; PRO E101/577/9; PRO E101/577/11;PRO E101/577/17.

42. *Records of Leicester,* ed. Bateson, vol. 1, pp. 127, 185, 250, 265.

43. G. W. Skinner, "Marketing and Social Structure in Rural China," *Journal of Asian Studies* 24 (1964-65): 3-43; C. Meillassoux, ed., *The Development of Indigenous Trade and Markets in West Africa* (Oxford, 1971); R. Beals, *The Peasant Marketing System of Oaxaca, Mexico* (Berkeley and Los Angeles, 1975).

44. These issues will be explored in greater depth in part 4 of this book.

45. PRO C143/1 no.22, transcribed in *A Formula Book of English Official Historical Documents,* ed. H. Hall (Cambridge, 1909), vol. 2, pp. 89-90.

46. *The Roll of the Shropshire Eyre of 1256,* ed. A. Harding, Selden Society, no. 96 (London, 1981), pp. 161-62.

47. PRO C143/1 no.21.

Chapter 7

1. *Abbreviatio Placitorum. Richard I - Edward II,* ed. G. Rose and W. Illingworth (London, 1811), pp. 147-48.

2. Assuming a total population greater than 5 million and an urban share of 20 percent. C. Dyer, *Everyday Life in Medieval England* (London, 1994), p. xv; R. M. Smith, "Demographic Developments in Rural England, 1300-48: A Survey," in *Before the Black Death,* ed. B. M. S. Campbell (Manchester, 1991), pp. 48-49.

3. P. Bairoch, *Cities and Economic Development* (Chicago, 1988), p. 22; D. Keene, *Survey of Medieval Winchester* (Oxford, 1985), pp. 370-71.

4. J. Tait, *The Medieval English Borough* (Manchester, 1936), pp. 70-77.

5. G. Duby, *Rural Economy and Country Life in the Medieval West,* trans. C. Postan (Columbia, SC, 1968), p. 128.

6. R. H. Britnell, *Growth and Decline in Colchester, 1300-1525* (Cambridge, 1986), pp. 41-47; J. A. Raftis, *A Small Town in Late Medieval England: Godmanchester, 1278-1400* (Toronto, 1982), pp. 133-34. See also D. Farmer, "Marketing the Produce of the Countryside, 1200-1500," in *The Agrarian History of England and Wales,* vol. 3, 1348-1500, ed. E. Miller (Cambridge, 1991), pp. 328-29.

7. *The Oak Book of Southampton,* ed. P. Studer, Publications of the Southampton Record Society, nos. 10 and 11 (Southampton, 1910-11), vol. 1, p. 69; Public Record Office (PRO) SC6/1248/8 (Northampton); O. Ogle, "The Oxford Market," in *Collectanea II,* ed. M. Bur-

rows, Oxford Historical Society, no. 16 (Oxford, 1890), pp. 14-15, 119; *The Ancient Usages of the City of Winchester,* ed. J. Furley (Oxford, 1927), p. 37.

8. See, for example, *Records of the Borough of Nottingham,* ed. W. Stevenson (London, 1882), vol. 1, pp. 82-83; N. S. B. Gras, *The Early English Customs System* (Cambridge, MA, 1918), p. 157.

9. A. Vince, "The Medieval Pottery Industry in Southern England: 10th to 13th Centuries," in *Production and Distribution: A Ceramic Viewpoint,* ed. H. Howard and E. Morris, British Archeological Reports International Series, no. 120 (1981), p. 319; M. McCarthy and C. Brooks, *Medieval Pottery in Britain* A.D. *900-1600* (Leicester, 1988), pp. 69-76.

10. J. Cherry, "Leather," in *English Medieval Industries,* ed. J. Blair and N. Ramsay (London, 1991), pp. 295-318; M. Kowaleski, "Town and Country in Late Medieval England: The Hide and Leather Trade," in *Work in Towns, 850-1850,* ed. P. J. Corfield and D. Keene (Leicester, 1990), pp. 57-73; H. Swanson, *Medieval Artisans* (Oxford, 1989), pp. 53-65; D. Farmer, "Marketing the Produce of the Countryside," p. 378.

11. See, for example, *Black Book of the Admiralty,* ed. T. Twiss, vol. 2, Rolls Series, no. 55 (London, 1871-76), vol. 2, pp. 184-207; R. H. Morris, *Chester in the Plantagenet and Tudor Reigns* (Chester, n.d.), pp. 553-62; *Patent Rolls of the Reign of Henry III, 1225-1232,* p. 483.

12. *Oak Book of Southampton,* ed. Studer, vol. 1, p. 69; PRO SC6/1248/8 (Northampton); Ogle, "Oxford Market," pp. 14-15, 119; *Ancient Usages of Winchester,* ed. Furley, p. 37.

13. R. H. Britnell, "*Forstall,* Forestalling and the Statute of Forestallers," *English Historical Review* 102 (1987): 89-102.

14. C. Platt, "The Evolution of Towns: Natural Growth," in *The Plans and Topography of Medieval Towns in England and Wales,* ed. M. W. Barley, Council for British Archaelogy Research Report, no. 14 (1976), pp. 48-56.

15. D. Keene, "Medieval London and Its Region," *The London Journal* 14 (1989): 99-111; Swanson, *Medieval Artisans,* pp. 134-49; M. Kowaleski, *Local Markets and Regional Trade in Medieval Exeter* (Cambridge, 1995); C. Dyer, "Market Towns and the Countryside in Late Medieval England," *Canadian Journal of History* 21 (1996): 17-36.

16. Kowaleski, *Local Markets and Regional Trade,* pp. 279-324; Keene, "Medieval London"; Swanson, *Medieval Artisans,* pp. 134-49; T. Adams, "Aliens, Agriculturalists and Entrepreneurs: Identifying the Market-Makers in a Norfolk Port from the Water-Bailiffs' Accounts, 1400-1460," in *Trade, Devotion and Governance,* ed. D. Clayton, R. Davies and P. McNiven (Stroud, Gloucestershire, 1994), pp. 140-57.

17. R. B. Dobson, "Admissions to the City of York in the Later Middle Ages," *Economic History Review,* 2nd ser., 26 (1973): 1-22; P. J. P. Goldberg, *Women, Work, and Life Cycle in a Medieval Economy* (Oxford, 1992), pp. 35-37, 49-63.

18. Dobson, "Admissions to York," pp. 11-12.

19. *The Gild Merchant,* ed. C. Gross (Oxford, 1890), vol. 2, pp. 14, 50, 196, 237; *Records of the Borough of Leicester,* ed. M. Bateson, (London, 1899), vol. 1, pp. l-liii.

20. Suffolk Record Office, C4/1, fos. 81v-91v. A partial transcription of the list can be found in *Ninth Report of the Royal Commission on Historical Manuscripts* (London, 1883), part 1, pp. 240-41. Technically, the foreigners were listed as *forinseci burgenses,* but payments for their privilege were made to the merchant guild of the town.

21. Cf. R. H. Britnell, "Minor Landlords and Medieval Agrarian Capitalism," *Past & Present* 89 (1980): 3-22.

22. Suffolk Record Office, C4/1, f. 83v.

23. The Shrewsbury lists were edited by C. H. Drinkwater and published serially in *Transactions of the Shropshire Archaeological and Natural History Society* as follows: "The Merchants' Guild of Shrewsbury," 2nd ser., 2 (1890): 29-59; "The Merchants' Guild of Shrewsbury. The Two Earliest Rolls," 2nd ser., 8 (1896): 21-43; "The Merchant Guild of Shrewsbury. Seven Rolls of the Thirteenth Century," 2nd ser., 12 (1900): 229-82; "Shrewsbury Guild Merchant and Other Rolls of the Fourteenth Century," 3rd ser., 2 (1902): 65-106; "Seven Shrewsbury Guild Merchant Rolls of the Fourteenth Century," 3rd ser., 3 (1903): 47-98; "Two Mer-

chant Guild Rolls of the Fourteenth Century," 3rd ser., 3 (1903): 351-62; "A Burgess Roll and a Guild Merchant Roll of 1372," 3rd ser., 4 (1904): 217-36; "Shrewsbury Guild Merchant Rolls of the Fourteenth and Fifteenth Centuries," 3rd ser., 5 (1905): 35-54. I have checked these against the originals in the Shropshire Record Office (3365/50-53) and found the quality of the transcription to be generally very good.

24. *Gild Merchant,* ed. Gross, vol. 2, p. 195.

25. *The Rolls of Burgesses at the Guilds Merchant of the Borough of Preston, 1397-1682,* ed. W. A. Abram, The Record Society for the Publication of Original Documents Relating to Lancashire and Cheshire, no. 9 (n.p., 1884).

26. *Gild Merchant,* ed. Gross, vol. 2, p. 200.

27. J. Masschaele, "Urban Trade in Medieval England: The Evidence of Foreign Gild Membership Lists," in *Thirteenth Century England V,* ed. P. Coss and S. Lloyd (Woodbridge, Suffolk, 1994), pp. 115-28.

28. Five women occur in the earliest list from 1210, but none in the lists from 1232, 1252 and 1319. There is one woman, a servant, in the 1268 list, and one in the 1281 list.

29. Masschaele, "Urban Trade," pp. 122-25.

30. In this set of data, simple locative names and compound locatives are not distinguished. Placenames are identified (and thus distances calculated) using the guidelines outlined in P. McClure, "Patterns of Migration in the Late Middle Ages: The Evidence of English Place-Name Surnames," *Economic History Review,* 2nd ser., 32 (1979): 167-82. It should be noted that the total number of foreigners included in this table is lower than the absolute number of foreigners recorded because modern equivalents could not be found for all placenames occurring in the lists. Positive identifications of placenames range from 78 percent of all locative names in the 1209-1210 list to 85 percent of all locative names in the 1232 and 1252 lists. One can, however, safely assume that the spatial distribution of irretrievable placenames is random and therefore does not materially affect the relative proportions presented in the table.

31. PRO SC 6/1248/8.

32. On municipal policies concerning the supply of foodstuffs, see A. B. Hibbert, "The Economic Policies of Towns," in *The Cambridge Economic History of Europe,* vol. 3, ed. M. M. Postan, E. E. Rich and E. Miller (Cambridge, 1963), pp. 172-79.

33. D. H. Owen, "Farming Practice and Techniques. Wales and the Marches," in *Agrarian History of England and Wales,* vol. 3, 1348-1500, ed. E. Miller (Cambridge, 1991), pp. 239-43; *English Historical Documents,* vol. 3, 1189-1327, ed. H. Rothwell (New York, 1975), p. 882.

34. Dobson, "Admissions to York," pp. 14-15.

35. On the prominence of Shrewsbury's wool merchants, see T. H. Lloyd, *The English Wool Trade in the Middle Ages* (Cambridge, 1977), pp. 132-33.

36. For other evidence documenting the textile industry in Shrewsbury, see *Calendar of Charter Rolls, 1226-1257,* p. 26; D. Hutton, "Women in Fourteenth Century Shrewsbury," in *Women and Work in Pre-Industrial England,* ed. L. Charles and L. Duffin (London, 1985), pp. 88-89; *Victoria History of the County of Shropshire,* vol. 4, ed. G. C. Baugh (Oxford, 1989), p. 60.

37. Keene, *Winchester,* vol. 1, pp. 251-55; R. H. Britnell, *Growth and Decline in Colchester,* p. 44.

38. The seven are Clun, Ellesmere, Ludlow, Newport, Oswestry, Wem, and Much Wenlock. M. Beresford and H. P. R. Finberg, *English Medieval Boroughs: A Handlist* (Newton Abbot, Devon, 1973), pp. 150-54; J. Willard, "Taxation Boroughs and Parliamentary Boroughs, 1294-1336," in *Historical Essays in Honour of James Tait,* ed. J. G. Edwards, V. H. Galbraith, and E. F. Jacob (Manchester, 1933), p. 433.

39. *Victoria History of the County of Shropshire,* vol. 4, p. 66.

40. I include members from the following places among suburb dwellers: Abbey Foregate, Coleham, Edgebold, Frankwell, Hencott, Shelton, and Sutton.

41. R. Eyton, *Antiquities of Shropshire* (London, 1854-60), vol. 6, pp. 38-39.

42. Ibid., vol. 6, pp. 38-39 (John de Berrington); ibid., vol. 8, p. 195 (Thomas de Cherrington); ibid., vol. 10, p. 91 (Thomas de Rosshall).

43. *Victoria History of the County of Shropshire,* vol. 4, p. 32-33.

44. Eyton, *Antiquities of Shropshire.*

45. The following description is based on *Victoria History of the County of Shropshire,* vol. 8, ed. A. T. Gaydon (Oxford, 1968), pp. 73-77; W. Fletcher, "The Shropshire Lay Subsidy of 1327" *Transactions of the Shropshire Archaeological and Natural History Society,* 2nd ser., 11 (1899): 378-79; Eyton, *Antiquities of Shropshire,* vol. 6, pp. 308-17.

Chapter 8

1. H. E. Hallam, ed., *The Agrarian History of England and Wales,* vol. 2, 1042-1350 (Cambridge, 1988); J. A. Raftis, *The Estates of Ramsey Abbey* (Toronto, 1957).

2. The quote is drawn from W. Gilpin, *Observations on Several Parts of the Counties of Cambridge, Norfolk, Suffolk and Essex* (London, 1809), p. 18. On the medieval fenland in general, see J. Ravensdale, *Liable to Floods* (Cambridge, 1974) and H. C. Darby, *The Medieval Fenland* (Cambridge, 1940).

3. British Library (BL) Add. Ch. 33141.

4. *The Lay Subsidy of 1334,* ed. R. Glasscock, Records of Social and Economic History, no. 2 (London, 1975), p. xxvii.

5. *Inquisitions and Assessments Relating to Feudal Aids, 1284-1431,* vol. 2, pp. 467-74; *Rotuli Hundredorum,* ed. W. Illingworth and J. Caley (London, 1812-18), vol. 2, pp. 591-687. The earldom of Huntingdon was further fragmented by its association with the Scottish crown and the confiscations that resulted from this association in the reign of Edward I. See W. Farrer, *Honors and Knights Fees* (Manchester, 1925), vol. 2, pp. 296-301. Important manorial complexes in Huntingdonshire were held by the Earls of Hereford in Kimbolton and by the Segraves in Alconbury Weston.

6. Raftis, *Ramsey Abbey,* p. 20; *Royal Justice in the Medieval English Countryside,* ed. A. R. DeWindt and E. B. DeWindt, (Toronto, 1981), p. 110.

7. PRO C47/1/4.

8. BL Harl. Ch. 58.E.40; BL Harl. Ch. E.41.

9. E. A. Kosminsky, *Studies in the Agrarian History of England in the Thirteenth Century,* trans. R. Kisch (Oxford, 1956), p. 90.

10. *Rotuli Hundredorum,* vol. 2, pp. 607-10 (Brampton), 610-14 (Alconbury Weston), 650-52 (Glatton).

11. Kosminsky, *Studies in Agrarian History,* p. 90.

12. J. A. Raftis, *A Small Town in Late Medieval England: Godmanchester, 1278-1400* (Toronto, 1982); PRO C133/95, m.12. The other places in the county noted in M. Beresford and H. P. R. Finberg, *English Medieval Boroughs: A Handlist* (Newton Abbot, Devon, 1973) were all ancient demesne and thus paid the urban rate in the 1319 lay subsidy.

13. For densities in other counties, see R. H. Britnell, "The Proliferation of Markets in England, 1200-1349," *Economic History Review,* 2nd ser., 34 (1981): 210. Another measure of density is the ratio between the number of markets and the number of villages. In Huntingdonshire, the theoretical density works out to about 6 villages per market. By comparison, G. W. Skinner found a density in the recent past of about 18 villages per market in

the areas of rural China he investigated. G. W. Skinner, "Marketing and Social Structure in Rural China," *The Journal of Asian Studies* 24 (1964-65): 18.

14. J. Masschaele, "The Multiplicity of Medieval Markets Reconsidered," *Journal of Historical Geography* 20 (1994): 255-71.

15. Ibid., p. 262.

16. *Hansard's Parliamentary Debates*, 3rd ser., vol. 313 (London, 1887), col. 1645; *Statutes of the Realm*, ed. A. Luders et al. (London, 1810-28), vol. 1, p. 107.

17. Printed in *Placita de Quo Warranto*, ed. W. Illingworth and J. Caley (London, 1818), pp. 292-309. A. DeWindt and E. DeWindt note that these pleas belong to the eyre of 1286. *Royal Justice*, ed. DeWindt and DeWindt, p. 115 n.1. On the relationship between pleas of Quo Warranto and franchise rights, see D. Sutherland, *Quo Warranto Proceedings in the Reign of Edward I, 1278-1294* (Oxford, 1963).

18. PRO E101/256/9.

19. R. D. Conner, *The Weights and Measures of England* (London, 1987), pp. 325-28; J. H. Johnson, "The King's Wardrobe and Household," in *The English Government at Work*, ed. J. Willard and W. Morris (Cambridge, MA, 1940), vol. 1, pp. 245-48; N. Williams, "Sessions of the Clerk of the Market of the Household in Middlesex," *Transactions of the London and Middlesex Archeological Society* 19 (1958): 76-89.

20. PRO E101/256/6; PRO E101/256/9; PRO E101/256/14.

21. BL Add. Ch. 39263.

22. *Nonarum Inquisitiones in Curia Scacarii*, ed. G. Vanderzee (London, 1807), p. 430.

23. PRO C133/95, m.12.

24. Masschaele, "Multiplicity of Markets."

25. Based on comparisons derived from *Lay Subsidy of 1334*, ed. Glasscock, pp. 136-39.

26. C. Platt, "The Evolution of Towns: Natural Growth," in *The Plans and Topography of Medieval Towns in England and Wales*, ed. M. W. Barley, Council for British Archaeology Research Report, no. 14 (1976), p. 51; H. Clarke, *The Archaeology of Medieval England* (London, 1984), p. 37.

27. The town plan is included in Royal Commission on Historical Monuments (England), *An Inventory of the Historical Monuments in Huntingdonshire* (London, 1926), p. 157.

28. Ibid., p. 174.

29. Ibid., p. 210; *Victoria History of the County of Huntingdonshire*, vol. 2, ed. W. Page, G. Proby and S. I. Ladds (London, 1932), p. 189. At first glance, it seems as though the spacious Great Whyte would have been the location of the market, but its width is due not to the market but to the presence of a stream in the Middle Ages running from Wistow. The abbey was located next to the southeast corner of the marketplace.

30. *Inventory of Historical Monuments in Huntingdonshire*, p. 225.

31. C. F. Tebbott, *St. Neots* (London, 1978), pp. 1-12.

32. R. H. T. Smith, "West African Marketplaces: Temporal Periodicity and Locational Spacing," in *The Development of Indigenous Trade and Markets in West Africa*, ed. C. Meillassoux (Oxford, 1971), pp. 319-46; R. J. Bromly, "Contemporary Market Periodicity in Highland Ecuador," in *Regional Analysis*, ed. C. A. Smith (New York, 1976), vol. 1, pp. 91-122; R. Beals, *The Peasant Marketing System of Oaxaca, Mexico* (Berkeley and Los Angeles, 1975).

33. Bromly, "Market Periodicity in Ecuador," p. 98.

34. M. Reed, "Markets and Fairs in Medieval Buckinghamshire," *Records of Buckinghamshire* 20 (1978): 572.

35. D. Postles, "Markets for Rural Produce in Oxfordshire, 1086-1350," *Midland History* 12 (1987): 15.

36. T. Unwin, "Rural Marketing in Medieval Nottinghamshire," *Journal of Historical Geography* 7 (1981): 231-51. This is also the study that most explicitly adopts central-place theory to study patterns of marketing.

37. Based on the sources noted in Appendix 2. Huntingdon's market day is mentioned in a mid-fifteenth-century ecclesiastical document, printed in A. H. Thompson, *The English Clergy and Their Organization in the Later Middle Ages* (Oxford, 1947), p. 217.

38. J. L. Cate, "The English Mission of Eustace of Flay (1200-1201)," in *Etudes d'histoire dédiés à la mémoire de Henri Pirenne par ses anciens élèves* (Brussels, 1937), pp. 67-89.

39. C. Smith, "Introduction," in *Regional Analysis,* ed. idem, vol. 1, pp. 10-12.

40. P. Goodfellow, "Medieval Markets in Northamptonshire," *Northamptonshire Past and Present* 7 (1987-88): 305-23; *Victoria History of the County of Bedfordshire,* vol. 2, ed. W. Page (London, 1908), p. 88; D. Lysons and S. Lysons, *Magna Britannia* (London, 1806-22), vol. 2, pp. 79-288, corroborated by a search of the published volumes of *Victoria History of the County of Cambridgeshire,* and *Calendar of Charter Rolls.*

41. Survival has been determined by comparing medieval markets with those inventoried by A. Everitt, "The Marketing of Agricultural Produce," in *The Agrarian History of England and Wales,* vol. 4, 1500-1640, ed. J. Thirsk (Cambridge, 1967), pp. 466-592, reprinted in *Agricultural Markets and Trade 1500-1700,* ed. J. Chartres (Cambridge, 1990), pp. 15-141. Everitt omitted Swavesey, Cambridgeshire, from his list. The market was, however, functioning in the eighteenth century, and other evidence points to its medieval importance; it is thus characterized as a core market on the map. Brackley and Rothwell in Northamptonshire were assessed separately from the rest of the hundred in which they were located. For the purposes of these maps, I have compared them to the other settlements in their hundred.

42. *Rotuli Hundredorum,* vol. 2, p. 2; PRO SC11/10.

43. This conclusion assumes a continuity between medieval and later market days. Cf. C. Pickman, *The Tradesman's Guide* (London, 1727), p. 74. The Tuesday market was added in 1554. *Calendar of Patent Rolls, 1553-1554,* p. 276.

44. Reed, "Markets in Buckinghamshire," p. 572; Unwin, "Rural Marketing in Medieval Nottinghamshire," p. 235; Postles, "Markets for Rural Produce in Oxfordshire," p. 24.

45. Britnell, "Proliferation of Markets," Table 1, p. 210.

46. Three new markets were founded in Cambridgeshire in 1335 (in Abbington Piggots, Babraham, and Barrington), one in Huntingdonshire (Keyston in 1341), and one in Northamptonshire (Flore in 1333). No new markets were attempted in Bedfordshire after the chartering of Marston Moretaine in 1324.

47. Northamptonshire and Bedfordshire have particularly thorough Quo Warranto records surviving from the eyre revivals in 1329-30. *Placita de Quo Warranto,* pp. 15-80, 499-584. For a more thorough assessment of the Northamptonshire evidence see J. Masschaele, "Multiplicity of Markets." Quo Warranto pleas were heard in Cambridgeshire in 1299, but the royal justices were not as diligent in investigating market franchises there as they were in other circuits. *Placita de Quo Warranto,* pp. 99-107. The following Clerk of the Market records provide the most thorough coverage of markets in these counties: PRO E101/256/6; PRO E101/256/7; PRO E101/256/9. Like the justices in eyre, the Clerk of the Market paid less attention to markets in Cambridgeshire than in other counties. To make up for these deficiencies in the Cambridgeshire evidence, I counted as functioning markets sites that were recorded in the Hundred Rolls but not in later Quo Warranto pleas or visits by the Clerk of the Market. These data may not be as reliable as those for the other counties.

48. *Calendar of Charter Rolls, 1257-1300,* p. 427. Reach in Cambridgeshire may also fall into this category. It was a market site in the early modern period, but it was not included in the 1334 lay subsidy assessment.

49. Masschaele, "Multiplicity of Markets," pp. 264-68.

50. *Placita de Quo Warranto,* p. 64.

51. Beals, *Peasant Marketing System of Oaxaca,* p. 145. A *plaza* is a marketplace.

52. *Placita Anglo-Normannica: Law Cases From William I to Richard I,* ed. M. Bigelow (Boston, 1881), p. 201.

Chapter 9

1. On the relationship between development and transportation facilities, see W. Owen, *Transportation and World Development* (Baltimore, 1987); D. Hilling, *Transport and Developing Countries* (London, 1996), especially pp. 24, 316-17 on the issue of debt.

2. See, for example, W. T. Jackman, *The Development of Transportation in Modern England* (London, 1962); H. J. Dyos and D. H. Aldcroft, *British Transport: An Economic Survey from the Seventeenth Century to the Twentieth* (Leicester, 1969); W. Albert, *The Turnpike Road System in England, 1663-1840* (Cambridge, 1972); D. Hey, *Packmen, Carriers and Packhorse Roads* (Leicester, 1980); R. Szostack, *The Role of Transportation in the Industrial Revolution: A Comparison of England and France* (Montreal, 1991).

3. H. C. Darby, *The Medieval Fenland* (Cambridge, 1940).

4. Ibid., pp. 93-100; V. Parker, *The Making of King's Lynn* (London, 1971), pp. 6-10. Darby thought that the Wisbech outlet silted up in the latter part of the thirteenth century, but King's Lynn was already a leading port at the very beginning of the century, suggesting that it rather than Wisbech was already serving as the principal outport of the fenland waterways. N. S. B. Gras, *The Early English Customs System* (Cambridge, MA, 1918), pp. 221-22.

5. D. Hill, *An Atlas of Anglo-Saxon England* (Toronto, 1981), p. 13 gives an enlargement of Christopher Saxton's map of the fenland waterways drawn in 1576; John Speed's map, drawn ca. 1600, conveys similar information. J. Speed, *The Counties of Britain: A Tudor Atlas* (London, 1988), pp. 102-03.

6. *Cartularium Monasterii de Rameseia,* ed. W. H. Hart and P. A. Lyons, Rolls Series, no. 79 (London, 1884-94), vol. 1, p. 166.

7. J. Langdon, "Inland Water Transport in Medieval England," *Journal of Historical Geography* 19 (1993): 4-5.

8. *Royal Justice in the Medieval English Countryside,* ed. A. R. DeWindt and E. B. DeWindt (Toronto, 1981), p. 319; *Placita de Quo Warranto,* ed. W. Illingworth and J. Caley (London, 1818), p. 297.

9. *Curia Regis Rolls,* vol. 13, p. 89.

10. *Calendar of Liberate Rolls, 1226-1240,* pp. 89, 91, 107-8.

11. Langdon, "Inland Water Transport."

12. *Curia Regis Rolls,* vol. 13, pp. 88-89; *Calendar of Patent Rolls, 1321-1324,* p. 386; Parker, *Making of King's Lynn,* p. 9.

13. *Royal Justice,* ed. DeWindt and DeWindt, pp. 395, 476; *Placita de Quo Warranto,*, p. 308.

14. *Cartularium Monasterii de Rameseia,* ed. Hart and Lyons, vol. 2, pp. 325-26.

15. *Rotuli Hundredorum,* ed. W. Illingworth and J. Caley (London, 1812-18), vol. 2, p. 685.

16. *Cartularium Monasterii de Rameseia,* ed. Hart and Lyons, vol. 1, p. 432.

17. Ibid., p. 175.

18. B. P. Hindle, *Medieval Roads* (Aylesbury, 1982); idem, "The Road Network of Medieval England and Wales," *Journal of Historical Geography* 2 (1976): 207-21; J. Edwards, "The Trans-

port System of Medieval England and Wales—A Geographical Synthesis," (Ph.D. diss., University of Salford, 1987).

19. *The Map of Great Britain, c. A.D. 1360, Known as the Gough Map,* issued by the Bodleian Library in association with the Royal Geographical Society (Oxford, 1958); *Ordnance Survey Map of Roman Britain* (London, 1978), south sheet. A tidier illustration of these data is given in B. P. Hindle, "Roads and Tracks," in *The English Medieval Landscape,* ed. L. Cantor (London, 1982), p. 197.

20. Edwards, "Transport System," pp. 34-37.

21. Public Record Office (PRO) E101/622/21.

22. *Ordnance Survey Map of Roman Britain,* south sheet.

23. *The Place-Names of Cambridgeshire and the Isle of Ely,* English Place-Name Society, no. 19 (Cambridge, 1943), pp. 30-31.

24. W. G. Hoskins, *Leicestershire* (London, 1957), p. 101.

25. M. Clanchy, *From Memory to Written Record* (London, 1979).

26. Sources for this paragraph include: *Victoria History of the County of Huntingdonshire,* vol. 2, ed. W. Page, G. Proby and S. I. Ladds (London, 1932), pp. 338, 339; M. Beresford and J. K. St. Joseph, *Medieval England: An Aerial Survey* (Cambridge, 1979), p. 182; E. W. Moore, *The Fairs of Medieval England* (Toronto, 1985), pp. 144-45; *Registrum Antiquissimum of the Cathedral Church of Lincoln,* ed. C. W. Foster, Lincoln Record Society, no. 27 (Hereford, 1931), vol. 1, pp. 129-30; *Calendar of Patent Rolls, 1340-1343,* p. 169; British Library (BL) Add. R. 34804; BL Add. R. 34363; *Descriptive Catalogue of Ancient Deeds,* vol. 4, p. 100.

27. R. H. Britnell, "Essex Markets Before 1350," *Essex Archaeology and History* 13 (1981): 18-19; M. Kowaleski, *Local Markets and Regional Trade in Medieval Exeter* (Cambridge, 1995), pp. 49-50.

28. See the map in J. A. Raftis, *A Small Town in Late Medieval England: Godmanchester, 1278-1400* (Toronto, 1982), p. 6.

29. *Rotuli Hundredorum,* vol. 1, p. 49; vol. 2, p. 359; F. W. Maitland, *Township and Borough* (Cambridge, 1898), p. 172.

30. *Rotuli Hundredorum,* vol. 2, pp. 626-27.

31. Beresford and St. Joseph, *Medieval England,* p. 88. The map is reproduced in *Victoria History of the County of Huntingdonshire,* vol. 3, facing p. 48.

32. A. B. White, *Self-Government at the King's Command* (Minneapolis, 1933, reprt. 1974).

33. Darby, *Medieval Fenland,* pp. 155-68; A. Owen, "The Records of a Commission of Sewers for Wiggenhall 1319-1324," *Norfolk Record Society,* no. 48 (Norwich, 1981): 9-16.

34. *Public Works in Medieval Law,* ed. C. T. Flower, vol. 2, Selden Society, no. 40 (London, 1923), p. xxvii.

35. *Calendar of Patent Rolls, 1334-1338,* p. 70.

36. *Calendar of Patent Rolls, 1313-1317,* pp. 241-42; *Calendar of Patent Rolls, 1321-1324,* p. 386.

37. *Cartularium Monasterii de Rameseia,* ed. Hart and Lyons, vol. 3, pp. 121-57. Further details on this case can be found in chapter 10.

38. *Public Works,* Flower, vol. 1, Selden Society, no. 32 (London, 1915), pp. 310-11.

39. *Royal Justice,* ed. DeWindt and DeWindt, p. 319; *Placita de Quo Warranto,* p. 297.

40. *Calendar of Patent Rolls, 1370-1374,* p. 35.

41. *Victoria History of the County of Huntingdonshire,* vol. 2, p. 131.

42. *Public Works,* ed. Flower, vol. 2, p. xvi.

43. F. Pollock, *Oxford Lectures,* vol. 3, (London, 1890), pp. 80-83.

44. *Leges Henrici Primi,* ed. L. J. Downer (Oxford, 1972), p. 249.

45. Ibid. Royal property rights continued to form an important part of the notion of a highway in subsequent centuries. Henry Bracton's definition of *via regia,* for example, occurs

in the context of a discussion of boundaries. Bracton draws a distinction between common property and royal property, and gives the king's highway as an example of the latter. *Bracton On the Laws and Customs of England,* ed. G. E. Woodbine, trans. and rev. S. E. Thorne (Cambridge, MA, and London, 1977), vol. 3, p. 61.

46. Ibid., p. 130; W. S. Holdsworth, *A History of English Law* (London, 1938), vol. 10, p. 301.

47. *Bracton,* ed. Woodbine, trans. and rev. Thorne, vol. 3, pp. 61, 136.

48. *The Court Baron,* ed. F. W. Maitland, Selden Society, no. 4 (London, 1890), pp. 71-72.

49. Ibid., p. 98.

50. *Leet Jurisdiction in England,* ed. F. J. C. Hearnshaw, Publications of the Southampton Record Society, no. 5 (Southampton, 1908), pp. 43-64; J. Beckerman, "The Articles of Presentment of a Court Leet and Court Baron, in English, c.1400," *Bulletin of the Institute of Historical Research* 47 (1974): 231-32.

51. For Wistow, see BL Add. R. 34898. For Broughton, see BL Add. R. 39459 and BL Add. R. 34363. For Elton, see BL Add. R. 34321. For Upwood, see BL Add. R. 34803.

52. For an example from Elton, see PRO SC2/179/12. For Upwood, see BL Add. R. 34798. For Ramsey, see BL Add. R. 34770. For Weston, see PRO SC2/179/18.

53. BL Add. R. 39464.

54. PRO SC2/179/18.

55. BL Add. R. 34770.

56. For an example from Wistow, see BL Add. R. 34896. For Little Stukely, see BL Add. R. 34908. For Upwood, see BL Add. R. 34805. For Elton, see PRO SC2/179/30. For Warboys, see BL Add. R. 34895. For King's Ripton, see PRO SC2/179/18.

57. For an example from Ramsey, see PRO SC2/179/18. For Over, Cambridgeshire, see PRO SC2/179/18.

58. D. F. Harrison, "Bridges and Economic Development, 1300-1800," *Economic History Review,* 2nd ser., 45 (1992): 240-61.

59. Raftis, *Godmanchester,* p. 3; *Cartularium Monasterii de Rameseia,* ed. Hart and Lyons, vol. 2, p. 214; *Victoria History of the County of Huntingdonshire,* vol. 2, p. 337.

60. *Royal Justice,* ed. DeWindt and DeWindt, p. 320. A fourteenth-century reference occurs in *Calendar of Patent Rolls, 1345-1348,* p. 188.

61. P. Goodfellow, "Medieval Bridges in Northamptonshire," *Northamptonshire Past and Present* 7 (1985-86): 144, 155-57.

62. *Victoria History of the County of Huntingdonshire,* vol. 2, pp. 354-55, 379; vol. 3, p. 97.

63. Goodfellow, "Medieval Bridges in Northamptonshire," pp. 143-58.

64. Harrison, "Bridges," pp. 255-56.

65. *Calendar of Patent Rolls,* passim.

66. *Public Works,* ed. Flower, vol. 2, p. xli. One of the articles of the Magna Carta was that only those vills or men who "by custom and law" had been distrained to build bridges would be so distrained in future. J. C. Holt, *Magna Carta* (Cambridge, 1965), p. 322.

67. *Abbreviatio Placitorum. Richard I - Edward II,* ed. G. Rose and W. Illingworth (London, 1811), p. 148.

68. *The Rolls and Register of Bishop Oliver Sutton, 1280-1299,* ed. R. Hill, vol. 4, Lincoln Record Society, no. 52 (Hereford, 1958), p. 163.

69. *Calendar of Miscellaneous Inquisitions, 1307-1349,* no. 1069 (1329); *Calendar of Close Rolls, 1364-1368,* pp. 39-40; *Calendar of Close Rolls, 1369-74,* p. 140; *Calendar of Close Rolls, 1374-1377,* p. 523.

70. *Calendar of Close Rolls, 1364-1368,* p. 39.

71. PRO E101/622/21.

72. *Calendar of Patent Rolls, 1345-1348,* p. 188; *Bishop Sutton's Register,* ed. Hill, vol. 4, p. 188; *Calendar of Patent Rolls, 1385-1389,* p. 479.

73. J. Langdon, *Horses, Oxen and Technological Innovation* (Cambridge, 1986).

74. J. Langdon, "Horse Hauling: A Revolution in Vehicle Transport in Twelfth- and Thirteenth-Century England," *Past & Present* 103 (1984): 37-66.

75. *Patent Rolls of the Reign of Henry III, 1225-1232,* p. 483; *The Black Book of the Admiralty,* ed. T. Twiss, Rolls Series, no. 55 (London, 1871-1876), vol. 2, pp. 197-98.

76. J. Masschaele, "Transport Costs in Medieval England," *Economic History Review,* 2nd ser., 46 (1993): 269-70; PRO E101/577/17.

77. J. Langdon, "The Economics of Horses and Oxen in Medieval England," *Agricultural History Review* 30 (1982): 40; *Early Huntingdonshire Lay Subsidy Rolls,* ed. J. A. Raftis and M. P. Hogan (Toronto, 1976), pp. 117-27; J. A. Raftis, *The Estates of Ramsey Abbey* (Toronto, 1957), pp. 211-14; *Manorial Records of Cuxham, Oxfordshire,* ed. P. D. A. Harvey, Oxfordshire Record Society, no. 50 and Historical Manuscripts Commission Joint Publication, no. 23 (London, 1976), passim.

78. Langdon, *Horses, Oxen and Technological Innovation,* pp. 158-59. A Lincolnshire sheriff's account recording expenses incurred to find and maintain a number of horses to send to the king in Berwick in 1301 reveals expenditures of about 6d. per week per horse for food, an amount that corroborates Langdon's finding. PRO E101/684/72/1.

79. Langdon, *Horses, Oxen and Technological Innovation,* pp. 179-96.

80. *Huntingdonshire Lay Subsidy Rolls,* ed. Raffis and Hogan, pp. 31-34.

81. Ibid., pp. 34-36.

82. *Manorial Records of Cuxham,* ed. Harvey, pp. 712-14.

83. G. H. Martin, "Road Travel in the Middle Ages," *Journal of Transport History* 3 (1976): 167, 172.

84. M. Taylor, "Justices of Assize," in *The English Government at Work,* ed. J. Willard, W. Morris and W. Dunham (Cambridge, 1950), vol. 3, pp. 236-37.

85. PRO E101/550/19.

86. PRO E101/550/10.

87. PRO E101/552/7.

88. PRO E101/577/8.

89. D. Postles, "Customary Carrying Services," *Journal of Transport History,* 3rd ser., 5 (1984): 1-15; D. Farmer, "Marketing the Produce of the Countryside, 1200-1500," in *The Agrarian History of England and Wales,* vol. 3, 1348-1500, ed. E. Miller (Cambridge, 1991), pp. 347-49.

90. *Rotuli Hundredorum,* vol. 2, p. 626.

91. Ibid., p. 628.

92. Ibid., pp. 638, 639.

93. Ibid., p. 628; *Cartularium Monasterii de Rameseia,* vol. 1, pp. 476-77.

94. Masschaele, "Transport Costs".

95. Ibid., p. 274.

96. These costs have been calculated using the method outlined in ibid., pp. 277-9.

97. PRO E101/552/13.

98. D. Farmer, "Prices and Wages," in *The Agrarian History of England and Wales,* vol. 2, 1042-1350, ed. H. E. Hallam (Cambridge, 1988) p. 734.

99. PRO E101/552/14; PRO E101/552/16; PRO E101/552/17.

100. PRO E101/552/33.

101. A. R. DeWindt, "Redefining the Peasant Community in Medieval England: The Regional Perspective," *Journal of British Studies* 26 (1987): 163-207.

102. C. Dyer, "Were Peasants Self Sufficient? English Villagers and the Market, 900-1350," in *Campagnes médiévales: L'homme et son espace*, ed. E. Mornet (Paris, 1995), pp. 657-60. On yields in Huntingdonshire, see J.A. Raftis, *Estates of Ramsey Abbey*, pp. 173-77, 185.

103. *Black Book of the Admiralty*, ed. Twiss, vol. 2, pp. 184-207; R. Morris, *Chester in the Plantagenet and Tudor Reigns* (Chester, n.d.), pp. 554-58.

Chapter 10

1. Domesday documents a village of 15 hides, with 3 ploughs on the demesne and 18 ploughs in the possession of 38 villeins. No other tenants are mentioned. *Victoria History of the County of Huntingdonshire*, vol. 1, ed. W. Page and G. Proby (London, 1926), p. 345.

2. *Rotuli Hundredorum*, ed. W. Illingworth and J. Caley (London, 1812-18), vol. 2, pp. 640-43.

3. R. H. Britnell, "Burghal Characteristics of Market Towns in Medieval England," *Durham University Journal*, n. s., 42 (1981): 147-51; R. M. Smith, "A Periodic Market and Its Impact on a Manorial Community: Botesdale, Suffolk and the Manor of Redgrave, 1280-1300," in *Medieval Society and the Manor Court*, ed. Z. Razi and R. M. Smith (Oxford, 1996), pp. 450-81.

4. *Nonarum Inquisitiones in Curia Scacarii*, ed. G. Vanderzee (London, 1807), pp. 429-30.

5. *Curia Regis Rolls*, vol. 1, pp. 449-50.

6. *Curia Regis Rolls*, vol. 12, pp. 513-14.

7. The siege is described in *Victoria History of the County of Bedfordshire*, vol. 3, ed. W. Page (London, 1912), pp. 10-11.

8. *Curia Regis Rolls*, vol. 12, pp. 414-15.

9. British Library Stowe 941, fos. 55-56.

10. *Rotuli Hundredorum*, vol. 2, p. 685.

11. *Calendar of Letters from the Mayor and Corporation of the City of London*, ed. R. L. Sharpe (London, 1885), Letter II62.

12. *The Records of the Borough of Northampton*, ed. C. A. Markham and J. C. Cox (London and Northampton, 1898), vol. 2, p. 198; *Rotuli Hundredorum*, vol. 2, pp. 640-41.

13. Norfolk Record Office Y/C4/54; Y/C4/55; Y/C4/59.

14. E. Ekwall, *Studies on the Population of Medieval London* (Stockholm, 1956), pp. 132-36.

15. Corporation of London Record Office, Recognizance Roll 1, m.2; *Royal Justice in the Medieval English Countryside*, ed. A. R. DeWindt and E. B. DeWindt, (Toronto, 1981), pp. 141-42.

16. V. Parker, *The Making of King's Lynn* (London, 1971), p. 4.

17. E. M. Carus Wilson, "The Medieval Trade of the Ports of the Wash," *Medieval Archeology* 6-7 (1962-63), p. 195.

18. *The Making of King's Lynn*, ed. D. M. Owen, Records of Social and Economic History, n. s., no. 9 (London, 1984), pp. 41-42.

19. Ibid., pp. 42, 306, 307, 310, 313.

20. The record of the proceedings in this case is taken from *Cartularium Monasterii de Rameseia*, ed. W. H. Hart and P. A. Lyons, Rolls Series, no. 79 (London, 1884-94), vol. 3, pp. 121-57.

21. Ibid., p. 142.

22. *Curia Regis Rolls*, vol. 13, pp. 88-89.

23. E. W. Moore, *The Fairs of Medieval England: An Introductory Study* (Toronto, 1985), p. 14.

24. *Calendar of Charter Rolls, 1257-1300,* p. 427.

25. Public Record Office (PRO) C143/19, no. 23.

26. J. R. Maddicott, *The English Peasantry and the Demands of the Crown,* Past & Present Supplement, no. 1 (1975); M. Prestwich, *War, Politics and Finance under Edward I* (Totowa, NJ, 1972), pp. 114-36; H. J. Hewitt, *The Organization of War under Edward III, 1338-62* (Manchester, 1966), pp. 50-74; *A Lincolnshire Assize Roll for 1298,* ed. W. S. Thomson, Lincoln Record Society, no. 36 (Hereford, 1939), pp. lii-lxxxvii.

27. See, for example, *Calendar of Patent Rolls, 1292-1301,* pp. 314, 388, 578, 609; *Rotuli Scotiae in Turri Londoniensi et in Domo Capitulari Westmonasteriensi Asservati, 19 Edward I - Henry VIII,* ed. D. Macpherson et al. (London, 1814-19), vol. 1, pp. 150b, 157a, 170a, 184b.

28. PRO E101/552/5; PRO E358/2, m.7; PRO E358/3, ms. 7, 14.

29. PRO E101/552/4.

30. William de Haliwell and John de Earith are two examples. See PRO E101/552/16; PRO E101/552/17; Moore, *Fairs of Medieval England,* pp. 276, 277, 314, 316, 331.

31. PRO E101/552/11; PRO E101/552/16; PRO E101/552/17.

32. PRO E101/552/5.

33. PRO E358/3 m.3r; PRO E101/577/8. In 1334, large quantities of goods were also shipped from Alwalton.

34. See, for example, PRO E101/552/17; PRO E101/552/25.

35. According to PRO E101/552/11, the 29 barrels acquired for the purpose held a total of 188 quarters plus advantage of flour, or about 7 quarters each. Similar capacities are recorded in accounts from other counties; see, for example, PRO E101/25/16.

36. PRO E101/552/14; J. Masschaele, "Transport Costs in Medieval England," *Economic History Review,* 2nd ser., 46 (1993): 277.

37. *Rotuli Parliamentorum* (London, 1783), vol. 2, p. 269; C. Given-Wilson, "Purveyance for the Royal Household, 1362-1413," *Bulletin of the Institute for Historical Research* 56 (1983): 145-63.

38. E. Perroy, *The Hundred Years War,* trans. W. B. Wells (London, 1951), pp. 33-59.

39. R. H. Hilton, "Medieval Market Towns and Simple Commodity Production," *Past & Present* 109 (1985): 3-23.

Conclusion

1. C. Geertz, *Agricultural Involution: The Process of Ecological Change in Indonesia* (Berkeley and Los Angeles, 1963).

2. R. M. Smith, "Families and Their Land in an Area of Partible Inheritance: Redgrave, Suffolk 1260-1320" in *Land, Kinship and Life Cycle,* ed. idem (Cambridge, 1984), pp. 139-44; R. M. Smith, "A Periodic Market and Its Impact on a Manorial Community: Botesdale, Suffolk and the Manor of Redgrave, 1280-1300," in *Medieval Society and the Manor Court,* ed. Z. Razi and R. M. Smith (Oxford, 1996), pp. 450-81.

3. Marshall Sahlins has argued that this cultural emphasis is the distinguishing characteristic of western societies. M. Sahlins, *Culture and Practical Reason* (Chicago, 1976).

4. G. Snooks, "The Dynamic Role of the Market in the Anglo-Norman Economy and Beyond, 1086-1300," in *A Commercialising Economy,* ed. R. H. Britnell and B. M. S. Campbell (Manchester, 1995), pp. 27-54; N. Mayhew, "Modelling Medieval Monetisation," in ibid., pp. 55-77.

5. M. Bailey, *A Marginal Economy? East Anglian Breckland in the Later Middle Ages* (Cambridge, 1989).

6. R. H. Britnell, "Commercialisation and Economic Development in England, 1000-1300" in *A Commercialising Economy,* pp. 7-26.

7. M. Mate, "Medieval Agrarian Practices: The Determining Factors," *Agricultural History Review* 33 (1985): 22-31.

8. P. Hill, "Two Types of West African House Trade," in *The Development of Indigenous Trade and Markets in West Africa,* ed. C. Meillassoux (Oxford, 1971), pp. 303-5.

Appendix 1

1. The *Wealth of Shrewsbury in the Early Fourteenth Century,* ed. D. Cromarty and R. Cromarty (Shrewsbury, 1993), pp. 40, 80.

Index

Index